This is a wonderful book about couple therapy.  of one of America's most thoughtful and skillful provides the sort of practical guide to practice fo yearn. Building on a wide-ranging integrative t ple therapists understand the intricacies involved experiencing common problems and stressful situ money, stepfamily issues, and sexuality. This book should be required reading for every graduate course in couple therapy and will be of great value to every couple therapist.

—Jay Lebow, PhD
Editor, *Family Process;* Senior Scholar and Senior Therapist,
The Family Institute at Northwestern and Northwestern University

Art Nielsen has written a tour de force, applying his comprehensive, flexible, integrative approach to couple therapy to the common struggles couples present. Blending systemic, psychoeducational/behavioral, and psychodynamic theories and techniques in a systematic manner, Nielsen shows beginning and advanced clinicians how to bring these multiple perspectives to issues of money, issues of division of domestic labor, the balance between work and relationship time, affairs, couples on the brink of divorce or already engaged in that process, and stepfamilies. Based on science, therapeutic craft, and artistic use of metaphor, and with great attention to sustaining a working alliance, Nielsen provides a detailed roadmap for helping couples with these common challenges. This book is an essential text for couple therapists at any level of training and experience. Highly recommended and highly engaging!

—Peter Fraenkel, PhD
Associate Professor of Psychology, The City College of New York,
former Vice President, American Family Therapy Academy, and
author of *Last Chance Couple Therapy: Bringing Relationships Back
from the Brink*

In a comprehensive work that reflects a vast knowledge along with years of wisdom and experience as a couple therapist, Nielsen successfully integrates psychotherapy couple treatment models, drawing upon the most up-to-date research and scholarship and offering all sorts of gems about how to conduct therapy along with helpful tools that will prove indispensable to your practice. Definitely a must-have on your bookshelf!

—Rhonda Goldman, PhD
Professor, The Chicago School of Professional Psychology, and
author of *Case Formulation in Emotion-Focused Therapy* and
The Clinical Handbook of Emotion-Focused Therapy

Art Nielsen has done it again! Like his first book, this sequel is another clear, well-written, user-friendly guide that draws on the author's 40 years of clinical experience, seemingly encyclopedic knowledge of the couple therapy and related literature, and ability to translate complicated concepts into plain English. Both are books I wish I'd had when I saw my first couple, and yet I still learned from them over 30 years later.

—Carla Leone, PhD
Faculty, Institute for Clinical Social Work (Chicago); Secretary, International Association of Psychoanalytic Self Psychology; author of numerous papers on the application of self psychology to the treatment of couples and families.

Couple therapy is a very difficult field. Art Nielsen's *Integrative Couple Therapy in Action* is a master class in how to integrate diverse therapeutic approaches to treating couples. Drawing on decades of experience and from the depth of his thinking about couple therapy, Nielsen integrates lessons from systems, psychodynamic and behavior therapies to produce a guide that is at once practical and wise. The book offers support to therapists with a wide range of approaches and a deeper understanding of the shoals upon which couples frequently flounder. It is a book to keep at hand for moments when therapists need a guide for navigating their way through clinical problems.

—David E. Scharff, MD
Co-Founder and Former Director, International Psychotherapy Institute; Former Chair, International Psychoanalytic Association Committee on Couple and Family Psychoanalysis; Co-author, *Object Relations Couple Therapy,* and Co-editor, *Psychoanalytic Couple Therapy*

Following on Art Nielsen's landmark *Roadmap for Couple Therapy*, which mapped the integrative territory of couple therapy, Nielsen's new book focuses on the major intersections in that territory—sex, conflict, intimacy, money, etc. Not only does he focus on understanding those intersections, this book is full of his wisdom on how to successfully traverse them. Nielsen's unique wisdom is his ability to seamlessly move back and forth from the depths of the psyche to the complexities of changing behavior in the here and now. Beginners can use this book to learn "how to" and old folks like me can use it to sharpen and expand what we know. Another gift to the field and to the couples we treat.

—William Pinsof, PhD, LMFT, ABPP
Past President, The Family Institute at Northwestern University; Clinical Professor of Psychology Northwestern University; Lead Author, *Integrative Systemic Therapy: Metaframeworks for Problem Solving with Individuals, Couples, and Families*

In this second comprehensive text, Art Nielsen again brings his brilliantly integrative mind to the task of teaching the science and art of couple therapy. Whether he is summarizing the major theories that have shaped the field, teaching essential clinical concepts and principles, or offering specific and helpful case illustrations, one senses Nielsen's scholarly grasp, clinical wisdom, and basic humanity and empathy (including empathy for the reader) on every page. The result is a sophisticated primer that teaches therapists at all levels how to offer distressed couples the complex, often-multidimensional, therapeutic help they actually need.

—Steven Stern, PsyD
Author of *Needed Relationships and Psychoanalytic Healing* (2017) and Clinical Associate Professor, Department of Psychiatry, Tufts University School of Medicine and Maine Medical Center

In this generous book, Dr Nielsen provides a far-ranging view of the most common topics that couples in therapy bring to their therapist—problems with money, job issues, children, sex, affairs, and so on. He digs down in each of these broad topics, detailing all the different nuances, subtopics, and hidden issues that can be involved as well as providing extensive research references, case vignettes, and practical tips for both therapists and couples. For novice therapists, this book is a treasure trove of concentrated expertise and experience. For more experienced clinicians, it is a wonderful tool for refreshing, expanding, and focusing your thinking about the couples who come to you with their problems.

—Prudence Leib Gourguechon, MD
Past President of The American Psychoanalytic Association and Past Dean of The Chicago Psychoanalytic Institute

At a time when our field is riven with narrow partisan advocacy, Art Nielsen has pursued a very different path. He draws from the best of each major line of thought and arrives at an approach marked by both depth and clinical wisdom. An invaluable guide to clinical work with couples.

—Paul L. Wachtel, PhD
Distinguished Professor, Doctoral Program in Clinical Psychology, City College of New York; Co-founder of The Society for the Exploration of Psychotherapy Integration (SEPI)

Art Nielsen provides a comprehensive guide to couple therapy, offering both the beginning and more advanced clinician a wide array of helpful interventions with couples in distress. Using an integrative lens, and bringing the reader into the therapist's thought process, this book offers concrete suggestions for successfully working with a variety of common couple struggles.

—Mona Fishbane, PhD
2017 APA Family Psychologist of the Year (Division 43); Author of
Loving with the Brain in Mind: Neurobiology & Couple Therapy

Integrative Couple Therapy in Action

Integrative Couple Therapy in Action offers a comprehensive, user-friendly guide to handling the most common problems and crisis situations seen by couple therapists.

Drawing on the latest literature and the author's experience of over 40 years, Nielsen investigates what makes certain issues, such as sex, or situations, such as extramarital affairs, so stressful for clients and challenging for therapists. Unlike most graduate programs and texts on couple therapy that focus on theory and technique, *Integrated Couple Therapy in Action* fills in the details. The chapters cover common presenting problems (sex, money, children, and the stresses of time, work, and simply living together) and then discuss catastrophic crisis situations (couples reeling from affairs, contemplating divorce, divorcing, or living in stepfamilies after divorcing).

Integrative Couple Therapy in Action provides one-stop shopping for readers of all skill levels interested in understanding the subject matter that bedevils so many couples.

Arthur C. Nielsen, M.D. is Clinical Associate Professor of Psychiatry at Northwestern's Feinberg School of Medicine, Associate Director of the Integrative Psychoanalytic Couple Therapy Program at the Chicago Psychoanalytic Institute, and the author of *A Roadmap for Couple Therapy: Integrating Systemic, Psychodynamic, and Behavioral Approaches.*

Integrative Couple Therapy in Action

A Practical Guide for Handling Common
Relationship Problems and Crises

Arthur C. Nielsen

Routledge
Taylor & Francis Group

NEW YORK AND LONDON

Cover image: © Getty Images

First published 2022
by Routledge
605 Third Avenue, New York, NY 10158

and by Routledge
2 Park Square, Milton Park, Abingdon, Oxon, OX14 4RN

Routledge is an imprint of the Taylor & Francis Group, an informa
business

© 2022 Arthur C. Nielsen

Library of Congress Cataloging-in-Publication Data
A catalog record for this title has been requested

ISBN: 9781032272160 (hbk)
ISBN: 9781032272177 (pbk)
ISBN: 9781003291848 (ebk)

DOI: 10.4324/b22905

Typeset in Bembo
by Apex CoVantage, LLC

In memory of my parents, Art & Patty Nielsen, who loved me and taught me so much

A relationship science has emerged over the time and the history of couple therapy . . . that provides considerable guidance for practice and helps separate this activity today from the well-meaning ideas of opinionated uncles or cable relationship experts.
—Jay Lebow, Editor, *Family Process* (2013)

"Tell us please, what treatment in an emergency is administered by ear?"
"Words of comfort," I said to my father.
—Abraham Verghese, *Cutting for Stone* (2010)

Contents

PART III
Upgrades to Address Common Stressful Situations　　129

Acknowledgments

I am indebted to the many colleagues and contributors to the field who have shared their ideas, experience, and research findings; to my students who have helped me clarify my thinking; and to feedback from a study group of senior couple therapists with whom I have been able to share safely not only my successes but also my failures and conundrums. Certain colleagues deserve special thanks for their careful reading and the resulting helpful suggestions they made to drafts of various chapters: Richard Carrol, Mona Fishbane, Peter Fraenkel, Rhonda Goldman, Charles Jaffe, David Klow, Jay Lebow, Jennifer McComb, Sara Schwartzbaum, Alexandra Solomon, and Steven Zuckerman.

I was especially fortunate to have, again, the services of my loyal editor, Chava Casper who, though not an expert in the field of couple therapy, brought to the book her years of relationship wisdom and her astute editorial suggestions.

I also want to give a shout-out to my editor at Taylor & Francis (Routledge), Heather Evans, for her assistance throughout the arduous process of bringing this book to print.

To my many clients—some of whose stories appear here in disguised form—I want to thank you for allowing me into your lives, for trusting me with your deepest concerns, for helping me to hone my craft, and for making it possible for me to pass along to the next generation of therapists what we learned together under considerable duress. I wish you well.

And, finally, I want to acknowledge the support of my wife, Sheila, whose devotion to her own writing served as a shining star for me and who has taught me so much about the joys of married life.

Permissions acknowledgments

Excerpt(s) from *Cutting for Stone: A Novel* by Abraham Verghese, copyright © 2009 by Abraham Verghese. Used by permission of Alfred A. Knopf, an imprint of the Knopf Doubleday.
Publishing Group, a division of Penguin Random House LLC. All rights reserved.

Thanks to **JOHN WILEY AND SONS** for granting the license (5158451210554, 5158911349628 and 5159011460490).

Thanks to **Oxford Publishing Limited** for grating the license.

From *The State of Affairs* by Esther Perel. Copyright(c) 2017 by Esther Perel. Used by permission of **HarperCollins Publishers**.

About the Author

Arthur C. Nielsen, MD, is a board-certified psychiatrist, psychoanalyst, and couple therapist practicing in Chicago, Illinois. He earned his undergraduate degree at Harvard College and his MD at Johns Hopkins, completed his psychiatry residency at Yale, did family therapy training at The Philadelphia Child Guidance Clinic, and graduated from The Chicago Psychoanalytic Institute.

Professor Nielsen is Clinical Associate Professor of Psychiatry and Behavioral Sciences at Northwestern University's Feinberg School of Medicine and serves on the faculty of The Family Institute at Northwestern University and the Chicago Institute for Psychoanalysis, where he is Associate Director of the Integrative Psychoanalytic Couple Therapy Program.

For many years and until recently, he was the coordinator of a popular for-credit course he developed for Northwestern undergraduates, *Marriage 101: Building Loving and Lasting Relationships*. In recent years, he has lectured nationally and internationally and has taught courses on couple therapy in many venues, including to students in Iran and China. He has authored/published more than 40 professional papers in the fields of psychiatry, psychoanalysis, and couple therapy, together with the textbook, *A Roadmap for Couple Therapy: Integrating Systemic, Psychodynamic, and Behavioral Approaches*.

He lives in Winnetka, IL, with his wife, Sheila, and is the proud father of three adult daughters and grandfather of two granddaughters.

Introduction

Couple therapy is hard. Therapists must deal with two clients who are often at war with each other and who have differing psychologies, histories, agendas, and commitments to therapy. It is emotionally demanding because it evokes intense emotions. The subject matter is challenging, including pragmatic topics, such as sex, money, and childrearing, and abstract ones like power, commitment, and love.

The good news is that precisely because couple therapy is complex, deals with life's great challenges, and allows us to help people who are suffering, couple therapy can be deeply gratifying, intellectually interesting, and personally rewarding. It can also improve our individual therapy since, unlike in individual treatment, it allows us to see what happens behind closed doors, not just what clients *tell* us happens there. Given these challenges and rewards, my goal in writing this book is to help you feel less of the stress and confusion and more of the satisfaction as you practice this challenging form of therapy.

In my earlier book, *A Roadmap for Couple Therapy: Integrating Systemic, Psychodynamic, and Behavioral Approaches*, I discussed the components of a comprehensive, integrative model for conducting couple therapy. My goal there was to describe the unique value of each of the three principal approaches to couple problems and treatment—those identified in the book's subtitle—and to show how therapists can interweave and sequence interventions based on those approaches. This book takes up where that book left off, by filling in more details and adding suggestions for handling both common problems and major crises that lead couples to seek our help.

While my previous book focused on how to help couples talk to each other—constructively, collaboratively, lovingly—this one focuses on the details of what they are talking about, the subject matter that is both commonplace and sometimes catastrophic. Even when helping clients to listen to each other and fight fair (as in Behavioral Couple Therapy), to "soften" and heal attachment wounds (as in Emotionally Focused Couple Therapy), to "solve the moment" (as in Dan Wile's Collaborative Couple Therapy), or to recognize their transferences and own their projected insecurities (as in psychodynamic approaches), there remain the details of what they should do!

DOI: 10.4324/b22905-1

This book aims to fill that gap by providing domain-specific knowledge, as it discusses the psychology and dynamics of common problems (with sex, money, children) and stressful situations (affairs, divorce, stepfamilies). We will investigate each topic to identify what makes it so stressful, so hard to face, and so challenging to resolve. If you're like me, many of these topics will not have been covered in graduate school or professional training, where the emphasis tends to be on teaching techniques of therapy rather than on the specific, complex problems that bring people to us. Like most of us, couples have also received little education that might help them cope and, consequently, they can use our guidance.

As was my earlier book, this one is based on my 40-plus years of experience with more than 500 couples; on an extensive review of the clinical and research literature; and on many years of teaching, supervising, and interacting with others in the field. While there are separate books and still more individual articles on the topics covered here, this text aims to provide one-stop shopping and a synthesis of the best available ideas. Knowing that some readers may want to learn still more about particular topics, I have flagged references along the way that I have found particularly illuminating. The chapters here, however, should provide a good enough scaffolding to facilitate work with couples facing these problems, sometimes providing more suggestions than I (even after having written them) can keep in mind.

My motivations for writing this book are both professional and personal. On the personal side, my early failed marriage and my later, far happier one—now 40 years and three grown daughters later—have convinced me of the wrenching pain of marital discord and of the joy that is possible when a marriage is going well. These experiences have fueled my curiosity about how marital success can be achieved and about how therapists can foster this worthwhile endeavor. From a professional perspective, this book provides a better map than the one I had years ago when I began to treat couples. Much of what I have learned, I have learned the hard way—by trying to understand why I wasn't getting better results—and much occurred when flying by the seat of my pants. This book spells out some of that hard-earned knowledge so that others can have an easier time of it and be more expeditiously and predictably successful.

The importance of couple therapy

The following statistics illuminate what is at stake:

- Approximately 80% of American women marry for the first time by age 40 (Copen et al., 2012), and about 90% of both men and women eventually marry (Whitehead & Popenoe, 2002).
- Despite the rise in cohabitating couples and single-parent families, most young people want to marry, marriage having "evolved from a marker

of conformity to a marker of prestige . . . a status one builds up to" (Cherlin, 2004, p. 855).

- One in five first marriages will fail within the first five years, and 40–50% of first marriages end in divorce (Copen et al., 2012).
- Twenty percent of married couples report significant marital distress at any point in time (Bradbury et al., 2000).
- Among clients seeking treatment for "acute emotional distress," problems with intimate relationships are the most frequently cited causes (Foran et al., 2015; Swindel et al., 2000).
- Marital success augments general well-being, physical health, and economic success (Doherty et al., 2002; Proulx et al., 2007; Waite & Gallagher, 2000); and relationship success is probably the best predictor of overall happiness (Carr et al., 2014; Heller et al., 2004; Lee et al., 1991; Lyubomirsky, 2013).[1]
- Marital conflict, unhappiness, and divorce cause declines in all the just-mentioned areas and generate similar problems in the next generation (Booth & Amato, 2001; Cummings & Davies, 1994; Hetherington, 2003; Wallerstein et al., 2000).
- Marital distress is associated with broad classifications of anxiety, mood, and substance use disorders and with almost all narrower classifications of specific mental disorders (Whisman & Uebelacker, 2003).
- Half of all psychotherapists in the United States do some couple therapy (Orlinsky & Ronnestad, 2005), though many find it daunting or even frightening (*Psychotherapy Networker*, Nov–Dec, 2011).
- On the positive side, couple therapy has been shown to improve marital success and happiness in approximately two-thirds of unselected distressed couples (Gurman, 2011; Lebow et al., 2012), with effectiveness rates that are "vastly superior to control groups not receiving treatment" (Lebow et al., 2012, p. 145).
- There is considerable room for improvement in couple therapy, as less than 50% of couples entering therapy reach levels of marital satisfaction seen in nonclinical couples (Baucom et al., 2003), many come for only a short time and are not helped much (Owen et al., 2019), and many who improve later relapse (Jacobson & Addis, 1993; Owen et al., 2019; Rathgeber et al., 2019).

In summary, relationship success matters greatly, is often compromised, and improves with couple therapy, a practice with room for improvement.

Terminology

Couple therapy

I have chosen to use *couple therapy* rather than *couples therapy* or other possible variations, by analogy with *individual therapy* (never termed *individual's therapy*) and because the leading anthologies in the field use that term (Gurman, 2008a, 2010).

Marital or couple

For purely stylistic reasons, I sometimes use the more restrictive terms *marital* and *spouse* interchangeably with the more inclusive terms *couple* and *partner*, with the understanding that, in most situations, it makes little difference whether the individuals are formally married or not, since what I am discussing throughout are people in committed, intimate relationships.

They *instead of* he/she, s/he, he and she *or alternating occasions of* he *and* she

For quite some time, it has been considered unacceptable to use *he* as a generic, singular pronoun for a person of either gender. Because the other options, listed above, make for awkward prose, I will often employ the (grammatically incorrect) plural pronouns *they* or *their*, as has become common practice in everyday speech and is now accepted as correct APA style.

Outline of the book

Part I: Synopsis of A Roadmap for Couple Therapy reviews and summarizes the three main approaches to couple treatment: systems theory, psychodynamics, and behavior therapy (psychoeducation) and then discusses how to sequence them. This distills the content of my earlier book while conveying its most important practical suggestions. In my model (Nielsen, 2016, 2017a), integration proceeds from the unadorned, conjoint meetings of Couple Therapy 1.0 to an early focus on the couple's maladaptive processes, the vicious cycles that interfere with problem solving and erode friendship, intimacy, and trust, which, when allowed to repeat and intensify, often lead to divorce. Each of the three major approaches to couple treatment provides useful options (upgrades) for remediating these maladaptive vicious cycles. After describing each of these approaches in more detail, I discuss how to sequence and choose among them. Part I concludes with an illustrative case example.

The remainder of the book provides more fine-grained improvements/upgrades that do not simply follow intuitively from this aerial view of couple therapy. After beginning with hopeful expectations for a happy future, all marriages face some predictable life challenges that may unhinge and destabilize them. Some will also face unexpected crises, such as illness or financial hardship. When faced with such challenges, some couples will work as a team and grow in commitment, respect, and love. Others will fight maladaptively over how to proceed, perhaps agreeing on ill-advised courses of action. And some will come to therapy for help.

When they do, optimal assistance will come from therapists armed with both strategies for helping couples to talk to each other (the subject of Part I) *and* domain-specific knowledge (the subject of Parts II and III), for instance, about how best to deal with a difficult teenager, an out-of-control budget, or a lagging sex life. Even couples who are fundamentally solid in the three overarching areas of process, psychodynamics, and communication skills may require help tailored to their specific developmental challenges.

Part II: Upgrades Addressing Common Problems applies the comprehensive, integrative model of Part I to some common problems seen in couple therapy, including those life challenges that lead the list of manifest reasons couples seek our help: problems with sex, children, money, division of labor, and simply living under the same roof (which I call *domestic problems*). The final chapter discusses common issues related to stress from work, balancing work and family life, and managing limited time. These topics are often the bread and butter of couple therapy content, each with nuances that can help or hinder working out solutions.

Part III: Upgrades Addressing Common Stressful Situations discusses situations that create marital crises and are often catastrophic. These are the most challenging, gut-wrenching marital cases, ones that almost should not be assigned to beginners: couples reeling from extramarital affairs, impending or recent divorces, and attempting to manage stepfamilies. In all these situations, partners are questioning the foundations of their union and their commitment to each other. Each of these circumstances presents hidden mine fields, serious countertransference challenges, and problems related to maintaining neutrality when couples take up vastly different positions. There is much to learn here, which explains why these are some of the longest chapters in the book.

How to use this book

If you haven't read my first book, be sure to read Part I, since it will be assumed that you have done so in the case examples that come later. (If you enjoy Part I but have not yet read my first book, you may, at some point want to read it, since it contains far more detail, practical suggestions, and illustrative examples than I could squeeze in here.) After reading Part I, many of you will want to simply read this book from cover to cover, as in a graduate school course; the book is easier that way, as it flows from somewhat simpler problems to more complex ones. As an alternative—especially for those who have not been assigned the book in a course—separate chapters can be read as stand-alone resources when you are treating couples with particular problems.

An empathic field guide

Across all the topics covered in this book, my aim is to provide a sort of field guide to help readers know where to look and what to look for. Unlike a guide for bird-watchers, this book should allow readers to also achieve greater empathy for the suffering of the clients we treat. Just as partners tend to blame and pathologize each other, therapists can fall into similar internal states of mind, even if we don't act them out in therapy. To really help people, we must feel our way into their varied lived experiences. It is my hope that, after reading this book, you will have a far better empathic understanding of the many challenges of married life, including the emotional struggles that lie beneath the surface of these external problems and marital crises.

Note

1. In their review of 13 relevant studies, Heller et al. (2004) found an average correlation of .42 between marital satisfaction and overall life satisfaction.

Part I

Synopsis of Integrative Couple Therapy

1 Couple Therapy 1.0

The intimidator and the novelist: a prototypical case

Tom, a 35-year-old retired professional football player, and Jennifer, a 33-year-old novelist, presented with the manifest conflict of deciding whether to move to another city.[1] There were clear plusses and minuses to relocating that they had "discussed" endlessly—he, using what he considered logical arguments, and she, becoming exasperated and shutting down. Jennifer remained unwilling to consider Tom's arguments, as she felt that her needs, though somewhat unclear even to herself, were not being considered. Both were despondent, not only about the deadlocked decision, but about their sex life, which had almost ceased, and about the viability of their six-year marriage.

Couple Therapy 1.0

"Just Talk to Each Other."

Had I seen Tom and Jennifer when I began doing couple therapy as a psychiatric resident in 1975, I would have suggested they meet with me to talk to each other while I watched and tried to mediate. I call this relatively unstructured, here-and-now, talk-to-each-other model Couple Therapy 1.0. It is the Model T of couple therapy and still provides the scaffolding for my work. It makes intuitive sense because, like Tom and Jennifer, virtually all couples coming for couple therapy complain of a breakdown in communication. As with many forms of instruction—music, sports, or dance—the model assumes that *talking about* how a person interacts (or plays) is insufficient for revealing what is going on. Rather, the therapist (or teacher or pro) must *observe* the client in action.

The format of *conjoint* meetings to deal with marital problems was uncommon until the 1960s, although *marriage counseling* began in the 1920s (Gurman & Fraenkel, 2002). Couple Therapy 1.0 builds on conjoint couple counseling meetings where partners met together with a mediator by adding some rudimentary recommendations to help couples communicate more effectively. It is distinguished from the upgraded forms I will describe later

DOI: 10.4324/b22905-3

by the absence of sophisticated methods for attending to and improving the interpersonal couple process. I chose to make this conjoint, talk-to-each-other model the basic 1.0 version (rather than the earlier or later formats) for two reasons: first, because it is still commonly employed by many untrained counselors (peer and religious) and individual therapists who know that they must encourage couples to interact, but don't know what to do beyond simple mediation; and second, because it is the foundation for the various approaches that improve on it.

The basics of Couple Therapy 1.0

Prior to tackling our central topic—the integration and sequencing of advanced options—I will offer some basic guidelines for Couple Therapy 1.0 that also inform more complex versions. Here and throughout, recommended interventions will be shown as italicized bullet points.

- *As in all forms of psychotherapy, offer empathy, hope, safety, and containment in a professional environment that prioritizes the therapeutic alliance* (Friedlander et al., 2006; Sprenkle et al., 2009).
- *Allow the couple to choose problematic topics and attempt to work them out* (Pinsof, 1995).
- *Observe, monitor, and sometimes question partners about what their spouses have said.*
- Assist clients who do not want to talk to each other.

Most clients prefer to talk to *you*, rather than to *each other*. They want to tell you how they see things and why their partners are wrong, bad, or mentally ill (Christensen & Jacobson, 2000). To counter their desire to talk only to me, I tell them, "As in music, sports, or dance lessons, I need to see you doing what you do to help you improve."

- *Assert control and manage the emotional room temperature.*

In the ideal session, the couple respectfully engages emotionally significant issues. "Getting feelings out," while necessary, risks being only destructive. Couple therapy requires far more structuring than individual therapy. Several interventions are helpful for adjusting the emotional room temperature and providing containment. I include these under Couple Therapy 1.0 not only because they are basic and powerful but because they will quickly occur to almost any novice therapist and, thus, do not deserve more advanced upgrade status.

- *Cool things down by putting yourself in the middle.*

Exploiting clients' preference for talking to you, reduce the room's emotional temperature by coming between them (sometimes literally) and allowing them to return to what feels less intense: talking to an empathic therapist or, more soothing still, listening to you talk to them.

- *Heat things up by applying the interventions used in psychodynamic individual therapy to reduce anxiety and defensiveness.*

These include gently encouraging clients to describe the calamities they fear will occur if they become more emotionally present and forthcoming.

- *Heat things up by moving out of the middle and instructing the partners to interact with each other directly, an option not available in individual therapy.*
- *Work to remain neutral.*

Couple therapists must not be perceived as *consistently* biased in favor of one of the partners, a situation correlated with poor outcomes (Lebow et al., 2012), even as maintaining overall neutrality while encouraging partners to change can be challenging (Friedlander et al., 2006).

When Couple Therapy 1.0 is sufficient: rarely

The unadorned conjoint model of Couple Therapy 1.0 may be successful when couples must resolve important disagreements (e.g., dealing with a difficult child) or need to discuss their feelings about a recent stressful life event (e.g., undergoing chemotherapy). It works well when the conflicts and feelings are not proxies for deeper, more long-standing issues, and when the discussion is not impeded by serious character pathology or maladaptive patterns of relating. More often, however, it fails because it lacks the power for dealing with these complications (Gurman, 2008b; Snyder & Mitchell, 2008). This leads us to the next chapter and our first "upgrade": focusing on the couple's interpersonal process.

Note

1. All the couples I describe are disguised and some are composite versions of couples I have treated.

2 The First Upgrade

Focus on the Interpersonal Process

"Upgrades" here are analogous to technological advances that increase the functionality of computer operating systems. This metaphor avoids the problem of name-branding, since existing brands of therapy and new innovations can all contribute improvements to the underlying, bare-bones Couple Therapy 1.0 model. As with computer upgrades, we must be sure the elements work together.

The first upgrade to Couple Therapy 1.0 is focusing on the couple's interpersonal process

The "pathological dance," in which the emotional music generally matters more than the lyrics, must become the principal concern of both the therapist and the couple. Virtually, all experienced couple therapists agree on this, though, as discussed later, they approach it from different angles. This is a systems theory upgrade that views much couple behavior as an *emergent property* of individual interactions, where what emerges is more than the sum of the individual contributions. While Couple Therapy 1.0 emphasizes the here and now of couples talking to each other, it does not specify that the *process*, rather than the *content*, should be the early and primary focus. This process focus should be considered a crucial upgrade to working with couples, as it was at the dawn of the family therapy movement. Indeed, a failure to utilize this upgrade probably explains the disappointing results obtained by untrained counselors and individual therapists undertaking conjoint therapy.

Why process should precede content

There are many reasons to focus on process. Most importantly, research shows that negative process predicts poor outcomes in marriage and interferes with problem-solving (Gottman et al., 1998; Gottman & Gottman, 2017; Lebow et al., 2012), whereas improved collaboration reduces the number of problems to be solved, facilitates problem solving post therapy, and correlates with positive outcomes (Gurman & Fraenkel, 2002; Sullivan & Baucom, 2005). Improving system dysfunction is also easier than changing personality

DOI: 10.4324/b22905-4

dysfunction (Pinsof, 1995), while "solving the moment" strengthens intimacy (Wile, 2002), "shared purpose" (Friedlander et al., 2006), and "we-ness," independent of resolution of couple problems that can be "perpetual" (Gottman & Levenson, 1999).

Improved process as a shared target

Targeting negative interaction cycles can help us begin to integrate systemic, psychodynamic, and behavioral approaches, including those of Dan Wile (2002), whose interventions center on establishing "collaboration"; Les Greenberg and Sue Johnson (1988) and other EFT therapists whose research shows the benefits of "pursuer/blamer softening" and "distancer engagement"; and Howard Markman, Scott Stanley, and Susan Blumberg (2001), who teach the speaker–listener technique. Consequently, rather than referring to specific authors or branded therapies, we can classify interventions into three broad categories: *Systemic theories* stress how negative process can stem from the cyclical amplification of initial conditions (somewhat independent of the partners' individual psychologies) and the structural challenge of sharing power equitably in a two-person polity (among other things); *psychodynamic theories* explain maladaptive process via hidden issues, divergent meanings, transferences, and projective identification; and *psychoeducational and behavioral theories* add that people can be taught better approaches to managing difficult conversations, regulating emotions, and solving problems.

The Cheshire Cat complication

Having just declared that interpersonal process should usually be the early focus of therapy, we must acknowledge that it is impossible to discuss process in the abstract, without *some* concrete content. In *Alice in Wonderland*, the Cheshire Cat's smile existed without the cat, but in real life, "process" always requires "content," if it is to be seen. This suggests a recommendation sometimes at variance with the guideline of letting couples choose topics for discussion:

• *To improve the benefit and sustainability of focusing on process, encourage couples to begin with more workable, less emotionally charged content.*

This may not always be possible, especially when the consultation is driven by a serious rupture of trust, such as infidelity. In such cases, we should begin with the topic that is most pressing, even though it may render examination and remediation of the couple's process more difficult. Emotional intensity aside, there are many days when we should follow the problem-centered focus of Couple Therapy 1.0 and allow couples to focus on content rather than spotlighting process. Although improved process fosters more successful management of most marital problems, thorny problems *are* important (Fincham & Beach, 1999) and will eventually need to be addressed.

Systemic interventions that begin to alter negative interaction cycles

- *Focus on the cycle and label it as the enemy.*

Focusing on the pathological cycle will usually, in and of itself, improve that process. It accomplishes this in three interrelated ways. Giving the vague marital problem a diagnostic label ("a systems problem") defines and demystifies it (just as diagnosing a physical malady does). Objectifying it makes it a shared enemy the couple can attack jointly, in what White (2007) termed an "externalizing conversation." And focusing on the pathological dance reduces blame by countering linear narratives of victim and villain.

- *Use the chemical reaction metaphor.*

To convey the idea of a systemic problem—one with additive, circular, and emergent properties—I use the metaphor of a chemical reaction. The partners are likened to two colorless reagents in separate beakers that, when mixed, become drastically altered: perhaps becoming explosively hot, ice cold, or foul smelling. One of the reagents might think, "I was just fine before: not hot, cold, or smelly. This sudden change, in which I don't recognize myself, must be due to that other damn chemical!" This metaphor powerfully illustrates how group process is not reducible to individual behavior and is experience-near for individuals who are feeling blamelessly victimized by their partners.

- *Explain that the "punctuation" of negative cycles is arbitrary.*

Most people "punctuate" their narratives by beginning with some misdeed or insensitive action of their partner. Therapists can point out that this starting point is usually arbitrary.

- *Normalize off-putting demands: drowning swimmers.*

Escalation commonly consists of one or both partners speaking increasingly loudly, impatiently, and aggressively, perhaps while nagging, guilt-tripping, or swearing. These ineffective attempts to influence a partner tend to occur and intensify when the partner appears unresponsive. Therapists can normalize these counterproductive behaviors by explaining them in systemic terms. One metaphor I use is of a drowning swimmer calling for help from an unresponsive lifeguard. The more the swimmer fears drowning, and the longer the lifeguard fails to respond, the louder the swimmer screams. Often, in escalating negative couple cycles, it is more accurate to characterize *both* partners as drowning swimmers, even though one may superficially appear to be an unresponsive lifeguard.

- *Normalize flight: firefighters battling forest fires.*

Just as escalating anger can seem appropriate in some situations, so can flight. Withdrawal becomes more comprehensible and acceptable if one remembers that firefighters facing a raging forest fire must sometimes retreat temporarily. Therapists can help couples consider the perspectives of meta-phorical fleeing firefighters (Why do they think the situation is hopeless?) and advancing forest fires (What is making the pursuer so hot and insistent?).

•   *Introduce the goal of "making a short story long."*

After giving the couple a preliminary outline of the cycle that is simulta-neously captivating and torturing them, I explain that we can gain a deeper understanding by "making a short story long" (Scheinkman & Fishbane, 2004): slowing things down, as in a slow-motion video replay that can allow us to examine it in detail.

In the next two chapters, we discuss ways that psychodynamically informed therapists and behavior therapists have found useful to work with negative interaction cycles and to further deepen the treatment.

3   Psychodynamic Upgrades

As described in more detail in separate papers (Nielsen, 2017b, 2019b), psychodynamically informed thinking encourages us to:

- *Focus on underlying issues, personal meanings, transferences, resistances, projective identification, and acceptance.*

The initial goal of the psychodynamic approach is to reduce defensiveness and blame via "reframing" and "making a short story long" as we explore personal meanings and allergic reactions stirred by surface conflicts. Transference hopes and fears, intrapsychic conflicts, and idiographic sensitivities are explored with the goal of elucidating what powers the counterproductive behaviors of the negative interaction cycle. In all cases, therapists can point out that less-than-perfect behavior is common when people face their negative transference expectations or believe that their central needs are not being met (Leone, 2008; Shaddock, 2000).

Once we uncover and reframe an issue in one partner, the other will often become more understanding. When this does *not* happen, the therapist can work to help him or her respond more sympathetically by uncovering issues that stand in the way.

The next step after the initial exploration of hidden issues depends on the psychodynamics and content uncovered: Work on projective identification, families of origin, forgiveness, and acceptance usually evolves organically as specific hidden issues emerge in an increasingly safe setting.

Projective identification is a powerful conceptual tool for couple therapists. It is an interpersonal defense that moves beyond misidentifying others (transference) to inducing them to play roles in some interpersonal drama. It allows projecting partners to locate unacceptable parts of themselves in their partners or to use them to work out unfinished issues from their past (Catherall, 1992; Nielsen, 2019b). In either form, it interferes with couple intimacy and problem solving.

As advocated by others (Pinsof et al., 2011; E. Wachtel, 2017), when I am uncovering and working with psychodynamic issues (meanings, hopes, fears, defenses), my preference is to focus on the here-and-now couple

DOI: 10.4324/b22905-5

process before exploring historical origins. This is because hearing a negative transference labeled by the therapist ("Perhaps you fear asking for things from your wife because you believe she will become critical of you like your mother?") is usually less effective than encouraging clients to test out their (transference) fears in the present—here, a fear of making requests. If clients achieve better results than they expected, the historical explanation is interesting and may help them remember and make sense of their undue fear, but it pales in comparison to the therapeutic impact of their corrective experience. This here-and-now preference also makes it less likely that the spouse will pile on with, "See, I've always said you act like I'm your mother!"

That said, not all psychodynamic work occurs *during* examination of the couple's process. As it turns out, *unpacking the interpersonal process is often the royal road to discovering the individual intrapsychic problems that haunt a marriage* and serves as the starting point for what I term episodes of "witnessed individual psychotherapy." Here, I proceed as I would in an individual psychodynamic therapy, with the added benefit that partners get to observe and learn more about one another's deepest concerns, sometimes adding their own insights.

•   *Work on forgiveness and acceptance.*

With some couples, such as those who begin therapy reeling from a recently exposed affair, issues concerning forgiveness and reconciliation arise from the start, and therapy often begins as crisis intervention. This is why I have diagrammed "Betrayal/Forgiveness Therapy" in Figure 5.1 (p. 24) as a separate (challenging) form of therapy evolving rapidly out of the limitations of Couple Therapy 1.0. When the presenting problem involves betrayal, we need to focus on the immediate crisis, including the meaning of the betrayal, the loss of trust, possible apologies, and the need to control unacceptable behavior. Once things have settled down—and assuming the partners elect to continue their relationship—work can proceed in the usual manner, focusing on negative cycles, psychodynamics, and skill deficits, and progressing to discussions of the specific issues that may have led to the violation of trust. For other couples, specialized forgiveness work will occur later in treatment, when it becomes safe or relevant to bring up a long-past betrayal.

For most couples, work on *acceptance* will almost always come later, after attempts at problem solving and compromise have shown their limitations (Jacobson & Christensen, 1996), which is why this psychodynamically informed module is shown as a rectangle of its own at the bottom of Figure 5.1. Work on acceptance is important because research shows that many couple problems are "perpetual" and unlikely to change (Gottman & Levenson, 1999). To some extent, acceptance is a background theme for all therapeutic interventions, as we work to help clients learn to live with their less-than-perfect partners *and* their less-than-perfect selves. (Working on self-acceptance also reduces projective identification, because clients who can accept negative aspects of themselves no longer need to locate or induce them in their partners.)

• *Aim for more than conflict resolution.*

When using psychodynamic interventions, *we seek not only to reduce conflict and enable productive problem solving, but to facilitate empathy, intimacy, self-esteem, and love.* Among other things, couples learn to trust each other with more honest self-disclosure and to balance the existential conflict between meeting their own needs and those of their partner. These more far-reaching goals may explain the more enduring and intensifying benefits found in some follow-up studies of couple therapy emphasizing psychodynamics (Johnson & Greenberg, 1985; Snyder & Mitchell, 2008).

• *Pay attention to countertransferences.*

Throughout couple therapy and independent of intervention category, therapists must monitor their emotional reactions to clients, their countertransferences. During psychodynamic work, this facilitates guesses about the role relationships and expectations in play (Tansey & Burke, 1989). To assess these, I imagine what it might be like to be married to each of the partners and ask myself whether I would experience the same sorts of frustrations and disappointments they are describing. If it seems likely that I would, I feel more confident that those problems are worthy of attention. If I see different problems not yet mentioned, I may wonder why a spouse is so complacent. If I am not much bothered by the problems mentioned, I am more likely to wonder whether the complaining spouse is having allergic reactions. All these musings depend on my having a working knowledge of my own personal biases, emotional allergies, and current concerns.

I pay particular attention to negative countertransferences. Noticing a reflexive inclination to side against an obviously offensive partner often leads to my coming to that person's aid. This stems partly from systems thinking: A whining, annoying, or stridently defensive spouse is often the one holding the fewest cards, having the least power, and therefore acting the most symptomatically. In couple therapy, the squeaky wheel is often the partner who is not getting needed psychological grease. When I find a client particularly repellent, I consider the possibility that he or she is not doing a good enough job representing his or her position or needs. If I can reframe, uncover, or give coherent voice to the client's concerns, this often improves the repellent behavior, the marriage, and the therapeutic alliance.

4 Behavioral/ Psychoeducational Upgrades

Behavioral and psychoeducational interventions that aim to improve couple process encourage us to:

- *Teach communication and emotion regulation skills.*

Early in treatment, I give clients handouts and recommended readings that discuss skillful communication (e.g., Markman et al., 2001). The readings help develop a shared vocabulary of do's and don'ts for difficult conversations, presenting the material more systematically and in greater depth than makes sense in therapy sessions. I then offer individualized relationship training, as necessary: communication skills when we encounter recurring maladaptive ways of speaking and listening, emotion regulation skills when emotion tolerance is repeatedly exceeded, and problem-solving and negotiation skills when we discuss specific concrete conflicts (see Nielsen, 2016, for detailed recommendations).

When doing this, I regularly toggle between psychodynamic work and skills education. When couples fail to follow recommended communication rules, I explore their internal psychological obstacles. And when they *do* successfully follow the rules, we often uncover previously hidden issues and witness corrective experiences (Segraves, 1982). For instance, in one typical pursuer–distancer couple, the sheepish husband who perennially feared displeasing his wife was overjoyed to see how sticking to the role of active listener almost guaranteed him success with her. Both spouses also had corrective experiences after the wife followed the rule that the speaker keep remarks to a manageable duration. That allowed this timid man to experience his wife as less overwhelming and allowed her to experience him as more responsive (in contrast to her negative expectation, which had powered her off-putting pursuit).

As mentioned before, the timing of teaching skills is critical: too soon, and the therapist may fail to connect with the couple's pain; too late, and the couple may be deprived of powerful tools that can arrest their persistent negative cycles. Sometimes, I offer educational structuring right out of the gate. When teaching communication skills, I begin by emphasizing restraint from speakers ("*not* doing what comes naturally") and curiosity and empathy from listeners.

For most clients, following "communication rules" feels awkward and artificial, so it can help to remind clients of other beneficial procedures that

DOI: 10.4324/b22905-6

initially feel unnatural: a medical team using a pre-surgery checklist, a PTA meeting adhering to Robert's Rules of Order. While some therapists have argued that skills training is pointless because clients already know how they "should" behave but can't perform that way under pressure, research (e.g., Baucom et al., 2008; Roddy et al., 2016) and clinical experience demonstrate that many people benefit.

With volatile clients, I explain how to initiate and manage timeouts and how to downregulate intense emotions, as per Linehan (1993) and Atkinson (2005). And, to lower the intensity of conjoint sessions, I sometimes supplement them with individual sessions. Psychoactive medication can also help.

The following therapeutic recommendations are listed in this chapter on educational upgrades because they often require a combination of education and therapist directiveness, although, to be effective, they will also require therapists to be aware of underlying psychological (psychodynamic) concerns and impediments.

- *Work toward resolving specific tangible problems.*

Once we have a workable interpersonal process, we can target concrete areas of couple conflict. In later chapters we will look into this challenge in detail. Here, I simply want to note that all along, couples will have been discussing *some* specific issues that have elicited conflict and hard feelings, even as we have been focusing on their maladaptive process, their underlying psychodynamics, and their communication skills. But it is only now, after we have cleared away some of the structural constraints to productive problem solving, that couples will make headway in settling their more thorny and chronic disagreements. As we do so, we will almost always uncover additional *specific topic-related* underlying issues (psychodynamics) that will require attention and facilitate conflict resolution.

- *Suggest relevant self-help readings.*

In this phase of treatment, couples often benefit from self-help readings pertaining to the topics they are discussing (stepparenting, financial planning, caring for an aging parent).

- *Teach problem-solving and negotiation techniques.*

Sometimes, it helps to teach problem-solving and negotiation skills over and above rules for talking to each other safely, such as brainstorming and systematic problem assessment, as per Markman et al. (2001) and Fisher et al. (2011). Clients can then continue to access these resources after treatment ends.

Success in achieving practical and equitable solutions takes the heat out of pathological dancing and is strongly correlated with future marital happiness (Roddy et al., 2016). While work to improve process must often come first, resolution of highly distressing problems (e.g., managing an ex-spouse in a new stepfamily) may ultimately be what couples remember as most beneficial.

Concurrent interventions

The following interventions are theoretically separable from ones aimed at improving negative interaction cycles or practical problem solving and can run concurrently with them.

- *Encourage positive interactions.*

Beginning as soon as I believe there is a reasonable chance of success, I encourage date nights and other pleasurable activities, occasions explicitly designed to be free from conflict and stress. I help couples brainstorm and work with them to identify and reduce impediments, including the responsibilities (childrearing, work) and activities (solo recreation) that many chronically distressed partners focus on as alternatives to marital satisfactions. Although this idea is familiar to behavioral couple therapists, it is a valuable upgrade for therapists who might otherwise attend only to interpersonal process or who were trained to be nondirective.

- *Work to restore sexual intimacy.*

Sexual problems are extremely common in the general population (Laumann et al., 1999) and are almost universal in couples who present for couple therapy. We will discuss these in detail in a later chapter. Except for couples whose leading complaint concerns sex, most couples will choose to put this topic on hold until later in their work, as they assume, often correctly, that their lack of sex is secondary to their negative feelings toward each other.

It might seem logical that sexual encounters would resume spontaneously after overt conflict declines and cordial feelings return, but this is often not the case. For such couples, physical and sexual contact is often the final frontier requiring our help, something insufficiently addressed in many couple treatments that assume that this area of life will take care of itself (Gurman & Fraenkel, 2002; McCarthy & Thestrup, 2008).

While clients come to trust their partners to fight fair, many will remain reluctant to trust them with their strong, literally naked, desires for love and affection. As a result, I have found it helpful to think of myself as a ballroom dance instructor of frightened middle schoolers, the instructor who declares that it is now time to choose a partner and master the anxieties of dancing together. I begin slowly, encouraging the couple to hold hands, to hug, and to engage in sensate focus exercises, as needed, prior to erotic contact. Along the way, we may encounter specific sexual problems that need skillful, individualized attention. I designate this an upgrade because to address sexual problems successfully, therapists must be both proactive "dance instructors" and informed experts on what works beyond basic couple therapy.

5 Sequencing Interventions

It remains much easier to create a generic model of what to do than to state the order in which to proceed with those activities.

—Jay Lebow (1997, p. 10)

Couple therapy engages us in a complex, recursive process of interlocking activities: data gathering, hypothesizing, planning, sharing our ideas with clients, and processing their feedback. These activities proceed almost simultaneously, allowing us to continuously refine our working models of what the problems are and what we can do to help. This complexity can be both stimulating and overwhelming. While much of what I do now in couple therapy has become automatic, some attitudes and behaviors require constant vigilance, even after many years. In this chapter, I offer some overarching recommendations for conducting therapy and then discuss the sequencing of interventions in detail.

Categories of interventions

Table 5.1 lists the main categories of couple therapy interventions that I have described in previous chapters. These interventions are like pieces on a chessboard or tools in a toolbox, each with its own strengths, functions, and limitations. Our challenge is to know how to make them work together and in what order.

Overview of sequencing

The sequencing of interventions depends on the details of the problem at hand and on the stage of therapy. Some moves will get us off to a good start, and others will have to wait. While couple therapy will always be an unpredictable, nonlinear activity—unlike building a bridge, for which steps can be outlined in advance—experience and research show that therapy goes better if therapists pay attention to sequence, notwithstanding the varying sequences recommended by different schools of therapy.

DOI: 10.4324/b22905-7

Table 5.1 Categories of Couple Therapy Interventions

- Allow the couple to talk to each other, with minimal assistance from the therapist, about problems that concern them (Couple Therapy 1.0).
- Focus on their process: their negative interaction cycle.
- Focus on their psychodynamics: underlying issues (hopes and fears), personal meanings, transferences, and projective identification.
- Focus on acceptance and forgiveness.
- Teach communication skills.
- Teach emotion regulation skills.
- Teach problem-solving and negotiation skills.
- Teach adaptive, domain-specific solutions to particular problems.
- Discuss and encourage positive activities.

As noted by Scheinkman (2008), a sequencing map can be useful for beginners and experienced therapists alike. For beginners, often flooded with too many options, it offers direction. For experienced therapists, with their ingrained personal preferences, it offers an alternative array of options.

The ideal sequencing map should be relatively comprehensive—allowing improvisational use of diverse interventions as required by specific circumstances—but not so complex or encyclopedic as to give practitioners brain freeze. The ideal map should also prioritize interventions that are most likely to work and to work quickly (Pinsof, 1995). Unlike some therapists, I do not assume that the most expeditious therapy will necessarily begin with attention to behavior, to surface concerns, or to medications, since sometimes these foci just delay getting to the heart of the matter. In what follows, I describe my sequencing preferences and their rationale, including (a) what to try first, (b) what to try next should that prove insufficient, and (c) what to do when success has created the foundation for further work. Figure 5.1 provides a visual summary of sequencing options, beginning at the top and moving as indicated by the arrows.

Couple Therapy 1.0 interventions

I begin with the conjoint format of therapist and couple meeting to discuss the couple's presenting problems. This will be foundational to all that follows and offers a measure of structure, safety, and hope in the context of a professional, helping relationship.

1. *Begin with the couple's choice of a problem to discuss.* It is almost always best to start the therapy itself, and most subsequent sessions, with the client's choice of a pressing problem. I reserve the option of bringing up topics that have been avoided or that seem promising, and I will sometimes steer partners to more workable topics early on, leaving more difficult issues until later, when their relationship to each other and to therapy is stronger.

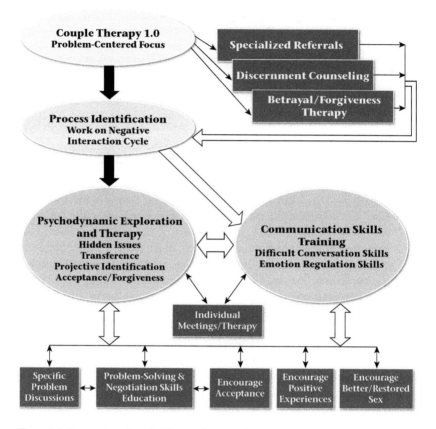

Figure 5.1 Sequencing Couple Therapy Interventions.

In general, interventions flow from top to bottom and then horizontally, as indicated, with the ovals representing the earlier and more important options. Rectangles at the top represent a rapid alteration of the conjoint format. Those at the bottom represent therapeutic foci made possible by earlier interventions. The exception is the rectangle of individual therapy or individual meetings with the couple therapist, which may be a necessary or concurrent step supporting the entire enterprise.

2. *Allow the couple to begin to talk unassisted.* After the topic has been opened, encourage the partners to talk to each other about it.[1] If they are doing well, utilizing only the symbolic holding provided by the therapeutic setting and the minimal structuring offered by your presence, allow the dialogue to progress and enjoy watching the couple move forward to the next step of minimally assisted problem solving. If things are not going well, proceed to options further down the list. This illustrates an important general principle: *If they are doing well on their own, stay out of it.* As noted by Pinsof (1995), "Excessive therapist competence leads to an underadequate and underachieving patient system," one that is too dependent on the therapist (p. 104).

3. *Attempt assisted problem solving.* Some couples begin talking reasonably well about a delimited topic (parenting a difficult teenager, coping with an aging relative) but then bog down because they have too little information or insufficient problem-solving skills. In such circumstances, I offer the practical assistance the couple appears to need while helping them to hear each other's feelings and positions more completely. It may be that extensive therapy will not be required if they can succeed with the help of minimal practical mediation and guidance. The test of this is whether the couple actually works out a compromise or solution themselves.

Ancillary or modified treatment formats based on presenting problems

The typical conjoint format must sometimes be modified immediately, as follows:

4. *If divorce seems imminent because one partner is only tenuously committed to the marriage, propose "discernment counseling"* (Doherty et al., 2016). This format is described in detail in Chapter 13.
5. *If serious psychopathology, depression, substance abuse, or extensive intimate partner violence are present, make appropriate referrals for specialized treatment; sometimes, this may run concurrently with the couple therapy.*
6. *If betrayal of trust is central at the outset, begin with a conjoint therapy tailored toward forgiveness.* I will have lots more to say about this in Chapter 12, which deals with extramarital affairs.

Negative process identification

In most cases, Steps 1 through 3 (Couple Therapy 1.0) will prove inadequate and more assistance will be needed, as follows:

7. *Focus on the couple's interpersonal process.* When minimally structured discussion and practical guidance have failed, focus on the pathological group process and identify the steps in the couple's negative interaction cycle. Most of the time, I begin to do this in the first diagnostic session. Almost all contemporary couple therapists begin here. This focus allows us to label the systemic process as the enemy and to suspend work on other presenting problems until the partners improve their manner of relating.

A fork in the road

After they have identified the behavioral steps in the couple's negative interaction cycle (e.g., a pursuer–distancer cycle), therapists of different persuasions take different paths. Behaviorally inspired therapists will choose to label specific problems in communication and teach better tactics. Psycho-analytically informed therapists, EFT couple therapists, and others who favor a more experiential approach will focus on the psychodynamic issues that lie below the surface of most "communication problems."

Whichever path we take, if either partner is experiencing too much distress, no new learning or useful dialogue will take place. Our job is to help partners to calm down sufficiently to talk to each other safely—sometimes by uncovering and validating deeper emotional concerns, sometimes by teaching rules that direct conversations into less volatile channels. Partners must be relatively calm and receptive for them to engage in problem solving or in planning positive activities.

Sprenkle, Davis, and Lebow (2009), after reviewing many studies of this choice point, concluded that "therapists do better offering insight-oriented procedures to clients who are more self-reflective, introspective, and intro-verted. Conversely, therapists should offer skill-building and symptom-focused methods to clients who are more impulsive and aggressive" (p. 52).

Consistent with their advice, I take a pragmatic approach tailored to clients' personality styles and receptivity. For reasons to be described shortly, I usually begin with a psychodynamic, uncovering approach. Should that prove ineffec-tive, I shift quickly to teaching rules for safe dialogue and techniques for emotion regulation. With high-intensity couples who lack psychological-mindedness, uncovering deeper anxieties—say, about commitment or respect—may be inflammatory. Teaching such couples how to talk more safely will often enable them to access deeper concerns later in the therapy. That said, some volatile couples will not hold still for such practical instruction, so you may need to do some empathic interpreting as a prelude to relationship education.

Psychodynamic interventions

8. *Focus on underlying issues, personal meanings, transferences, and resistances.* The principal reason to focus here first, before teaching fair-fighting skills, is because asking people to behave themselves when they don't want to and don't understand why they should, can feel inauthentic and forced, and may result in a failure to facilitate genuine emotional healing. With this problem of authenticity in mind, my usual preference—after labeling the components of the negative interaction cycle and noting its circularity—is to try to access the deeper, hidden issues that tend to maintain such cycles.

While virtually all couples can use instruction in the optimal ways to han-dle "difficult conversations," many couples will converse collaboratively soon after the therapist helps them address their underlying concerns. One cou-ple I treated had been fighting endlessly over whether the husband should or should not work harder on his career. This surface disagreement became accessible to discussion soon after I helped them see that the road to compro-mise was blocked by the emotional issues connected with both the content and the process of their disagreement: the husband feeling shamed and controlled, the wife feeling powerless to avoid reliving the economic hardship she had experienced as a child. In situations like this, uncovering therapy can move things along rapidly, whereas teaching skills like empathic listening can feel like stalling and can actually increase anxiety if partners feel that their complaints remain painfully unaddressed. Indeed, there is suggestive evidence—albeit from research conducted by proponents of this strategy—that choosing this experiential fork in the road yields superior results to choosing behavioral or problem-solving interventions (Johnson & Greenberg, 1985).

As noted in Chapter 3, where to go after the initial exploration of hidden issues depends on the psychodynamics and the content uncovered: Work on projective identification, acceptance, forgiveness, and families of origin usually evolves organically, as specific hidden issues are explored in an increasingly safe setting.

9. *Work with projective identification.* Viewing couple problems through the lens of projective identification flows naturally out of explorations of unacceptable feelings. Such work holds exceptional promise for effecting long-lasting change. Since projective identification involves motivations to keep the spouse at a distance, successful work here will also improve communication and intimacy. Many couple polarizations spring from the couple *process* itself: Specifically, when each partner voices a part of the truth, but fails to acknowledge the merit of the opposing side, both partners will become more extreme and insistent in maintaining their positions. This type of inductive process can often be interrupted relatively easily by using the "You're Both Right" intervention. When projective identification stems from more characterologically entrenched defensive patterns, however, therapeutic attention must be directed at deeper concerns, since clients aiming to disavow painful states will not so easily concede that "both are right."

10. *Explore each client's family of origin and past history.* Clients will often recall relevant historical material spontaneously as they try to understand specific underlying issues, hopes, and fears. When reviewing historical events, my focus is on how past events are *currently* active and how they shape the present (Breunlin et al., 2011; Cooper, 1987). Reviewing formative traumatic life events in detail almost always makes current sensitivities more comprehensible, and that makes everyone more sympathetic. When I feel fairly certain that a current pattern is long-lived, I ask directly about its historical origins: "Has this always been a sensitive area for you? When did it start?" Or, after we have uncovered a particular historical event, I might ask, "How do you think that has affected you and your relationships?"

11. *Work on acceptance.* As noted earlier, for most couples, work on *acceptance* will almost always come later, after attempts at problem solving and compromise have shown their limitations.

Behavioral/educational interventions

12. *Teach communication and emotion regulation skills.* As previously noted in Chapter 4, early in treatment, I give clients handouts and readings that discuss skillful communication. After this, most of my teaching of communication skills then unfolds organically in the context of the couple's discussions, not unlike most lessons in sports, dance, or music, in which individual lessons focus on strengths and weaknesses. I offer individualized relationship training when it seems appropriate: communication skills when we encounter recurring maladaptive ways of speaking and listening, emotion regulation skills when emotion tolerance is repeatedly exceeded, and problem-solving and negotiation skills when we discuss specific concrete topics (sex, money, parenting). As indicated by the horizontal arrows in Figure 5.1, there is usually a back-and-forth focus between psychodynamics and skills education, including moving to explore psychodynamic obstacles to following recommended communication rules.

As mentioned before, the timing of teaching skills is critical. Too soon, and the therapist may fail to connect with the couple's pain. Too late, and the couple may be deprived of powerful tools that can arrest their repetitive negative cycles.

I teach communication skills more extensively and more systematically in two (sometimes overlapping) situations: with concrete thinkers who are deficient in psychological-mindedness and with emotionally volatile couples. With clients who are nonabstract thinkers less comfortable with—or capable of—introspection, I teach communication skills in a formal manner, early in the treatment. Most of these couples seem grateful for this early shift to relationship education, which offers them explicit rules that help them do better. This is like teaching helpful rules of etiquette to people who would be hard-pressed to explain their psychological basis. This also gives these couples a sense of getting something tangible from me, in keeping with their relatively concrete, nonpsychological manner of relating.

I also move more quickly to systematic didactic teaching with highly volatile couples, including teaching emotion regulation skills and the nuts and bolts of timeouts. To break up the intensity of the conjoint sessions, I sometimes also supplement my work with such emotionally turbulent couples by adding individual sessions.

Specific problem-solving interventions

13. *Work toward resolution of specific tangible problems.* Once we have a more workable interpersonal process, we can begin to target concrete areas of couple conflict. Of course, all along, couples will have been discussing *some* specific topics that have elicited conflict and hard feelings, even as I tried to focus their attention on their maladaptive process,

their underlying psychodynamics, and their communication skill deficits. But it is only now, after we have cleared away some of the structural constraints to productive problem solving that couples will make headway on their more thorny and chronic disagreements. Discussing presenting problems in new and satisfactory ways has been shown to be a frequent characteristic of "pivotal moments" in couple therapy (Helmeke & Sprenkle, 2000).

At this point, we should recall the research that has found that, in the majority of naturally occurring couple arguments, no practical problem solving is required at all. This is because most such dustups arise from partners' inadvertently touching each other's hot buttons. When this has been the core of a couple's deteriorating marriage, therapy is a matter of teaching the partners to better understand each other's sensitivities (via psychodynamic exploration) and to reconnect (via the empathic apologies that are the heart of recovery conversations, as discussed in detail in Nielsen, 2016, pp. 158–160).

Nonetheless, in many cases, substantive issues and conflicts will still require attention. But now, having improved their interpersonal process and ability to work together, partners will have a far better chance of making workable decisions than they had when they entered therapy. Remaining mindful of the couple process, the therapist's attention can now shift to the details of the couple's ongoing disputes. This means returning to Steps 1–3 and allowing the couple to have another go at problem solving, with the therapist sometimes offering domain-specific suggestions. Couples in this phase of treatment will also benefit from self-help readings pertaining to the topics they are discussing (stepparenting, financial planning, caring for an aging parent).

14. *Teach problem-solving and negotiation techniques.* Once we have a more workable interpersonal process and have begun to discuss concrete areas of couple conflict, we can again observe how the couple does on their own. Sometimes, it will help to teach problem-solving and negotiation skills over and above the rules for talking to each other safely, but I do this only after determining that it will add value. One advantage of doing this at least once during a course of therapy is that clients will then have these skills available to them after therapy has concluded.

Concurrent interventions

15. *Along the way, encourage positive interactions.* As discussed in Chapter 4, beginning as soon as I believe there is a reasonable chance of success, I encourage date nights and other pleasurable times spent together, time explicitly prescribed to be free from conflict and stress. I help couples brainstorm and work with them to uncover possible impediments. In the process, it is frequently necessary to *challenge other social obligations that conflict with their time together.*

16. *Along the way, work to restore sexual intimacy.* For many couples, physical and sexual contact may be the final frontier requiring our help. Even when couples do not explicitly complain about sexual problems, therapists should assess sexual satisfaction, both as a measure of how they are doing and as an important target for assistance.

17. *Along the way, consider recommending individual psychotherapy.* For many clients, couple therapy is a minimally stigmatizing way to begin to rework lifelong sensitivities and personality deficits. After a course of couple therapy, many clients will stop blaming their partners, assume more responsibility for their marital problems, and acknowledge that these problems stem from their own ongoing emotional issues. In such cases, referral for individual treatment or psychoanalysis is often welcome. Requests for individual therapy referrals are fairly common at the termination of a successful couple treatment.

Whether to recommend individual treatment *during* an ongoing treatment is more debatable. My preference is to try not to complicate matters by doing so and to wait, instead, until couple issues are considerably improved. The main exception is when serious psychiatric or personality pathology either does not seem to be improving or is grossly interfering with the couple work. In such cases, separate individual therapy may be essential to enabling the couple treatment to succeed (Graller et al., 2001).

Repetition and nonlinearity

Although the decision tree that I have presented appears linear, actual therapy is far more circular, chaotic, and repetitive. Important changes take time and practice before they sink in. Clients rarely understand this: They expect that their partners will simply change after being told to do so, and they are surprised when therapy takes so much time and patience. We must therefore help clients replace the discouragement of "Here we go again." with the more hopeful attitude of "OK, things are heating up. What have I learned that can make this work out better for both of us?" Therapists also need not become overly discouraged when, week after week, couples make the same mistakes and follow the same patterns. Change is most often slow and difficult.

Mixing psychodynamic and relationship/educational interventions

While interventions will often follow one after the other in the sequence I described, skillful therapy will sometimes interdigitate intervention types, for instance, moving back and forth between psychodynamic exploration and educational didactic modes (Wachtel, 2014). Leone (2008) provides a good example of this in her account of how she directed and challenged a husband to be more verbally present and then elicited his reactions:

We talked about my direction and encouragement to Mike. Ann said it was one of the first helpful things I'd done in the 18-month treatment ("Finally!"). Mike acknowledged that if I directed him like that too frequently, he might start to feel controlled and dominated by me as he did with Ann. However, he said that in this case he had appreciated the direction, especially because it was a suggestion, not an order. He also described a mixed experience of feeling embarrassed that I'd have to tell him something he "should have known," but also pleased or flattered that I'd seen him as capable of doing it. He had imagined I'd be thinking, "This is important stuff I'd better handle this, Mike will screw it up!" We explored extensively Mike's sense of himself as "not good at these things," and related it to the fact that no one had comforted him or helped him learn how to comfort someone else.

(p. 95)

This example also illustrates the benefits of obtaining client feedback. Some clients will eagerly seek and absorb skills training while others will resist it as superficial or controlling. Some clients will flourish once we begin to explore and integrate past traumatic events; others will resist and never quite see the relevance. Asking clients how they have experienced an intervention, as Leone did, can help us tailor our interventions to client receptivity.

Relationship education and psychodynamics are also intertwined when, after teaching a skill, like the speaker–listener technique, we find clients unable to perform it. Here, we must become curious about the underlying dynamics that interfere. *More than most relationship education or behavioral couple therapies, this roadmap emphasizes working with the psychological issues (the psychodynamics) that make it hard for clients to follow adaptive rules for communicating or problem solving.* In doing so, this becomes an integrative therapy practiced with a "psychoanalytic accent" (Wachtel, 2014, p. 110).

In other cases, the psychodynamics become clearer *after* a client successfully follows our directives about better ways to communicate. This was true for the pursuer–distancer couple described briefly in Chapter 4. Not only did teaching the speaker–listener technique help them do better, but, more powerfully than my prior verbal interpretations, the fleeing husband's actual success and the pursuing wife's experience of being listened to illuminated to all of us his unrealistic, inhibiting fears of failure and her unrealistic fears that he didn't love her.

More than most purely psychodynamic approaches, this roadmap employs teaching and encouraging rules for safe communicating to achieve the "softening," lessened defensiveness, and corrective experiences that are the desired outcomes in emotionally focused therapies and in other therapies based on attachment theory or psychodynamics.

Finally, as noted by Fraenkel (2009), many of our best interventions are *simultaneously* relationship/educational and psychodynamic, and some will advance the goals of almost all schools of couple therapy:

[T]eaching (or at least encouraging) a couple to use more equitable, non-aggressive communication is simultaneously supported by a cognitive-behavioral theory promoting acquisition of skills; by a feminist couple approach that seeks to promote greater equality and less intimidation between partners; by a structural couple therapy that promotes increased closeness between partners; by emotionally focused couple therapy that values the opportunities for couples to express deeply held, vulnerable emotions; by a psychodynamically-informed couple therapy focused on increasing each partner's capacity to reflect on the mind of the other; by an attachment-based therapy seeking to improve neuro-physiologically determined emotional regulation (Atkinson, 2005); by a family-of-origin approach seeking to interrupt inherited distance-promoting interactions; and by a narrative couple therapy that values opportunities for each partner to share their respective perspectives in order to attain a more "preferred story."

(p. 238)

Direction versus non-direction

Separate from client feedback and the decision tree I have outlined, we should base our sequencing choices on the immediate structural pros and cons of possible interventions, including the trade-offs between being directive and providing a safe, nondirective space for client initiative. As has been emphasized for years by psychodynamically informed therapists, if we give direct advice, we may fail to uncover and discuss the ambivalence and anxiety that block authentic action. Whether clients follow our premature advice or rebel against it matters little, since important life decisions based on the preferences of others are unlikely to last or suffice. By contrast, our failing to give helpful, timely advice risks depriving clients of the information they may need to make educated choices.

Not only do greater or lesser amounts of directiveness impact clients, but pursuing one or the other shapes our own mindsets. When I am in teaching mode, I am trying to be systematic and convincing. When I am allowing space, I experience more of the free-floating curiosity and openness that are the hallmarks of the listening psychoanalyst. Both are useful, but they are somewhat antithetical states of mind. To achieve balance, I try not to allow myself to get too caught up in one to the exclusion of the other.

Still more generally, the relevant dichotomy here is between having a plan for what should happen next and going with the flow. Therapists who lack a plan will become lost and may fail to recognize landmarks they have visited before, whereas therapists with too strict an agenda will miss improvisational opportunities that emerge out of the give-and-take of the moment. As in so many areas of life, the key to optimal functioning is balance.

In the final chapter in this section, we return to our prototypical couple to illustrate this integrative approach to couple therapy.

Note

1. A study by Butler, Harper, and Mitchell (2011) supports giving priority to assisting couples with *talking to each other* (what they call "enactments") and offering input as needed, rather than using a more controlled therapist-directed format from the start. The researchers randomly assigned couples to enactments followed by therapist-directed work or the reverse sequence. Results strongly favored the former.

6 The Intimidator and the Novelist

An Illustration of the Integrative Model[1]

Recall that this couple came to therapy stuck in the zero-sum problem of deciding whether to move away from Chicago. In our first meeting, both Tom and Jennifer described the negative cycle that emerged whenever they tried to discuss this conflict. When I encouraged them to talk to each other rather than to me, I got to observe it directly. And when I attempted to mediate a discussion of the pros and cons of moving, their negative cycle impeded my efforts. As often happens, this attempt at bare-bones Couple Therapy 1.0 proved insufficient. We did, however, now have a handle on a working diagnosis, as their description, their unaided process in the room, and their imperviousness to straightforward assistance all pointed to their negative interaction cycle as the culprit needing attention.

A business school graduate after ending his professional sports career, Tom was very competitive. He interfaced with his wife—and the world—in a dogged, excessively logical manner, but his detailed charts showing the advantages of moving had no effect on Jennifer. Her reluctance—not only to move, but even to *discuss* moving—remained mysterious, especially since they both knew that Tom was growing increasingly depressed since the job opportunities he sought and the recreational activities he loved were unavailable locally.

The couple had met in college, where both were active in sports, and had bonded over this common interest and other shared values. Jennifer had been attracted to Tom's self-assurance but had resisted when he pressured her against her wishes to meet his needs. This was true in the bedroom, as well; although she had initially enjoyed sex with him, she had lost interest, feeling he imposed on her when she wasn't in the mood. Her rejection only added to Tom's frustration and feelings of inadequacy. Both his depression and his insistence that they move intensified. Clearly, the same negative interaction cycle was interfering with this other important area of their marriage. This was another reason, distinct from our inability to solve their presenting problem, to shift our focus to the pathological dance itself: to address multiple problems simultaneously.

"Tom," I began, "to the extent that you forcefully and repeatedly try to influence Jennifer with what you believe is impeccable logic, Jennifer feels increasingly dominated and withdraws still more into her angry, confused state of mind. When she retreats and refuses to participate in this crucial

DOI: 10.4324/b22905-8

discussion, you feel unimportant, anxious, and out of control. As a result, you redouble your efforts to force her to talk, and around you go."

My first goal here was to *interrupt* the negative process by labeling its steps and showing how they led to their standoff and escalating unhappiness. I also wanted to validate each partner's emotional reasons for continuing to dance as they did, by offering empathic explanations, sometimes directly ("Tom, it's hard for you to remain calm when your career and self-respect are blocked by Jennifer's reluctance to engage these issues.") and sometimes indirectly, representing one to the other ("Tom, I think what Jennifer would like to tell you, if she could be more direct and less afraid of hurting your feelings, is that when you get all worked up and insistent, it makes her feel like you're not interested in *her* needs. This makes her angry, and then, feeling uncomfortable with her anger, she shuts down.").

This combination of labeling the steps in their vicious cycle and providing empathy—a melding of systemic and psychodynamic approaches—almost immediately helped to slow them down and give them hope. It also cleared a space where we could further explore the underlying issues that both powered the cycle and were concealed by it. Specifically, as I continued to validate Tom's frustration with Jennifer's indecisiveness and block the guilt-inducing/controlling tactics he was using to deal with it, he became more patient, and we were able to uncover the reasons for her hesitation.

As the mood lightened, we found an amusing and telling image for an aspect of their dance: It turned out that, in sports, both had been known for "intimidating" their opponents. Significantly, this had been the *sole* area of Jennifer's life where she had allowed herself to be satisfyingly aggressive. Her anger was otherwise channeled indirectly, through characters in her novels who stood up to authority figures. I worked to help her express, overtly, the resentment she felt at being pushed around by Tom, now labeled "The Intimidator." In the process, she began to reflect on the origins of her difficulty expressing her needs. We learned of a career-ending sports injury and how she believed that she had allowed others, including her domineering father, to bully her into a surgery that made things worse. We also uncovered considerable internal conflictedness about her parents, who lived nearby, and about their expectations that she remain in the area to assist with family responsibilities.

Calling Tom "The Intimidator" might seem like a put-down, but he liked the title, which reminded him of times when he had felt strong and capable, so that he accepted being ribbed for being too dominating in his marriage. Further, reminding Jennifer of *her* past glories as an "intimidator" energized her to find a more assertive voice.

To help them experience a more balanced form of communicating, I taught them some speaking and listening skills, which helped Tom restrain himself and encouraged Jennifer to speak in ways that Tom could hear. Tom proved to be particularly coachable (he had, after all, been a professional athlete). He became almost a co-therapist, drawing Jennifer out about her family and her wish to never again go along blindly with plans proposed by others.

Tom's more patient and empathic presence made it possible for Jennifer to hear him as he spoke movingly of his fears of being like other professional athletes who ran through their earnings, of his shame at being unemployed, and of his lifelong love of the outdoor sports he could not pursue in Chicago. The difference was that now Jennifer, as she "softened," could hear him and be moved by his pleas to relocate. More fundamentally, they experienced moments of real intimacy and connection in my office, and their sex life picked up at home (unlike many couples, who require special attention to resuscitate sexual contact).

As their interpersonal process improved, they became a team working together to solve their external problems. On their own, they decided in favor of the relocation Tom favored, and, equally important, they worked together to deal with the resulting fallout from making a choice contrary to Jennifer's parents' wishes.

It may appear that Jennifer "resolved" her marital conflict by simply resorting to her old pattern of capitulation, but I don't believe that is what happened. What we discovered was that the major obstacle to her acceding to Tom's wish was her semiconscious guilt over displeasing her parents. Unearthing this problem, coming to accept that she couldn't please everyone, and choosing marital happiness (her own, as well as Tom's) over fulfilling her parents' wishes that she care for her disabled brother, allowed her to settle her disagreement with Tom and agree to move.

After solving the specific problem that had brought them to therapy, and using a problem-solving template I had taught them, Tom and Jennifer became better at managing other conflicts (e.g., which new house to buy), demonstrating that they were prepared to handle future episodes of conflict. Their depressed mood lifted, and their pleasure in their shared life was palpable, then and a year later, when they returned for a follow-up visit.

This case is typical of many successful cases: A couple presents with a specific problem and some level of chronic unhappiness. Their sex life is compromised, and they are growing increasingly estranged from each other. They may be considering divorce. What helps, beyond providing a safe forum for them to talk to each other, is directing early attention to their negative interaction cycle, labeling it, and working to expose its roots, enabling them to feel and act more sympathetically and collaboratively with each other. Teaching communication and problem-solving skills also helps, and improved systemic process exposes previously concealed personal concerns (psychodynamics). Intimacy, problem solving, and overall happiness improve concurrently.

Note

1. This case was previously described in Nielsen (2017a).

Introduction to Parts II and III

Domain-Specific Knowledge

We are now positioned to discuss the principal subject of this book: the specific topics and situations that most often bedevil our clients. In all cases, our goal will be to help couples work as a team to solve the problems at hand. In doing so, we will need to use everything that we have discussed previously, especially techniques to improve maladaptive processes by identifying vicious cycles, uncovering underlying issues, and teaching rules for optimal communication and problem solving. This is because, in most cases, conflict between the partners will be part of the problem that interferes with discussion, whether it is about how much money to spend, how often to have sex, or what rules to set for the children. Couples will face what I term the *co-captains problem*—the structural challenge of decision-making in a two-person group—as they attempt to work out satisfying, effective, and equitable decisions that they can agree on.

While focusing on the couple's vulnerability cycles should remain our *first* concern, most couples will not be satisfied until their presenting conflicts and problems concerning money, children, in-laws, division of labor, etc. are actually settled. Work on *process* is thus often a prerequisite but *not* the be-all and end-all of couple therapy—as we might think if our only goal were to work on the pathological dance or the underlying psychodynamics. In practice, couple therapy success usually depends on artfully weaving attention to interpersonal process, underlying human needs, and practical problem solving.

Practical decisions will work best if they are not settled by cultural convention or pat prescriptions. Solutions will also be better if we consider both the external issues at stake (e.g., the need to save money) together with the individual hopes and fears of the partners (e.g., the excessive fear of poverty based on having had a father who was chronically unemployed). We begin Part II with one of the most common, challenging, and delicate subject areas: sex.

DOI: 10.4324/b22905-9

Part II

Upgrades to Address Common Problems

7 Sex

Sexual problems are extremely common in the general population: 43% of women and 31% of men reported problems in one much-cited national survey (Laumann et al., 1999); and in our consulting rooms, where some 30% of couples coming for "relationship therapy" report sexual problems (Peloquin et al., 2019). Problems with sex are not only common, they are consistently a *leading* reason couples seek therapy (e.g., Ellison, 2002). As journalist Stephens-Davidowitz (2015) reports:

> On Google the top complaint about marriages is "not having sex" where searches for "sexless marriage" are three and a half times more common than "unhappy marriage" and eight times more common that "loveless marriage." There are 16 times more complaints about a spouse not wanting sex than about a married partner not being willing to talk.
>
> (p. 6)

Sexual problems are almost universal in the couples who present to me, though many do not mention them unless I ask. And contrary to what one might wish, sexual problems do not usually resolve spontaneously as marital harmony improves. Doing good couple therapy requires us to look closely at sex, which turns out to be as fascinating as it is complicated. After discussing the unique importance of sex in relationships, this chapter will focus on the three most common problems encountered by the couple therapist: difficulties talking about sex, arguments about how often to have sex (desire discrepancies), and diminished interest in sex.[1] I will conclude the chapter with a brief discussion of some additional sexual problems couples may have, especially those related to sexual fantasies and pornography; in a later chapter, I will discuss extramarital affairs.

The emphasis here will be on practical interventions to assist couples in restarting a dormant sex life and in keeping marital sex alive. Most couple therapists have insufficient training in this area, which leads them to be reluctant to ask about or treat sexual problems (Harris & Hays, 2008). This chapter should fill in some of the gaps and justify making the treatment of most sexual problems a subspecialty of couple therapy, rather than an

DOI: 10.4324/b22905-11

esoteric thing unto itself (Weeks & Gambescia, 2015). In this regard, my experience is like that of my colleague, Carla Leone (unpublished, 2020):

> In the case of significant, intractable or unusual sexual difficulties, it may be best to refer to a specialist in sex therapy, which I am not; however, in my experience this has rarely been needed. In most cases it has clearly seemed better for the couple to continue with me and for me to seek consultation from a specialist when needed.

Sexual problems secondary to nonsexual issues

Almost all the couples I see with chronic or severe marital problems are having trouble in the bedroom. The most common reason is simply that their anger, hurt feelings, fear of asking for what they desire, or other nonsexual issues interfere with approaching and enjoying each other sexually. Not only do they feel unsafe with their partners, but they feel little inclination to provide their partners with sensual pleasure and may have experienced a decline in their own level of sexual desire in tandem (Murray et al., 2017; Vowels & Mark, 2020). In less extreme cases, couples have "grown apart" while living busy parallel lives and neglecting the verbal intimacy that makes sexual contact feel natural. For these couples, sex may gradually wither on the vine. For all couples who have stopped having sex entirely, or where sexual frequency has greatly diminished, restarting the sexual dance is often a considerable challenge and will usually have to wait until therapy has warmed the relational atmosphere.

Primary sexual problems and circular impact

Sometimes, marital problems begin with problems specific to sexuality. Some partners suffer from excessive guilt about sex, others from fears about performance. Some couples have incompatibilities around favored sexual scenarios; others simply do not line up on how often they want to have sex. In these situations, marital satisfaction will decrease, perhaps more so for men, for whom dissatisfaction with sexual intimacy tends to be more strongly associated with dissatisfaction with the relationship (Bradbury & Karney, 2010). Should the couple also have difficulties in nonsexual areas, especially when it comes to managing conflict, their sexual problems and their nonsexual problems will frequently be intertwined, and usually increase as each exacerbates the other (studies cited in Bradbury & Karney, 2010, pp. 308–310; Weeks & Gambescia, 2015). While we generally see such circular aggravation of sexual and nonsexual problems, good sex can offset other marital problems for some couples, and otherwise high-quality marriages can offset mediocre sex for others.

The importance of sex

Of all the things that couples identify as necessary for a successful marriage, a "good sex life" is second only to fidelity (Pew Research, 2007), and, whether primary or secondary, sexual problems are especially detrimental to overall couple well-being (Peloquin et al., 2019). Conversely, as with other areas of shared pleasure, the return of sexual pleasure can be highly effective in restoring morale. More than in many other areas of life, the quality of the sexual relationship is a key indicator of how the couple is doing—to the couple, as well as to the therapist. This is due, in part, to the normative expectation for monogamy. Because sex outside the marriage is usually viewed as a violation of marital faithfulness and trust, the quality of marital sex becomes a more salient measure of the success of the marriage. (Other activities partners may choose to do with others—say, watching football or shopping—are comparatively innocuous.)

Sexual life also gains special significance because sex is never just about "sex" narrowly defined as a form of sensual pleasure. Instead, sexual activity engages our deepest human concerns and satisfactions—especially hopes and fears concerning trust, mutual acceptance, specialness, caretaking, and pride in being a man or a woman.[2] This is another reason why understanding sexual behavior is so challenging: While sex includes an appetitive inborn quality, like hunger seeking satisfaction in food, we are drawn to sexual connection by a combination of almost all other human desires, including the wish to be the object of our partner's desire.

As it engages our deepest concerns, sex can be either intimate or not, with intimate sex requiring sharing, coordination, and willingness to adjust to the needs of one's partner, as expressed by Scheinkman (2019):

> Sex tends to be experienced as intimate when it is shared between people who care about each other or are developing a bond. Sex can be a way of knowing the other person or a space for expressing different feelings; it can be a time for self-abandonment, self-discovery, or repair. It can also be simply an activity for being close. In intimate atmospheres, sex becomes infused with feelings and meanings such as "I love you," "You are special," or "You are the one I choose to do this with." While sexual intimacy takes the subjective experience of the other person into account, sex is usually experienced as non-intimate when it is objectifying, mechanical, or dutiful and the feelings of the other person are ignored or obliterated. In situations in which sex is demanded or imposed by force, the experience can be profoundly traumatic and toxic.
> (p. 563)

Slow to recover and important to monitor

Positive sexual interaction is frequently one of the slowest problem areas to improve in couple therapy, and it usually needs our explicit attention before it does (Iasenza, 2010; McCarthy & McCarthy, 2014). This is because trust and emotional safety must be restored before sex can get back on track, and these are usually slow to recover. With this in mind, therapists should monitor each couple's sexual satisfaction as an ongoing indicator of mutual pleasure and trust. If the partners are not having satisfying sex, there will often remain a sense of deprivation and lack of connection (for one partner if not for both) that will fuel irritability and uncertainty about commitment. So, while the couple therapist must be patient in this area and advocate similar patience in clients, it is equally important to test the waters from time to time by discussing the sexual situation openly, a challenge that we take up next.

Difficulty talking about sex

Most of us have difficulty talking about sex with our partners (Gottman, 2011). One study found that 54% of a random sample of more than 21,000 American couples were "dissatisfied with their level of openness in discussing sexual topics" (Olson & Olson, 2000, p. 124) and another study of couples married ten or more years found that partners knew only 60% of what their partners liked sexually and only about 20% of what they didn't (Miller & Byers, 2004). Contrary to the romantic fantasy that sex just happens, talking about sex in marriage is uniquely challenging and commonly helpful (Jones et al., 2017; Weeks & Gambescia, 2015). As with the far less erotic act of back scratching, there is just no getting around the requirement that partners must tell each other what they want.[3]

There are many reasons for this inhibition, which can be explored to help couples to communicate more clearly.

- *Children learn that sex should not be talked about.* Adverse early socialization is perhaps the most common impediment to discussing sexual problems. This occurs through anti-sex instruction of children ("Only bad little girls and boys touch themselves there!" or, still worse and now less common, "Masturbators will burn in Hell!") and by the absence of open discussion of the obvious bodily pleasures children feel when they do touch those forbidden places: Children hear Dad exclaim about the wonderful game he saw on TV last night, but not about the wonderful sex he had with Mom! In some families this lack of discussion includes not naming sexual organs properly and not discussing puberty.[4]
- *We risk having others see us as weird or abnormal if we talk about sex.* This danger follows because many sexual fantasies contain taboo, potentially embarrassing elements, including aggressive, dependent, passive, cross-gender, and/or age-inappropriate wishes and behavior.
- *We risk feeling painfully needy or dependent if we talk about sex.* Even "plain vanilla" sex, when unpacked, exposes our deepest wishes to be loved and desired. These deeper concerns, despite our adult desire to believe that we have them under control, make talking about sex something that is vaguely anxiety-producing for almost everyone, as we encounter how much we depend on our partners. Talking about sex can expose our difficulty "asking for things," especially our fear of rejection, since most talk about sex in marriage involves requests that our partner change.

- *We risk being exposed as naïve or ignorant if we talk about sex.* This danger follows from the taboos about talking about sex that limit information access, from the great variety of sexual scenarios that exist and from the assumption that not knowing about sex is especially shameful.
- *Talking about sex may expose concerns about physical attractiveness or sexual performance—ours or our partner's—loaded topics that may damage our pride or hurt our partner's feelings.*
- *Talking about sex runs the risk of our becoming aroused and then embarrassed.*

Therapist anxieties

Helping couples overcome these impediments to talking openly about their experiences and preferences is an obvious essential first step toward helping them with their sexual problems. To do so, we may have to overcome our own personal constraints. Therapists, even when simply asking questions about sex, are not immune from similar anxieties (Dimen, 2003; Kahr, 2009; Risen, 2010). In addition, we may feel insensitively intrusive or voyeuristic. We may fear becoming aroused or embarrassed by possible arousal. We might not want to hear things that seem personally distasteful or be exposed as ignorant about some sexual practices. And we may fear not knowing what to do should we discover a sexual problem. Nonetheless, we must not give the impression that we are afraid to discuss a couple's sex life. Most of us must work in therapy or supervision to overcome personal issues that interfere with open discussions of sex. As with learning to become comfortable talking about other distressing topics—despair, injustice, death—it gets easier with experience, but it remains challenging when we allow ourselves to really connect with the feelings involved.

Some suggestions for opening discussions of sex

Therapists may have to initiate discussion of sexual difficulties

Do not assume that couples who do not bring up sexual problems do not have any. Do not assume that you know what goes on in the bedroom. (For example, when my colleague Jennifer McComb was treating a couple dealing with the husband's erectile dysfunction, she was surprised when they revealed that, during sex, the wife no longer touched her husband's penis, something that had not been an issue when they were younger.)

If it is known that sexual problems are central, interview the partners separately at least once

This will make it easier for them to be honest with you and with themselves. Partly for this reason, I conduct individual interviews with all clients in the initial diagnostic period. I also do so later in therapy when I encounter serious sexual problems. The following important topics can be more easily assessed in individual interviews: the person's past sexual history; the history and presence of affairs; whether problems are/were present with all partners; sexual orientation and preferred sexual practices (do not assume that "heterosexual couples" are heterosexual in their orientation); dissatisfaction with the partner's appearance or performance; masturbation fantasies; and the extent of pornography use and the frequency of masturbation.

Whether in private sessions or conjoint meetings, begin by saying something like, "Would it be OK to talk about sex? I know it may be uncomfortable, but it should become easier as we go along." Later, when you want to ask about specific practices, begin with, "Some men [or women] . . . sometimes . . . Has this ever happened to you?"

Questions to ask about sex

The following are some particularly useful questions (see also Risen, 2010). To help me remember them when I'm interviewing clients, I divide these questions into three categories: those about the client's *sexual history*, those about the context and events *leading up to* sex, and those about the details of what goes on *during* sex. Don't feel that you must ask them all, but this list will give you ideas about topics that can be revealing.

Development and history

- Family influence questions (for women; you should modify these for men, and for clients raised by single parents): How were nudity and other bodily issues handled when you were growing up? What did your parents tell you about sex? How did your mother dress when she went out to a romantic dinner with your father? How did she feel about her body? How did she react to sexually confident women? How did she relate to her body as she got older? How did your parents touch, kiss, and relate affectionately? How did your father react to your interest in boys?
- What sort of sex education and religious teaching about sex did you receive?
- How did you experience puberty and your body developing?
- What were your first kiss and your first sexual experience like?
- What have been your peak sexual experiences?
- Did you have any unpleasant, confusing, embarrassing, or disturbing sexual experiences growing up? If so, how do you think those experiences affect your sex life now?
- [For LGBTQ clients] What was your coming out experience like?

Context and events leading up to sex

- How do you feel about being sexual with your partner?
- What leads up to and follows sex?

- What determines when you feel ready to be sexual with your partner? What are you feeling when you wish to be sexual with your partner?
- [If relevant] Why do you *not* feel like being sexual with your partner?
- How do you signal your interest?
- How comfortable are you talking to your partner about your sexual preferences?
- What do you usually fantasize about when you masturbate? What imagery in pornography most draws you? Do you ever fantasize about sexual behaviors you would be reluctant to do?

During sex

- How do you have sex as a couple? Can you describe a mental videotape of a recent sexual encounter? How does your partner look, smell, act? What do you do and how satisfying it is? Who takes the lead? Do you know what your partner likes? Does he/she know what you like? Do you take turns pleasuring each other, or do you think that giving and receiving should be done simultaneously [something that is difficult for many partners]? Do you share fantasies or act out scenarios? Do you have private sexual fantasies? Does anyone touch the clitoris during sex? For women: Do you experience pain during intercourse? What do you do and how do you feel if one of you has trouble coming?
- Are you distracted during sex by thoughts about external stressors, obligations, resentments, or expectations that it won't be satisfying?

Across all these topics, it is important to track themes of shame, guilt, and boundary violations. The following case example illustrates problems talking about and having sex due to adverse childhood socialization and expectations.

Parental ghosts in the bedroom: Joel and Mary Ann

Joel came to me, referred by his wife, Mary Ann, after she had discovered him once again conducting flirtatious email exchanges with other women. Joel didn't want to lose Mary Ann. He admired her as an excellent mother to their children, as a responsible professional like himself, and as a good friend with whom he had shared 15 mostly satisfying years of marriage. He *was* angry about the infrequency of sex, which occurred only once every few months. But more than that, he was hopeless and distressed about his inability to elicit excitement and pleasure in his wife when they made love.

Joel took to our individual psychodynamic therapy easily and quickly saw how his email affairs were serving as a "home remedy" for him generally, not just a substitute for infrequent sex.[5] What he most treasured in these email connections that he had established over the years was his ability to captivate these women by his use of words. A salesman in his day job, he was, indeed, a skilled wordsmith who won over his sexual correspondents with his blend of romantic, intellectual, and erotic prose. What powered this desire for admiring responsiveness were the many disappointments in that area he had experienced as a child. His insecure mother had little to offer him, as she was preoccupied with her various obsessive household projects and with her anger at her domineering husband; and his father, a physician celebrated for his devotion to his patients, had little time for Joel and was almost mute with him during their rare times together. As Joel and I explored the same themes of lack of enthusiastic connection, he gained momentum from his sense that I was attentive, responsive, and impressed by his many talents. His interest in his Internet women disappeared and was replaced first by his attachment to me and the therapy (his correspondence with women gave way to his recording his dreams), and then by his restarting his amateur acting career (where he received the accolades he longed for), and finally by taking more chances with intimate conversations with his wife. It became clear that he had grown hopeless in a parental transference to Mary Ann, as someone who was into her own career and had little interest in taking risks or having fun with him.

At this point, I encouraged him to try to talk to Mary Ann more frankly about their sex life and to consider what might be limiting her involvement. We learned then of the ghosts that constrained Mary Ann's ability to talk about and enjoy sex. Mary Ann had grown up in a strict Catholic family where "nice people" never spoke of sex and where her stern father frequently criticized both her academic knowledge (despite her almost perfect grades) and what he judged to be her excessively revealing clothing. In talking with Mary Ann, Joel learned of her (unrealistic) fear of Joel calling her "a stupid slut!"—an insult that condensed her father's criticism of both her intellect and her sexuality. Joel told me how he thought she got around this fear of his paternal criticism by only initiating sex with him when he was asleep!

We came to see how they had been locked in a mutually confirming ("interlocking") transference cycle: Joel would criticize Mary Ann for being emotionally unresponsive (like his parents), especially sexually, and then Mary Ann would feel traumatically criticized about her sexual behavior (as she had been by her father). She would then shut down both sexually and verbally, refusing to talk further and retreating into a defensive silence that further reminded Joel of his father. Mary Ann's flight would intensify Joel's frustration and criticism, and their pursuer–distancer cycle would escalate, until both gave up and Joel went to the Internet as his escape valve.

Now, in what amounted to a couple therapy at a distance, Joel was able to stop himself and attempt to reverse their transference cycles. He engaged Mary Ann patiently, supportively, and nonjudgmentally, and helped her overcome her expectation that he would act like her critical father. She told him of her internalized view that her sexual desires were sinful (she had some rape fantasies) and how she was sure he would agree. When he not only failed to confirm her fear that he would see her as "slutty," but told her of his admiration for her and her courage in sharing this with him, she became more the emotionally responsive woman he desired. Not only did their sexual frequency and pleasure improve, but their overall happiness with each other grew as they came to feel increasingly comfortable in each other's presence. Mary Ann did not totally change her ingrained attitudes toward sex, but her attitudes shifted sufficiently to allow for a vast improvement in their sex life. As Mary Ann got out of her head and let herself go, she could show her husband that she was enjoying his company in bed, the very thing that turned Joel on the most. Soon thereafter, Joel ended his individual therapy, a much happier man.

Psychoeducation: providing accurate information about sex

Because many couples lack accurate information about sex—due, in part, to inadequate sexual education that focuses on biology, adolescence, and risky behavior (Russell et al., 2020)—I often present facts and research relevant to specific problems. Often, this helps lower the bar on perfectionistic views of sex. As noted by McCarthy and McCarthy (2014, p. 7), "Naïve, repressive myths have been replaced by unrealistic, performance-oriented myths." In movies, arousal is quick, no talking is required, and both orgasms arrive quickly, even when everyone is standing up! Pornography adds to the unreality. Possibly as a result, three-quarters of men believe that their penises are too small, and most men have great difficulty believing a woman can respect a man with any sort of sexual problem. Many couples also unfairly compare their own early romantic sexual encounters (partly fueled by novelty and uncertainty about whether their partners will desire them) with the sex in their long-term relationships.

Nonetheless, in real life, "less than half of the sexual experiences of well-functioning couples involve equal desire, arousal, and orgasm . . . . Of total sexual experiences, 5 percent to 15 percent are mediocre, unsatisfying, or dysfunctional" (McCarthy & McCarthy, 2014, pp. 8–9). The following myths frequently make sexual problems worse, and, when relevant, therapists should dispel them:

- That vaginal intercourse in the missionary position is sufficient or optimal for most women.
- That men's erections should be spontaneous and should not require extra stimulation.
- That men should know all about sex and how to please their partners (an attitude especially prevalent in Latinx and African American cultures).
- That women can leave everything up to the man.

More generally, as pointed out by Barry McCarthy, most men learn about sex by themselves while masturbating, while most women learn in interaction with partners. This difference suggests what each gender needs to learn later: Men must learn to value intimacy and attunement, not to fear imperfect performance, and to gain pleasure other than from orgasms. Women must learn the benefits of sexual fantasies, sexual techniques that work for them, and a more self-centered attitude of "ruthless excitement."[6] And, sadly, both genders may have to unlearn generalizations from prior misadventures and sexual traumas.

Desire discrepancies

Joel and Mary Ann not only had trouble talking about sex, but they are an extreme example of a couple disagreeing about how often to have sex. Such disparities are a frequent source of marital unhappiness, impacting one in three women and one in seven men, with these disparities increasing with age (McCarthy & McCarthy, 2014). Desire discrepancies interfere not only with overall relationship satisfaction but also with satisfaction during sex itself (Mark & Lasslo, 2018). While men complain of insufficient sex more often than their partners—men, overall, have been found to have a greater sex drive by every measure and in every study (Bradbury & Karney, 2010)—the complaint of too little sex from wives is often more shameful to them because of cultural assumptions that all men are sexually rapacious. Even in Wallerstein's sample of happily married couples, only 50% matched each other in desired frequency, with equal numbers of men and women in the remaining 50% wanting more frequent sex than their partners (1995, p. 190). This accords with the almost equal number of Google searches for "Won't have sex with me" by men and women (Stephens-Davidowitz, 2015, p. 6). This discrepancy is not static and may change if one spouse's desire declines due to depression, illness, or worry or, conversely, if one partner desires more frequent sex to assuage distress from other life problems.

Helping couples to uncover and discuss the emotional wounds of desire discrepancies can prove extremely helpful. Commonly, higher desire partners feel not only frustrated, but rejected, while lower desire partners feel guilty for not going along or angry and resentful for being pressured against their will. Couples can say or think things that injure their partners and further damage the marriage: "You don't have the need to feel closer to me; you're just a sex maniac" or "If you weren't so controlling or selfish, you'd accept that I'm not as physical as you are and you would leave me alone!" (Weiner-Davis, 2003). Once the problem becomes established, it can grow worse if partners avoid sex due to the struggles that lead up to it or engage in it grudgingly, angrily, or guiltily. And absent agreement on how often to have sex, couples commonly stop touching and showing affection in nonsexual ways, growing more irritable with each other and drifting apart.

The key for both partners is to make this a shared *couple* problem that they must work on rather than allowing it to remain an ongoing source of dissatisfaction and struggle. It will not do for lower desire spouses to expect their partners to remain monogamous and feel deprived while failing to work on sexual satisfaction within the marriage. Nor is it acceptable for higher desire partners to always prevail in their wish to have sex on demand. Each has a "relational claim" on the other (Fishbane, 2010), while they should also recognize that guilt-inducing statements from one side ("If you loved me, you would have sex with me more often!") can be countered by similar ones from the other side ("If you loved me, you wouldn't ask so often!"). Therapists can work to help couples see that intimacy and emotional closeness must take precedence over the frequency of sex.

When discussing this problem, therapists can point out other areas of life where the partners do not line up identically on their preferences (like attending sporting events or shopping for household furnishings), with the best examples being ones the partners have already discussed in therapy. As with discrepancies elsewhere, some compromise will be required. Sometimes, this will be that the higher desire spouse masturbates to meet their needs ("the do-it-yourself solution"), which is understood as an accommodation to the lower desire spouse rather than a form of unfaithfulness or a lack of attraction.

Beyond compromising, higher desire spouses must learn that, while they cannot force the issue, they can work to facilitate receptivity. Higher desire spouses can become more empathic by recalling situations where they found they could not simply turn their feelings on or off on demand or times when they were so preoccupied with worry or focused on some problem that they could not relax. And perhaps, if this is a relevant concern for their partner, they can recall a time when they felt ashamed of their body and didn't want anyone to see some part of it.

Since being in the mood is especially important for many people, partners should learn how to facilitate this—whether through music, compliments, or doing housework! Lower desire spouses can help by describing what helps them "get in the mood," beyond simply feeling safer and happier about the relationship. Sometimes, "romantic" evenings—dressing up and going out to dinner, with or without dancing, or simply lighting a couple of candles—can facilitate getting in the mood. More generally, higher desire partners can foster receptivity by telling their partners how important they are to their well-being and how appreciative they are of their efforts on behalf of the couple and the family. For many lower desire partners what helps most is discovering why they "have the brakes on" prior to sex, often due to negative experiences or socialization (as in Mary Ann's case).

For many women with low desire, it helps to challenge the linear model of sexual desire described by Masters and Johnson (1970), in which erotic desire must *precede* sexual activity. Simply beginning sexual activity ("being willing" to "just do it") can often lead to erotic feelings.[7] To make this point, I remind couples that this is true for other activities: You may have low interest in an activity beforehand—like going to a social event or trying a new game—but find it enjoyable once you get into it. Lower desire spouses will do better if, instead of asking their partners to stop pressuring them, they ask for help to increase their desire and satisfaction, fostering "responsive desire." As discussed in the next section on diminished sexual desire, therapists can also work with low-desire partners to rekindle desire, including by asking them, "What might make sex worth wanting?" (Kleinplatz, 2010).

This problem is made worse when the higher desire spouse not only wants more sex but wants the other to initiate it. Women who want their partners to initiate sex more often may feel worse than men in this situation because of our culture's (erroneous) assumption that most men are sex-starved animals who always want more sex than their female partners. Again, open discussion of the problem, including the underlying assumptions and feelings involved, will help. With luck, the higher desire spouse of either gender will learn not to take this lack of initiative as the acid test of their desirability or worth. But in the end, the higher desire spouse, here the woman, will often have to accept that, just as she may never get her husband to go shopping with her unless she brings it up, she must initiate sex more than she would like.[8]

Diminished or low sexual desire

Desire discrepancies often appear or grow worse when one partner becomes less interested in sex, something that is common in midlife. Indeed, low desire, itself, is the most common sexual complaint, accounting for more than 50% of all sexual problems in women and 25% of those in men (Peloquin et al., 2019).[9] The maintenance of sexual desire has been empirically identified as one of the key factors promoting relationship satisfaction and strongly affecting the maintenance of relationships (Hinchliff & Gott, 2004; McCarthy et al., 2006).

Of the many references on this subject, the most helpful to me as a professional have been Basson (2010), Iasenza (2010), Kaplan (1995), Levine (1999), McCarthy and McCarthy (2014), and Morin (1995). For clients, I recommend Goldstein and Brandon (2004) for both genders; Margolies (2001) and Murray (2019) for men; and Weiner-Davis (2003) for women. While the most common cause of diminished desire in couples coming for couple therapy is general marital dissatisfaction, some couples struggle in this area despite few conflicts elsewhere (e.g., Ferreira et al., 2015) so that other causes must be considered, as shown in Table 7.1. Perhaps more than is commonly appreciated, diminished sexual desire should be seen and evaluated as the outcome of a diverse set of biopsychosocial variables.

Marital problems and extramarital stress

Diminished desire in women tends to get more press, but diminished desire in men is real and is often due to stress either within or outside of the marriage. That desire should fall off when external danger threatens makes sense from a Darwinian perspective—couples who continued copulating when a lion was nearby are underrepresented in our current gene pool! Sexual desire for both men and women, like our ability to fall sleep, can be easily disrupted by pressing external concerns.

Table 7.1 Causes of Diminished or Low Sexual Desire

- Marital dissatisfaction generally.
- Stress and tiredness (work, children).
- Sexual abuse or trauma.
- Adverse socialization and guilt about sex.
- Physical causes: depression, aging, smoking, alcohol, obesity, medications, (antidepressants, antihypertensives), prostate surgery, vascular or peripheral nerve disease (diabetes, atherosclerosis).
- Anxiety: performance anxiety (shame); body image concerns (shame); fear of pregnancy; distress and anxiety about infertility treatment.
- Adverse accommodations to low desire (**grudging sex**, faked orgasms, "Let's get this over with.").
- Reduced attractiveness of the partner (obesity, illness, surgery, aging).
- Parenthood, Inc. (focus on needs of children, desexualized view of mother, Madonna–whore complex).
- Boredom, routinization, lack of novelty (too much safety).
- Hidden sexual alternatives: extramarital affair(s) or liaisons (prostitutes); same–sex relationships (by a seemingly heterosexual individual); porn addiction; paraphilias.

Sexual abuse and trauma

Since some clients have always had low desire, therapists should ask about the time course of libido problems. Most commonly, these are victims of sexual abuse or clients who have experienced little positive physical closeness with caretakers, though for some, low desire may be purely physical/constitutional.

Formative negative experiences need not consist of rape or child molestation (though those are disturbingly common events) but can include submitting to the wishes of boyfriends in adolescence or otherwise engaging in sex to maintain relationships. Sexual abuse of boys, though less frequent, is often experienced as more shameful. Such experiences may reduce trust in others and trigger painful memories that lead to avoidance of sex.

Sexual abuse survivors who knew the perpetrator (most cases) also tend to blame themselves, more than those raped by strangers. Additionally, some survivors may have incorporated rape fantasies into their sexual scripts and then shut down even more, due to shame and guilt. In all cases, individual therapy that goes slowly, reworks aspects of the trauma, and moves first to establish satisfying masturbation may help. After that, sensate focus (SF) exercises (discussed in detail later in this chapter) can be especially useful, as described by two recognized experts: "Nowhere is the diagnostic power of Sensate Focus more evident than when working with [sexually] traumatized clients. Sensate Focus can help uncover triggers and teach skills to manage reactions, thoughts, associations, and negative defenses associated with the trauma" (Weiner & Avery-Clark, 2017, p. 113). These authors emphasize building safety slowly and recommend that survivors be in charge of touching sessions, which can begin with partners fully or partially clothed.

Adverse socialization

Separate from the issue of sexual trauma, some people (women more often than men) have never become comfortable with their own sexual potential and have never experienced orgasms, and some have simply had negative socialization toward sexual pleasure. Many have been socialized to prioritize their partner's needs above their own and to be mostly the objects of desire, rather than desiring subjects. This can make it difficult for them to surrender to their own "ruthless" excitement (Bader, 2002), which may explain why many women describe sex as like work or childcare. Others have had negative experiences with caretakers that make them averse, later, to close physical contact involving smell, touch, or simply "sharing air" (Solomon & Tatkin, 2011). With the latter group, as with all couples who have not had sex in a long time, working on simple touch via SF exercises can be helpful. In addition, for women who have never been comfortable with sex, I have found it useful to prescribe remediation in the form of erotica, vibrators, and visits to the OMG Yes website (www.omgyes.com) where such matters are sensitively discussed, and women's sexual pleasure is encouraged.

Concerning socialization or emotional development more broadly, therapists can help anxiously attached clients learn that sex can be about their pleasure, not just about securing a partner; and avoidant clients can learn to experience intimacy during sex rather than using it mainly to enhance their self-esteem (Mikulincer & Shaver, 2007).

Illness and aging

Although many studies show that while sexual *frequency* declines with age (e.g., Laumann et al., 1999), sexual *pleasure* may increase (Lodge & Umberson, 2012). Diminished libido with aging in men is related to decreasing testosterone, while the biology responsible for the common menopausal decline in women is currently unclear. Prevalent nonhormonal conditions causing reduced libido include depressive disorders, alcohol use, medication side-effects (especially antidepressants and antihypertensives), and peripheral nerve disease (from diabetes, hypertensive vascular disease, and other neurological diseases). Since purely physical causes can contribute to this problem, clients with noticeable changes—including, especially, men with absent morning erections or clients with diminished desire for all contemplatable partners—should be referred for physical evaluation. Despite our recommendations, some clients with known physical causes for their dysfunction may still drag their feet in seeking medical treatment due to shame and embarrassment or to rationalize avoiding sex with their partners.

There is currently much discussion in the literature concerning the causes and treatment of the frequent falloff in libido in perimenopausal and postmenopausal women (Basson, 2007, 2010; Dennerstein, 2010; Goldstein & Brandon, 2004; Levine, 1999; Meana, 2010). Low or no sexual desire is the most common sexual complaint of women of all ages, with concerns present in some 30%–40% of women (Basson, 2007). Many sexually functional and satisfied women—especially those in established relationships—do not experience spontaneous sexual desire, so "arousability" or "responsive desire" has become the preferred model for female sexual progression, replacing Masters and Johnson's model, in which arousal always comes first. Among other things, arousability will depend on a woman's sense of being desired rather than used, and on her body image and current mood. As concerns the impact of aging and hormonal decline, Rosemary Basson (2007), a recognized expert on this topic, notes that while many women tell her, "I have a hormonal problem," she has come to attribute declining sexual interest more to women's broader life context, consistent with her summary of a recent large-scale study:

> Of 3,000 North American women of different ethnicities close to or entering perimenopause, the frequency of feeling desire was not associated with menopause status, night sweats, or hot flashes but *with negative attitudes toward aging and higher levels of perceived stress*—these being negatively related to feelings of desire. By contrast, starting a new relationship and perceiving sex as important were positively related. . . . The consistent theme is that biological insults (radical hysterectomies, hormonal changes of perimenopause) create a vulnerability to sexual dysfunction but contextual, personal, past experiential, and cultural factors determine the presence or absence of problems.
>
> (pp. 32–33, italics added)

Consistent with this view, replacement of sex hormones per se has limited value (although they can improve vaginal wall atrophy and insufficient lubrication). It appears that we have yet to discover the physical causes of declining sexual interest in women, something Levine (1999), emphasizing biology more than Basson, argues may be more generalized, that is, related to "aging" and (possibly) to decreased hormone receptors.

Anxiety and adverse reactions to sexual problems

Masters and Johnson (1970) usefully stressed that performance anxiety and "spectatoring" self-consciousness both create and aggravate sexual dysfunction. Most clients will have adverse psychological reactions to their diminished desire, whatever its cause, and these reactions can make matters worse (Lodge & Umberson, 2012). Some clients will feel ashamed of their aging bodies or of their uncertain erections (especially if Viagra or other PDE5 inhibitors fail to help). Some will have undisclosed anxiety about becoming pregnant, while others will have sex marred by infertility treatments, which prescribe sex at specific times and about which some spouses may be anxious or ambivalent. Some will feel diminished desire for overweight or aging partners, or partners whose bodies have been altered by surgery (e.g., mastectomy). Many will feel distressed by their partner's diminished desire, and some will take this personally. Some clients will make grudging accommodations to the sexual problem ("OK, let's get this over with!") or fake orgasms. All such reactions can increase sexual avoidance and couple distress. Bringing these issues out in the open in couple sessions will often, though not invariably, reduce their negative influence.

Body image concerns and attractiveness

The perception of physical attractiveness matters but not as much as people fear. One large study of 3,024 couples (Silveri & Samayoa, 2018) found that it correlated significantly with marital satisfaction in all five cultures studied (the U.S., the U.K., China, Turkey, and Russia), though the relative importance varied by culture when compared to other important variables (e.g., intelligence, kindness, access to resources) and explained far less of the variance than measures of "compatibility." Despite aging and the length of their marriages, husbands and wives in these five cultures continued to perceive their partners as attractive and as substantially more attractive than their partners considered themselves.

Consequently, real and feared loss of physical attractiveness can impede sexual pleasure and activity, especially in women, where it may be comparable to performance anxiety in men (Paine et al., 2019). This is exacerbated by impossible standards for appearance and body weight presented in the media. Concerns about weight can then fuel a vicious cycle if women avoid sex because they consider themselves overweight, if husbands suffer lowered desire from their wives' weight gain, and if food is then used to calm ensuing distressed feelings. And since many women are excited by their ability to arouse men sexually, this sequence can become a 180°-negative shift to "I hope Brian won't want to make love tonight!"

Men whose wives criticize them for failing to lose weight—sometimes more out of concern for their husbands' health—can become caught in similar vicious cycles, as what these men perceive as nagging leads them both to eat more and to avoid sex with their wives.

A related sexual conundrum linked to body image is that many women are conflicted about being desired as sexual objects. It can be a great turn-on ("He wants *me*!") or a big turn-off if the woman feels objectified ("He only wants to *use me* to get his rocks off!"). Open discussion of these issues often helps, but it can be challenging. Men will be assisted here by being allowed to admit that they often do, indeed, want to have their sexual itch reduced, but that the sex is, nonetheless, more than assisted masturbation.

Misconceptions about sex

As discussed earlier in this chapter, inadequate sex education combined with contemporary media portrayals often create unrealistic expectations that reduce desire. Educating couples about the real facts of sexual life may help them enjoy sex more and keep images of how it's done in the movies from spoiling it.

Parenthood, Inc.

Sexual problems often increase after couples have children, usually long before illness or physical decline manifest themselves. Gottman and Gottman (2010) found that three years after the first child was born, men wanted sex on average three times per week, while women wanted it once every two weeks. Esther Perel (2006) attributes some of this heightened mismatch to the love affair that mothers have with their babies, which not only exhausts them, but partially satisfies their need for physical contact. Other authors note the desexualizing impact the maternal role has on some women and that some men begin to see their wives as asexual mothers (the Madonna–whore complex). Kernberg (2011) finds that some parents, once they have children, are unable to lock their bedroom doors because of intensified sexual guilt. Perel (2006) observed a common pattern in boys who had to care for or protect their mothers, sometimes from aggressive fathers: They have a "love–lust split," such that they are drawn to a woman who is "anything but fragile. She is sexually assertive, even demanding, and never reminds him of his victimized mother or his overwhelmed wife. Her confidence and availability are a turn-on that frees him from any caretaking responsibilities" (p. 197). Whichever psychodynamics apply, therapists will see that open bedroom door policies or, more generally, prohibitions on sex when kids are at home ("They'll hear us!") can serve as rationalizations for avoiding physical contact that has become problematic.

Novelty vs. safety

Setting aside contributions from aging, illness, and parenthood, there remains substantial debate about why sexual interest frequently declines in committed relationships, often contributing to extramarital affairs. Perhaps surprisingly, recent biologically based studies find that women lose sexual interest in their partners sooner than men do and as a direct function of time spent together (Lyubomirsky, 2013). Writers such as Perel (2006), Mitchell (2002), and Schnarch (1991, 1997) suggest that sexual excitement—like excitement in other areas of life (roller coasters, foreign travel)—depends on some amount of uncertainty and novelty. Perel notes how common it is for partners to fantasize about sex with strangers.[10] These authors argue that when relational safety becomes a preeminent goal in marriage, sexual desire will decline for partners who now seem too predictable and familiar. They also suggest that such safety is partly illusory, based on a false sense of truly knowing one's partner. Perel observes that some people desexualize their partners, "clipping their wings" to reassure themselves that their partners will not stray.

By contrast, there is excitement in really seeing one's partner as a separate individual. True intimacy with a partner seen clearly as separate and "differentiated" from the self is both more risky and more exciting. It is also ultimately more satisfying and better glue for the marital bond. It is this kind of (total) sex that many happily married couples find most satisfying. By contrast, pornography, hooking up, and prostitution can be viewed as "sex lite"—activities that provide less risk and less psychological reward.

Others attribute the decline of sexual interest to a routinization or "institutionalization" of both the relationship and specific sexual activities, with sex becoming "more an obligation, rather than a suspension of the mundane" (Meana, 2010, p. 105). As Suzanne Iasenza (2010) puts it:

> Imagine going to a restaurant and ordering the same meal every time. Imagine expecting you and your partner to want the same menu item or the same number of courses each time you dine out. Sometimes you are not hungry but go out to eat with your partner anyway because you want to be together . . . . The sexual menu helps couples understand the need to be more specific and flexible about sexuality in a light-hearted way. It offers the couple a nonjudgmental way of expressing preferences while normalizing differences. One may prefer fast food (a quickie) one day and a leisurely meal (making love) next time. It encompasses the need to know what one wants, to express it clearly, and to negotiate differences. I get my way and have Italian food tonight, and then am willing to go for Chinese, your favorite, next week.
>
> (p. 303)

Iasenza suggests that we help couples brainstorm by creating separate lists of sexual menu items. When doing this, they should put aside their partner's preferences and try hard not to censor themselves by excluding items that seem too tame or too kinky.

Other authors, like Gottman (2011) in his more recent work, stress the importance of trust and safety in maintaining sexual connection, a theory supported by the dramatic fall-off in sex between partners once trust is lost. This may be truer for women, who tend to see feelings of closeness as a *prerequisite* for sex, whereas men typically feel close and more trusting *after* sex. For both genders, the excitement of sharing sexual fantasies requires safety and trust.

Both sides of this debate make good points—both safety and some level of novelty/uncertainty are required, just as they are in other invigorating activities (again, think roller coasters)—thus explaining why ongoing sex in marriage is challenging to achieve.

Monogamy

While sex can be the glue that holds couples together, it can also be the dynamite that blows marriages apart. Some thinkers contemplating the waning of sexual desire in marriage and the frequency of affairs followed by divorce blame our overvaluing of monogamy (Coontz, 2005; Perel, 2006; Scheinkman, 2005). They note that, for most of human history, multiple wives, prostitution, and extramarital liaisons have been accepted, if often hidden from plain view; and they point to contemporary practices of polyamory and open relationships, particularly in the gay male community, that function with different expectations (Morin, 2012). Whether most contemporary humans could truly accept that their partners were having sex outside their relationship or whether such activity amounts to playing with fire seems to me an empirical question. Couples considering non-monogamy can consult the self-help book by Taormino (2008), and therapists considering helping them should examine their own beliefs about non-monogamy and, should these be negative, refer the couple to a colleague.

My experience has been that, for most people, monogamy is a requisite component of marital commitment that is gravely threatened by extramarital sex. We will discuss extramarital affairs in more detail in a later chapter, but here we should note that they are not invariably the result of unsatisfactory sex inside the marriage.

Hidden sexual alternatives

Sometimes, the decline in sexual interest is due to clandestine sexual practices—affairs, porn addiction, sex with prostitutes, or (for apparent heterosexuals) same-sex activity—that diminish desire for sex within the marriage. Such hidden alternatives should be considered when more overt and obvious causes fail to account for a loss of interest.

The take-home lessons for sustaining sexual interest are to try to foster *both* safety and novelty, qualities that are not mutually exclusive. Couples will do better in bed as they share their inner lives outside the bedroom more fully, as they keep getting to know each other, and as they sometimes experiment with novel sexual practices. The choice of novel sexual practices can be left up to the couple and need not include trapezes. Instead, sharing fantasies, watching erotica, experimenting with different positions, and trying out sex in different settings may work quite well. Suggestions for improving sexual desire and satisfaction are listed in Table 7.2.

Further suggestions for keeping sex alive

Table 7.2 shows that many ways to increase sexual desire follow directly from identifying their causes. We can also learn from studies of couples who have succeeded in keeping their sex lives vital over many years (Gottman & Gottman, 2010; Kleinplatz, 2010; Mark & Lasslo, 2018; Morin, 2012). All such studies find that, contrary to common belief, such couples work at it.

Table 7.2 Possible Solutions for Reduced Sexual Desire

- Improve marital satisfaction generally.
- Reduce external stress.
- Refocus on the importance of sex.
- Schedule medical evaluation(s) to assess physical causes and provide remediation.
- Psychotherapy for sexual abuse in childhood or for inhibited desire due to excessive negative socialization.
- Prescribe vibrators/erotica/masturbation for women who have never experienced orgasms or who were negatively socialized concerning sex.
- Focus on "reclaiming desire" and "sexual selfishness" in women who locate need/ desire too much in others (children/husbands).
- Reduce unrealistic expectations, especially about performance, body image, and orgasms.
- Treat specific sexual dysfunctions (premature ejaculation, erectile dysfunction, vaginismus).
- Improve the physical environment during sex (warm baths, special oils, candles, music).
- Assign sensate focus and gradual resumption of physical contact.
- Experiment with novelty, fantasy, and role-playing.

As Morin puts it, "Routine is not the problem; it's the secret!" The following conclusions emerge from these studies:

- The quality of the couple relationship is foundational. Couples showed mutual respect, caring, acceptance, and admiration. They let their partners know that they were sexually desirable. They gave compliments and surprise gifts and wrote poems or daily messages that said, "You are special to me." They expressed nonsexual physical and verbal affection often. As one subject put it, "It's not great technique that makes a good lover. It's involvement."
- Couples made sex a priority. They had "maintenance" or "intentional" sex and were game to try even when they weren't horny. They had "quickies," as well as gourmet sex, without having a long list of prerequisites for having sex. They thought that frequency mattered ("use it or lose it") and that sex was an important source of positivity in their relationships—a beneficial habit, almost like working out or taking vitamins.
- Couples had agreed-upon rituals for initiating and declining sex, which helped them not take it personally when they were out of sync.
- Couples felt unselfconscious, uninhibited, and safe with each other, so that they were willing to take risks and were able to lose themselves in the moment.
- Couples commented on sexually attractive body parts of their partners (biceps, breasts), in what Morin termed "lusty objectification."
- They looked for novelty in bed and out.
- They explored and accepted each other's sexual fantasies and sometimes used erotica.
- They paid attention to their physical health and appearance.

- They accepted masturbation (together or separately).
- They mentioned unlearning some things, much of it from culture and the movies: that a beautiful woman was sufficient for a man, that just letting the guy do it would work for the woman, that talking wasn't required, that no planning was needed, that orgasms were the measure of success.
- Less-than-perfect sex was OK, and if the couple started to have sexual problems, they discussed them, just as they did other marital problems.
- More important than technique was a willingness to read feedback. In Kleinplatz's studies, great sex took time to learn. Interestingly, kissing was the act that really counted. (Speculating, this may be because kissing involves the central challenge of great sex—to simultaneously experience and give pleasure in a way that responds to feedback.)

In addition to these research findings, couples can work to improve their sexual *environment* at home: adding music, soft lighting, lingerie, and cologne, and eliminating distractions.

These couples who kept sex alive talked about and played with their sexual fantasies. Most such fantasies contain a curative wish concerning a childhood trauma or adult anxiety, and thus turn out to be endlessly pleasing when enacted in the bedroom (Stoller, 1991). Sometimes, helping a spouse accept the favored sexual scripts of their partner will also revitalize their sex life, but this may not always be possible. More generally, helping couples discuss their wishes without shame will prove useful and may require tackling inhibitions, as described earlier in this chapter. While studies show that couples do better when they can accept less-than-perfect sex, working to improve its quality also makes sense. As Kleinplatz (2010) sometimes tells her clients who complain of low desire, "If I had the kind of sex you've been having, I wouldn't want it either!" Here is where it helps to learn the details of the couple's sex practices, even as asking about them may make non-sex therapists uncomfortable.

Suggestions for restarting sex in couples when it has become infrequent

While most suggestions for improving desire, receptivity, and sexual quality make logical sense to couples, getting them back on track after a long drought can prove challenging. What usually blocks the way is both simple and fundamental: Partners fear feeling vulnerable as they again touch each other while naked. This is where we can help. Once tempers are under control enough to make affectionate physical contact attractive, therapists can prescribe specific exercises to get over this awkward stage of reconnecting. By directing the couple in this way, we partly solve the problem of neither partner wanting to risk "going first."

Think of this like the sequence of adolescent behaviors, beginning with affectionate touching, then hugging and kissing, and then more erotic touching of naked bodies. I usually begin by encouraging couples to hold hands and then hug in our sessions. They are usually self-consciously reluctant and then relieved to have bridged the gap. Later, I suggest that they continue this outside our sessions, including Schnarch's (1991) exercise of "hugging till calm," where couples hug every time they meet and focus on achieving personal relaxation. If a partner continues to look uncomfortable, however, we discuss this, in keeping with Rancourt's (2016) finding that women with sexual problems frequently have aversive reactions to their husband's simply touching them.

Once they can manage such basic touching, we can move on to "non-demand pleasuring" or "sensate focus exercises" (SF), as developed by William Masters and Virginia Johnson (1970) and modified by subsequent sex therapists (Kaplan, 1974; Weiner & Avery-Clark, 2017). SF shifts attention from anxious thoughts about sex ("Will I get an erection?" "Will I be orgasmic?" "How do I look?"), to being present (mindfully) in the moment, and serves as a bridge between affection and eroticism, emphasizing pleasure over performance. It challenges the view that sex concerns only genitals, intercourse, and orgasm. It encourages feedback about what works and what doesn't. And it replaces the rigid roles learned in adolescence when, most often, the boy took charge. Because of these features and because it is done as a joint project, non-demand pleasuring does more than just help restart and improve sexual activity and may be superior to ordinary sexual activity for fostering couple intimacy (McCarthy & McCarthy, 2014).

Before launching into non-demand pleasuring exercises, it sometimes helps to have clients, more often women, explore their bodies and erotic minds in private. Virtually, all sex therapists agree that intentional self-stimulation is the most effective way for women to learn how to achieve reliable orgasms.

Table 7.3 lists some specific instructions that you can print as a handout to help couples gradually get back on track while improving the quality of their sexual experiences. This list proceeds all the way to orgasm, although you will want to advise most couples to progress slowly. Following Weiner and Avery-Clark (2017), I recommend that couples formally schedule these exercises for about 30 minutes, every two or three days. While the instructions are written for heterosexual couples, they apply equally to same-sex partners.[11]

Because focusing on *sensation* alone can be difficult, it is preferable to instruct clients to report *whatever happens* in the moment. Allowing them to simply notice what happens, including distracting thoughts, will help you work with intrusive, pleasure-killing thoughts that cannot be banished simply by instructions to do so (Iasenza, 2010). In this way, SF may uncover problematic love-making techniques, as well as embodied, procedural, automatic, out-of-awareness experiences that may have been missed in the sexual history (Pacey, 2019).[12]

Erectile dysfunction

Erectile dysfunction (ED) is often secondary to insecurity about subpar sexual "performance," although therapists should not assume that it is determined

Table 7.3 Sensate Focus Exercises

- Optional: Begin with a shower or bath alone or, alternatively, together with each soaping the other.
- Set up the environment for comfort and privacy, free of pets, children, phones, and other potential distractions.
- Prior to touching, begin with deep breathing and muscle relaxation.
- Set a timer for the giving and receiving pleasure exercises that come next, so that you don't have to pay attention to the time. Alternate roles every 5 to 10 minutes.
- Begin by alternating roles of pleasure giver and pleasure receiver. Pay attention to only one role at a time until you get better at it.
- The role of the pleasure giver is to explore, observe, and experiment.
- The role of pleasure receiver is to be passively relaxed and aware of thoughts, feelings, and bodily sensations. Notice whatever happens, including distracting, pleasure-killing thoughts.
- Begin with nonsexual touch: back scratching/massage and/or foot massage with oil.
- After doing this several times, progress to alternating between nonsexual and sexual touch, first with the woman as giver. The man should have his eyes closed. Erections can be allowed to come and go.
- Shift to the man as active. He should experiment, allowing himself to be playful while aiming to create good feelings, not only to "turn her on." Again, mix genital and nongenital touching.
- Optional and *without* the timer: Have the woman initiate the transition to intercourse, guiding intromission.
- Afterwards, hold each other and, after that, discuss the experience. What did you like? What did you learn? What would make it better? Write down your experiences and bring your reports to therapy for further discussion.
- Some additional exercises to try:
  o Synchronized breathing.
  o Touching objects with your eyes closed and describing them.
  o Close your eyes, while facing each other, and explore each other's face and hair, moving down the body, describing what you feel and notice.
  o "Female anatomy lesson" with the woman lying with her back supported and legs apart and the man with his head between her legs, assuming the attitude of a curious medical student. The woman describes her anatomy, including labia and clitoris, and how she likes to be touched. You can also do the male version of this exercise.

solely by self-doubt. Men and women alike will avoid sex, like other activities, that provoke shame. And asymptomatic partners may mislabel the cause as due to anger at them or to their lack of attractiveness. Difficulty with erections and ejaculation are obvious, all-or-nothing, events. While orgasms in women can be faked, this is less than optimal sex. Orgasms cannot simply be willed, and they are paradoxically made less likely by efforts to do so. The SF exercises just described were originally developed by Masters and Johnson as treatment for ED, with the aim of decreasing the performance anxiety and "spectatoring" that so often interfere with male arousal and orgasm. After physical causes have been ruled out, and (in some cases) PDE5 inhibitor drugs like Viagra have been tried, the aforementioned exercises can help. In addition, therapists can educate couples that sexual arousal and orgasm in aging men and women are aided by "multiple sensation stimulation" (she stroking his testicles, he touching her breasts, both kissing, fantasizing, etc.), and by helping partners become less shy about asking for more erotic stimulation. Many partners just need more of the touching that worked before. For men who lose their erections at the point of penetration, we can counsel becoming more comfortable getting and losing erections, followed by pleasuring their partners with nonvaginal orgasms. Partners can help by playing with the penis around the vagina to gain practice in stimulating and guiding the penis, including deciding when to transition to intercourse. One common pattern is that men who are worried about ED move too quickly to intercourse (understandably, due to their fear of losing their erection). Wanting to penetrate ASAP, they do so too soon and then lose their erection after entry. Therapists, alert to this dynamic, can caution against penetrating too soon.

Therapists can help women with analogous issues of becoming aroused and reaching orgasm by challenging the idea that it is the man's responsibility "to make the woman come." Rather, she should guide him and find her "sexual voice," showing him what works for her. This will often include informing him that for most women, unlike for most men, touching genital areas before women are mentally aroused is a turn-off and going faster and harder as orgasm approaches may not be welcomed.

Premature ejaculation

Premature ejaculation (PE) similarly causes shame and sexual avoidance and can also be treated by modified SF exercises. Women may incorrectly believe that the man could have controlled his timing and may then feel used and that their sexual pleasure was unimportant to him. Her negative response then increases his anxiety and makes the problem worse. Women may complain not only because of "pleasure interruptus," as vaginal intercourse ceases too soon, but because many men react maladaptively to their problem, with undue timidity, hurried lovemaking, or off-putting excesses of bravado and control (Margolies, 2001).

Men who ejaculate prematurely most commonly suffer from what Margolies terms "excessive sexualized arousal." As she describes it, "The sexualizer is in such a state of anxious anticipation when it comes to sex that he seems to leapfrog his way to early orgasm" (p. 55). These men are usually uninterested in foreplay. Focused solely and anxiously on their orgasm, they are out of touch with whatever else is going on interpersonally with their partners or physically with their own bodies. Not knowing what is going on in their bodies makes it impossible for them to control their pacing. The most common treatment for PE is fostering enhanced awareness, not by promoting distraction, but by slowing down at the point of ejaculatory inevitability, with slowing down assisted by the "squeeze technique" with the woman in the superior position (see Weiner & Avery-Clark, 2017, pp. 83–85, for detailed instructions). Men can begin to work on this problem on their own using the stop–start technique (Metz & McCarthy, 2003). Selective serotonin inhibitors (SSRIs) may also help to delay ejaculation.

Sexual fantasies and scripts: valuable and problematic

Humans, unlike other animals, fantasize during sex to increase pleasure and arousal. Indeed, for most people, the brain is the body's biggest sex organ. In this section, we will see how exploring clients' sexual fantasies can facilitate couple therapy, and how sexual scripts can cause problems.

Many sexual fantasies contain socially unacceptable or transgressive elements (e.g., sex with strangers, watching others, threesomes, bondage). Some scripts are common (rape fantasies), some are idiosyncratic and rare (sex with amputees), many are highly repugnant to those who do not enjoy them (painful masochism, "golden showers"), and others are illegal (pedophilia, exhibitionism). This extensive diversity of sexual fantasies and enactments has long called out for explication (Bader, 2002; Dimen, 2003; Freud, 1905; Iasenza, 2010; Kahr, 2007; Kaplan, 1995; Kernberg, 1991; Morin, 1995; Stoller, 1991).[13] Contemporary explanations of sexual fantasies (whether imagined or enacted) view them as psychologically meaningful, similar to wishful daydreams and children's play, and intended (a) to restage and reverse or master painful childhood traumas (e.g., children who had painful surgical procedures later enjoy forms of painful sex); (b) to overcome sexual guilt or inhibition by disclaiming responsibility (e.g., rape fantasies); (c) to transcend or integrate opposites (e.g., active vs. passive, responsible vs. abandoned, male vs. female, adult vs. child); or (d) to increase excitement by staging meaningful, uncertain dramas that require overcoming obstacles (e.g., sex with strangers). It appears that sex added to almost anything makes it feel good! In many sexual fantasies, anxiety moves to security, weakness becomes strength, guilt transforms to freedom, and indifferent partners become enthusiastic. As Morin (1995, p. 142) puts it, "High states of arousal flow from the tension between persistent problems and triumphant solutions."

For therapists, sexual fantasies are like dreams, often the royal road to understanding our clients' deepest hopes and fears, not only in the bedroom but in their relationships more generally. But because most sexual fantasies take shape automatically and unconsciously early in life, most people are unaware of the motives just mentioned and feel vaguely uncomfortable and guilty about revealing their fantasies to others. To access preferred sexual fantasies and their possible meaning, Morin asks clients to

> Imagine yourself really wanting to be sexually aroused but, for some reason, you're not. Based on everything you know about your sexuality, describe the fantasy that would be the very most likely to arouse you. What are your ideas about what makes this fantasy so exciting?
>
> (p. 27)

Sexual fantasies can help us understand our clients, but they can also create problems.

Sexual inhibition

Most of us know what turns us on, but not why. When people are uncomfortable with their own fantasies and preferences, they may avoid the sexual activity that calls them forth. This is particularly ironic when we consider that many sexual fantasies aim to allow sex to go forward by freeing us from guilt and responsibility. Such inhibition can become a problem early in a marriage, when the pressure to have sex falls off and a person's latent discomfort with sex may become exposed. When sexual fantasies involve (usually disguised) parental figures, sex can dwindle after the wedding or after the first child is born. Fantasies that involve a need to preserve the wife as "pure" account for the Madonna–whore complex, where husbands unconsciously feel they must go outside the marriage for sex. In all these cases, therapy can often help by exposing the sexual fantasies, which usually turn out to be pretty tame and then by helping the person to own them as playfully acceptable. In doing so, we can help to clarify that sexual fantasies are not identical to sexual actions. The woman who might imagine being ravished by many powerful men is not saying that she wants to be gang-raped. The man who occasionally fantasizes about three-way sex may not want to do this in real life.

And because sexual fantasies are pretty much immutable in adults, we will sometimes have to help clients to accept fantasies that they find distasteful, such as "feminists who are aroused by rape fantasies; liberals who have sadistic erotic fantasies; and macho men who are turned on by masochistic fantasies of being dominated by a woman" (Kaplan, 1995, p. 153). Clients often feel liberated as we help them normalize, depathologize, and "de-criminalize" their fantasies.

Incompatible scripts

In some cases, couples learn that the preferences or requirements for successful sex of one partner clash with the needs or aversions of the other. Ideally, couples would have learned this prior to marriage. But in some cases, as with the sexual inhibition problem just mentioned, the incompatibility has been hidden in the early stages of the relationship. Therapy here resembles our work in other areas of apparent incompatibility. Couples are encouraged to talk honestly about what they prefer and what they dislike, while working toward compromises. For instance, one couple I treated ultimately agreed that the husband's preference for sometimes wearing pantyhose during sex was something they could manage.

As our culture has changed, some couples have become less likely to be completely thrown off by the desires of one partner for fantasy enactments that involve fetishes, bondage, rape, masochism, or cross-gender play.

Helping some clients to be less critical and more playful, and others to accept their partner's aversive reactions can reduce ongoing resentment, as well as sexual avoidance. While preferred sexual activities and fantasies will rarely change, many partners can come to accept and work on their differences.

Some partners will not be able to meet each other's desires. In such cases, we can help them discuss the consequences for their marriage. In my experience, either the partner whose needs are not met will feel chronically resentful or that person may go outside the marriage for satisfaction.

Noxious paraphilias

The so-called noxious paraphilias, almost all confined to men, include behaviors that are illegal or abusive (e.g., pedophilia, voyeurism, exhibitionism). Sex for these couples was often satisfactory early in the relationship, but then the man's desire for marital sex declined. Women who have blamed themselves for being unattractive or poor partners may be relieved as much as shocked when the man's secret is revealed. Noxious paraphilias most often come to light when the man is arrested or loses his job following exposure. According to McCarthy and McCarthy (2014):

> It is quite difficult, and usually impossible, to transfer variant arousal to couple sex. . . . The pattern develops in childhood or early adolescence and is reinforced by thousands of experiences of masturbating to images of deviant arousal. It . . . serves as the man's "secret sexual world." . . . Couple sex cannot compete with this distorted fantasy and secret world.
>
> (pp. 60–61)

For some clients, the prognosis may not be quite so bleak, but what to do next will depend greatly on the couple and the crime and may well stress the marriage to the breaking point. As with other external crises, couple therapy may help the partners clarify how to move ahead.

Porn and compulsive sexual behavior

Compulsive sexual behaviors—including serial affairs, cyber or phone sex, visiting prostitutes, frequenting strip clubs, and masturbating excessively—usually adversely impact other areas of life, as well. What all of these have in common is sex without intimacy, which is not to imply that intimacy is required for "sexual health."[14] When disapproved of by partners, when done to excess, or when at variance with the person's own moral/religious values, these activities can cause serious marital problems. In this section, I will focus on Internet porn use as representative of this group of behaviors, even as many clients find it less troubling than some of the other activities just mentioned.

For many people, Internet porn—with its easy access any time of day or night, affordability, variety, and anonymity—has become increasingly captivating. Control over the sexual script is complete, including over the "partner's" willingness and acceptance of that script. (In this, it resembles prostitution, which often serves as a work-around when partners are unwilling to engage in certain activities.) While masturbating to erotica has come to be seen by most people as benign (including as an alternative when partners were unavailable), the current epidemic—with porn accounting for perhaps 25% of Internet searches and 35% of downloads (Maltz & Maltz, 2008)—has stirred much discussion and debate about possible adverse social consequences.[15]

Castleman's (2016) review of the relevant statistics concluded that generalized panic over these developments is probably unwarranted, as he found only a slight increase in men viewing porn since the advent of the Internet, with porn now accounting for about 10% of Internet traffic. Nonetheless, some experts report that Internet video porn—unlike pornographic photographs and independent of porn *addiction*—has a more deleterious impact on men's sexual desire and attitudes toward women and hinders sexual performance with real-life partners (Maltz & Maltz, 2008; Park et al., 2016; Rasmussen, 2016). As concerns ED alone, some researchers have found no association with the use of porn (Landripet & Štulhofer, 2015), while others have found an association but only in "problematic [frequent] users" (Grubbs & Gola, 2019). So, the jury still is out on this issue.

Distinct from ED, Internet porn can interfere with sex with a real partner, who may seem inferior compared to the images on the screen. And, as one site or video leads to the next, there is often an escalation in kinkiness that users, themselves, may find unsettling. As one user put it, "Porn gives you what you want, but makes you want things you didn't start out wanting" (Maltz & Maltz, p. 88). Many people are horrified by what their partners watch and experience a sense of betrayal comparable to that associated with an extramarital affair (see Nielsen, 2019a, for a detailed case example). They become uncomfortable having sex, and the couple's intimate life deteriorates further.

Porn also impacts relationships if it becomes compulsive—like an addiction to a drug—leading to a neglect of work, family, and other responsibilities. Some men lose their jobs when caught using porn at work. Like other compulsive behaviors, "porn addiction" can be hard to give up. For these reasons, compulsive Internet use, much of it involving pornography, has become increasingly mentioned in divorce cases.[16]

Working to help clients give up their "sexual addictions" aims to promote sex that prioritizes intimacy over an exclusive focus on fantasy and orgasms (Maltz & Maltz, 2008; Marcus, 2010). This includes encouraging couples to use SF exercises to direct attention to touch, sensation, and loving feelings that offer more opportunity for shared pleasure and connection. (For an excellent, fictionalized account of movement from porn to intimacy, see the 2013 film, *Don Jon*.) Such sex not only pulls the porn abuser away from porn, but it can also heal the partner who has come to doubt the porn abuser's love and desire for her. Of course, we will ultimately want to know what led the person toward so much porn in the first place; the answer, as in the case of Joel, discussed earlier in this chapter, will often relate to sexual and nonsexual marital problems that deserve attention.

In her nuanced discussion of porn, Solomon (2020) cautions against taking extreme views and encourages partners to voice their concerns:

> Our larger cultural conversation about porn tends to get stuck in binaries. Individuals sometimes identify themselves as pro-porn or anti-porn. Dialogue gets framed in simplistic ways: porn is bad/porn is good; porn oppresses women/porn liberates women; porn is addictive/porn isn't addictive; using porn destroys a relationship/using porn helps a relationship. So, it makes a ton of sense that couples get stuck here as well, pointing fingers, blaming, and shaming. When this happens, both partners walk away feeling judged and unheard.

Solomon notes the common divide between men and women in such discussions:

> [A woman enters such conversations] as someone who has lived in a culture where evidence of objectification and exploitation of women is everywhere. Even if she is not a survivor of sexual trauma herself, to live as a woman is to live trauma-adjacent. It is painful to feel as if her partner is participating in an activity that fuels the objectification of women and violence against women, [whereas men are more often afraid of being shamed for their use of porn, something] he has likely had a longer-standing relationship with than the one with his partner. It may be a private space that he has turned to over many years—for self-soothing, escape, and exploration.

Specialized programs are available to help clients with various forms of compulsive sexual behaviors, including 12-step, group programs, in-patient programs, intensive individual psychodynamic psychotherapy (Marcus, 2010), and psychoanalysis (Goldberg, 1999). In all cases, the goal is to improve client's capacity for intimate connection with real partners, including their capacity to regulate their emotions without recourse to maladaptive compulsive behavior.

Fred and Beth: Fostering sexual happiness and reconnection

When they began therapy, Fred and Beth were hardly ever having sex. Like most of my couples, their feelings for each other had been so negative that the thought of being that close and vulnerable made little sense. One year of weekly therapy sessions later, sex was returning but far slower than their ability to talk or to enjoy other pleasurable activities together.

With my encouragement, Fred was able to complain openly about his "monastic life." When Beth responded that, "He only wants me for sex,"

I expressed my doubts about that conclusion, telling her that for many men, sex is one activity where they permit themselves to reveal their emotional needs. Fred's next thoughts then surprised us with the depth of his pain, as he told Beth that whenever she refuses him sexually, he feels certain that she doesn't really love him. He next voiced his fear that she had married him only because he was a "safe bet" and really preferred her prior boyfriends, with whom she had had more passionate sex.

While Beth reassured Fred that she did indeed love, respect, and appreciate him, thus countering his deepest fears, it remained true that she had often wondered, guiltily, about what had happened to the passion she had had with other men prior to her marriage. Partly, it seemed that the anti-sexual socialization of her childhood had been on temporary hold in her rebellious premarital life, held at bay by men more self-confident about their sexual needs than Fred and by her desire to maintain connection with them. Just talking about sex, as we were now doing, made it clear how uncomfortable Beth was with her own sexuality.

In the sessions that followed, I helped Beth see how she had located her (sexual) desire in Fred while denying that she, herself, had sexual needs. Recall how she had disdainfully said that she knew what *he* wanted! After interpreting this example of projective identification, I suggested that she experiment with masturbation and explore her sexual fantasy life. The positive results surprised Beth and made clear how she had let her own sexual pleasure go without protest (in keeping with her puritanical parents, who had rarely touched her affectionately and had disparaged sex). As she re-owned her sexual–sensual side, Beth soon talked softly of how, when Fred was away on business, she greatly missed having him in bed next to her. Fred, delighted at this transformation, deepened the process further by talking for the first time about how he also missed her when they were separated, not just for the sexual pleasure, but as his life companion.

Like many perimenopausal women, Beth rarely felt desirous of sex, and Fred had become afraid to initiate it because of fear of rejection. It helped to talk about this openly as a "desire discrepancy" and a common couple problem, as we made it a joint project to help Beth become more "willing" and "receptive." We learned that she felt far sexier after getting dressed up to go out for a romantic dinner together. She was also helped by Fred paying more attention to his appearance and to the appearance of their bedroom. Sex began to be re-established as a predictable event, which freed Fred from the anxiety of initiating it and Beth from the guilt and anxiety of never being in the mood.

As with other couples, as their sex improved, Fred and Beth exhibited less of the mutual crankiness that had characterized their early sessions with me. Both slept better and became less irritable. Going forward, the couple's improved sex life went hand in hand—as they now did as they left my office—with greater emotional contact and commitment.

Notes

1. A cultural/historical caveat: This chapter deals, for the most part, with contemporary American couples and their sexual problems. During much of human history and still in some countries, there exist significant, distressing problems not covered here: Clitoridectomies, marital rape, and death sentences for infidelity are among the most egregious.
2. This last will often be more complicated for LGBTQ clients but can give added pleasure after they overcome heterosexist norms.
3. One contribution to men's lack of interest in such discussions may stem from their notoriously easy arousal when young, as in the following quip from comedian Jerry Seinfeld, "There's very little sexual advice in men's magazines, because men think, 'I know what I'm doing. Just show me somebody naked!'"
4. In his wonderful article about fostering "sexpertise" in therapists, Kahr (2009) shares numerous historical anecdotes showing both professional and public discomfort and prudishness about sexual talk. My favorite is his account of a near-riot on the opening night of John Millington Synge's now-classic drama, *The Playboy of the Western World* in Dublin in 1907, when one character's "mere mention of undergarments caused so much outrage that members of the audience began to shout death threats toward the author, and to storm the stage" (p. 13). Kahr uses such anecdotes to encourage therapists to develop a "sexual skin" that will allow them to undertake a full sexual history and facilitate discussion of sexual material without shame, undue anxiety, or fears of being intrusive or becoming excited.
5. I treated this man many years ago when I was less experienced. My current preference with such "Identified Patient Couples"—couples where one partner refers the other to me to be "fixed" or set right—is to press harder than I did then to begin with conjoint couple therapy (see Nielsen, 2016, pp. 76–77).
6. McCarthy's suggestion about women and sexual fantasies may need updating in light of Kahr's (2007) extensive research showing the high prevalence of sexual fantasizing among adult women, even though, as with many men, they often feel ashamed about using fantasy during sex.
7. A caveat to this "just do it" advice: Kleinplatz (2010) has found that when spouses "repeatedly accommodated" their partners while not getting into and enjoying the sex, this adversely impacted both the sex and the relationship.
8. For a detailed example of such a case, see "Sally and George" (Nielsen, 2016, pp. 104–107).
9. The technical diagnostic term for low sexual desire in women has been changing in recent years: Some authors use Hypoactive Sexual Desire Disorder (HSDD), while DSM-V uses Female Sexual Interest/Arousal Disorder (FSIAD).
10. This was confirmed in Kahr's (2007) extensive research. Kahr found that "the vast majority of adults" sometimes imagine someone other than their current partner during sex, in what he calls an "intra-marital affair."
11. My list is a composite and personal modification of lists presented by others. The biggest difference between my list and the extensive instructions of Weiner and Avery-Clark (2017) is that they strongly recommend "touching for interest" rather than touching to induce pleasure:

> [W]hile touching the partner, the Toucher focuses on his or her own sensory experience by turning attention to the reliable sensations of temperature (cool or warm), pressure (hard or soft), and texture (smooth or rough.) This means that the person touching is doing so with a non-demand attitude of interest, curiosity, and exploration rather than with a goal-oriented, pleasuring mindset. This is the *complete opposite of a massage* during which the person touching contacts the partner's body with the expressed intent of trying to make relaxation, enjoyment, or pleasure happen for the Touchee.

(p. 33)

To me, this takes the homework exercises down a notch and may not be required for couples to simply restart sex, as contrasted with couples with more long-standing, intractable, or narrowly defined sexual problems (vaginismus, premature ejaculation, or sexual trauma), who are the typical clients of those authors. Indeed, in such cases, they often begin with "self-Sensate Focus" (touching without a partner) and start with touching nongenital areas to avoid triggering distress. Thus, they go far slower and employ more safeguards to reduce anxiety. Unlike Weiner and Avery-Clark, my colleague Jennifer McComb reports that in her sex therapy practice, couples find it easier to focus on their partner's pleasure than on their own sensations. So, my recommendations may work better for most couples.

12. This excellent article summarizes the experience of ten senior psychoanalytic couple therapists who used SF in their work. All found SF useful, especially with women who had been physically or sexually abused.

13. While all these authors are worth studying, readers will most enjoy psychoanalyst Brett Kahr's (2007), *Who's Been Sleeping in Your Head: The Secret World of Sexual Fantasies.* His mixed methods research included his many years of therapy practice, his intensive study of 122 people in semi-structured interviews, and 22,000 (*sic*) sex fantasies collected online from an extremely diverse sample of "ordinary British and American adults," men and women, aged 18–90+. His writing is entertaining, and his examples, questions, and conclusions are convincing. Noting that people often wonder, "Do our fantasies represent just a bit of private fun, or do they have more profound implications for how we lead our lives?" Kahr concludes that "a significant majority of adults maintain a most uncomfortable relationship with their private sexual fantasies, although most fantasies culminate in orgasm," which he refers to as "the masturbatory paradox" (p. 22). He convincingly presents many cases that show a close correlation between childhood traumas and the details of adult sexual fantasies, as the latter both represent them and rewrite them as wishes with a happy ending. He catalogues 14 separate functions of sexual fantasies that involve creative combinations of wishes, self-comfort, trial action, discharges of aggression at self or others, and reversals and mastery of painful situations, both past and present. On the question of whether couples should or should not share their private fantasies, Kahr allows that this can be either helpful or disastrous!

14. Sexual health no longer consists of avoiding disease and unwanted pregnancies. In a summary adapted from the WHO, the respected sex therapist Doug Braun-Harvey adds the following five principles to qualify: consent, non-exploitative, honest, shared values, and pleasure (www.theharveyinstitute.com/six-principles-of-sexual-health; downloaded 4/2/2021); notably, intimacy is not required.

15. In this regard, there is now debate over whether to use the term *porn*, rather than *erotica,* since the former has a more negative connotation.

16. I have put "porn addiction" in quotes because there is currently controversy about the proper term for such behavior. Notably, the American Association of Sexuality Educators, Counselors, and Therapists (AASECT) "does not find sufficient empirical evidence to support the classification of sex addiction or porn addiction as a mental health disorder" (www.aasect.org/position-sex-addiction; downloaded April 29, 2021). That said, WHO is scheduled to authorize the term "Compulsive Sexual Behavior Disorder" for such activities where people report that their behavior feels out of control and deleterious, not simply frowned upon as immoral.

8 Children and Extended Family

If I were asked to identify the most common problem presented to me in three decades of therapeutic work with children and families, my answer would be unequivocal: As parents, we are, unwittingly, too critical of our children.

—Ken Barish (2012, p. 57)

Don't have a tantrum back!

—T. Berry Brazelton (TV interview, cited in Barish, 2012)

Of course, the unrealistic factor in this advice about friendly firmness is that a mother can't help getting cranky after hours of needling from her child, whether the needling is gentle or fiendish.

—Benjamin Spock (1954, p. 219)

Children as a topic

Sex, children, and money are the three most common topics of discussion in couple therapy. Unlike problems with sex or money, problems with children are rarely the opening issue for couples presenting for "couple therapy" as opposed to "family therapy" or "child therapy." (Stepfamily couples are a notable exception.) Preoccupied with marital issues, parents are routinely blind to the impact of those problems on their children, so therapists should be skeptical when told that "the kids are fine" and remain prepared to discuss parenting concerns later in treatment.

As with all topics that trouble couples, problem solving in this area will usually have to take a back seat as we focus first on the couple's interpersonal process. The good news is that helping couples improve their interpersonal relationship *by itself* can help their children, since longitudinal studies "generally show that families whose parents start off with worse marital functioning tend to have children with poorer adjustment later on" (Knopp et al., 2017, p. 452), and many studies show the bidirectional impact of parents' and children's problems (e.g., Fosco et al., 2014; Sears et al., 2016). Nonetheless, work on the marital relationship alone is frequently insufficient to prevent or remediate children's problems (Cowan & Cowan, 2012; Hahlweg et al., 2010).

DOI: 10.4324/b22905-12

When discussion turns to children, we usually begin by talking to the parents alone, just as we do with other topics; sometimes direct involvement of the children later on will be beneficial. Distinct from working on problems around sex or money, negative interaction cycles with children are common complications and have many characteristics familiar to us from working with couples. Whether working with parents alone or in sessions including their children, we must be sensitive to the danger that parents will think we are criticizing them as "bad parents." Instead, we should applaud their concern for their kids and affirm their unique power to help.

Children on the scene

The addition of children frequently destabilizes couples, and many studies have found that relationship satisfaction declines following the transition to parenthood (Keizer & Schenk, 2012). Lyubomirsky (2013) summarizes research on this topic:

> An analysis of more than a hundred studies revealed that couples who were followed before and after the birth of a child suffered seemingly permanent declines in their relationship satisfaction. Surveys also demonstrate that, despite many parents' professions of joy and elation at their role, if you are female, young, not married, and unemployed—and if your children are very young or adolescent, step, or troubled—then being a parent likely makes you less happy, and less satisfied with your life and partner (if you have one), rather than more. . . . Furthermore, marital satisfaction soars after the last child leaves the home.
>
> (p. 85)

Lyubomirsky softens the disillusionment such data can elicit by reminding us that "Loving our children is not the same as loving parenting" (p. 86), and that "When people are asked confidentially about their biggest regrets in life, scarcely anyone ever says that they regret having been a parent. Instead, 95% agree that, despite the heavy costs, the rewards of being a parent are worth it" (p. 87). Children offer opportunities for (literally) creating shared meaning, for vicariously returning to childhood, for growing as a person, and, if parents are fortunate, for deep, reciprocal love.

Some of the common parental tribulations identified in the Olsons' (2000) national survey—in which 84% of the sample reported reduced marital satisfaction related to their children—were: "The father is not involved enough with our children" (68%), "We disagree on discipline" (66%), "I am dissatisfied with how childrearing is shared" (66%), and "My partner focuses more on the children than on the marriage" (64%), with unhappy couples complaining substantially more often about each of these issues. So, our charge will be to help couples do better than average in these problem areas.

Equity, careers, finances, and couple process

Children put considerable economic, physical, emotional, and time demands on their parents, leaving less of those resources available to support the marriage. Surprisingly, then, one large German study found that "After holding constant the *financial and time costs* of parenthood, fathers and mothers of all groups showed significantly *higher* levels of life satisfaction than childless men and women" (Pollmann-Schult, 2014, p. 329, italics added). The take-home point from this study is that problems with *parenting*, narrowly defined, are only part of the explanation for the decline in marital and life satisfaction after children come on the scene.

Almost universally, couples will now experience substantially increased conflict between their work and family lives: This was true of 70% of North American couples in one large study (Bond et al., 2003). This conflict is magnified in countries like the United States, where family leave and childcare resources are often inadequate (Teti, 2019).[1] As parents struggle to find time for work and family, what often suffers most is time together (Amato et al., 2007) and, less appreciated, time alone (Neilson & Stanfors, 2018). Equity issues and increased conflict enter here, as many studies show that women devote more time to their families than men do, though this disparity has lessened in recent years (Young & Schieman, 2018).

Consequently, as with manifest complaints about sex, money, or in-laws, skillful therapy must attempt to sort out how much any stated parenting problem is specific to parenting, including to children with problems, and how much is secondary to other social or marital issues.

The transition to parenthood

As many as 90% of couples report declines in marital satisfaction after becoming parents, with steeper declines in couples who have been together for less time and who communicate poorly (Doss et al., 2009). Fatigue, arrangements for childcare, and concerns about parenting adequacy and the baby's health become central challenges (Lower, 2005; Perry-Jenkins & Schoppe-Sullivan, 2019). Most mothers (60–80%) experience "baby blues" in the weeks after birth, while more severe postpartum depression affects approximately 20%, and 10% of fathers experience postnatal depression (Perry-Jenkins & Schoppe-Sullivan, 2019).

During the later stages of pregnancy and the first months post-delivery, most women have little interest in sex, and many husbands feel neglected or guilty for feeling selfish, making maintaining sexual satisfaction another common problem. Having children can also reawaken or create problems with in-laws, who may now seem either too intrusive or too distant.

Couples may benefit from reading John and Julie Gottman's self-help book, *And Baby Makes Three* (2007), or by attending a parenting education workshop, like their *Bringing Baby Home* program.[2]

Becoming a parent clearly raises issues of identity and self-esteem ("What kind of parent will I be?" "What kind of parent will my partner be with me?"), but most of the formal research on this challenging transition has focused on changes in paid employment and housework:

> In general, both types of work are more traditionally divided after the transition into parenthood: New mothers devote more time to household labor and less time to paid labor, whereas the opposite pattern is witnessed for new fathers . . . [such that] the general understanding in the literature is that new parents become less satisfied with their relationship because of these increased gender differences in labor.
>
> (Keizer & Schenk, 2012, p. 760)

According to these same researchers, however, the impact of mothers' work hours and of more household chores post-childbirth are relatively small, and *not* the main sources of relationship decline, since that decline remained after their influence was factored out. My clinical experience is that after the first child is born, couples face a multiplicity of new areas of increased stress and potential conflict, any one of which can be destabilizing. While issues differ from couple to couple, the net impact is that new parents almost universally take a hit in marital satisfaction.

Protecting couple time

Of course, one important source of disputes is that time has become far more limited. And less time means not only more disputes over whose more limited time will go to family responsibilities, but it also means less time for couple togetherness. In 1975, couples with children spent only 13 hours per week with each other compared to 35 hours for their childless peers. These numbers fell still more for couples in 2003, to only 9 hours versus 26 hours (Finkel, 2014). Not only do couples spend less time together, but when faced with a scarcity of time, couples may adapt poorly: Those who are tightly bonded will have trouble allowing their children in; others will grow apart as their accommodations to insufficient time result in parallel lives.

Once children are on the scene, arguments about insufficient time (e.g., who will take a sick child to the pediatrician) often overlap with discussions of partners' life goals (e.g., whose career is more important). Couples will now often have serious disagreements about career, financial and religious preferences that they have not discussed previously.

Infertility and conflicts about having children

Some couples come to us while stressed by infertility. Infertility treatments almost invariably stretch budgets, interfere with intimacy, and raise doubts about one's adequacy as a man or woman (if the source of the problem is identified). Distress over repeated failures to conceive and/or recurrent miscarriages can be intense. Therapists can assist such clients by allowing them to share their anguish openly, offering realistic hope and uncovering latent meanings of events (e.g., that having children is essential to self-esteem and happiness). Should infertility treatments not succeed, therapists can help couples mourn the plan for biological children and decide whether to pursue adoption.

Other couples argue over the desirability of having a first child or an additional one. While one might expect that couples would discuss whether to have children prior to marriage, many do not and some partners change their minds. The decision over whether to enlarge the family is made more complex in remarried couples, especially where one partner already has children, and the other does not. Unsurprisingly, the age and health of the couple, their finances, and the impact of children on careers and other life projects need to be discussed. Considering these potential issues up front, including by not minimizing likely consequences, can assist clients in making a reasoned decision and in accepting, ahead of time, the changes that will be necessary.

When discussing having children, it helps to uncover expectations about what being a parent will entail and mean. Over the years, I have seen many couples with one partner strongly opposed to having children due to the irrational certainty of repeating painful scenarios from his or her childhood. Once these were examined and found to be unlikely, almost all these couples decided to move ahead to have children.

Open discussion also helps couples who ultimately choose not to have additional children. Sometimes, it becomes clear that the additional child is a hoped-for "home remedy" that is better replaced by some other solution, including greater marital closeness. Some disappointed spouses can become more accepting of a smaller family after learning that their partners have little interest in assisting with childcare. And partners who convince their spouses not to have more children are often able to openly express gratitude for that sacrifice, a crucial cushion to the other partner's deeply felt disappointment.

Additional sources of problems

Socioeconomic constraints and family diversity

Our clients live within a rapidly changing social context. The parenting suggestions in this chapter are constrained by that context, which—currently in the United States—is woefully deficient in supporting parents and children due to a lack of adequate paid maternity leave, quality daycare, local grandparents, family friendly jobs, and mental health care. As Paul Wachtel (2014) notes:

> All of our theories of development assume that when parents have time to be with their children, and when that time is relaxed, attentive, and responsive to the child's needs, the outcome will be better . . . . Our journals and case reports are filled with accounts of patients' parents

depicted as narcissistic, depressed, or lacking in empathy . . . however . . . it becomes apparent that nurturingly engaged parental availability is also powerfully dependent on aspects of the larger social context, including matters as simple and straightforward as how long a commute Mom and Dad have to and from work.

(p. 177)

When keeping these social constraints in mind, we must eschew simplistic ideas about what is "functional" or "normal" concerning families and parenting. In 1960, 73% of children lived in families with both parents in their first marriage, but by 2015, that had dropped to 46% (Pew Research Center, 2015). So, as Froma Walsh (2012b) cautions:

In the mental health field and the larger society, those who did not conform to the reified standard of the "normal family" tended to be pathologized and stigmatized, reinforcing their sense of failure and deficiency. Interventions often aimed inappropriately to mold all families into a "one-size-fits-all" model that didn't fit their lives.

(p. ix)

Instead, optimal functioning will mean helping diverse families to successfully meet their needs for nurture, protection, growth, and intimacy, when faced with both normative stressors (e.g., adolescent children) and unexpected, untimely, or severe stressors (e.g., the death of a child) as family members progress through time. While a life-stage analysis frequently points to predictable issues (e.g., coping with the "empty nest"), many contemporary families span a number of stages simultaneously, such as Walsh's (2012a) telling example of a "remarriage family comprised of a 50-year-old husband, his 35-year-old wife, their toddler twins, and his adolescent children, in shared custody with their mother" (p. 7).

Families must make trade-offs among many goals: career priorities that interfere with family functioning or vice versa, marital harmony over parental conflict or vice versa, and devotion to parenting that adversely impacts couple well-being or vice versa. Our job as therapists will be to help clients create roles and work things out on an individual basis, including in stepfamilies, dual-earner families, and same-sex families—all of which differ from the idealized model of the 1950s household "comprised of an intact, two-parent family unit headed by a male breadwinner and supported by his full-time homemaker wife, who devoted herself to household management, childrearing, and elder care" (Walsh, 2012a, p. 11).

Structural family problems

Some unhappily married people involve their children in their marital problems, and some children so involved will become symptomatic and aggravate

their parents' marital problems. In my practice, the most common such patterns are: (a) one parent enmeshed or too close to a child (or children),
while the other parent is alienated, acting out, or seeking happiness elsewhere—with either partner originating this vicious circle; (b) both parents
overly focused on the children, a situation that can be secondary to marital
problems or the cause of them, which may or may not cause problems for
the children, and which leads to trouble when the children leave home; and
(c) parents arguing over real or exaggerated child misbehavior as a defensive
proxy for similar, unstated disagreements they have with each other (e g ,
over the child's poor school performance when Dad is out of work, or over
a teen's curfew when the couple's sex life is troubled).

This last situation is a form of scapegoating, in which children may be
induced in a form of projective identification to play requisite roles, though
some children may resist such pressure. In this way, some parents misuse
their children by locating and inducing unacceptable parts of themselves in
them—inadequacy, sexuality, defiance, lack of responsibility—as they cast
their children in unidimensional, problematic roles. Any aspect of life that a
parent feels is not going well for them can be seen, denied, or "remote controlled" in a child. Some children will be encouraged to live the lives parents
cannot allow themselves to live, and some of these will be (paradoxically)
punished for doing do.[3]

Such "family processes" were central to the development of the family
therapy movement, which coined the term "*identified patient*" (IP) for children caught in these family patterns. Structural Family Therapy (Minuchin,
1974; Minuchin & Fishman, 1981) called attention to misalliances across
generations, and Bowen's Family Systems Therapy (Titelman, 2010) noted
how children can be misused (triangulated) to stabilize couples.

Left to their own devices, IP children who have been scapegoated or
unfairly blamed for what are fundamentally parental problems will frequently
blame themselves, as did one client of mine who remained convinced years
later that she had caused all her parents' fights and their subsequent divorce,
since most of their overt arguing followed (legitimate) requests that she had
made to one of them.

For cases in which children are used as proxies for parental problems, it is
usually best to begin treatment *not* by questioning the parents' assessment of
the problem, but, instead, by working with them to come up with a solution. In doing so, therapists will often be working on latent problems in the
partners (Who listens to whom? Who is aligned with whom? What affects
cannot be contained and are being projected?). Only after an alliance with
the therapist has developed can one interpret and work to reduce what may
have seemed an obvious displacement.

That said, one can also see couples whose marriages have been severely
tested and disrupted because of the stress of managing disturbed or delinquent children. So, when a child is presented as the problem, one should
never simplistically assume that a marital problem is the cause.

Ghosts in the family: how the past shapes parenting

Having children inevitably evokes memories of one's own childhood and stirs hopes and fears about the future. Parents' fears most often derive from personal experiences that they worry will repeat. A mother hesitant to return to satisfying work when all her children were in grade school had had too little parental attention as a child. A father reluctant to allow his daughter to drive had witnessed horrific auto accidents as a policeman. Parents like these—partly aware of their past suffering—will often overcorrect in an attempt to protect their children. Many parenting conundrums will only be resolved after we uncover the historical precedents and traumas that account for parental inflexibility.

As described by child psychologist Selma Fraiberg in her famous paper, "Ghosts in the Nursery" (Fraiberg et al., 1975), parents who have repressed or minimized their painful childhood experiences will often re-enact them. Never having fully registered how her mother's depression left her alone and neglected, a young mother may ignore her baby's crying. Still believing his father was right to harshly shame him for minor mistakes, a husband may repeat this with his children.

A third way history shapes parenting occurs with parents who never presented a particular problem to their parents as children. Such parents are often unprepared for and flummoxed by novel situations with their children, for instance, when they, the parents, had been "good kids" who never acted out, stellar students who needed no help in school, or only children who never faced sibling issues.

Because past traumas and learning deficits help explain current impasses, we will frequently see problems emerging when children reach developmental stages that correspond to the parent's own past troubles. A parent who "missed adolescence" after his father died when he was 12 will predictably start having trouble with his children when they reach puberty.

We can also help parents to become aware of the personal goals they hope to meet through their children, some shaped by their past histories. These include wishes to redo or simply repeat their childhood, to leave a legacy, or to create a supportive extended family. A certain amount of this is healthy and helps motivate parental attention and caretaking. As noted by Shaddock (2000), "All parents need the gratification of seeing the child as a 'chip off the old block,' but pathogenic parents are so hungry for that gratification that the child cannot be seen as anything more than a chip" (p. 165). These are the proverbial Little League Parents enacting their own agenda and constraining the lives of their children. Other children can be "misidentified" or "delegated" to play the roles of dead or absent family members, or to play out other selfobject roles, like providing excessive admiration or companionship.

Other parents find their children abhorrent simply because they resemble significant people from their past. One father cut off his son—failing to respond to the son's appeals for closeness, including that his father attend his wedding—in large part because the son reminded him of his first wife, his son's mother, who had committed suicide.

Children witnessing parental problems

Distinct from parents misusing their children, we should be concerned about children living in homes where parents are in conflict with each other for any reason, especially out in the open. These children will understandably be worried, if not overtly symptomatic, about their parents, who are the foundations of their lives. Many studies show a *bidirectional* "spillover" or contagion of problems transferring from marital strife to children and then back from children to parents (Fosco et al., 2014; Sears et al., 2016).[4]

Ideally, as therapy fosters improvement in couples, therapists can encourage parents to discuss this situation openly with their children, including normalizing some episodes of parental conflict, apologizing for the suffering they have caused, and helping their children to distinguish normal disagreements from destructive ones.

Children with problems

> The child teaches the adult something else about love: that genuine love should involve a constant attempt to interpret with maximal generosity what might be going on, at any time, beneath the surface of difficult and unappealing behavior. The parent has to second-guess what the cry, the kick, the grief, or the anger is really about.
>
> —Alain de Botton (2016, p. 112)

Just as troubled marriages can cause troubled children, troubled children can cause troubled marriages. While the previous section focused on the negative impact of parental problems on children, this section discusses how to help parents with problems that emanate more from their children. In optimal circumstances, parents will find that working together to help their children can bring them closer and make their relationship stronger (Morrill et al., 2010).[5]

Couples may bring up diverse problems they are having with their children—physical, mental, or social—but it is usually *not* necessary that we see the child; we can help the parents work on this issue as we would any other. Sometimes, however, seeing the child with the parents will greatly aid diagnosis and foster family harmony and may become the start of a productive family therapy. If you do this, don't forget to include the "well siblings," who can often provide useful information and who may turn out to be quietly suffering themselves.[6]

Many parents have never witnessed good-enough parenting, and some are unaware of what to expect and how to facilitate their children's development. Many are controlling, overly anxious, or expect too much or too little at different developmental stages. Couple therapists can educate parents about child development and provide emotional support for the hard work that parenting requires. Challenging topics will include children's sleep routines, eating and other health issues, developing a conscience and learning to follow rules (from "the terrible twos" on past adolescence), peer relationships, use/misuse of "devices" and social media, school performance, and extracurricular activities. Alcohol, driving, and sex pose realistic dangers during adolescence and often frighten both therapists and parents. As topics come up, therapists will do well to acquaint themselves with current best practices for facing particular problems.[7]

Self-help books

Relevant self-help books can provide information and normalize the stress parents feel with their children. For general issues with young children, I like Anthony Wolf's *The Secret of Parenting* (2000), and for adolescents, his better-known *Get Out of My Life, but First Could You Drive Me and Cheryl to the Mall: A Parent's Guide to the New Teenager* (2002). Two other helpful general parenting books are Siegel and Hartzell's *Parenting from the Inside Out: How a Deeper Self-Understanding Can Help You Raise Children Who Thrive* (2003), and Barish's *Pride & Joy: A Guide to Understanding Your Child's Emotions and Solving Family Problems* (2012). But my current favorite general, go-to self-help book is Lafrance and Miller's *What to Say to Kids When Nothing Seems to Work: A Practical Guide for Parents and Caregivers* (2020).

For children with special needs, I recommend Andrew Solomon's wonderful *Far from the Tree: Parents, Children, and the Search for Identity* (2012). Solomon documents the frequency of divorces when children, per the book's title, differ from their parents but also relates stories of parents who credit their parenting challenges with making them better people. For children who are exceptionally angry, oppositional-defiant, or explosive, a great resource is Greene and Ablon's *Treating Explosive Kids: The Collaborative Problem-Solving Approach* (2006), about which I will say more shortly.

Some parents will have emotional blocks to knowing and relating to their children—blocks that may make them excessively controlling, critical, or distant. We need to help them become able to "happily hold their child in mind," as Martha Edwards (2013) of The Ackerman Institute has termed this capacity. Edwards recommends a specific intervention to help parents get on track. When a parent complains that a child is "too selfish," Edwards asks, "What would you like to see, instead?" to which a parent might respond, "Sharing." Having shifted the discussion from a presumed moral failing to a desired behavior, the therapist can then say, "OK, let's discuss how we can get there." By doing this, we block parents from explaining their children's misbehavior as due to nefarious motivations, something that has been shown to lead to further deterioration (Patterson, 2005).

When we succeed in helping parents with any specific parenting problem, a beneficial circular process will ensue: As parents gain confidence, their kids will do better, which will reinforce the parents' feelings of pride, competence, and pleasure in being parents, which will further improve their "parental alliance" and success with their children, et cetera.

Limits and *understanding: the problem of polarization*

Good parenting inescapably requires that parents be an educating, civilizing, limit-setting force in their children's lives. As Alain de Botton (2016) notes:

> The role of being a good parent brings with it one large and very tricky requirement: to be the constant bearer of deeply unfortunate news . . . . Out of love, parents must gird themselves to speak of clean teeth, home-work, tidy rooms, bedtimes, generosity, and limits to computer usage. Out of love, they must adopt the guise of bores with a hateful and mad-dening habit of bringing up unwelcome facts about existence just when the fun is really starting. And, as a result of these subterranean loving acts, good parents must, if things have gone well, end up as the special targets of intense resentment and indignation.
>
> (pp. 125–126)

Possibly because of this onerous parental role requirement, the most common arguments I encounter as a couple therapist concern the need for more discipline and rules versus the need for more understanding and unconditional love. Of course, children need both, but in specific instances, it is not always clear just how much of each is appropriate. While parents can apply limits with understanding, enforcing family rules is never fun and, like other unpleasant duties, is sometimes neglected. In some families, both parents fail to set limits, and their kids run amok.

Other couples become polarized, as we see them do in other areas, as one plays the role of bad cop (disciplinarian), and the other is not so much the good cop as the consoling friend to the misbehaving or underachieving child. Separate from the problems being debated, such parental polarizations will negatively impact family structure. Children will gravitate to the more lenient parent, causing resentment in the tougher parent, who will find it harder to be close to the child. Parents may drift apart and become distressed when they witness their partners undercutting their interactions with the child. And both parents will fear acceding to the other: The disciplinarian will worry about more bad behavior, while the parent asserting the need for understanding will fear that going over to the other side will leave the child defenseless against a wall of negativity. As with other polarizations, therapists can help each side be heard as they work toward effective compromises. Here is a sampling of the suggestions Lafrance and Miller (2020) offer for how parents might talk respectfully to each other about their differences:

To the "tougher" parent:

"I can understand why you'd object—it might seem like she's got me wrapped around her little finger and that would be a problem."

"It must be frustrating when it looks like I'm choosing to do more for her and sacrificing some of the precious little time we have together."

To the "softer" parent:

"I get it why you'd think I'm too hard on him. He's a little guy, and you don't want him to get overwhelmed, shut down, or act out even more."

"Sounds like you're worried he's going to take it personally and feel worse about himself."

(pp. 194–208)

Because parents will usually have enduring preferences for "limits versus love," helping them talk about one problem area in this way will ideally generalize to other conflicts. At the same time, when helping couples reduce their polarized logjams, therapists should keep in mind that usually the best cure for any parental polarization is better management of the child's problem. In the typical good cop/bad cop polarization, what is left out is not just that there is "truth on both sides," but that when a child isn't doing what would be best, there is a reason, not just that the child is lazy, getting away with something, or playing the parents. Most kids would prefer to do better but are somehow stuck. So, after reducing polarization, specific problem-solving sessions will help, as will sometimes letting one parent take the lead for a specified length of time and then revisiting the parenting plan.

In the following sections, I describe some basic guidelines for reducing behavioral/emotional problems in children.

Some behavioral basics

Parenting education programs have been found to be quite helpful when grounded in basic behavioral, social learning principles (Forgatch & Kjøbli, 2016; Lebow, 2014, pp. 81–82). As summarized by Cowan and Cowan (2015):

> There is reasonable agreement in the research literature on children's development that authoritative parenting—a combination of parental warmth, structure, limit stetting, and appropriate demands for maturity—provides a context in which children are more likely to develop effective cognitive skills, better relationships with peers, and fewer behavioral problems. Other parenting styles are less effective. Authoritarian parenting is harsh and structured. Permissive parenting is warm but laissez-faire, with few if any limits. Neglectful or uninvolved parenting is neither warm nor structured and demanding.
>
> (pp. 364–365)

Therapists and clients alike will benefit from learning about evidence-based programs for bringing about positive behavior change, such as the

Parent Management Training model, developed in Oregon (Patterson, 1982) and referred to as PMTO (Forgatch, 1994; Forgatch & Kjøbli, 2016) or, more recently, as The Triple P—Positive Parenting Program (Sanders & Turner, 2019). Supported by 40 years of research, this program teaches parents the key components of success:

- Encourage positive behavior.
- Institute systematic, mild consequences for negative behavior, and set limits.
- Monitor the child
- Problem solve with the child.
- Be involved in positive activities with the child.

More recent refinements add setting realistic expectations for children, taking care of oneself as a parent, and providing partner support.

To demonstrate the importance of encouragement coupled with direction, Wenning (1996) asks parents to recall their "best boss" (an analogous parental role) and tells them, "He or she probably was a person who had a good sense of humor, paid attention to your work, was supportive, helpful, and attentive" (p. 54).

Here's a selection of additional practical suggestions for parents based on social learning and behavioral thinking:

- When giving a directive, you must mean it, and speak as you would to a friend: "Please hand me that frying pan," not "I don't suppose you'll lift a finger to help." Do not make your request contingent, "If you don't do this, I'll . . ."; instead, rely most often on your child's natural desire to please you by being helpful.
- When giving a directive, focus on what you want the child to do, not on what you want them to stop doing, what Kazdin (2008) calls "the positive opposite."
- Praise effort.
- When a child is difficult or noncompliant, do not get stuck thinking, "My God, at this age, he should be able to handle not getting his way!" If you do, you will vacillate between blaming the child and blaming yourself for this apparent learning deficit. Instead, stay "in the now" and work on a plan to improve the situation.
- When you have frustrated your child's wishes, help him or her manage this by:
  o Registering the child's desire and not pathologizing it: "I know it would have been fun to stay longer."
  o Agreeing that delay may still lead to a desired outcome: "It's hard when you're really excited and have to wait until after dinner to play catch."
  o Suggesting how the child might channel current energies in some other way: "You can't throw that ball in the house, but why don't you try throwing it up against that wall out back?"

o   Admitting your own contribution: "Daddy is working on this project right now. Can we read that story after I get done, in about 15 minutes?"

- When giving a penalty (a better word than *punishment*), don't go on and on explaining yourself too much.
- Have your children earn some privileges that they can lose by not following family rules.
- Create positive rituals, including at bedtime. Review the good things the child did during the day and praise good behavior. Tell relevant personal stories. Know that "The effectiveness of our time-outs depends largely on the quality of our time-ins" (Kazdin, quoted by Barish, 2012, p. 122).
- Persist in your parenting plans; they will often take time to work.

Individualized, deficit-focused, and emotion-focused approaches

While behavioral approaches are both popular and frequently effective, they have their limitations and have recently been strongly critiqued and amended by approaches that focus on understanding the individualized reasons why children have trouble complying with parental requests (Barish, 2012; Gottman et al., 1996; Greene & Ablon, 2006; Lafrance & Miller, 2020; Siegel & Bryson, 2015; Siegel & Hartzell, 2003).[8] Most behavioral approaches assume that children misbehave because of reward contingencies ("getting away with it" or "getting attention"). The clinician-researchers just cited, however, suggest that children continue to misbehave, despite punishment and rewards, for more complex reasons, most notably as they become caught up in the emotional moment due to frustration, anxiety, shame, or anger. The problem then becomes how to help children do better when they are losing it.

We want our children to grow up able to handle life's frustrations without becoming either too distraught ("I just don't know what to do!") or insisting that the world give them what they want ("You have to change your mind or I'm going to quit this job!"). Left to their own devices after parents apply time-outs or punishments, however, many children fail to learn to cope. While some parents object that a focus on children's feelings will make them more entitled as adults, the opposite is far more likely. As Greene and Ablon (2006) put it:

> Reward-and-punishment programs don't effectively treat other learning disabilities—reading, writing, and arithmetic—and they don't effectively treat a learning disability in the domains of flexibility/adaptability, frustration tolerance, and problem solving either. In other words, reward-and-punishment programs do not train a child to shift cognitive set more readily, reflect upon how a problem has been solved previously, consider the likely outcomes of alternative solutions, enter a group competently, recognize that someone is sad, let other people know how

he is feeling, or stay calm enough to think clearly. To reiterate, focusing on cognition helps adults move beyond popular motivational "explanations" for children's maladaptive behavior: "She's doing it for attention," "She's not motivated to do well," "She just wants control," "She just wants things her own way."

(p. 36)

As we proceed to discuss the details of how to help children regulate their emotions and manage frustration better, we should note that research has found that the experiences children have with their parents in moments of distress largely shape how they regulate emotions later in life (Sroufe, 2000), that deficiencies in these capacities are found in aggressive children and others with "externalizing" behaviors (Lockman et al., 2019), and that competence in naming and managing emotions correlates strongly with later success in intimate relationships (e.g., Gottman et al., 1996).

All the just-mentioned authors provide guidance to help parents assess and then overcome specific deficits. They also make suggestions to help parents manage their own emotions when working with their children (recall Brazelton's "Don't have a tantrum back!"). For many parents, the challenge is to register the pain their child is feeling; for others, it can be facing their own guilt, shame, or powerlessness. Parents will need our help to access and contain these feelings without resorting to defenses that make things worse: blindness to their child's feelings, proscribing their protests ("You can't talk to me like that!"), or perceiving their child as "too needy" or "inconsolable."

The Three Plan approach

Greene and Ablon's (2006) "Collaborative Problem-Solving Approach," with its "three plans" provides an overarching context for ameliorating deficits that create parent–child problems:

> The first option, known as "Plan A," involves the imposition of adult will . . . in other words, adults insisting that their expectations be met. This is, of course, an extremely popular option. The second option, known as "Plan B," involves engaging the child in a collaborative process of problem solving so as to resolve whatever concerns or factors are interfering with expectations being met (this option is far less popular). The third option, "Plan C," involves reducing or removing expectations, at least temporarily (this is a fairly popular option as well).
>
> (p. 42)

The problem with Plan A, even when parental expectations seem realistic, is that it greatly heightens the likelihood of explosive, oppositional outbursts. Adults often respond to these with intensification of incentives and threats of punishment, making things still worse. Most American adults tend to assume that such reactions are simply the child's method for "getting his way," and, consequently, they resist giving in to such coercion. Plan B is generally not on their radar screens, and Plan C seems like capitulation (although it can be a sensible short-term option). The goal of addressing deficient problem-solving and emotion-regulation skills is met only by Plan B, since Plan A, at best, achieves only compliance with adult expectations, and at worst, makes parent–child collaboration less likely.

Greene and Ablon note that, while many parents rely on Plan A because they think it will be faster, the reality is that Plan B saves time since

> time spent problem solving together is generally far less than what is required in dealing with a child who has spiraled out of control and become violent or destructive . . . And unsolved problems are, of course, far more time-consuming than solved problems.
>
> (p. 47)

In many families, one parent emphasizes Plan A and the other Plan C—in the bad cop/good cop, limits-versus-unconditional love polarization discussed earlier, where I asserted that both parents have a point. In another sense, however, both are wrong or unnecessarily incomplete, since neither limits nor empathy, alone or in combination, may be sufficient. Plan B will help *both* parents as they meet to discuss how to help their child develop the requisite skills to do better.

When I introduce Plan B to parents, I tell them that they will function as "surrogate frontal lobes" for their child. This helps orient parents who already know that their children need them to teach them how to read, ride a bike, or look both ways when crossing the street. Plan B fits the advice of other contemporary child specialists (including the Triple P System) by encouraging parents to remain calm, provide empathy and interest in the child's concerns and perspective, define the problem clearly, and then brainstorm possible solutions with the child as collaborator.

Notice how similar this is to my recommendations for "difficult conversations" between adults, including to remain calm, consider the needs of *both* people, and brainstorm possible solutions (Nielsen, 2016). One difference, of course, is that parent–child discussions take place in a power hierarchy that needs to be maintained. This creates some problems. Perhaps surprisingly, one big one is the need to reassure children that they haven't lost the fight at the beginning: "I'm not saying that you can't do X, or that you can, I'm saying that we need to discuss this, get our concerns on the table, and problem solve." When handled sensitively, these collaborative conversations will reassure children that their input will not be rejected out of hand and can even influence solutions.

In some cases, adult expectations are unrealistic and should be labeled as age-inappropriate or otherwise excessive. Greene and Ablon (2006) note further that "adults are notorious for failing to acknowledge children's legitimate concerns and, even when such concerns are briefly acknowledged, minimizing their importance and supplanting them with adult concerns" (pp. 52–53). They observe that all acceptable solutions appear to fall into three categories: asking for help, compromising or meeting in the middle, and trying something new and different.

Parents will do well to begin Plan B discussions with "I've noticed that" as in "I've noticed that homework has been a bit of a struggle lately, and I know that's no fun for you. What's up?" They will then have to dig deeper to discover the child's specific problem ("I don't understand the assignments," "I'm too tired," or "It's too noisy.") since coming up with a workable cure depends on making a proper diagnosis. Recall that this is just what we therapists do with clients who balk at doing things that seem reasonable to us or to them, or when clients seem excessively upset about some event in their lives. Lafrance and Miller (2020) infuse their empathic statements with affirmations that convey parents' appreciation for the child's basic goodness. ("I know you're frustrated because you take your work seriously and worked hard on that project, but it didn't turn out as well as you had hoped.")

Notice that Plan B is quite different from Anthony Wolf's (2000) recommendation cautioning against extensive discussions with the child, which he sees as simply stalling and putting off the child's painful experience of not getting what he or she wants. He does have a point, but note that the Plan B option, especially if done proactively, can better address some extremely challenging situations, including ones where parents have little objective power but want to communicate their concerns (e.g., with teens about unprotected sex).

Additional suggestions for working with parent–child problems

- Begin with a nonreductionistic, biopsychosocial approach to problem maintenance.
- Look for biological contributions (attention deficit disorder, depression, constitutional shyness, specific learning disorders), but don't assume that medications or educational tutoring will be the whole answer.
- Consider that parents may have similar problems to those they complain about in their children, like difficulty in emotion regulation.
- As with all interpersonal problems, problem assessment should begin with learning how the children and parents *experience* the problem, rather than with simple behavioral descriptions.
- While dysfunctional family structure frequently makes problems worse, do not assume, a priori, that it is the upstream cause.
- Vicious cycles occur between parents and kids, just as they do between parents. Helpful rules for respectful "difficult conversations" are remarkably similar in both situations.
- Help parents quiet their own unruly emotions (their "shark music") so that they can "chase the why" of their children's problems (terms from Siegel & Bryson, 2015).
- Teach parents that, just as you want to be there when your children do well, you want to be there when they are having trouble. Parenting to develop secure attachment doesn't stop with holding and rocking a

crying baby. Ideally, parents need to see their children's emotional distress as an opportunity to connect with them.

- To start conversations with children who don't want to talk to parents or therapists, break the ice by asking them *what is unfair* about their lives (Barish, 2012).
- Encourage repair conversations and "do-over" attempts to work things out (Lafrance & Miller, 2020). Children need to learn that bad feelings can be addressed and that people, including parents, can apologize. An example from Siegel and Hartzell (2003): "I'm so sorry. Sometimes grown-ups lose their tempers and I know when I do that, it can frighten you. I was afraid that you would fall out of that tree and hurt yourself, so I didn't really see that you were being careful or really think how you wanted to show me how much fun you had been having up there."
- A selection from Siegel and Bryson's "Discipline Mistakes that Even Great Parents Make" (2015, pp. 238–240):

  o We talk too much and forget to focus on *how* we say what we say.
  o Our discipline becomes consequence-based instead of teaching-based.
  o We assume the worst before letting our kids explain.
  o We expect too much.

Helping parents slow down, regulate their emotions, and understand their children

To succeed via Plan B and the other recommendations just mentioned, parents must resist offering knee-jerk, blanket responses, such as those described by Lafrance and Miller (2020): reassuring ("Everything will turn out OK."), cheerleading ("Don't worry, you're actually good at math."), downplaying ("It's no big deal."), or should-ing ("There's no reason to feel like that."). These may be well-meaning, but they are too often ineffective, as they foreclose examination of the problem.

Sometimes, the problem is that parents have their own agenda (getting the kids in the car for a trip) that conflicts with taking advantage of a "teachable moment" and can lead them to say things like, "You're going because I said so!" So, sometimes Plan B will have to wait. Other times, parents will be overcome by distress ("parental countertransference") and can use our permission to take "parental timeouts," or to use mindfulness meditation or other methods to calm themselves before trying to tackle the parenting problem. As noted child psychoanalyst Anna Ornstein (2015) remarked:

Parenting . . . is a much more difficult task than is ordinarily acknowledged, especially for caretakers who are responsible for children who have become demanding, negativistic, or otherwise symptomatic. Because the child's behavior is interpreted in terms of its meaning to the caretaker and not in terms of its meaning to the child, caretaker empathy in relation to a symptomatic child is likely to erode over time. By the time the child becomes demanding and destructive to self and others because its motives have been originally misinterpreted and/ or ignored, an interaction has been set into motion where the symptomatic behavior makes it increasingly more difficult to ascertain the child's original motives . . . . In treating children, caretakers are asked to recognize the symptomatic behavior for what it is: an expression of psychic pain behind the noisy and provocative behavior.

(p. 132)

Ornstein goes on to note that this is where therapists come in: by first providing clients with an experience of empathy for the parenting challenges they face and then helping them comprehend their child's needs, much as we couple therapists often translate or explain one partner's needs to the other. What Ornstein adds here is the qualification that, while we can teach and advocate for Triple P and Plan B approaches, parents will often need us to be part of the mix.

Teens and older children

Adolescents

This chapter would not be complete without some comments about the specific challenges of raising adolescents. Everything I've already said about balancing limits and love, about Plan B, about showing interest and empathy, and about vicarious living through children still applies, although teenagers do seem to be a species all their own, presenting parents and therapists with unique conundrums.

Prior to adolescence, parents have been narrating the story and controlling the action by both their words and their superior physical strength. As teens, children wage intensified battles with parents to become the authors of their lives. Such battles can render them foreign, devaluing, and rebellious to their parents, as captured in the following vignette by Cusk (2015):

> Lately I've become aware of a dissonance, a dislocation, as though a familiar text had suddenly become illegible to me. What she [my daughter] needs is different from what I think she needs . . . . Sometimes—when I'm brushing my teeth or chopping vegetables, when I'm not thinking about her at all—she'll come and stand next to me and say, "Give me attention." At other times, like now, I feel I'm forcing myself on her, like an insistent hostess forcing food on her guests. . . . [A friend has brought her teenage son to the author's home for a visit, and she continues.] Once we carried these children in our arms; at other times we pushed them in strollers or led them by the hand. Now he follows his mother in like a pet

lion on a leash, a proud, taciturn beast who has consented, temporarily, to be tamed. My daughter has the same aura of the wild about her, as though beneath a veneer of sophistication she is constantly hearing the summons of her native land, somewhere formless and free that still lies inside her head and to which at any moment she might return.

(pp. 40–42)

Anthony Wolf's book title, *Get Out of My Life, but First Could You Drive Me and Cheryl to the Mall*, similarly captures the teenager's pursuit of autonomy, coupled with their hostile denial of continuing dependency. Indeed, studies show that conflicts with parents normatively increase during adolescence, with the underlying dispute most often between adolescents' desire for autonomy and parents' desire for socialization and safe life choices (Campione-Barr & Smetana, 2019).

Sex, drugs, and driving (rock and roll is really no threat) enter the scene in adolescence, intensifying parental anxieties because of their inherent peril and because parents are generally not present when danger threatens. At the same time, the gravitational pull of the peer group increases and competes with parental authority and moral values. Some good news is that, although teens may complain fiercely about parental rules, they may also be relieved to be able to use them to combat peer pressure to do things that are unwise or unsafe ("My parents are really strict about curfew. Gotta go." *Whew.*).

Much research confirms that authoritative parenting, which combines responsiveness to adolescent needs with high expectations for maturity, achieves the best outcomes (Sorkhabi & Mandara, 2013). Parents may have less power, but they can still set limits, monitor whereabouts, and enforce some consequences ("I can't control when you come home, but there will be a price to pay if you come home after 11 PM."), and they should continue to make recommendations about healthy and ethical behavior ("I can't stop you from doing what you're planning and in the end, it's your choice, but I think it will be hurtful and I think it's wrong."). Above all, parents will have to depend more on what has been their main source of power all along: their children's desire to please them. In this regard, when children talk back, parents should try to help them distinguish between "disrespectful talk" and "honest expression." That said, a certain amount of devaluing of parents as a way to individuate should be expected and accepted. Parents will benefit from recalling their own adolescent misadventures and disputes with their parents, even as they have been long repressed by their more sensible adult minds.

Older children, parents, and in-laws

Couples will sometimes bring up problems with their young ("emerging") adult children, some of whom may return ("boomerang") home for a time; with their married children and their families; or with their own parents. Again, there is much to say and too little space to do more than cover some basics.

In my experience, the most common issues powering problems between adults and their older offspring concern boundaries ("Why can't we spend more time together?" or "Don't tell me how to raise my children!"); competing allegiances ("You spend more time with your mother than you do with me and our kids!"); and doubts about love, support, and respect, often related to prior traumatic events ("I'll never forgive you for how you treated me when I was in college!").

Conflicts concerning how to relate to in-laws are common. Typically, the conflict is over the wish of one partner to be close to his or her family of origin and to have the spouse participate, or tension may erupt over a spouse's experience of not being welcomed by in-laws (Leone, 2008, p. 81). While an appropriate boundary around the couple is important, healthy boundaries also need to be permeable enough that outside relationships can continue. Family obligations, such as caring for ailing parents or disabled siblings, can also be a source of strain and conflict, just as, by contrast, parents and siblings can be important supports for the couple. Many permutations are possible, and therapists will be wise to get the lay of the land, even when these issues are not the primary subjects of debate between partners.

As in other areas of potential couple conflict, partners may attempt to finesse or hide their true preferences, as in these examples from Hibbs (2010):

> "Oh, didn't I tell you that my son and daughter planned to throw me a sixtieth-birthday party? I thought that would save you the trouble." (Hidden claim: I don't want to have to choose between you and my kids. Let's not get into that again.)
>
> "I got a real deal on the flight to spend the holidays with my folks! Isn't that great?" (Hidden claim: I want to spend the holidays with my family, and I was afraid you wouldn't, so I made the plans without checking with you first.)
>
> (p. 195)

Coping with new babies and aging parents can reactivate old wounds and unfinished business, or sometimes foster healthier partnerships. Children and parents will frequently have to give up idealized wishes about one another as they come to see each other, warts and all, as flawed humans shaped by past circumstances and opportunities. Children will be helped to accomplish this by imagining their parents as the children of their grandparents. In this way, we can help adult children to "wake from the spell of childhood" and reject a narrative in which they view themselves too much as helpless victims trying to "seek damages at the wrong address" (Fishbane, 2005, p. 548) by repeating painful interactions they had with their parents with their own children.

Family meetings with the therapist may be surprisingly helpful in offering a forum where adversaries can air their painful feelings and try to accept and forgive each other, so as to move into a better future (Fishbane, 2005, 2009, 2010; Framo, 1976; Wachtel & Wachtel, 1986). In this regard, Walsh (2016) makes the important point that relational healing across generations has often (mistakenly) been discouraged by therapists and friends as impossible since parents have been identified as the source of a client's problems. Following her mentor, Murray Bowen, she believes that therapists will do best if they have tried this themselves and succeeded, and, in her just-cited article, she offers a moving example of her efforts to reconnect with her father.

Mona Fishbane, who has written extensively on this subject, calls such family meetings with the therapist "Loving Updates." She makes the following recommendations for conducting them:

- To avoid a "blame-fest," prepare the adult child first, by helping them develop realistic expectations, including by preparing them to be somewhat disappointed with how their parents may respond.
- Clarify boundary issues, possibly using Fishbane's "Fence Exercise," as in this example with her client, Barbara, who felt overly responsible, reactive, and disappointed with her mother:

> The therapist suggests to Barbara that she imagine her mother as her neighbor, with a clear fence between their yards. The fence is symbolic—perhaps a picket fence—rather than a brick barricade. If her neighbor is planting flowers that Barbara thinks are inappropriate, for example, sun-loving flowers in a shady spot, Barbara might or might not choose to offer her advice to the neighbor. If the neighbor rejects the advice and has a poor outcome with her flowers, Barbara can still enjoy her own yard; she doesn't have to ruin her own summer in aggravation over her neighbor's flower bed. The therapist adds that if her neighbor is planting poison ivy that will creep into Barbara's yard, Barbara does need to protect herself and her property.
>
> (Fishbane, 2005, p. 552)

- Have children invite their parents to attend the meeting by expressing their love and wishes for help; and their desires to be better understood, to get to know their parents better, and to do better in the future.
- Have both the child and parents consider that what children experience as excessive control and criticism often flows from parental anxiety about how their child will turn out, sometimes driven by traumatic experiences in the parents' lives. Parental criticism can also be reframed as a response to the adult child keeping the parent at arm's length (often to reduce such criticism), with parent and child now caught in a vicious circle.

My own experience with such meetings between adult children and their parents, sometimes initiated by the children and sometimes by the parents, has almost always proven beneficial. One major danger is that people will assume that the therapist is biased and has been captured by the narrative of the client they have been seeing. I try to be clear that I am interested in helping everyone, and I begin family sessions asking each person to share what they are hoping to accomplish. As sessions draw to a close, I again poll the group, now asking them what they found helpful and what remains problematic. We can then decide whether and in what ways to continue meeting.

In one memorable case, I had been meeting with an elderly couple who were at odds with each other and with their adult children. In the family sessions that followed some groundwork with the couple, I learned that the wife and children all agreed that the father was "impossible" and that all had given up on him. (He had recently been prohibited from flying on an airplane after he got into a yelling match with a flight attendant.) What then emerged was that this patriarch's narcissistic entitlement was mostly a maladaptive reaction to feeling shut out by his family, who kept themselves defensively aloof (which the flight attendant had been unable to do!). As we worked on this vicious cycle, all members of the group benefited: Marital harmony returned, the wife's depression lessened, family get-togethers became rewarding again, and the work relationship between father and son was vastly improved. As with couple therapy generally, an important resistance to convening such meetings lies in therapists who dread sessions with multiple participants. But therapists willing to take a risk will often be rewarded with surprising benefits.

Notes

1. A recent study (Glass et al., 2016) comparing the United States and other countries concluded that, "The negative effects of parenthood on happiness were entirely explained by the presence or absence of social policies allowing parents to better combine paid work with family obligations" (p. 886).
2. The jury is still out on the value of couple relationship/parenting education during the transition to parenthood. Some studies have found minimal improvement (Trillingsgaard et al., 2014), while others have found benefits (e.g., Gambrell & Piercy, 2015). Many studies have found improvement in husband involvement, which correlated with improved parenting and marital satisfaction, including wives experiencing their husbands as being more "on the team."
3. Now almost forgotten, Adelaide Johnson (1949) called attention to a group of parents with "superego lacunae" (holes in their consciences), who induced and identified with their children's misbehavior while simultaneously complaining about it. Years ago, I saw one such mother in the Yale New Haven Psychiatric Emergency Room. This straitlaced, upper-middle-class woman was there with her 14-year-old daughter who was suicidal after becoming pregnant. While proclaiming her disapproval of her daughter's premature sexual behavior, the mother eagerly read to me from a pornographic romance novel she had found in her daughter's room and exclaimed, "I just can't seem to do anything about such things: This is my third daughter who's gotten pregnant before she turned 18!"
4. Studies by Fosco et al. (2010, 2014) show all possible problematic combinations of interaction between parents and their adolescent children: children misused to triangulate or detour parental conflict; children who become aggressive or symptomatic to interrupt parental conflict; and situations where parental fighting and hostility simply "spilled over," as parents vented on their children, and children, in turn, reacted aggressively or symptomatically. Most generally, the more children witnessed

parental arguments, the more they became aggressive, first within the family, and then outside it.

5. Morrill and colleagues (2010) found that cooperation and mutual support in *parenting* correlated with *marital* happiness, and Solomon (2012) demonstrated benefits when parents stick it out and work together on a wide variety of children's problems. Similarly, Zeytinoglu et al. (2017) reported that 15 of 17 couples raising a child with cleft lip and/or palate said this brought them closer and made their relationship stronger. Open communication was considered essential, while support and assistance from doctors, friends, family, church, support groups, and websites were also identified as helpful.

6. For a wonderful example that addresses the "family therapy anxiety" of therapists not used to conducting sessions with children, see Leone (2019).

7. In researching this chapter, I read Benjamin Spock's (1954) classic, *Dr. Spock Talks with Mothers*. I was struck by his reassuring tone and generally sensible recommendations, which suggested, far more than I feel today, that easy answers were readily available to parents. Spock's answers were based on a far simpler developmental schema, including one that assumed traditional gender roles for parents and children, did not have much to say about childhood mental disorders (e.g., ADHD, constitutional shyness, childhood depression, eating disorders, self-cutting), peer and academic problems, or problems during "emerging adulthood." It now reads as "a good start," that reveals the greater challenges we now face, some of them paradoxically due to our far greater sophistication concerning children's needs and problems.

8. The importance of teaching children to regulate their emotions has become mainstream in formal parenting education programs and was listed as the first of seven content areas taught in "quality programs" in a recent review (Morris et al., 2020).

9 Money

Money seems simple to us because in a certain sense it is thoroughly one dimensional, possessing quantity but none of the qualities that so complicate and enrich our lives. When it comes to money, there is only *more* or *less* . . . And yet, almost nothing is more symbolic in its very nature.

—Paul Wachtel (2014, p. 171)

Money is probably the most emotionally meaningful object in contemporary life; only food and sex are its close competitors as common carriers of such strong and diverse feelings, significances, and strivings.

—David Krueger (1986, p. 3)

Financial issues are the number one argument starter and area of conflict in first marriages[1] and loom large in many unhappy marriages (Stanley et al., 2002; Papp et al., 2009; Parker-Pope, 2010). The American Psychological Association's annual "Stress in America" studies repeatedly find "financial concerns" leading the list of potential "personal stressors" (American Psychological Association, "Stress in America," 2019 and 2020). This is understandable, given that studies conducted *between* the Great Recession and the coronavirus pandemic (cited in Dew et al., 2020) found that 49% of participants said it was "somewhat difficult" or "very difficult" to keep up with their monthly bills, 51% indicated that they had no money set aside to handle unexpected expenses, and only 33% had $5,000 or more saved for retirement.

Many studies have found strong correlations between economic resources and marital conflict and satisfaction (e.g., Hardy & Lucas, 2010), that "financial strain" increases couple conflict and the risk of divorce (Sobolewski & Amato, 2005), and that marital happiness is lower when partners feel their spouses "handle money poorly" (Dew, 2015). Children also suffer, as parental job loss has been linked to poor school performance, increased mental illness, negative family interactions, and increased "harsh parenting behavior" (Gassman-Pines & Schenck-Fontaine, 2019).

Respondents in Olson and Olson's national study (2000) showed a large difference between happy and unhappy couples on the assertion, "We agree

DOI: 10.4324/b22905-13

on how to spend money" (89% vs. 41%), and the total sample scored high on, "We have trouble saving money" (72%), "I wish my partner was more careful in spending money" (72%), "We have problems deciding what is more important to purchase" (66%), and "Major debts are a problem for us" (56%). Debt prior to marriage—a sort of reverse dowry—is now the leading source of conflict for newlyweds (Parker-Pope, 2010).

Although many couples struggle with money, low-income couples have it worse (Gassman-Pines & Schenck-Fontaine, 2019). One national study of 6,012 people weighted toward low-income couples found that *low income per se*—rather than "less value placed on marriage" or "less marital skillfulness"—accounted for higher divorce rates in low-income families (Trail & Karney, 2012).[2] Another study of 431 low-income newlyweds followed for four years—couples who faced additional stresses from living in poor neighborhoods with high drug and crime rates, inferior schools, systemic racism, and so on—did *not* find that "lower income marriages were less satisfying," but did find that external stresses, many related to money, created greater *fluctuations* in marital satisfaction that might well explain higher divorce rates (Jackson et al., 2017). So, while "money isn't everything," *worrying* about having insufficient funds, together with the realities associated with less money, often destabilizes marriages, more often in low-income couples.

Like food, money is constantly on people's minds, because there is no day "for any adult when money is not used, thought of, spent, saved, or worried about . . . ; money is deemed a significant issue for so many couples partly because money 'events' are so frequent" (Stanley & Einhorn, 2007, p. 294). And, like disordered eating or extramarital affairs, the financial misbehavior of one partner—done privately or unilaterally—impacts the other and often seriously erodes trust.

Achieving financial health is a complex, multifaceted task that includes maintaining employment, budgeting, saving, estate planning, and insurance coverage—all of which, like remaining physically healthy, require planning, knowledge, and, often, help from professionals.

Facing and talking about money problems

As with maintaining physical health, many clients are lax in facing their financial problems and slow to seek professional help. And, like sexual issues, most people—therapists included—have had insufficient education about financial matters and feel uncomfortable talking about them. Couples may feel constrained when talking about money because, as suggested by Atwood (2012),

> American society stipulates that people should marry for love and not money so that any discussions about money are defined as tainting the pure love union. Simply bringing up money could bring an ugliness into the discussion that smacks of mistrust and lack of good feeling.
>
> (p. 11)

And therapists may feel constrained, as they can when asking about sexual details, because asking about specific dollar amounts can seem voyeuristic, when, in truth, the devil is often in the details.

Conflict

Independent of financial stress, couples who achieve *agreement* on key financial decisions and goals have been found to be more content in their marriages (Archuleta, 2013). As with other important areas where joint decisions are required, couples will face the *co-captains problem*, the structural challenge of decision-making in a two-person group. Debates here will focus on how much to spend or save, what to spend money on, and how much to merge financial resources. The problem will be to manage such disagreements amicably. Everything we therapists know about helping couples manage conflict and work toward adaptive solutions will help.

Hard choices

Reaching agreement is difficult because financial conflicts deal with hard realities that cannot be settled by agreeing to disagree and, sometimes, can only be settled by compromising. Trade-offs will often be required as partners must decide both what they can afford and what matters most to them. Important decisions must be made about location and type of housing, careers that generate more or less money or require travel, whether partners will work or stay at home with children or pay for daycare or nannies. Couples must decide how much they value expensive celebrations, vacation travel, summer camp for kids, private school education, saving and paying for college, providing funds to relatives in need, and (in more serious situations) needed health care, including, let's not forget, psychotherapy itself.

Values and compromise

Many apparent arguments about money are best viewed as arguments about values: how much to give to charity or relatives in need; whether to ask for money from relatives or choose independence instead; how much parents should pay for their grown children's expenses; whether private or public schooling is better preparation for "real life"; how to distribute money in estate plans, especially if not all children are shared; how much to spend on bar mitzvahs, weddings, and other life-cycle events.[3] Again, couples cannot simply agree to disagree, since important actions will be taken or not. Sometimes, compromises are possible; sometimes, they're not.

Many financial conflicts are hard fought because powerful cultural, religious, and other value differences come into play. Some illustrations from my practice have involved debates over whether to foot the bill for a 3,000-person Indian wedding, whether to send children to a religious summer camp, and whether to relocate the family to advance a teenager's athletic career.

When couples can't agree on priorities, marriages can be threatened. Two common deal breakers concern how much money to spend on step-children and whether to relocate for one partner's career. Some couples in the latter situation will agree that relocation decisions will rotate, as in, "Last time, we moved for your career. This time, I want to not move so I can stay close to my friends and parents." Other couples will find a way to compromise, with one or both partners commuting long distances for work. Many couple therapy sessions will involve helping couples arrive at decisions that are less than perfect, ones that one partner must "accept," with that acceptance made easier by appreciation from the partner who got what he or she wanted (Nielsen, 2016, Chapter 10).

Interpersonal significance

Because financial decisions have important consequences, they inevitably carry strong interpersonal meanings for the couple: who has the power to decide, whose needs are more important, who is behaving "responsibly" and can be trusted, who is "carrying their weight," and whose religious beliefs or future goals are more important.

Interpersonal process

While real-life consequences, value differences, and interpersonal implications make financial discussions momentous, the way couples talk to each other also matters. When coping with financial stress, couples who resort to the pathological dance of demand–withdraw (pursuer–distancer) do worse, whereas couples who express more gratitude do better (Barton et al., 2015). Other studies show that superior interpersonal problem solving can buffer the adverse impact of economic adversity even after controlling for education, income, and "conscientiousness" (Masarik et al., 2016), and that such skills targeted to specific financial situations can be taught, leading to improved couple satisfaction and financial well-being (Falconier, 2015). More recently, a study of relationship satisfaction, measured before the coronavirus pandemic and later during it, found that—independent of financial stress and income level—what mattered was *how couples managed conflict*, whether as a team or by blaming each other's character flaws (Williamson, 2020).

As we'll explore shortly, actions related to money can carry hidden idiosyncratic meanings, often stemming from early life experiences. As in other areas of couple conflict, these will have to be uncovered and discussed to clear away roadblocks to conflict resolution.

Too little conflict

A caveat at the close of this section on conflict: While many couples come to us needing help to resolve financial *conflicts*, others get into trouble when both partners fail to behave responsibly—like two people who drink too much. In such cases, we will have to help them face unpleasant realities and give up maladaptive behaviors such as spending too much or investing recklessly.

Debt, unemployment, and unequal incomes

Conflict and distress follow financial calamities: loss of jobs, stock market crashes, unexpected medical expenses. Some couples will break up over imprudent financial decisions or mismanagement (a dating couple over excessive student loan debt, a married couple over gambling debt), while others will remain together, unhappily, because funds are limited. Whatever the cause, insufficient money is a stressor that commonly leads to depression, irritability, reduced self-esteem, and a lessened ability to manage other concurrent stressors. Consequently, *sometimes conflict over spending is less about a need to reconcile a disagreement and more about the stress of simply not having enough money.*

Couples who carry more consumer debt have been found to argue more often, and not just about money (Dew, 2015). And couples with one unemployed or underemployed partner experience stress in many areas of their lives. A *New York Times*/CBS News survey of 708 recently unemployed US citizens—conducted on December 15, 2009, as the financial crisis of the Great Recession took hold—found that 75% of those with unemployment benefits thought it "very or somewhat likely" that their benefits would run out before they found a new job; 61% said unemployment benefits were not enough to cover costs of basic necessities; 53% had borrowed money from family or friends; 26% had been threatened with eviction or foreclosure or had lost their homes; 47% were without health insurance; 54% had cut back on doctor visits or medical treatments; 48% had experienced "emotional issues like anxiety or depression"; 48% "had more conflicts or arguments than usual with family and friends"; and 46% had felt embarrassed or ashamed about being out of work. All these numbers were higher for those who were unemployed longer. Unsurprisingly, when asked, "Has the job loss you experienced created a major crisis in your life, a minor crisis, or no crisis at all?" 46% said "major"; 40% said "minor"; and 13% said "no crisis." News reports after recent government shutdowns lasting only a single month have disturbingly revealed how dependent the average American is on steady work, and distress due to unemployment during the coronavirus pandemic has been far worse than during the Great Recession (Williamson, 2020; *Family Process*, Special Issue on COVID-19, September 2020). Economic downturns also adversely impact the mental health of continuously employed adults (Gassman-Pines & Schenck-Fontaine, 2019), probably due to a combination of job uncertainty and interaction with others who have lost their jobs.

As with other calamities (say, the serious illness of a child), money problems brought on by unemployment can bring partners together or drive a wedge between them. Frequently, the anxiety about unemployment will lurk in the background and manifest as displaced irritation about other issues. But the problem is never simply financial. Employment organizes and gives meaning to people's lives. The person with the career problem will find it hard to maintain self-respect, and the couple may argue over whether the unemployed person is pulling his or her weight. In a culture where a husband's full-time employment is strongly associated with a lower risk of divorce (Killewald, 2016), unemployment usually disturbs men more than women, as it violates the cultural norm that they should be breadwinners and make more money than their wives.[4]

In dual-earner couples where one works less than the other, or where one works at a job that is emotionally gratifying but low-paying, couples may argue about fairness. Partners who make the lion's share of the family income may feel more pressure and sometimes resentment, whereas partners who make less or are stay-at-home parents may feel guilty or resent what feels like a return to childhood dependency when they receive an "allowance." Impending or actual retirement by one or both partners may also evoke distress and conflict concerning equity, dependency, financial security, or life goals.

In all these situations, therapists can help couples discuss both practical and emotional issues and face the considerable anxiety created by unemployment or insufficient funds; otherwise, these concerns will be misplaced and incessantly acted out.

Couples who seemingly have plenty of money may also argue or worry about how much money is enough, perhaps if one has neurotic fears of poverty stemming from childhood experiences. Other couples will create anxiety by overspending "to keep up with the Joneses" or with their own lifestyle expectations. Some will deplete their funds by foolish investments, shopaholism, or gambling, which can begin as "home remedies" for unhappiness in life or marriage, but which then create financial distress.

Our money or my money?

Debates over whose money is whose or whether all assets are to be considered jointly owned are common and engage concerns about autonomy and about how fully and safely bonded the couple feel. Prenuptial agreements—which "require thinking explicitly about the relationship coming to an end even as the foundation is being laid" (Stanley & Einhorn, 2007, p. 296)—can raise fears that a partner is holding back on total commitment, although for some people, they provide the safety needed to marry. Some individuals who continue to keep tight control over "their money" will seem not fully married, and their partners may complain about this. When this occurs, it will help to uncover the hidden distrust that explains the partner's reservations and prevents "going all in." Like it or not, couples should know that the IRS and other creditors do not view their funds as separate. Additionally, fully merged and transparent finances are a powerful symbol of couple "we-ness," and their absence can, over time, erode feelings of trust and fairness. Research bears this out, as separate bank accounts appear to be a risk factor for divorce (Kurdek, 1993), whereas pooled accounts become more common (78%, up from 58%) once couples have children (Eikmeyer et al., 2019), presumably indicating growing commitment. Pooling of funds seems to both signify commitment and contribute to it.

While many partners find it expedient to maintain separate bank accounts and plan who will pay which bills from which account, the important issue is whether each has an equal say in how the money is spent.[5] Therapists can point out that, although couples may bring in different amounts of money each month, fairness usually dictates that each partner gets one vote and a veto when deciding how to spend it. Most couples allow autonomous deci sions for routine or inexpensive items but have threshold amounts above which purchases must be discussed.

A sensible recommendation is that all earnings be deposited initially into one joint bank account (Chambers, 2014), and that most bills should be paid out of this account. Separate accounts can then be created for saving (for retire- ment, children's education, major travel, etc.) and for individual discretion- ary spending. These sensible practices are recommended by many financial planners (Parker-Pope, 2010) and prevent the malignant marital process of one spouse having to ask the other for an "allowance." It also helps partners avoid conflict over discretionary spending ("I can't believe you just bought another . . . ?!"), including at times when the partners must cut down on overall expenses: One partner can still choose to save to spend on sports tickets, the other on clothing. Couples will still have to work out and fine- tune how much money goes to savings and discretionary spending accounts.

Whether to spend or save

Many couples debate how much to save and how much to spend. In such situations, "conflicts about money often involve one partner's need for the selfobject experience of safety and security provided by saving versus the other's need to feel affirmed, stimulated, soothed, or otherwise enhanced by buying or spending" (Leone, 2008, p. 81).

Parker-Pope (2010, p. 220) cites evidence that opposites attract on this dimension more than in other areas: A person who favors controlled spending may be powerfully attracted to a person who is less constrained, and vice versa. As with other "fatal attractions" (Felmlee, 1998), this will almost certainly lead to conflict later. Many couples "resolve" such conflicts by subterfuge. But when partners feel restrained about spending and then do so secretly, they risk diminishing trust when their partners discover this and feel betrayed. Some partners manifestly champion saving but secretly enjoy their partner's spending while complaining about it. Others blind themselves to their own spending while continuing to blame their partner for the leak in the couple's financial boat.[6] Helping the frugal to see that there is more to life than saving for a rainy day and shopaholics to see that happiness can be achieved without so many possessions can be an important goal of couple treatment.[7]

In all cases, therapists can help by making this saving-versus-spending polarity explicit, exploring its origins and meanings, and facilitating compromises that strengthen the couple's relationship.

Budgeting: income must exceed expenditures

Everything I have read on how to be financially healthy stresses the point made famous by Charles Dickens that success depends on spending less than you make.[8] I have devoted many sessions trying to help couples, at all financial levels, achieve this goal. Sometimes, the work is on the income side—for instance, helping unemployed clients overcome anxiety about networking to find new work. Other times, therapy focuses on jointly making a budget and cutting expenses.

Like people who avoid going to doctors for fear of what they might find out, many clients dread looking at what they spend because they fear they will have to cut back. Others think that doing a budget will be too onerous and require hours of obsessive labor. Therapists should not let such beliefs stop the process and should encourage couples to work out rough estimates of their expenditures. To get them to do this, I cite two relevant aphorisms, "The perfect is the enemy of the good," and "Failing to plan is planning to fail."

As in other areas of life where people put off planning, one benefit of having a plan is simply that it reduces the nagging awareness that you haven't made one! A plan also allows one to sustain effort toward a distant, future goal, as when planting and tending a garden. The goal might include remodeling the kitchen, a trip to Europe, or buying a home. More complicated goals include returning to school to get the education that will enable a career change. Focusing on, and committing to, goals have the advantages of just that: focus and commitment—and, if all goes well, satisfaction when the goal is achieved. After setting their goals, couples can work out how to attain them, including assessing their monetary inflows and outflows.

Planning starts with a budget. While *detailed* budgets have not proved particularly helpful to the couples I have seen, what has been instructive is having couples track yearly expenses by category: housing, food, education/childcare, health care, vacations/entertainment, holiday/birthday gifts, charitable contributions, insurance, dues, taxes, and any other recurring categories that require substantial outlays. Couples can next separate essential spending from discretionary, big ticket items, and work from there to decide which discretionary items they can forego. In some cases, therapists can help couples reduce major expenses that previously seemed fixed, such as by moving to a smaller, less expensive home. Once the numbers are on the table—either in my office or in the clients' homes—this task often resembles helping people mourn or accept what they *cannot* have (at least for now), whether it's a redecorated kitchen or an expensive vacation. It will also help to uncover the specific meanings of such foregone expenditures.

Besides helping the couple decide on their long-term goals and where they can cut back, keeping track of spending can reduce the tendency for partners to blame each other for the shortage of cash, since people often do not count what they themselves pay for as anything other than essential.

When financial crises abate, I mention the importance of saving and estate planning since, like routine doctor visits, action on these fronts is frequently neglected and can have long-term consequences. Most experts recommend some method that makes saving routine and sacrosanct, with money automatically transferred each month (barring emergencies) to accounts for college, retirement, and perhaps some other specified savings purpose, say, for a home down payment or a family vacation.

If they don't already have one, couples can be referred to a financial advisor who can make additional practical suggestions and who couples may allow to settle some of their disputes. Some couples will learn the basics of financial literacy, and others will benefit from tax and estate planning. Financial planning is a complex task that "requires the planner to have specific knowledge about investments, taxes, retirement planning/distribution, estate planning, insurance, education funding, and a variety of market/economic and individual contextual factors that can influence the likelihood of success" (Dew et al., 2020, p. 620). Most therapists probably underestimate the value of such referrals, although one study found that such assistance generated an additional annual monetary return of 1.65% (Dew et al., 2020).

Of course, high-end financial planning makes little sense for many people. Moderate- and low-income individuals who are in financial trouble can be referred to financial counselors who can help them with debt and to credit counselors who sometimes work as intermediaries with creditors.

For couples who might benefit and for therapists with more interest, I recommend the excellent self-help book by Jenkins et al., *You Paid How Much for That?! How to Win at Money Without Losing at Love* (2002). This book is singularly helpful since it gives equal weight to the emotional and financial facets of a couple's financial life. It also teaches the basics of the PREP approach to marital success (Markman et al., 2001).

Money and happiness

Studies show that Americans generally hold the mistaken belief that having more money will make them happier. While true for the genuinely poor, for most of the population, more money does not lead to much more happiness, whereas success in relationships does (Jenkins et al., 2002; Lyubomirsky, 2013).[9] Jenkins and colleagues make the case for challenging this belief when we see it in clients, noting that the pursuit of money leads people to neglect other activities that would be more rewarding and runs the risk of excessive debt with its resultant suffering:

> When we invest our energy in obtaining more money and the stuff it buys, the consequences are worse than simply ending up with lots of nice trinkets. The real tragedy is that we too often end up failing

to invest our time and energy in ways that could bring real happiness in life . . . . There are two unfortunate consequences to following the wrong path . . . . Imagine setting out with your family for a wonderful picnic by a lake. But you take a wrong turn and end up at a contaminated swamp! . . . This is the kind of exchange we see couples making when they believe the myth that more money equals happiness. They not only miss out on joy and well-being, but they also land in places full of stress and less material wealth—the mucky swamp of debt.

(pp. 42–43)

More meanings of money and the things it can buy

While somewhat over-rated as the source of happiness, money and material possessions can connote pleasure, security, love, and much more (Patterson & Datchi, 2019). Some people think that "diamonds are a girl's best friend," and others will feel secure as they review their portfolios of aptly named "securities." One client worried that her boyfriend would lose interest in her after his substantial promotion reversed the relative contributions to their pooled finances. Other clients have been severely wounded by parents, sometimes irreparably, when expected funds were withheld (e.g., through curtailing college tuition or by disinheritance), adding a gut-wrenching relational injury to unanticipated financial stress.

For those who grew up in financially strapped families, money may simultaneously relieve fears of economic hardship and shame. For many clients, money and possessions are "how you keep score" in life, how you measure success and status.[10] Clients with uncertain self-esteem may be more taken by the pursuit of wealth and more distressed when it is not available. Others will see expensive gifts as reassurance that they are lovable. Some will live vicariously through overspending on their children.

The different values that men and women often give to possessions can make it hard for them to understand the others' buying preferences: boats, power tools, and cars as "phallic symbols" of power and status for men; home furnishings and fashionable clothes as more important for women (excluding the stereotypical exceptions of gay men, African American men, and Hindu men at their weddings).

When we buy things, some meanings may be obvious (we get to "treat ourselves" to a night out); others are idiosyncratic (we triumph over a childhood when our parents couldn't afford a fancy restaurant). The lesson for therapists is that when couples fight over expenditures, it almost always helps to unpack the specific values and meanings at play (see, especially, Shapiro, 2007; Jenkins et al., 2002, pp. 58–71). Just as we saw that arguments about sex are not *only* about sex, arguments about money are rarely *only* about money. As noted earlier, such arguments may also include important interpersonal issues of control, commitment, caring, integrity, recognition, fairness, and autonomy.

Cultural expectations and childhood memories may differ and complicate the discussion. It often helps to ask how the family of origin handled money and whether there were financial setbacks. Some clients will have (transference) fears based on childhood experiences with parents or with prior partners, worrying, for instance, that their husband will be inept in business, that their wife will be a shopaholic, or that their partner will conceal purchases or bank accounts. For many clients, the meanings of spending are outside their awareness or considered obvious truths about life. Couples who come to us saying, "We fight about money all the time!" will often be surprised to learn what they are really fighting about.

A leaky roof, an upright piano, and a Peloton bicycle

The following vignette illustrates how uncovering idiographic meanings can help a couple manage differences and grow closer. Steve and Stephanie were two urban professionals in their mid-40s who had recently relocated to Chicago. Their move had helped Stephanie's career and made Steve's more difficult (his main office was in the city they had left). They were having what seemed to me an incomprehensible, ongoing debate about when and whether to repair the roof of their new home. (Don't you always have to repair leaky roofs?!) Their debate became comprehensible and resolvable once Steve was able to see that dragging his feet on the roof repair was connected to anger at the relocation and to Stephanie's having prevailed in deciding which house to buy. (He'd preferred a newer one that needed fewer repairs.) Later, the couple would decide to purchase a small apartment, a pied-à-terre, in the city they had come from that, though seemingly extravagant and unnecessary, helped even the score as it enabled Steve to remain in touch with his central work office and to enjoy the city where he'd grown up, including the museums he had used as an escape from his divorced mother's depressed mood.

Later, when their marital happiness was dragged down by Stephanie's job stress and minor depression (reminiscent of Steve's mother's mood), they got a shot in the arm when Steve agreed to another purchase: a piano for Stephanie to play (as she had as a child) and share with their daughter. Stephanie was moved by Steve's willingness to spend on something special for her. To get to that purchase, though, we needed to understand her past, especially her difficulty asking for what she needed, including financially, when she was a child.

A more mysterious argument followed Steve's ordering an expensive Peloton bike as a Christmas gift for Stephanie; her gym had closed during the COVID pandemic, and he thought this would elevate her mood as the piano had. The confusion over the Peloton cleared up when Stephanie confessed, with some embarrassment, that she wanted that bike "all to myself"—Steve had mentioned sharing it with her—since she felt that so much of her childhood had been sacrificed to the needs of her parents and her troubled sister. Steve, who had other ways to exercise, appreciated her sensitivity and accepted this limitation. While all these financial conundrums might seem humdrum, their exploration led to more significant themes (the unbalanced relocation, the issue of "depressed family mood," and the Virginia Woolf-like desire for "a bike of one's own"). Consistent with Stanley and Einhorn's (2007) research demonstrating the importance of "commitment" and "dedication to a future together," exploring the meanings of these family purchases helped this couple work as a team committed to a shared future—one that included a solid roof, a pied-à-terre for Dad, a Peloton for Mom, and enlivening piano music for all.

Notes

1. Conflicts about children take first place for stepfamilies and remarried partners.
2. These authors concluded, "Programs that promote economic stability in low-income communities (e.g., programs to increase steady employment or assist with debt relief and housing) may have significant effects on marital outcomes in those communities, even if those programs never target marriages or relationships directly. Whatever bolsters the financial prospects of low-income couples may remove barriers to marriage and/or forestall divorce for couples struggling with financial problems" (p. 424).
3. Many premarital couples discuss with me how much to spend on their weddings, balancing this expense with saving for future needs. As with engagement rings, spending on a wedding can symbolize just how committed the couple are to the marriage. Some couples who wish to skip the wedding may be signaling a lack of commitment, if not a stinginess, that could foretell a marriage lacking in pleasure—too much like Scrooge, too little like Mr. Fezziwig in *A Christmas Carol*. However, when overdone, wedding spending can create lasting debt and unhappiness. Couples stalled on how much to spend can be helped to uncover the underlying anxieties that come together as they face these concrete spending decisions. Encouraged by the wedding-industrial complex, many couples engage in magical/obsessional planning/spending, unconsciously believing that "the perfect wedding" will guarantee lasting happiness, not just a wonderful day. As Stanley and Einhorn (2007) put it, "The current, apparently growing, hyperexpression of investment in the ceremonial launching of marriages may be occurring precisely to counter the terrifying fragility of marriage" (pp. 296–297). For this reason, I often find myself questioning this and trying to refocus attention away from table settings to doubts about the future and shaky relations with parents that lie below the surface of such detailed planning and excessive spending.
4. "House husbands" or husbands who prioritize their wives' careers are frequently stressed in this way, as are many African American husbands I've treated, when their wives earn considerably more money than they do. The classic film treatment of this issue, related more to a discrepancy of fame than finances, is *A Star is Born,* in its many versions. With luck, this gender-role problem will recede in the future.
5. Predictably, research finds a strong link between gender equalitarian ideology and gender equalitarian money management (Çineli, 2020).
6. For a painful film example of such a marriage, see the award-winning documentary *The Queen of Versailles* (2012). On a personal note, my father—a child of the Great Depression who subsequently did very well in business—blinded himself to the considerable amount of money he spent on travel (his passion), camera equipment (his hobby), cars (for status), and tennis and golf equipment (his sports), while complaining frequently about the money my mother spent with her interior decorator, a man he referred to as "Basil, the Bastard." My mother kept a separate, somewhat

clandestine, checking account with money she'd inherited from her father, for those and other expenses he disapproved of.

7. While the stereotypical shopaholic is female, the classic movie portrayal of such a character is male: Charles Foster Kane in *Citizen Kane* (1941). When his relationships with people increasingly failed him, Kane, like his real-life model, William Randolph Hearst, resorted more and more to collecting material possessions, on the model of his transitional-object sled, Rosebud.

8. Dickens, who endured childhood poverty, had Mr. Micawber in *David Copperfield* put it this way: "Annual income twenty pounds, annual expenditure nineteen [pounds] six [pence], result happiness. Annual income twenty pounds, annual expenditure twenty pounds ought and six, result misery."

9. This seems to be the current consensus among social scientists, but it is largely based on studies showing no overall increase in happiness over time in industrialized countries despite rising buying power. What is omitted from such analyses is the obvious fact that happiness declines precipitously—as described earlier—when people have *sudden* financial calamities, like losing their jobs. In such cases, it is obvious that more money would have helped. Nonetheless, the point here is different: that people are mistaken in seeking money as their main source of happiness.

10. For an extensive example in which monetary success was linked strongly to status and self-esteem, see the case of Matt and Rachel (Nielsen, 2019b). Here, the wife's inability to contain distress over her business failure led her to seriously consider divorcing her husband for his failure to "keep up with the neighbors" financially.

10 Domestic Problems and Division-of-Labor Disputes

> Marriage is not just spiritual communion; it is also remembering to take out the trash.
>
> —Dr. Joyce Brothers (quoted in Parker-Pope, 2010, p. 193)

So far, we have covered the three topics that couples consider most radio-active: sex, children, and money. But these are not the ones that research shows they argue about the most. Much more common are arguments about the equitable division of labor and squabbles about "how things should be done." Friends don't generally have such problems, but living with another person, whether a spouse or roommate, can be a minefield. Living together requires people to work out who does the dishes, how late people can stay up, and how neat to keep the apartment. Such *domestic problems* became more intense and frequent during the COVID-19 pandemic, when couples who quarantined together had even more time for close-quarter friction. We can see a similar intensification of such problems when partners retire and start spending more time at home together.[1]

These domestic battles drag many couples down. They tend to erupt episodically and are rarely discussed in ways that lead to change or under-standing. Many count as *perpetual problems* based in personality differences that will forever plague a marriage, as in the aphorism, "When you marry a person, you marry one set of problems; if you'd married someone else, you would have married a different set." Researchers note that such problems often seem to be about nothing very important.[2] Sometimes, these dis-satisfactions smolder under the surface as people try to "put up with" each other—but this can gradually erode marital happiness, in a domestic version of the death by a thousand cuts. We begin by examining division-of-labor problems, which have received more research attention.

Division-of-labor problems

In the Olsons' large national survey (2000), cited previously, 49% of the cou-ples showed some concern about the unfair division of housework, and there

DOI: 10.4324/b22905-14

was a large disparity between happy and unhappy couples on satisfaction with "who did what" (81% vs. 41%) and with whether decisions had been made jointly (89% vs. 57%). Other research shows that "couples who learn to negotiate compromises involving household chores and caregiving are happier in both their marriages and their jobs" (Parker-Pope, 2010, pp. 206–207). Research also supports the commonsense expectation that people are most satisfied when there is equity in their relationships, not only equity of outcomes ("distributive justice") but also perceived fairness in the *procedures* for making decisions ("procedural justice") (Collett, 2010; Nelson et al., 2018).

While most research studies of the division of labor between couples focus on housework ("the chore wars"), clinical work with couples on this subject should be broadened to include equity and responsibility for all the tasks necessary to maintain a household, such as helping with science projects, paying bills, preparing taxes, getting cars serviced, and fixing computers (tasks more commonly performed by men), and buying children's clothes, scheduling doctors' appointments, and arranging babysitters (tasks more commonly performed by women). Partners also need to get credit for time spent doing paid work. And don't forget that these debates about fairness occur within the overall context of a "marital quid pro quo" (Lederer & Jackson, 1968), such that when partners feel less loved and less connected, they often become more sensitive to inequities concerning who changes light bulbs.

Most couples fail to discuss explicitly how they will apportion their shared responsibilities (Knudson-Martin, 2013). Instead, they generally fall, without discussion, into roles that become more gender-stereotypical and inequitable after the first child is born (Parker-Pope, 2010). Clients who would not expect others to perform tasks without discussion at work often act as though this is realistic at home. Not talking, however, has the usual disadvantages.

Part of the problem is that domestic tasks have come to be relatively devalued when compared to work for pay, making them a less obvious topic for serious discussion. As historian Stephanie Coontz (2005) points out:

> Women's traditional tasks—growing food for the family table, tending animals, dairying, cooking, repairing household implements, and making clothes—though no less burdensome, were no longer viewed as economic activities. In the older definition of housekeeping, women's labor was recognized as a vital contribution to the family's economic survival. Wives were regularly referred to as "helps-meet" and "yoke mates." But as housekeeping became "homemaking," it came to be seen as an act of love rather than a contribution to survival.
>
> (p. 155)

Another problem in working out an equitable division of labor is that partners often do not witness tasks performed by each other and, consequently, each may assume that he or she is doing more than their fair share. Cheryl Rampage, a friend, colleague, and well-known champion of women's rights in marriage, likes to relate that when she first married, she and her husband, Larry, were each convinced that they were doing more work around the house than was fair. They agreed to keep records for one week and then compare notes. When they reconvened, they discovered that each was far busier than they had realized and equally as busy as the other—thus ending this chore war. I often share this anecdote with couples who argue about such inequities, and suggest that they do a similar research project, but over a longer time span, recognizing that some tasks, like doing income taxes or taking children to the doctor, are intermittent.

With some exceptions, the Rampages' experience is consistent with recent research that has found the overall workloads of mothers and fathers to be "relatively equal," with men doing more at home than their fathers did, but with the division of tasks "remaining gender specialized, with women doing more in the home and men doing more in the marketplace" (Bianchi & Milkie, 2010, p. 718). These same authors reported inequity when more work became required—say, after children were born: "[M]others (but not fathers) curtailed employment in the face of overwhelming demands from work and family" (p. 709).

Domestic problems: arguments over how things should be done

Domestic arguments are not just about who should do what but also about how they should do it and when. Many of these will be about seemingly trivial issues. Paradoxically, this can make these squabbles more worrisome, as partners notice that they are unable to agree on minor, everyday procedures, as in the following quote from de Botton (2016):

> Not all domestic concerns carry equivalent prestige. One can quickly be made to look a fool for caring a lot about how much noise the other person makes while eating cereal or how long they want to keep magazines beyond their publication dates. It's not difficult to humiliate someone who cleaves to a strict policy of how to stack a dishwasher or how quickly the butter ought to be returned to the fridge after use. When the tensions which bedevil us lack glamour, we are at the mercy of those who might wish to label our concerns petty and odd. We can end up frustrated and at the same time too doubtful of the dignity of our frustrations to have the confidence to outline them calmly for our dubious or impatient audiences.
>
> (p. 55)

But of course, there are reasons for these recurring skirmishes. The explanations often lie in differences over what feels acceptable or necessary concerning priorities, neatness, organization, and timeliness. Arguments over dishwashing or bill paying will not only touch on these topics, but may, for instance, engage underlying themes of caretaking and control. All of us have histories with these issues, and some of us are more sensitive about some of them than our spouses. Partners who felt dominated by parents may drag their feet when spouses ask them to pick up their clothes (especially if "picking up clothes" feels insignificant to them), and partners whose requests for action fail to get results may feel neglected and unimportant as they may have felt in childhood (especially if orderliness is a high priority for them).

For some people, it is not so much childhood sensitivities but rather some almost biologically determined, comfortable set point for order versus randomness, for productive work versus relaxation—like the correct room temperature during the winter—that leads to misunderstanding and repetitive arguments. John Gray, author of *Men are From Mars, Women are From Venus* (1992), relates numerous funny anecdotes about such differences (which he attributes to biology), in which wives want their husbands to do chores around the house while husbands want to watch sports on TV.

Many arguments revolve around order and neatness, which may be a matter of personal taste or something determined by a person's psychology. Two clients of mine, one an architect and the other an art dealer, got into repeated arguments with their respective wives about the arrangement of furniture in their homes. What helped me to understand these men was how, without conscious awareness or my permission, they similarly rearranged items in my office (a clock, a tissue box, a small statue) to suit their need for aesthetic/visual/spatial harmony. I saw their preferences as more baked in the cake (i.e., biological), something that had helped in their careers but caused trouble in their marriages to people with different aesthetic or spatial set points.

Others, who learned in childhood to organize their possessions or, conversely, to let things go, can get into recurring arguments with spouses whose preferences differ. And demands for neatness (or timeliness) get worse when marriages seem "out of control" or unrewarding, so that the "personal religion" of orderliness, in which things are done "the way I like them," may seem essential. By contrast, spouses who feel beset by demands from work, partners, and children may be more prone at such times to let things go, resulting in greater disorder in the home. Vicious cycles and domestic battles often ensue.

More generally and underlying many fights about who will do what and how, is the simple wish not to be bothered. People who work hard during the day, exerting self-control with their bosses and subordinates, often harbor an unspoken wish to be pampered and cared for at home. The adult equivalent of Anthony Wolf's "baby self at home" (2000), such people (most of us?) object when asked to do "just one more thing." This background wish to be cared for makes partners less willing to hop to when asked to do home repairs, pick up the dry cleaning, or modify their inner set points for temperature, timeliness, or neatness. And again, such reluctance will intensify in marriages where other needs are not being met.

Couple therapy for domestic squabbles and division-of-labor disputes

Couples who constantly fight about the division of labor and about how things ought to be done can use our help to uncover, discuss, and then adjust based on a better understanding of what is really at stake. The key is to begin with curiosity about underlying issues and unmet needs. When we succeed, the answers will look something like those in the following example from Leone (2008).

> Ann needs the house neat and the bills paid on time to relax and feel soothed (to counter a sense of inner disorganization), and to feel she's with a competent and capable man who can take care of her. An orderly home is also a source of pride and self-esteem for her.
>
> (p. 81)

The key point is that the subjective meaning of these events for Ann extends beyond the observable facts of whether the bills are paid, or the home is orderly. Knowing this, her husband might be more understanding and less put out when these issues surface, just as he might be if he knew that Ann had a chronic shoulder injury that required him to modify his behavior. And Ann is likely to be appreciative when he does. As in other marital impasses, psychodynamic understanding might allow this couple to recognize what is really at stake and then work out amicable solutions.

But outside of therapy, many couples rarely discuss such subjective issues. Many prefer not to, either because they wish to "let sleeping dogs lie" or because they do not wish to relive the stresses they experienced separately during the day, at work or at home. One unfortunate outcome is that partners fail to receive emotional credit or support for hard work done out of sight—or for accommodations made to help the partner. This happens more extensively when distressed couples stop sharing their inner lives with each other. Compare this absence of communication with a spouse who says, "I had a hard day at work today and you just told me you did, too. Let's try to put the kids to bed as quickly as we can and then watch some TV together." In this scenario, the partners are a team facing an external enemy—the work/time crunch discussed in the next chapter.

To avoid resentment over perceived inequity and squabbles over who has or has not done their fair share "correctly" on a given day, couples need to talk. When they do, they will encounter our old friends: the problems of asking for things, of managing "difficult conversations," of negotiating fairly, and of unrealistic, wishful expectations. Additionally, when couples start talking—at home or in our offices—about how to divide up family tasks and live with different preferences, they routinely come up against some of the following difficulties:

- That the partner who is better at something might still not want to do it.
- That the partner who most wants something done urgently should not always be stuck with doing it.

- That couples can differ on what counts as "doing something right," just as they might differ on the merits of a particular film.
- That couples may need to challenge and renegotiate gender-based assumptions about who will do what.
- That the partner who delegates a task can then expect only limited control over precisely how and when it is done. I call this the "back-seat driver situation," which makes it instantly familiar to most couples. In the research literature on marriage, this comes up as the "maternal gatekeeper theory," described by Parker Pope (2010) as follows:

> While women claim that they want help with household chores, men say that their wives also want to dictate how the chores are done, such as the way a towel is folded, the way a baby is diapered, or the way a dishwasher is loaded. When the man doesn't do it the "right" way, the wives complain, criticize, or do it over themselves. As a result, men get angry, quit, or do it wrong the next time on purpose, so they won't be asked to do it again.
>
> (p. 203)

The truth is that when you delegate a task, you should get *some* say—just as a boss or expert might—but you must accept having less control and be aware of possible fallout from micromanaging.

- That what seems compulsive perfectionism to one partner may be the result of many attempts to find the best solution (like finding the best route when driving to work). At other times, perfectionism can be unpacked to reveal important emotional concerns, like Ann's need to have things done "correctly" to feel secure.
- That who is "in charge" of making sure that things get done is separable from who then does those things. Clarification here will help prevent spouses, usually husbands, from being surprised when their offers to "help out" are met with anger. Just as parents become annoyed when they must continuously remind their teenagers to do certain tasks (homework, cleaning their rooms), so spouses become burdened by the task of "being responsible for everything." Recall that the opening quote from Joyce Brothers mentions "remembering" to take out the trash.

In the end, it will help to make these and other latent issues explicit as couples face the challenging problem of sharing tasks equitably while living under the same roof. Having facilitated such discussions, therapists can also point out that "sacrifice" and "noncontingent giving" are indicators of healthier, happier marriages, and that constant scorekeeping regarding who has done how much is usually a sign of trouble (Beck & Clark, 2010; Gottman, 2011; Stanley, Rhodes, & Whitton, 2010).

Therapists can encourage clients to never stop saying "Thank you," after completion of routine tasks ("Thanks for picking up the groceries."), and to express appreciation when their partners shelve their own preferences to please them ("I know you didn't really want to clean out the garage today. I really appreciate that you did it anyway.").

Christina and Adam: domestic problems during COVID-19

Nine months into quarantining during COVID-19, at home with their two children (ages 3 and 1) while they each worked from home, this young couple could not contain their distress and blew up at each other. One day later, they had an emergency Zoom session with me during my vacation and told me how Christina had threatened to leave Adam and move home to live with her mother, who, she thought would supply better help with childcare.

I had been seeing this couple weekly for the previous four months, and we had made some headway on their vulnerability cycle. In these recurrent fights, Adam would angrily complain that Christina was too much like his critical father—expecting too much and never admitting that she was wrong—after which Christina would sullenly withdraw, confirming Adam's negative transference that she didn't respect him. Worse, when he would give up and stomp out, leaving Christina at home with the children, this pattern would confirm her sense that too much of the parenting fell to her. Of late, she had been able to speak up more, something that had been unacceptable in her family of origin, but the intensity of this recent blow-up scared the two of them and surprised me. Neither really wanted to get divorced, but it was now in the air.

How to explain this and what to do? Partly, it was my absence and the loss of my support during my vacation. Partly, it was COVID. All my couples were stressed, living under one roof, experiencing the full blast of domestic problems made worse by the additional caretaking required by school closures. Couples like Christina and Adam also missed contact with friends and with work settings that provided respite, variety, companionship, and simply "got them out of the house."

This couple was also anxious about money since Adam's career had taken a hit because of the pandemic and was now in limbo. His business had fallen off precipitously, forcing him, just now, to work out-of-town on a business opportunity. On the day of their big fight, Adam had driven the five hours it took to get home, arriving exhausted, uncertain of the outcome, after a week of trying to make that new business project a reality.

Meanwhile, the family finances depended on Christina's high-paying managerial job, which she now performed from home while taking care of the kids. The past week had been especially difficult for her, as well, since she had expected Adam to be gone only three days (during which her mother had come to help) but had now faced two extra days (without her mother) when Adam had to stay longer. So, when Adam arrived home to the usual bedtime pandemonium, both were exhausted and, as is typical of so many couples, ready to see their problems as coming from their spouse.

This was an example of the phenomenon I noted earlier: Neither had witnessed the stress of the other in recent days. And so, a fight began—with no empathy, little appreciation, and much mutual blaming.

Because of our prior work, Christina was no longer willing to be the long-suffering "mouse" in the marriage. That day, she not only blamed Adam for not holding up his end in childcare (when he was home, not just when he was out of town) but revealed a hidden hurt: her belief that he didn't value her as the current principal breadwinner. There was some truth to this characterization, which she drew from Adam's preoccupation with his career and lack of appreciation for her "holding down the fort," both in her job and with the kids while he was away. The conversation improved as I helped them uncover what felt like an unfair patriarchal value system, and then as I coached Adam to reassure Christina that he loved and appreciated her. She was correct that his attention was on his work problems (what wasn't working), rather than on her career (what was). But she had it wrong about how he felt about her. He really did appreciate her and her value, not just to the family finances but to his happiness and pride in being married to such a competent woman. His greater worry, he then said, was that she hated and devalued him! But this was the familiar father transference from before. All three of us recognized it, and Christina and I tried to help Adam see it as mostly due to his current insecurity following his somewhat disappointing week out of town.

We then returned to Christina's division-of-labor complaint: her anger at Adam for not doing more with the kids. At first glance, this seemed to be based on his having been out of town—that absence having aggravated her more long-standing complaint. But, in addition, some of Christina's experience of unfairness was due to her "maternal gatekeeping." How so? Aware that Christina was exhausted by the combined demands of work and childcare, Adam had repeatedly urged Christina to hire outside help. Now, in the context of the volcanic eruption of feelings on the prior day and fears of her marriage ending, she had to admit that she had rejected Adam's constructive attempts to get her the help she needed. She had done this not only because of uncertainty about whether a nanny might bring the COVID virus into their home, but, like many young mothers I see, because of a reluctance to trust other caretakers with her kids (something made worse by her feeling neglected as a child). Christina's reluctance, we learned, had also blocked Adam from taking the matter of obtaining babysitters into his own hands since he felt certain that if he had, Christina would have vetoed his choices of sitters.

As these issues were uncovered and met with compassion, the couple calmed down and recommitted to each other and to working with me on their marriage. The crisis seemed to be over. In the following months, we continued to discuss the issues that had surfaced in our emergency session, especially the belief each had that the other didn't appreciate their contributions to the marriage, and the concrete problem that contributed to that feeling: the need for more babysitting help for their kids. Our continuing therapeutic work on their *underlying emotional concerns* and *concrete external problems* was assisted by a growing improvement in their ability to collaborate in a cycle different from the (antagonistic) pursuer to (sullen) distancer cycle that had brought them to treatment.

Adam and Christina resemble other couples who struggle because they experience their partners as "doing less than their fair share." Their case shows how this belief is fueled not just by the facts on the ground (the time each spends on important family tasks) or by external stressors (here, delivered by the COVID pandemic)—though these do contribute. Most of all, it was due to these partners defensively retreating from each other. When partners retreat from each other they lose connection with precisely the person who can appreciate their contributions, sympathize with their suffering, and reassure them that they are committed for the long haul. When therapy helps them to reconnect, as it did here, they gain all of these back.

Notes

1. I use *domestic problems* to cover a range of problems that come up when people live under the same roof. I had thought of calling these *roommate problems* because the college students I teach instantly grasp the idea that it is harder to be a roommate than to be only a friend. I have also experienced some of these on golf trips with my buddies—where men suddenly discover that they would have trouble being married to a long-time friend who has different ideas about timeliness or neatness. No term quite captures the full range of problems, but *domestic problems* will do to cover a set of issues that cause trouble when people share more space and time living together.

2. "Our analyses of over 900 videotaped conflicts in our laboratory and over 1,000 play-by-play interviews about conflict at home have led us to the conclusion that most of the time most couples fight about what appears to be absolutely nothing" (Gottman & Gottman, 2010, p. 14).

11 Job Stress, Cultural Pressures, and Limited Time

Gorillas often spend more than fifty hours a week gathering and eating food; human hunter-gatherers, acting purposefully, typically spend only between fifteen and seventeen hours a week on feeding themselves, leaving them plenty of time for all sorts of other things. . . . If human beings are able to spend less time working than other primates, why do so many people now work as hard as gorillas?

—Lepore (2021, p. 66)

Spillover and crossover stress in the modern world

Social forces over which couples have limited control shape their lives for good and for ill, offering opportunities, constraining options, and stressing them out. Many studies have found that extradyadic (*spillover*) stress can have a negative impact on couple well-being, that intradyadic (*crossover*) couple conflict or maladjustment shapes functioning outside the marriage (causation goes both ways), and that how couples manage things when outside stress comes home matters greatly for their happiness and sense of commitment (studies cited in Falconier et al., 2015; Cooper et al., 2019). Similar results have been found for stress due to pretty much everything, including children, finances, work, illness, exams, and minority status. The list is still longer when we add the impact of crime, poverty, gun violence, incarceration, discrimination, migration, political unrest, and war. Unsurprisingly, stress adversely impacts sleep and sexual functioning, which then further compromise marital well-being (Yorgason et al., 2021). An illustrative longitudinal study of policemen found that work stress predicted men's hostility toward their wives, which, in turn, predicted wives' hostility toward their husbands, with hostility (and well-being) being moderated by couples' ability to regulate their emotions, their attachment security, and their shared time together (Roberts et al., 2013).

Trying to maintain a satisfactory work–life balance is an almost-universal stressor: In one study, it was mentioned by 90% of mothers and 95% of fathers (Williams & Boushey, 2010), and it is a problem for all ethnic and SES groups, though more so for low-income families (Fraenkel & Capstick, 2012). As noted by Schneider and Waite in their summary book on the topic (2005, quoted in Fraenkel, 2011, p. 250):

DOI: 10.4324/b22905-15

Nearly all mothers and fathers report conflicts between work and family, and when these conflicts occur, the family is more likely to suffer than work. For most working parents, trade-offs and compromises between family and work obligations appear to be unavoidable.

Nonetheless, Fraenkel and Capstick note some advantages dual-earner couples have over those in traditional marriages: greater security of income flow and buffering, should one person have a setback; greater mutual understanding of one another's roles; and the potential to challenge and work out gendered assumptions concerning power, roles, and finances. To this I would add the satisfactions that women can derive from working outside the home and those that men experience when they are more involved with their children. That said, virtually all dual-earner couples in the United States struggle to integrate and balance work and family responsibilities and satisfactions.

When facing external stresses, couples will be affected by the availability of jobs, quality day care, and health insurance, among other things. Economic concerns can sometimes trump issues of intimate commitment, as when lower SES women choose not to marry the fathers of their children and upper SES 20-somethings delay marriage to establish careers (Coontz, 2005). Many couples would prefer to have only one partner in the workforce while children are young but cannot afford that option. Some affluent career women leave the workplace to become stay-at-home mothers because their employers fail to provide flexible options that would enable them to combine a demanding job with the responsibilities of motherhood (Stone, 2010). Some couples choose to live separately due to the locations of their jobs (Lindemann, 2017).[1] And, as mentioned in Chapter 9, unemployment exacts a troubling toll on many couples and their families. Geographical mobility and relocation in the United States commonly interfere with social support networks of friends and family and add to marital stress.

Many studies document the deleterious impact of excessive work and job stress on family life (Fraenkel, 2011; Badawy & Schieman, 2021). While considerable research has found heightened distress among workers who lack power in the workplace, recent scholarship confirms that take-home stress also comes with positions of higher status and authority (Badawy & Schieman, 2021). Many workers are expected to work longer and harder in the wake of "downsizing," many are anxious about keeping their jobs now that people rarely remain at the same company for life, and many lack job security in the "gig economy." Shift work creates challenges for more than one in four dual-earner families (Fraenkel & Capstick, 2012), while unpredictable work schedules increasingly stress the families of low-income service workers (Ananat & Gassman-Pines, 2021).

Improvements in communication technology have changed expectations for how fast work must be turned around and have disrupted the worklife–homelife boundary (Nielsen, 2019a). Increased demands and unpredictable work schedules have intruded into the practicalities of therapy, too, as clients have become less able or willing to commit to regular weekly appointments. While detailing the complex external stresses that modern couples face is beyond the scope of this book, one key take-home point is clear: In many situations, therapists need to help couples make concrete plans to decrease the stress that can drain vibrancy and satisfaction from their marriages.

Two brief examples illustrate this point. As a psychiatry resident, I was treating a low-income, recently divorced single mother of three children, ages ten and under. As a future psychoanalyst, I thought my focus should be on the woman's transference to me (at times, she was quite testy, which made me wonder whether this was why her husband had left her). Fortunately for her, my faculty supervisor, Ruth Litz, focused me (then single, childless, and clueless in these matters) on helping this woman manage her time better and get her act together with those kids at dinner time. My client's depression and testiness were soon vastly improved!

More recently, a 30-something couple (also with three children under ten), whom I had helped previously after the husband's one-time sexual indiscretion, returned in September 2020, in the midst of the COVID-19 pandemic. Valeria, the wife, was working from home, and the kids were underfoot doing school remotely, while the husband, Juan, left home most days to work in his almost-deserted office. As the therapy got underway, Valeria complained that Juan was (again) "unfaithful" because he was "escaping" to work. Things got worse as their nanny (also stressed to the max, including after several wrangles with overstressed Valeria) quit on them. While long-standing issues that we had worked on before soon surfaced (her transference allergy to an absent father, his to a controlling mother), what helped them most in this three-session therapy was working out the details of childcare, hiring a new nanny, and enlisting help from Grandma.[2] Facing down these reality stressors—together and successfully—turned out to reduce Valeria's feeling that Juan was "abandoning" her and his that she was impossibly critical. It also helped that I normalized their stress coming from the pandemic (including their cabin fever) and that we brainstormed to come up with some fun, shared family activities (games, baking, and dancing).

Cultural pressures that add to these problems

Somewhat distinct from these external realities, cultural and religious norms concerning the proper behavior of men, women, and children often interfere with marital harmony and happiness (Breunlin et al., 2001; Hare-Mustin, 1978; Knudson-Martin, 2013): "Husbands must be good providers!" "Boys must excel at sports!" "Spouses (women especially) must not be selfish!" "Mothers must enjoy every minute of parenting!" "Parents must devote themselves to helping their children get into a top college!" Patriarchy, sexism, and other gender-based norms can add to couple conflict and stress, especially as couples try to balance home and work priorities. Many studies find that stress has risen due to increased societal expectations for involved parenting (Bianchi & Milkie, 2010). For other couples, the challenge is to create roles they have never seen before in a society where norms are in flux. Consequently, as a couple therapist, I frequently find myself attempting to help couples work together to question constricting social norms and expectations, many of which they take for granted.

Stop within-group blaming. Combat real external stressors!

To cope with external social stressors, couples must fight against them, rather than succumb to the temptations of blaming themselves or each other. In two relevant studies of 300 subjects, couples with the most nonmarital stress unsurprisingly had the most "couple burnout." Worse still, they blamed their spouses for their unhappiness more than they did their external circumstances and more than they should have, based on the opinions of presumably more objective, independent raters (Pines, 1996). Fraenkel and Capstick (2012) similarly opine that partners too often blame each other or themselves for overworking "rather than an understandable attempt to survive in an unstable, demanding employment culture" (p. 83).

To reduce such self-blame, therapists can cite the many studies documenting the near-universal stress couples experience when attempting to balance and manage the many demands of work and family. One can also uncover and then challenge internalized values that press for perfection and interfere with realistic happiness.

To further reduce fighting between partners, I explain how fighting (blaming) within a group sometimes serves as an illusory "social defense" against facing real *external* dangers, and I work hard to redirect them to the actual anxieties and challenges that they are avoiding. So that they will remember the defense I am highlighting, I illustrate it by referencing a war, an action, or a horror movie where characters delay their response to some external danger (enemy soldiers, natural disasters, or frightening monsters) and, instead, fight with each other.

Challenge the myth of unlimited time

While couples must contend with a wide variety of external challenges, there is one that transcends them all and, when mishandled, contributes to much marital unhappiness: the need to budget limited time. Time spent together correlates strongly with marital satisfaction (Bradford et al., 2019) and has greatly declined in recent years. For partners without children, time together declined from 35 to 26 hours per week between 1975 and 2003, while the corresponding numbers for couples *with* children declined from 13 to only 9 hours per week, with much of the additional decline due to intensified parenting commitments (Finkel, 2014).

Many couples I see are dual-earner couples with children living at home. Often, these couples argue endlessly over who is or isn't doing their fair share of household and childcare tasks. I see similar arguments in traditional couples (where one partner works and the other manages the household), in divorced parents, and in childless couples. When short on time, all varieties of partners tend to blame their "co-workers" and complain, as described in the last chapter, about the injustice of the division of labor. Further, people pressed for time are less giving and less loving.[3] When such couples become irritated with each other, the chore wars heat up, and some spouses act out as they avoid the family or passive-aggressively fail to do tasks they had promised to perform. This problem is made worse by workplaces that demand inordinate time and near servitude and by community pressures on parents to provide nonstop after-school enrichment for their children (organized sports, traveling teams, lessons, tutoring, etc.).

Frequently, the stress and time required to meet these copious social demands lead not only to marital discord but also to a retreat from the family to the islands of pleasure afforded by work (the workaholic doctor who lives at the hospital), by family commitments (the dutiful son/daughter who is always there for other family members but never home), by community service (the parent who volunteers for everything), by recreation (the "addicted" runner), or by more socially destructive escapes (extramarital affairs, gambling, drug and alcohol abuse). These attempted solutions usually make matters worse, and partners typically present to couple therapy exhausted, sleep-deprived, and depressed. Worse, because the partners have grown apart and things are not getting done, spouses are pretty sure that their partners are selfish people who do not love or care about them. In this context, it is no wonder that social commentators have described a "time famine" and advocated a counterrevolution (Doherty, 2003) or community (re)organizing by like-minded, similarly overstressed parents (Taffel, 2012). In my experience, *this thorny problem of limited time must be confronted if couple therapy is not to become mired in recurring recriminations or discussions of downstream symptomatology.*

A good way to begin to tackle this problem is to "reveal the hidden time structure" (Fraenkel, 2011) and expose the details of how family members spend their time. It is especially important to learn how couples handle things around and after dinnertime, the most common time for couple arguments. Just as we encourage couples to join to face other chronic problems and differences, the goal here is to get the couple on the same page, brainstorming about how to improve their distribution of time.

After learning how partners spend their time, we can begin to challenge the misconceptions and wishful fantasies that contribute to their time problems. Therapists must dispute the idea that quality family time will happen spontaneously and does not need to be planned—like almost everything else in family life. As noted by Fraenkel, one must also challenge the unrealistic beliefs that episodes of quality time can make up for a persistently low quantity of time and that things will get better if people would just work harder or become better organized. To be sure, better organization and time management can help, but discussions in that direction are frequently used to disguise the real culprit: the unwillingness to give up specific pleasurable or valued activities that would allow a more relaxed life together.

There is no way around the painful truth that some activities must be sacrificed or scaled back. Accomplishing this can be hard because of the losses incurred (many spouses semiconsciously believe that without the pleasure they derive from extra-familial activities, they could not bear the drudgery of their unhappy marriages), because of differences about what should be jettisoned (fishing trips, dance classes, or tutoring for the kids), or because the couple agrees on the importance or virtue of the activity to be scrapped (all those traveling baseball games, work for worthy charitable causes). Nonetheless, something must go! Just as therapists need to challenge the constraints imposed by gender-based norms, we often must challenge the necessity of various activities that spouses tell us they cannot live without.

To help make the point that external time demands—rather than inherent character flaws—account for a considerable amount of couple unhappiness, I examine how the couple does on a vacation or weekend away, when they are free of pressure from children and work (no mean feat in these days of cell phones and the Internet). If the couple's mood vastly improves, as it frequently does, one can use this observation to encourage them to let go of some of their unrealistic ideas about how to spend time at home. Other couples will not enjoy themselves, so that their strained relationship during their "weekend-away test" will demonstrate that external pressures are *not* the sole source of their troubles, contrary to what they may have been defensively asserting.

As we discuss the need for more time together and what might be given up to acquire it, we can offer some of the following additional suggestions:

- *Build a stronger boundary between work and home.* Be clear that being constantly on-call and, more generally, working at home have serious costs. When possible, partners should reassure their co-workers or clients that the work will get done, so as to allay their anxiety and free up at-home time.
- *Enlist more babysitters.* Couples can trade babysitting with other couples or get together as a larger group that allows children to be supervised while parents socialize. Get grandparents involved. Line up more babysitters, so that one being unavailable does not ruin parental plans. For older kids who need to be driven hither and yon, if parents can afford it, hire a local college student to drive the kids to some of those after-school activities.
- *Do housework, dinner clean-up, and childcare together.* Doing chores and being with the kids together, rather than separately, can make these tasks less onerous and more fun. Time passes faster when you share the events of the day and the fun and struggles of parenthood. While one-on-one parent–child time is important, too many parents think of this like tag team wrestling, where one parent comes to the rescue of the

other when the first parent becomes exhausted. Since solo time with little kids can be tiring or boring, adding an adult can help and provide more togetherness.

- *Work out ways to decompress from work.* Since so many couple fights occur when Dad or Mom arrives home, accept that this is a challenge and work on solutions. Help each parent plan how to decompress before reaching the front door or before meeting the onslaught of night-time family responsibilities. Discuss the problem of one parent eager to hand off childcare responsibilities to the other, who has finally arrived home from work.

All these changes may require working against underlying fears the partners have about spending more time together. But when the couple is ready and more time has been freed up, therapists can brainstorm with them about what shared activities are possible and will bring the most pleasure (see Nielsen, 2016, Chapter 14).

Additional suggestions for coping with external stress

Separate from helping couples to set boundaries with work, challenge social norms, and find more time for shared pleasurable time together, therapists can encourage some of the following coping strategies:

- *Discuss how family members can get enough sleep.* Sleep matters and can be disrupted for many reasons, including sleep apnea, young children, or spouses trying to avoid each other (Yorgason et al., 2021). Ask about this, and you will sometimes be shocked by what you learn.
- *Ask about hobbies and whether clients can allow themselves time off, just to play.* Unlike children, who love to play, adults can become strangely duty bound, work obsessed, and preoccupied with household chores, checking things off their to-do lists, and responding to emails. And watching TV doesn't really solve the problem; it's OK, but too passive. We can help some clients decrease the stress of the "greedy workplace" and helicopter parenting by encouraging them to do things that don't involve much responsibility and are simply fun. What these are will depend on the person: Some will find pleasure in gardening, solving crosswords, playing an instrument, reading detective stories, or cooking new recipes—all activities that can activate brain circuits devoted to PLAY (Panksepp, 1998).
- *Explore religious practices and connections that, especially when shared, have been shown to substantially reduce extradyadic stress* (Cooper et al., 2019).
- *In situations of severe intercurrent, extradyadic stress, therapists can encourage clients to reach out to friends, family, and relevant support groups.* Doing so made all the difference in a study of severe stress in the lives and marriages of law enforcement officers shaken by significant trauma, like watching a

buddy die or cleaning up a bloody suicide scene (Landers et al., 2020). In such situations, officers' married partners suffered vicarious traumatization (spillover is putting it mildly), and both partners benefited when they were able to talk to each other and get support from friends with similar experiences, formal support groups, and extended family. Officers also reported the value of spouses taking on additional responsibilities, sharing humor and exercise, and recalling positive times together.

The need for societal change

Having made these suggestions and believing strongly that happy marriages must come to terms with the weight of social demands and the limited time available to meet them, I remain deeply unsatisfied with the options currently open to most families. Work has taken over too much time and has expanded too far into off-hours (recall the quip about gorillas and hunter-gatherers that opened this chapter).[4] Real wages for the average worker have long been stagnant (even as CEO compensation has skyrocketed), and the minimum wage has stayed barely sufficient, as more and more couples have become dual earners with multiple jobs. Our economy provides little job security, especially for older workers. Labor union membership, which might counter some of these forces, is extremely low.[5]

These sociological realities contribute to job strain, spillover and crossover stress, and predictable couple unhappiness. They are also a major reason why studies continue to show that having children reduces marital well-being. My wish is that the United States, like some other countries, will come to its senses, especially about what can be expected of adults who are working and raising children.[6]

Although societal change would surely help, given the status quo and our limited role as couple therapists, our best option is to help our clients become aware of their priorities and of the costs of not noticing their choices. Sometimes, they will be able to buck the system, and sometimes, they will have to face the distress of not being able to "have it all." Ideally, they will do this with their eyes open and will not succumb to blaming each other or themselves for not being able to manage the impossible.

Notes

1. There have always been married couples who have lived separately—including because of immigration, occupations that require travel, or incarceration—but there are increasing numbers of couples who choose to live apart in the service of dual careers. Lindeman's (2017) interview study of 97 such couples found, surprisingly, a substantial minority who indicated that their noncohabitation enhanced their independence. These so-called "commuter marriages" resulted from four factors, all of which impact other contemporary relationships as well: married women's increasing participation in the professions; tighter, more competitive job markets; greater gender equality within marriage; and an increased societal emphasis on individualism.

Based on these findings, we should not assume that such relationships won't work or are inevitably stressful, as most of these couples reported that they relied heavily on each other and were in frequent contact via technology and often saw each other on weekends. Unsurprisingly, respondents said it worked well when each partner was a confident, capable, independent sort. I have seen an increasing number of dating couples for whom managing this geographical problem becomes an issue, especially if they have begun their relationships when living in different cities.

2. A recent study comparing 133 two-generation households to 129 three-generation households in China (where three-generation households are common) found that work stress for parents was "positively associated with child next-day negative affect, but only among two-generation families" (Musullo et al., 2021, p. 27). Grandparents matter!

3. Gladwell (2000) reports a pertinent social psychology study: Among seminary students who had just been studying the parable of the Good Samaritan, those who were told they were running late were less likely to behave charitably toward a stranger in need than those who thought they had sufficient time to get to a lecture.

4. Labor unions' call for shorter hours was largely won by the 1930s after Henry Ford accepted an eight-hour day and five-day work week in return for higher productivity and less turnover, such that economist "John Maynard Keynes predicted that, a hundred years in the future, the problem for workers would be too much leisure, since they would work no more than fifteen hours a week. Everyone would suffer from boredom." (Lepore, 2021). Keynes got that one wrong!

5. Outside of agriculture, about one in three Americans belonged to a union in the 1950s; that fell to one in five in 1983 and to one in ten in 2019 (Lepore, 2021).

6. We can look with some hope to countries like Germany: A study of 18,238 German women between 1984 and 2015 showed life satisfaction of women increasing such that the previous happiness gap between mothers (lower) and non-mothers (higher) no longer held and neither did the happiness gap before and after having a child (Preisner et al., 2018). The authors attributed this to a combination of changed cultural norms more conducive to allowing women to work while having children or to choose not to have children, coupled with better state-supported parental leave and childcare that provide more support for working mothers.

Part III

Upgrades to Address Common Stressful Situations

12 Extramarital Affairs

Affairs have a lot to teach us about relationships—what we expect, what we
think we want, and what we feel entitled to. . . . When a couple comes to me
in the aftermath of an affair, I often tell them this: Your first marriage is over.
Would you like to create a second one together?

—Esther Perel (2017a, pp. xiii, 17)

The discovery of an extramarital affair almost invariably shakes the foundations of a marriage. Whether a one-time sexual encounter or a long-standing
relationship, all affairs violate norms of commitment, loyalty, honesty, and
sexual fidelity. All violate the assumption that you can trust your partner to
place you above all others. All call into question whether you can count on
your partner to "have your back," to care about your feelings, and to draw a
protective boundary around the two of you. Treating the resulting relational
crises that follow in the wake of aptly named "infidelity" is one of the most
complex and challenging situations we face as couple therapists.

In my experience and that of others in the field (Baucom et al., 2009;
Enright & Fitzgibbons, 2000; Greenberg et al., 2008, 2010), such couples
require a distinctive approach, especially in the early stages of therapy. This
is because one partner is sharply defining the other as the offender and
demands an apology and reassurance that the offense will not recur. Another
defining feature of such couples is that injured partners are preoccupied with
the betrayal and have great difficulty letting go of their anger. Forgiveness,
when possible and acceptable, is often decisive in enabling these couples to
recover and sometimes, per Perel's opening quote, to work to improve their
relationships (Greenberg et al., 2010).

A subcategory of betrayals

Extramarital affairs are a subcategory of serious marital betrayals, a topic I have
discussed previously (Nielsen, 2016, Chapter 10). Much of what we will cover
in this chapter on affairs will apply to other betrayals, such as intimate partner
violence; failing to support a partner or family member who is seriously ill; or

DOI: 10.4324/b22905-17

concealing consequential, injurious behavior like risky investments gone bad. Like other interpersonal traumas, there is an initial shock that

> is partly caused by the dissimilarity between the event and previous assumptions about how the world and relationships operate. Furthermore, as injured partners often take on the role of victim, the range of emotions varies from intense anger at being betrayed and "victimized," to depression and loss of self-esteem.
>
> (Gordon & Baucom, 1998, p. 13)

Terminology

Leading authors who have studied affairs and other betrayals differ in what they call the partners and the offense. Many employ *betrayed/betrayer* or *offended/offender* (the terms I favor), while Greenberg and his colleagues (Greenberg et al., 2010) use *injured* and *injurer*. Gordon and Baucom employ less-intense terms: *injured partner* and *participating partner*, and some prefer *Extradyadic Involvement* (EDI) to the more value-laden *infidelity*. Such variety derives, I think, from the challenge of working scientifically with an ethical breach of conduct and with the variable intensity of such violations.

Statistics

According to The Kinsey Institute at Indiana University (2013):

- Approximately 20–25% of men and 10–19% of women engage in extramarital sex at least once during their marriage.
- Infidelity is the single most cited cause of divorce in over 150 cultures.
- In Western countries, infidelity is cited as the primary cause of divorce in 25–50% of divorces, with approximately 50% of divorced men and women reporting that their former spouse had engaged in extramarital sex.

Other studies agree that infidelity is one of the most common reasons couples divorce and/or seek therapy (Atkins et al., 2005; Heintzelman et al., 2014), and that when marital dissatisfaction contributes to the affair, men's dissatisfaction centers more on sexual issues, whereas women's centers more on emotional ones. This may partially explain why women's affairs are generally more threatening to marriages (Brown, 2001).

As with divorce and sexual activity generally, historical and cultural influences have greatly shaped the incidence of, opportunities for, and attitudes about extramarital sexual activity (Brown, 2001). In many cultures, infidelity was grounds for vengeful murder, while prostitution or polygyny were normative. Currently, the Internet contributes to forms of "cheating" not previously possible (Nielsen, 2019a). While infidelity has become more common in the United States, it continues to be viewed almost universally as immoral.[1]

Many varieties

Affairs come in many varieties. Some involve habitual philandering; others are triggered by developmental challenges or by unmet or idiosyncratic sexual needs. Many are fueled by combinations of stressful life events and marital dissatisfaction. Alcohol and business travel often contribute (see Abrahamson et al., 2012, for a review of typologies). As noted by Leone (2013b):

> Like snowflakes—and people—no two affairs are just alike. Affairs differ in their causes, functions, meanings, and impact . . . . Affairs can be sexual but not emotional, emotional but not sexual, or both emotional and sexual. They can be motivated by a wish for sex, love, closeness, nurturance, or emotional intimacy; by the thrill of the chase, the thrill of being chased, or the thrill of living dangerously. They can involve anything from anonymous physical pleasure to the glorious "high" of infatuation or romantic love—the intoxicating experience of adoring and being adored, of oneness or merger, of feeling deeply understood and known without words. Affairs can be an expression of anger or a need for revenge, and/or an effort to enact and perhaps attempt to heal something important and unresolved from the past. They can reflect an effort to call attention to important relationship dysfunction or longstanding unmet needs.
>
> (p. 284)

We will discuss the many motivations behind affairs later in this chapter, together with the various emotional responses of betrayed partners, although virtually all betrayed partners feel deeply wounded.

Presentation and therapeutic challenges

Post-affair couple therapy is usually requested by the injured partner shortly after he or she has discovered the affair. The offending spouse usually comes expecting to be blamed and frequently views therapy as a necessary penance toward reinstatement into their partner's good graces. The partners usually come with divergent agendas: The cheater hopes for a speedy return to normalcy, the wronged partner for sufficient time and dialogue to heal and regain trust, if not to punish the partner, and sometimes to decide whether to leave the relationship. *The challenge for the therapist and the couple will be to manage the acute crisis, with its asymmetry, while exposing and attending to the underlying causes of the infidelity.* Because of the great variety of affairs, no two treatments will be identical, but most begin with a rocky start.

In the wake of an affair, other areas of married life and conflict between the couple—children, money, chores—become more difficult to work out. Problems that may have contributed to the affair continue and aggravate the partners' distress. Anger and withdrawal may be so intense that no workable connection exists. Positive interactions, including sexual activity, usually cease. Finances are strapped if the offender is asked to move out.

Couple therapy in the wake of extramarital affairs demands all the skills we use with standard-issue couples and then some. Specifically, we will be stretched to help partners recover from trauma, work toward forgiveness, and—sometimes—desist from violence or suicide. This is really the Major Leagues of couple therapy, a content area viewed by therapists as only less stressful than working with substance abusers or people who say they have never loved each other (Baucom, 2014). Here are some additional reasons why this therapy is so challenging:

- *Couples are more distressed than average.* In a study of 530 couples who received couple therapy, the 145 couples who reported infidelity were significantly more distressed and more depressed at the start than the 385 couples who sought therapy for other reasons (Atkins et al., 2010).
- *Divorce may be a real possibility.* Either partner may be highly ambivalent about continuing the marriage, and some may already have secretly decided to divorce.
- *Morality is a central issue.* More than in most therapies, issues of moral injustice and moral failing are central to, and sometimes in apparent conflict with, the goal of discovering causes. Here, we are not simply discussing different choices (whether to move to a new town) or minor offenses (what counts as being late or disorganized). Rather, major ethical issues concerning trust and fidelity are on the table.
- *Partner agendas and subjective experience are almost universally different.* Far more than in most couple therapies where partners must come to terms with differences, these couples generally bring divergent agendas and have great difficulty listening to each other talk about them. While both partners usually agree that the offender has violated a marital norm, they routinely disagree on the magnitude of the offense and, even more, on any possible benefits or extenuating circumstances. As noted by Perel (2017a, p. 10), "An affair is a story that is experienced by two (or more) people in completely different ways."
- *Partners' time frames are different.* Offended partners will require a long time to heal, while offenders generally wish to move on quickly. Discussions of affairs frequently provoke debates about how long to "talk about past injuries" (see Nielsen, 2016, pp. 113–114).
- *Because partner agendas, subjectivities, and time frames are so different, therapists will have more difficulty than usual maintaining a neutral position vis-à-vis the partners.*
- *Partners frequently fear that being open will make matters worse.* Both partners are on edge and distrustful, understandably not wanting to do more damage to the precarious marital bond or make themselves even more vulnerable. Even raging partners, who might seem to be the exception, are usually hiding more vulnerable feelings of shame and anxiety.

- *Offended partners risk feeling blamed once discussion moves to marital contributions to the affair.*
- *Offended partners are often reluctant to give up control of the moral high ground if they forgive their partners and move on.*
- *Offending partners risk giving further offense if they share their prior dissatisfactions.*
- *Affair partners may still be active and on the scene, and partners must decide how to handle this.*
- *Outsiders may be advising or pressuring partners to leave the marriage or seek revenge or, conversely, because of the stigma associated with affairs, partners may have no one other than their therapist who they trust to help them through this crisis.*
- *Therapists feel the pressure of time, lest the marriage end before the therapy gets off the ground.*
- *Most basically: While couple therapy often works by helping couples see that their partners aren't as bad as they think—we try to show them how their negative views derive, in large measure, from a combination of romantic expectations, poor communication skills, vicious circles, and negative expectations from childhood and prior relationships—in the context of affairs, such attempts to help partners to see each other more favorably are obstructed by the hard reality of the affair, an event that confirms the wounded partner's negative perceptions.*

Research on couple therapy after affairs

So how have therapists done under these challenging circumstances? Keeping in mind that affairs come in many varieties, research shows that most clients experience significant benefits from couple therapy (Atkins et al., 2010; Gordon et al., 2005; Kessel et al., 2007; Marin et al., 2014; Wiebe & Johnson, 2016). That said, divorce rates for such couples are still quite high: 43% at 5-year follow-up for couples who came to therapy to cope with affairs vs. 23% for couples who came for other issues (Marin et al., 2014). Importantly, the same study found divorce to be far higher, 80%, when clients did not disclose an affair. The good news from this study was that couples who stayed together after affairs did just as well as couples coming for other reasons, which included positive trajectories post-therapy, indicating lasting therapeutic impact.

A more recent review found somewhat better outcomes for Emotionally Focused Couple therapy (Wiebe & Johnson, 2016), in which issues of anger, distrust, sadness, and fear were engaged during "in-depth processing of the injury," that is, pain was shared and an emotionally engaged apology was made, such that 63% of 24 couples were able to resolve the injury, forgive their partner, and continue to improve in therapy. These positive results were sustained when assessed three years later. None of the couples who failed to resolve the injury made any changes from pre- to post-therapy.

Other studies confirm the importance of processing the injury and working toward forgiveness (Abrahamson et al., 2012; Greenberg, Warwar, &

Malcolm, 2010), while Abrahamson's in-depth study of couples who were still suffering two years after an affair found that the ability to forgive was assisted by motivation to maintain the relationship and by learning from contrary examples of others who had remained angry and unforgiving.

Overview of therapist tasks

Based on this research, the clinical literature, and my personal experience, we can identify the following important tasks for therapy with these challenging couples:

- *Help couples work toward acceptance, if not reconciliation, and possible forgiveness.*
- *Help couples distinguish between exploration of contributions and exoneration.* The couple must ultimately see that a real transgression—worthy of apologies and promises to change—has occurred and that it had its reasons. One partner has acted unilaterally, destroyed trust, and broken the vow of monogamy, but most such events happen in extenuating circumstances and for important reasons. We can say to the wronged partner, "Can you accept that when we explore the causes of your partner's unfaithfulness, we are not condoning that behavior?"
- *Help couples face contributions they find difficult to accept and avoid premature foreclosure of such discussions.*
- *Help couples manage their different time frames for recovering and moving on.*
- *Help couples make changes based on exploration of the offense and the prior state of the marriage.* Real change, not just forgiveness, can come only after they gain deeper insight into what drove the offender to misbehave.
- *When relevant, help couples decide whether to remain together and, if not, help them to separate amicably.*

Countertransference challenges

Managing countertransference feelings can be very tricky, as some therapists find it hard to suspend their moral condemnation of the cheating spouse, while others have difficulty witnessing the wronged partner's continued vengefulness and unwillingness to consider forgiveness or context. Therapists' own experiences with betrayal and affairs, including with their parents when they were children, may make it harder or, ideally, may help them comprehend the shock, distress, and obsessing of clients who have been injured.

When I find myself becoming moralistic or impatient, I consciously work against that tendency since it interferes with, among other things, the curiosity, compassion, and neutrality that are essential in this work. To empathize better with betrayers, I remind myself of Goldberg's (1999) advice that when working with any form of ethical or legal transgression, one must consciously strive to understand the upside of that behavior from the client's point of view. I often recall when that helped me with two clients of mine:

a financially secure med student who (seemingly needlessly) enjoyed stealing food from grocery stores and an unhappy husband who risked his reputation by exhibiting his genitals to unsuspecting women. Both therapies went well once we understood the pleasures involved, even though the behaviors seemed abhorrent, weird, and unethical to me. To engage and treat clients who act out or behave badly, it is essential to recognize the emotional benefits they derive, benefits that they will now have to forgo.

To empathize better with betrayed partners and not flee from the full vicarious experience of their pain, I remind myself of how I felt in several situations (not affairs) where I was shocked and injured by people who unexpectedly mistreated me behind my back and failed to be loyal when I thought I deserved better. I also remind myself of times when I was young and jilted, an event almost all of us have had to cope with, when I similarly became preoccupied with a relational injury and took a severe hit to my self-esteem. This helps considerably when I am suffering with a client who "just can't get over it," and I find myself wishing that they would "just move on."

Most therapists strongly prioritize honesty and will reflexively condemn the dishonesty of "cheaters," forgetting that dishonesty was a prerequisite for the affair. Therapists who place less value on the excitement of autonomous action and more on relational fidelity (most therapists) will likely see the offender more as a transgressor and will have more trouble comprehending the motivations behind the crime.

Dishonesty will be still harder to handle if the client has also lied to the therapist about an ongoing affair or other matters. (I was upset and more surprised than I should have been when a man who had lied to his wife for years about an ongoing affair lied to me several times, saying his check was in the mail!) After recovering from such insults to one's sense of fair play, therapists may ask themselves why the client resorted to lying and recall that young children do it all the time to avoid blame and that, in extremis, lying can be lifesaving (e.g., a Jew pretending to be a Catholic in Nazi Germany).

Not only do therapists treating disloyal clients have to cope with immorality and dishonesty, but we must cope with the high probability of divorce and the possible feeling of personal failure that may follow. Here, I remind myself that the goal when treating couples in the wake of serious betrayals is to help them understand and change themselves for the better, whether or not the marriage survives. Partners who stay married without changing will either repeat the offense or continue the unhappiness that preceded it. Partners who divorce without understanding or making personal changes risk future repetitions. Some partners will be happier after splitting up. Whether partners choose to divorce or not is their decision so that therapy should not be judged simplistically by whether the marriage continues.

Stages of recovery and therapy

All serious students of affairs see treatment progressing through stages, although the reality is messier and more recursive than that implies. Keeping these stages in mind is helpful to therapists *and* to clients, who benefit from having a map of this unfamiliar territory (Olson et al., 2002).

Spring (2004) identified three stages in the healing process after an affair comes to light. First, both partners need to *normalize their feelings*; second, they must *decide whether they want to recommit* to their relationship or terminate it; and third, if they decide to recommit to the relationship, they must *undertake the process of rebuilding it.* This last stage involves *ending the relationship with the third person, earning back trust, communicating pain, becoming sexually intimate again* if intimacy had been interrupted, and *forgiving* the person who had the affair.

In their intensive study of 13 individuals recovering from affairs, Olson and colleagues (2002) used the following evocative terms to characterize the stages: *roller coaster, moratorium,* and *trust building.* When things went well, there was an additional stage, as partners reported some unanticipated positive changes, including "developing a closer marital relationship, becoming more assertive, placing a higher value on family, taking better care of oneself, and realizing the importance of good marital communication" (p. 430).

Baucom and his associates (2009), who have spent more time researching couple therapy following extramarital affairs than almost anyone, divide the treatment into three stages: an *impact stage,* where the injured person is struggling to stay afloat emotionally and to comprehend what has happened; a *stage of exploration, re-narration, and possible forgiveness*; and a final *stage of deciding how to go forward, together or separately.*

Meneses and Greenberg (2011) proposed a more interactive, recursive model of stages and processes, as they studied the differences between four couples who recovered and four who did not. Their most important conclusion was that:

> The ability of the injuring partner to tolerate and respond to the injured partner's anger and pain is at the heart of the couples' forgiveness process. This ultimately involves the injurer nondefensively accepting responsibility for the pain caused and expressing shame or empathic distress for the harm done.
>
> (p. 498)

When this happened, they observed a *Shift in View of the Other,* as injured partners came to see the offender more sympathetically and three-dimensionally, surely an important stage to track. Sometimes, this shift occurred after the offender *Accepted Responsibility* (another stage), and other times, after the offender's *Expression of Shame or Apology.* In addition, two of the four *injured* partners in the resolved couples *Assumed Responsibility for their Role in the Relational Conditions That Led to the Emotional Injury.* Finally, two processes/stages were observed exclusively in the *unresolved* couples: the offender's *Pressure to Forgive* and *Competition of Hurts* (emphasizing the offender's distress and reasons for the affair).

Summarizing: After studying how couple therapy can help some couples heal after affairs, all authors highlight distinct stages, processes, and tasks, some of which must wait until others have been completed. All identify a crisis stage during which the focus is on the offended partner. In many cases, this "stage" recurs and colors ongoing therapy, as flashbacks and distrust can linger for years. Regarding sequencing, most agree that sincere apologies and work toward forgiveness must precede full exploration of causes.

Based on this research and my clinical experience, I will now discuss treatment recommendations organized around the stages of impact/crisis, forgiveness/apology, and deeper understanding/personal growth.

The impact/crisis stage

In the impact/crisis stage, the injured partner's emotions are usually quite dysregulated, with rapid oscillations between anger, anxiety, disbelief, and despair. As in other traumatic situations, clients experience disrupted sleep, episodic numbness, and intrusive thoughts and feelings triggered by events associated with the affair ("flashbacks"). Often, they find it hard to concentrate on anything else, as their minds are colonized by thoughts related to the injury.

Basic beliefs about the spouse, the marriage, and the world are questioned. The injured partner feels less safe in a world where prior assumptions about fidelity and monogamy have been upended. This leads to anxiety, depression, doubt, and distrust over and above the damage specific to the betrayal and the relationship. Most partners will question their own worth or attractiveness. Some clients will become severely depressed or suicidal, and others may act out vengefully, including by making disclosures to third parties. Rage is fueled by feelings of humiliation, abandonment, and powerlessness. These painful states of mind cycle unpredictably.

Doubts about the self, the partner, and life in general are usually worse when offended partners have had prior life traumas or disillusionments. Partners who told themselves that they would never tolerate cheating now find themselves less sure about what to do.

Offenders are also often quite upset for having violated their own moral standards, distressed about possibly losing the marriage and their children, and/or fearful of being ostracized by their friends, families, or coworkers. Frequently, they are angry that they are being cast as more evil than they feel is fair. Some are shocked by their partner's reactions, which can be uncharacteristically vengeful or violent. Some debate internally whether to leave the marriage and continue the affair. Those who have split off the affair as "no big deal" or "not really anything to do with the marriage" are now confronted with painful truths.

Initial assessment

Pretty much everything useful when assessing couples may be relevant, including whether they are living together; current life stresses and developmental challenges; the emotional state of the partners, including whether they have thoughts of harming themselves or others; and their goals for therapy, especially their thoughts about divorce versus wanting to work on the marriage.

We will want to learn details about the affair: whether it is ongoing, the situation with the affair partner, who else has been told about it, and any impact on the children. Beyond this, we will gradually be exploring the meanings of the infidelity for both parties and possible contributions from prior marital or individual difficulties. It will help to ask about religious and cultural norms. As in other situations, where couples come to us in crisis, a common mistake is getting caught up in issues of the moment without gaining an understanding of how they are shaped and fueled by the partners' prior experiences.

Violence toward offenders or affair partners as acts of revenge "to settle the score" is sometimes a danger, since infidelity is a leading cause of intimate partner violence (Nemeth et al., 2012).

As concerns prognosis and some suggested targets for therapy, Perel (2017a) describes magnifiers and buffers of affairs: Some magnifiers include circumstances like pregnancy, economic dependency, ill health, past family history of affairs or losses, and personal insecurity. Buffers include a strong network of friends, job and dating prospects, financial resources, self-esteem, and the quality of the relationship itself.

If other therapists are involved, it will help to contact them to get their take on the situation, to assess their opinions or biases about the affair and whether the relationship should continue, and to offer to collaborate going forward.

Crisis intervention

Therapists should employ crisis intervention skills useful in other acute traumatic situations, including helping clients to maintain basic self-care and essential role functioning. Medications to assist sleep, reduce daytime anxiety, and decrease ongoing depression can also be beneficial and should be considered.

In this crisis stage, therapists should convey that they have been here before and understand that this is a terribly traumatic rupture of the couple's relational bond. The overall goal is to slow things down, to offer hope, and to discourage impulsive actions. To establish and maintain a therapeutic alliance, therapists should make clear that the goal is not necessarily to keep the couple together, but to work through the crisis and, after that, to examine the situation in detail so the partners can make informed decisions about what to do next.

In most cases, we will need to control the emotional temperature in the room during therapy sessions by having clients talk through us or *use us to talk for them in ways that their partner can hear*, per Dan Wile's doubling technique (Wile, 2013; also, Nielsen, 2016, pp. 14–15, 98–99). However, if unfaithful partners can express remorse and sorrow directly to their spouses, they should certainly do so.

At this stage, therapists will often have to work to help clients down-regulate their anger. Teaching emotion regulation skills and timeouts is especially useful. While it is usually necessary to allow injured partners some time to vent their venom during sessions, therapists can also encourage couples to set times and time limits *outside* the therapy for reviewing events. If clients haven't done so already, therapists can help them institute additional behavioral measures to manage intense feelings. These include planning what to do when partners are triggered and giving access to device passwords and partner locations.

Setting boundaries

Couples coping with the aftermath of an affair must work out boundaries with others: the affair partner, friends, and relatives (especially children). Therapists can help couples negotiate the details. If the affair is over, it is helpful to communicate this clearly to the affair partner and for the couple to clarify what interactions will be allowed should the two former lovers meet—at work or out-and-about in the community. To be clear about what the couple has agreed to, it can help to compose a letter from both partners to the affair partner, informing him or her that the affair is over, that the couple is committed to working in couple therapy, and that contact, unless required by work or other compelling circumstances, is over. Composing such a letter must balance the injured partner's wishes for verbal retaliation with the offending partner's desire not to further injure the affair partner who is now being rejected. As in other situations where revenge seems attractive, therapists can point out potential negative consequences: for instance, an offender may not be willing to send a too-hurtful letter or to enforce the boundaries it demands, and a narcissistically injured affair partner may become a loose cannon. Some couples will choose to have the offender read this letter to the affair partner over the phone, in a call witnessed by the offended spouse.

Couples will also want to discuss which of their friends and relations, if any, they will tell about the affair. Even when decisions on this are unilateral, it's best if each knows whom the other has told. Partners must balance their need for emotional support with the long-term damage to reputations and relationships that can occur when others know of the transgression. Friends and family may be too ready to encourage divorce and, as a colleague of mine cautions, "Even if *you* forgive your partner, *your mother* never will!" Because many clients intuit such problems or are inhibited by their shame from discussing the affair with others, sessions with an empathic, helpful therapist become even more crucial for maintaining client wellbeing. Journaling can also help to meet the need to reflect on the affair.

Children—including adult children—should be protected from the fallout of affairs, especially from being asked to take sides. Therapists should discourage clients from seeking alliances with their children by telling them about the "cheating." If clients don't know this already, we can warn them that mishandling the affair can cause lasting harm to their children (Ablow et al., 2009; Platt et al., 2008).

Hearing the story of the affair while placing limits on fact finding

Many injured partners understandably want to hear all the facts of the affair, including where it took place and what sexual acts were performed. Sometimes, it will help the victim to hear the "whole story" of the affair from the offender, so that he or she is not left to imagine that the offense was worse than it was or to anticipate additional damaging revelations in the future. Reviewing the transgression may also enable the therapist to uncover mitigating circumstances that had not been mentioned previously. Sometimes, hearing all the gory details seems to be a test of whether the offender will tell the whole truth now as a guarantor of future honesty. Other times, it is more an act of revenge, as the offender is forced to "fess up" in front of the therapist.

The danger of such interrogations is that they will unearth facts that make it harder for the injured party to put the affair in the past. More facts usually mean more triggers for post-traumatic stress. When witnessing such cross-examinations, I point out that investigating the underlying psychology in depth is far more important than learning what sexual acts took place and where the cheaters hung out. Nonetheless, some such grilling usually seems necessary, and so I go along for a time.

Obsessing/ruminating/understanding the injury

Offended partners almost always ruminate and obsess over the issues just mentioned, repeatedly asking themselves and their partner questions that, at bottom, demand to know, "Why did *you* do this to *me*?"

> Obsession takes the form of endless ruminating about the affair, asking the spouse thousands of questions, looking for answers, trying to "understand." It includes questioning, blaming, and attacking the straying partner . . . It may be loud and noisy, but it is a search for rational answers in hopes of avoiding the pain, fear, and powerlessness that come with betrayal . . . . In addition to avoiding the deep pain stemming from the affair, obsession functions as a way of avoiding issues and emotions that the couple hasn't been willing to face earlier in the marriage, and that the spouse still doesn't want to address.
>
> (Brown, 2001, p. 87)

As in the wake of other traumatic life events, therapists must listen empathically, allow obsessing to continue for a while, and then attempt to explore idiosyncratic personal meanings that emerge. Obsessions should be viewed as combinations of vengeful attacks, defensive simplifications, and fears concerning the future that need to be challenged and gradually modified, such as "I'll never trust anyone ever again" or "It's all my fault; I don't deserve to be loved." Such extremes of blaming the other or the self are familiar to us from many other situations that we treat.

As described earlier, therapist countertransference enters here, as some therapists may believe that the incessant blaming is justified, while most of us, like friends and family, will become worn out if it goes on month after month. As Brown (2001) writes, "It is just plain difficult to deal with obsessions. The tenacity of the betrayed spouse, the veiled nastiness and the repetitiveness of obsession [make it] . . . easy to get annoyed or feel sick and tired of listening" (p. 86). This is true not simply because of repetition, but because we know that, in the long run, "Obsession with the affair is the betrayed spouse's biggest enemy" (p. 90), since prolonged obsessing routinely leaves clients endlessly bitter and often alone in the role of lifelong victims.

Potential fears underlie and are hidden by such obsessing. For many women, it is that they have been found wanting as wives; for many men, it is not so much that they have failed as husbands, as that their "manhood" is insufficient. For those whose marriage has been a defense against fears of inadequacy or separation, those exposed nerves are touched.

It generally helps to view the intense anger as a "secondary emotion," per Emotion Focused Therapy (Greenberg & Goldman, 2008), and to uncover the underlying hurt and anxiety that are primary. When this anger includes wishes for revenge, it will still help to encourage wounded partners to say, "I am so angry at you!" rather than "You are a lowdown rotten excuse for a human being!"

Perhaps more than Emily Brown, Esther Perel (2017a) seems less in a rush to get rid of obsessions like "I don't know my partner anymore!" or "I should have seen it coming!" or "I must be terribly flawed," as she channels the offended person's need to ask such questions to consideration of more meaningful ones. Noting that *detective questions* about sordid details often prove self-destructive (as just discussed), she encourages offended partners to ask *investigative questions* about reasons behind the affair, since the latter need to be asked and answered. She adds that sometimes the former conceal the latter, as when "What kind of sex did you have?" is a stand-in for "Don't you like the sex we have?" Table 12.1 lists some potentially productive questions from Perel's *Infidelity Resource Guide* (2017b), which therapists can use to steer the exploration phase of therapy.

Offended partners will obsess less as a function of the therapeutic interventions that will become possible during later stages of the treatment.

Self-help resources

The following self-help resources can aid clients during the crisis stage, including by normalizing their situation and by giving them hope:

- Spring, J. A. (2004). *How can I forgive you?* New York: HarperCollins Publishers. Very sensible and possibly the best seller in the field.
- Chapman, G., & Thomas, J. (2006). *The five languages of apology: How to experience healing in all your relationships.* Chicago, IL: Northfield Publishing. Excellent recommendations on apologies.

Table 12.1 Meaningful Questions About Affairs

- What did you discover about yourself in that relationship? How did you feel about it?
- Did you discover new parts of yourself or recover lost ones in that relationship?
- Why do you think you could not express your needs to me—emotional, intellectual, or physical?
- Do you think you could show me those newly discovered parts?
- Are there parts of you that you want to bring into our relationship?
- Was your lover someone you thought you could build a life with?
- How important was sex?
- Did your affair have anything to do with something missing in our sex life?
- Were you drawn by the general idea of having an affair, or did you feel pulled toward this specific person?
- Are you sure that you want to be with me?
- Did you come back to me or to our family?
- What would be your biggest loss in the life we have built if we get divorced?

Source: Adapted from Esther Perel's *Infidelity Resource Guide* (2017b).

- Perel, E. (2017a). *The state of affairs: Rethinking infidelity.* New York: HarperCollins. Explores the depth psychology of both offenders and offended.
- Perel, E. (2017b). *Infidelity Resource Guide.* https://thestateofaffairs. estherperel.com/infidelity-resource-guide/. Includes great questions for clients to think about.
- Weiner-Davis, M. (2017). *Healing from infidelity.* Woodstock, IL: Michele Weiner-Davis Training Corporation. Separate chapters for offended and offending partners offer much sage advice that can help stabilize marriages, while also covering situations where affairs are continuing or divorce is likely. Weiner-Davis's advice makes up the lion's share of my Table 12.2, which offers specific behavioral advice to clients.

Trust

Trust is often the most momentous casualty of interpersonal betrayals, and its loss presents itself prominently in ruminations during the crisis stage. What was previously assumed to be safe—a spouse working late or going on a business trip—now arouses fears of a repeat offense. The trustworthiness and loving concern of the partner can no longer be taken for granted. If victims didn't see it coming, this will stir self-doubt, as well as doubt about others. And if offenders have previously accused the victim of being unduly suspicious or insecure, it will be still harder for victims to let down their guard. Restoring trust can begin in the crisis stage and continue in subsequent stages, often for many years, and may be the last component of a restored relational bond.

After reviewing possible definitions of trust, Gottman (2011) concluded that *trust includes the idea that one can depend on another in the face of limited information.* When your partner says she is having dinner with a friend, you shouldn't need to hire a private detective to corroborate her assertion.

Table 12.2 Practical Suggestions for Clients Coping with an Affair

For injured partners
- Spend more time together.
- Do not share anything about the affair with friends and family, only with a very trusted friend, if that.
- During the crisis stage, focus on self-care by setting simple daily behavioral tasks that can bring some satisfaction (e.g., "I will make myself a nourishing meal for dinner" or "I will make a plan to get together with a friend").
- When talking about the affair to your partner, express anger, but don't be intentionally hurtful. While your spouse needs to know how hurt and angry you feel, it isn't helpful for you to shame him or her or to become verbally abusive.
- Curtail marathon talk sessions (aside from therapy); instead, schedule time-limited affair talks.
- Notice what helps and share that information with your partner.
- Try to identify what needs to change in the marriage and what might make it better. What behaviors need to change to make this happen? What's lacking? Try asking for what you think your partner can do that will make things better. What has your spouse requested in the past that you didn't deem important at the time? How well have you each been at showing love in the other's "love language"?
- Continue to work toward forgiveness, something that will become easier as the quality of the marriage improves and need not precede other changes to the relationship.

For offenders
- End the affair soon if you really want to work on the marriage. While this may be hard to do, do so definitively so that you send a clear message to the affair partner.
- Spend time with your spouse.
- Tell the truth about what happened all at once, not in pieces over time; additional withholding or lying will make things worse.
- Be aware that expressing shame and guilt is good since it shows you have a conscience.
- Apologize and show remorse by sharing your feelings, rather than hiding them. If repeated, heartfelt apologies don't work, ask your partner what specifically you might do to make them feel you are truly sorry.
- Show empathy for how your partner is feeling.
- Evaluate what might improve your marriage, not just for yourself, but for both of you.
- Identify triggers that tempt you toward a replay or return to the affair. These will help you identify what needs improving in yourself and your marriage. They also point to danger situations to avoid (e.g., dinner alone with coworkers).
- Work toward mourning and self-forgiveness.

Source: Many of these are from Weiner-Davis, M. (2017). *Healing From Infidelity.* Woodstock, IL: Michele Weiner-Davis Training Corporation.

However, when fundamental trust can no longer be assumed, we begin to see spouses becoming, if not hiring, private detectives, as they assess the veracity of many things that would previously have gone unquestioned.

Distrust will make couple therapy more difficult, as each person retreats to positions of greater safety. Restoring trust will be made still more challenging for couples previously deficient in sharing their feelings and negotiating conflict.

To deal with distrust, we must label it as foundational to the relationship problem and affirm that it cannot be restored quickly. A painful fact of post-affair life is that restoring trust will take a long time. In the interim, therapists can help partners discuss supportive actions to help the injured partner feel safer (e.g., allowing access to the offender's cell phone). To facilitate such discussions and to make the subject of trust more concrete and less global, injured partners can be asked to complete sentences of the form: "I trust you to . . . ," "I trust you with . . . ," "I don't trust you to . . . ," "I don't trust you with . . . ," and "I have some but not full trust regarding . . ." (Baucom et al., 2009, pp. 321–322).

While restoration of trust can be aided by offenders allowing victims to check on their emails, texts, and whereabouts, Baucom cautions that such scrutiny can become counterproductive; at a certain point, he encourages victims to try to go without it. This amounts to response prevention therapy and will also help offenders feel less resentful and controlled.

My experience, in keeping with Greenberg's (2008, 2010) research, is that what is most helpful is hearing offenders discuss their shame, their guilt, and their wishes to restore, protect, and prioritize the relationship. This sharing of dispositions may have limited restorative power, however, if it resembles prior lying or gaslighting. Beyond sincere, repeated apologies, acts of sacrifice and generosity will count a lot. Trust must be earned. It will take time and behavioral evidence for it to return to pre-offense levels; in many cases, it never returns completely.

The forgiveness/apology stage

The crisis stage is usually followed by work on forgiveness, which is what can most help to get the crisis under control (e.g., Kimmes & Durtschi, 2016).[2] Deep understanding of reasons and causes will usually have to wait until after the matter of guilt and responsibility has been worked on and temporarily settled. That said, the reality is that there is a blending, inter-dependence, and recursiveness to these stages of crisis, forgiveness, under-standing, and future planning.

The psychology of forgiveness

Forgiveness is often poorly or simplistically understood by both clients and clinicians. Many clients begin by thinking that they "should" forgive, but after noticing that they "just can't," they give up on the idea. Both therapists and clients must understand that forgiveness is a complex psychological expe-rience, which—if it is to occur—requires time and work. They also must realize that the goal is not to "forgive and forget." Forgetting is simply not possible. Rather, forgiveness requires one to let go of a grievance about a still-remembered event. Such letting go is often frightening, as it can threaten the injured partner's conceptions of equity, safety, trust, and identity. Forgiving is far less like forgetting and more like giving up one's right to call in a debt.

By bestowing forgiveness, one shows mercy, absolving the perpetrator from living under the cloud of his or her transgression. Forgiveness can also be "a gift the forgiver gives him or herself," as one chooses personal happiness going forward over remaining mired in a state of injured self-righteousness.

Forgiveness, then, amounts to a "motivational transformation that inclines people to inhibit relationship-destructive responses and to behave constructively toward someone who has behaved destructively toward them" which depends on offenders expressing "affective empathy" (McCullough et al., 1997, p. 321). Gordon and Baucom (1998), in their foundational review of the forgiveness literature, offered a similar but slightly more extensive definition: "Forgiveness is conceptualized as attaining: (a) a realistic, nondistorted, balanced view of the relationship; (b) a release from being controlled by negative affect toward the participating partner; and (c) a lessened desire to punish the participating partner" (p. 425).

While forgiveness always includes letting go of the grievance, differing levels of empathy, reconciliation, and trust may be achieved. Forgiveness does not universally lead to healing the relationship or to reconciliation. Some partners will do well to acknowledge the irreparable damage and seek divorce. Others will develop empathy for the wrong-doer and continue the relationship. Whether to let down one's guard and allow trust to return will be a central question for betrayed partners who wish to get past an affair.

After reviewing the writings of experts in the field and comparing them with my own clinical experience, I find it useful to distinguish the following states, with each adding an element missing from the one prior: unforgiveness, acceptance (adding letting go of the grievance and the desire for revenge), forgiveness (adding understanding and empathy), and forgiveness with reconciliation (adding the continuation of the relationship).[3]

As described in my discussion of the crisis stage, unforgiveness is a painful state characterized by rumination on the offense and grave doubts about the partner, oneself, and life in general. Offended partners are emotionally stuck and unable to get on with their lives. This state of obsessive unforgiveness exists in relation to various complementary states in the perpetrator-spouse. These range from deep regret to defensive denial and include varying amounts of shame, guilt, suppressed anger, fears for the relationship, strong wishes that the partner move on, and doubts that the transgression will ever be forgiven.

Helping couples move past this state of distressing unforgiveness is not easy. In describing what can help, I will first discuss the situation from the perspective of the injured partner in isolation. For him or her, it is like mourning other traumatic life events and often requires clearing away constraints that inhibit moving on. I will then consider the role and psychology of the perpetrator in hindering or facilitating movement toward forgiveness.

Some injured partners forgive too easily, fearful of losing the relationship or facing their own deep hurt or because of characterological doubts about their personal value (Akhtar, 2002; Spring, 2004; Summers, 1999). This amounts to defensively sweeping the damage under the rug. The drawbacks of this strategy are that the defense will prove inadequate to suppress painful feelings, that the offense may recur, or that the relationship will continue to weaken. These injured partners may come for therapy years after the affair, either when their marital bond feels strong enough to allow discussion or when the hurt has grown unbearable.

More commonly, the process of getting beyond the injury becomes stalled in an openly unforgiving, ruminative state. As with other traumas in life (a tornado destroying a home, a reckless driver killing a child), the traumas of marriage (a husband hitting his wife, a wife cheating on her husband) will have both universal and individually determined significance for the victim. The therapist's task will be to facilitate discussions of the trauma while conveying empathy for the obvious losses involved, curiosity about idiosyncratic meanings, skepticism concerning simplistic accounts, and hope in the face of the client's pessimism about recovery.

Shame and revenge

In his article, "Unbearable shame, splitting, and forgiveness in the resolution of vengefulness," the psychoanalyst Melvin Lansky (2007) argues convincingly that unacceptable shame defended by hostile wishes to "get even" explains much of the stuckness of the unforgiving state of mind. Lansky notes how clients are held captive by their efforts to save face. As he sees it,

> [The vengeful state] offers intrapsychic defensive advantages—moral justification, firmness of purpose, and unquestioned certainty—when they effect reversals of disorganized, humiliated, and uncertain states of mind . . . . These defensive advantages, however, are costly ones. The certainty that is crystallized in the sense of being aggrieved, of being the recipient of injustice, being damaged by that injustice, and being entitled to justice seems in the mind of the vengeful person to override the practical, legal, and ethical considerations of doing harm, not just to the presumed offender or betrayer, but to the larger community and its standards.
>
> (pp. 573–574)

The therapist's task here should be clear: Free clients from their largely unconscious beliefs that they have been irretrievably shamed by their spouses so that they can let go of their defensive reversals, including their desire for vengeance.

A little bit of vengeance helps the grievance go down

Salman Akhtar (2002) suggests that clients are assisted in moving from vengefulness to forgiveness by small amounts of enacted revenge during the recovery phase, as perpetrators are called out for what they have done. Quoting Heinrich Heine, who in 1848 said, "One must, it is true, forgive one's enemies—but not before they have been hanged!'', Akhtar notes that experiencing the guilty pleasure of revenge, even in fantasy, helps victims move off their holier-than-thou stance and lay the groundwork for future empathy with the perpetrator.

Are we blaming the victim?

A problem arises, since Lansky's approach appears radically different from those who assert that forgiveness therapy must begin with all parties—the offending spouse, the offended spouse, and the therapist—agreeing unequivocally that the perpetrator has committed an injurious, morally reprehensible act (e.g., Enright & Fitzgibbons, 2000). Shouldn't we worry that focusing on the victim's shame or exaggerated "grievance story" (Luskin, 2002) amounts to "blaming the victim" for his or her continued suffering? How do we reconcile these two views?

Consider the case of a husband cheating on his wife with a younger colleague from work. This is an unacceptable offense and must be understood as such. When we look more deeply, however, we may find that for the wife to forgive, she will have to admit that it was not so much this one-time act of sex outside their marriage that stung, but the blow to her core sense of lovability on learning that her husband seemed to prefer someone else. Perhaps she has been wondering for some time whether she has been neglecting him emotionally, not just sexually, and that she is partly to blame for his dalliance. As we shall see shortly, this attack on her self-esteem should also be the subject of her husband's heartfelt apology, if he later becomes capable of giving one. Unless we access this woman's shame, we may remain stuck alongside her in her morally accurate, but psychologically superficial, account of events. In this and other situations, underlying shame is hidden from view, "drowned out by the blaring fanfare of the avenger's innocent victimhood" (Rosen, 2007, p. 603), but it must be accessed to allow mourning and authentic forgiveness to occur.

This necessity was confirmed in a recent study of EFT couple therapy in situations requiring forgiveness (Zuccarini et al., 2013), which found that *for couples to move past the angry surface of expressed hurt and defensive withdrawal, victims had to uncover and express the deeper personal meanings of the injury, often ones involving attachment insecurity.* Therapists must then take a dialectical view of the situation—that a serious "marital crime" has been committed *and* that we must investigate the psychology of the victim—if clients are to move toward acceptance and, possibly, forgiveness.

Therapists treating clients who have been betrayed will need to help them expose the shame the betrayal evoked and assist them in realizing that the shame is not fatal. *Forgiveness will include, perhaps surprisingly, a measure of forgiveness of the self.* As Lansky (2007) puts it, "Forgiveness in the depth-psychological sense here employed centers around the notion that the underlying shame, felt previously to be unbearable, has been unconsciously reassessed and is now felt to have become bearable" (p. 591).

Complexity and responsibility

Once their undue shame is exposed and re-evaluated, victims may become free to look for still more complexity in the narrative. This "reconsideration of the story" (Akhtar, 2002) is central to most conceptions of how people recover from trauma: Although victims cannot change the past, they can change how they view it in the present. In the new version, victim and perpetrator are more three-dimensional characters, their actions not so obviously black and white, the outcomes not so demoralizingly disastrous, and the victim more willing to separate the actor from the act. Now free of undue shame, victims can accept greater responsibility for the events leading to their injury (e.g., the wife who has been cheated on may admit that her prior verbal attacks on her husband's manhood had touched a nerve). Victims may become less self-righteous and more empathic toward offenders, a shift shown to correlate with later reconciliation in the relationship (studies cited in Greenberg et al., 2008).

Empathy for the offender will often also involve a re-owning of projected negative self-states, so that the offending "other" is no longer seen as so despicably "not-me," a person undeserving of understanding and forgiveness. In working toward this, injured clients often become aware of their own aggressiveness or hurtfulness, which allows them to accept it in their offending partners. They may also recall times when they sought to be forgiven. Forgiveness will likewise be facilitated when the victim recalls the good qualities and actions of the perpetrator, qualities and actions that may become more evident as the vengeful, obsessive state loosens its grip on the injured person's mind. Recalling good times from the couple's history and the potential benefits of a shared future can also help loosen the hold of the unforgiving state.

In some re-narrations, however, offenders may be seen as *more* responsible than previously. Victims may then blame themselves less and find it easier to reach out to friends and family; some will become less inclined to reconcile with their offenders.

Distrust and the power of the one-up position

Distinct from unconscious shame blocking forgiveness, victims may cling to the moral superiority of unforgiveness because it gives them control over their partner, now placed in the humbled, one-down role of supplicant on probation. Indeed, one core benefit of continuing to define oneself as victimized is having (or imagining one has) greater power over the previously out-of-control offender. In my experience, partners wish above all to control the attentiveness of offenders who had previously been neglectful and preoccupied outside the relationship. Victims may reap other benefits, as well—such as control over family decisions and resources—that may be hard to give up and may inhibit movement toward forgiveness. As long as the offense is still on the table and court is in session, the offender must sit attentively, maintaining good behavior, in the dock. The art of therapy includes helping victimized clients see that this can become counterproductive, as it generates resentment in their spouses. Simultaneously, therapists can help clients acknowledge when offenders remain attentive even after being freed from the holding cell of the offense.

Misconceptions about forgiveness

Some victims remain stuck in the victim role due to common misconceptions about what it would mean if they were more forgiving. Offended partners may see themselves as "weak" or "pushovers," whereas forgiving in the service of restoring a marriage actually requires emotional strength. It can help to point out that forgiveness does not require that the victim see things (only) from the perspective of the perpetrator. And it does not mean forgetting or condoning the injurious act or obligating one to forgo justice from the courts or restitution from the perpetrator (when the offense merits it). Nor does it determine whether one reconciles and continues the relationship. All of these depend, also, on the behavior of the offender. Absent the offender's expression of remorse and promises to reform, the best that can be expected of victims is "acceptance" of the offense.[4]

As with other behaviors influenced by circular causation, the capacity of victims to rewrite their grievance stories and let go of the moral high ground will depend powerfully on the offender's narrative and behavior, our next topic.

Forgiveness as transaction: the importance of witnessing

Genuine forgiveness that progresses beyond acceptance toward reconciliation is co-created and requires an interpersonal process in which the betrayal is discussed, and trust and attachment are restored (Macintosh et al., 2007). Forgiveness and renewed trust must be earned. Janice Spring (2004) gives an example of a wife who explained this to her husband:

> Shortly after he admitted his affair, he told her, "I'll never do it again, and I don't want to talk about it—or your grievances—anymore. It's ancient history." Jane's response cut to her bottom line: "If you don't want to hear my pain, I can't get close to you. I'm not trying to punish or manipulate you. I'm just telling you what I need to forgive you."
>
> (p. 123)

For healing to proceed, perpetrators must validate victims' experiences by listening carefully as they tell their stories. As Frommer (2005) puts it,

> Somehow, their recognition of the ways in which they have altered us feels crucial to our being able to do the intrapsychic work that might lead to our forgiving them . . . . Under this relational conception of

forgiveness, it is an error to conceive of the capacity to forgive in exclusively intrapsychic terms.

(pp. 36–37)

Note that some therapists (see, especially, Michael White, 2007) make witnessing central to *all* their couple therapy, not just to therapy following major betrayals. Much of the healing power of the work of Dan Wile, Sue Johnson, and others also derives from the impact of partners truly witnessing their spouses' stories.

Apologies

It is reasonable to expect that, after listening to the victim's account of the offense, the perpetrator will express remorse and convincingly promise to do better. This is a prerequisite to the injured partner's canceling the debt and regaining trust. Unsurprisingly, many studies have found that sincere apologies make forgiveness more likely (studies cited in Bradbury & Karney, 2010; Fife et al., 2013; Greenberg et al., 2010; Lewis et al., 2015; McCullough et al., 2000; Worthington & Wade, 1999). This research, clinical wisdom, and my personal experience suggest that optimal apologies should include the following elements:

- Offenders must take responsibility for the damage and must say, "This is what I did to you."
- In the early stages, offenders must not qualify their statements by attributing responsibility to the victim ("You hurt me, too!" or "You get hurt too easily!").
- Offenders must express regret and demonstrate a detailed awareness of what damage was done, including damage to trust ("I made you distrust me and our marriage.") and self-worth ("I made you doubt your value, not only to me, but to anyone.").
- Offenders must go beyond a simple confession ("I admit that I did this to you.") or a pro forma script (like those of public figures doing damage control). They must include convincing expressions of regret, concern, and empathic distress over their actions.
- Offenders must convey shame and guilt (personal self-criticism) about the offense.[5]
- Offenders must be patient and may have to repeat their apologies many times.
- Offenders must take an interest in understanding themselves, including how they came to wrong their partners and how they justified their actions to themselves.
- Offenders must promise not to repeat the offense. An optimal apology will include repentance, which includes not only remorse, but a promise not to repeat, combined with promises to do things to make

recurrence less likely (for affairs, this may include breaking off connection to the affair partner and reducing temptations to relapse). What makes repeated affairs so damaging and subsequent apologies so hard to accept is that the offenders have usually promised not to do it again, but have done so, nonetheless.

* Offenders must *ask* rather than *demand* forgiveness. Recall that "Pressure to Forgive" has been shown to impede forgiveness and reconciliation (Greenberg et al., 2010).

Repair beyond apologies

Students of forgiveness have identified additional actions that offenders can perform to facilitate forgiveness, including:

* *Acts of atonement and restitution.* While heartfelt apologies are crucial, concrete actions also help to undo damage. Some misdeeds immediately suggest appropriate corrective actions, but offenders can promote repair by soliciting suggestions: "What can I do that will help you heal?" "What can I do to show you that I still care about and love you?" "Is there anything I can do to make up for what I have done?"
* *Acts that reassure the partner that the offense will not recur.* In the case of an affair, the offender might change his or her phone number, formally end the relationship (perhaps in the presence of the partner), or change jobs, so as not to be around the former lover.
* *Acts that protect the partner from post-traumatic experiences.* Because the injured partner lives in a post-traumatic state, vulnerable to hurt and doubt, a truly remorseful offender should be aware of potential triggers and take responsibility for keeping them to a minimum. Examples include checking in more frequently without complaint, storing credit card and cell phone records in an accessible place, and generally looking out for the other protectively, in what Spring (2004) calls a "transfer of vigilance."

Homework letters

Should apologies and acts of atonement remain insufficient, *homework letters* may help clients communicate in a less triggering format. In their treatment study, Greenberg and colleagues (2010) had partners write letters to each other, which appeared to facilitate healing. Offenders wrote letters of apology that included: (a) *regret:* saying what they regretted and detailing their understanding of how they had hurt their partners, (b) *responsibility:* taking ownership of their role in the injury by specifying what they were taking responsibility for, and (c) *remedy:* articulating what they would do to help their partner heal.

Injured partners wrote letters describing where they were in the process of resolving, forgiving, and letting go of the hurt and anger toward their partners. They were to describe what they did not forgive or were not able to let go of, why it was difficult for them to resolve the injury, and what they needed from their partners to help them relinquish the hurt and anger so they could forgive. If they had already let go of the hurt and anger or had forgiven their partner, they were to write about whether they felt they were able to reconcile.

Impediments to apologizing

Not all offenders find it easy to apologize fully, and many victims make it difficult. Extreme artfulness is required of therapists as we try to work toward apologies while gradually interweaving exploration of causes. Almost always, we will face divergent accounts of events. Specifically, as noted by Baucom et al. (2009):

> Although infidelity seems to lend itself to the identification of a clear "victim" and "perpetrator," partners who participate in an affair may harbor their own resentments, hurts, or experiences of betrayal at the hands of the injured partner. Consequently, the participating partner may not be as contrite as the "victim" or therapist might expect, and this apparent lack of remorse may complicate therapy. Alternatively, the participating partner may have tolerated the injured partner's anger or abuse for so long that he or she finally refuses to offer further apology or restitutions.
>
> (p. 5)

Injured partners often make it harder for offenders to sincerely and convincingly apologize by endlessly pursuing details of the affair, by refusing to relinquish the pleasure of retaliation (it's hard to show remorse when a partner is insulting your integrity), by avoiding discussing an aspect of the affair that touches a core insecurity (e.g., sexual performance), or by invoking moral convictions that place affairs outside the pale and disallow exploration of reasons. All such constraints can become the focus of therapeutic attention.

Helping offenders in the forgiveness stage

Therapists can assist (willing) offenders by encouraging actions that are both morally virtuous and pragmatically efficacious—witnessing, apologizing, and performing acts of atonement and care—but often, we must do more than encourage such actions. Just as offended partners require assistance to move from unforgiveness to acceptance and possible forgiveness, so offenders will usually need our help before they can act unconflictedly to repair their relationships.

We should not assume that offenders are 100% on board with the repair agenda: Some will become so, some will apologize but will not wish to reconcile, and some will remain unrepentant. Their authentic choice will usually become clear only after their psychological concerns, including what they imagine forgiving to entail, are explored.

Shame and guilt

Somewhat paradoxically, the shame and guilt that offenders feel about their hurtful actions often interfere with their acts of contrition. We commonly see offenders sitting almost frozen, apparently unremorseful, as they listen to their spouses berating them for their actions. Often, they resemble children waiting for the reprimand to end rather than adults genuinely sorry for the hurt they have caused. Just as some clients are unable to tolerate sexual or aggressive feelings, many clients strive mightily to suppress or deny what, for them, is the extreme pain of self-criticism evoked by criticism from a loved one. Terrified of feeling their own badness or defectiveness, such clients may defensively flee or bizarrely assert their innocence.

One client's wife discovered his infidelity with several prostitutes after she developed a sexually transmitted illness. The couple came to therapy to deal with this betrayal and the many lies he had told to hide it from her. Anticipating that therapy would involve being shamed, and that this was the price he had to pay to avoid divorce, this man would begin most sessions with his head bowed, sheepishly soliciting punishment, saying, "OK, let's get this over with. Let me have it!" His wife often doubted the sincerity of his remorse—thinking him simply a narcissist who had been caught and herself the patsy listening to more of his lies (now, about his contrition)—but it turned out that this rush to penance was an attempt to avoid facing his crushing shame and guilt. A shame-prone person all his life, he dreaded the prospect of his wife berating him for the behavior that he himself saw as unforgivable. Gradually, in the safety of my office, he became less preoccupied with his shame and guilt long enough to use those feelings to express his genuine regret that he had wounded his wife and risked destroying the family he treasured.

In other cases, offending spouses initially imply that their only mistake was getting caught, maintaining that their partner is overly critical and that no significant damage was done. As was found in the South Africa Reconciliation hearings (Gobodo-Madikizela, 2008), such perpetrators are often able to commit their offenses by shielding themselves from identifying with their victims. As therapists help offenders to listen empathically, this defensive denial may collapse and allow heartfelt shame and guilt to emerge.

Clients who fear shame and guilt will be helped by therapists who reassure them that they are not the first to have sinned in this way and help them uncover mitigating circumstances and unmet needs that will allow a softening of their moralistic self-reproach. These people can be helped to overcome their beliefs that they do not deserve to be forgiven, that there is no way to heal the pain they have caused, and that their reprehensible actions make them unremittingly bad.

While many clients will come to feel genuine remorse, some will continue to minimize the damage they have done. Some non-sociopathic perpetrators whose split-off transgressive actions (such as serial affairs) remain ego-syntonic can benefit from intensive individual psychotherapy that focuses on the unconscious payoffs of their secret pleasures (Goldberg, 1999).

Fear of being one-down

Many offenders fear accepting responsibility for their transgressions because they believe that they will then be consenting to a perpetual one-down position in their relationship. As they see it, if they admit to the full measure of their crimes in the courtroom of couple therapy, they are handing their partner a "morality trump card" that can be used against them indefinitely (Ringstrom, 2014). The opposite is more often the case: Contrition will get offenders *out* of the marital doghouse and allow their marriages to recover.

Childhood experiences with forgiveness and apology

We can sometimes better understand clients' difficulty apologizing by asking about earlier experiences that impede apologizing, including (a) never having witnessed sincere apologies and forgiveness, so that they are unfamiliar with the process and the benefits; (b) having witnessed incessant fighting over who is to blame, so that admitting responsibility seems to invite disaster; (c) having witnessed repeated, insincere apologies ("I promise I'll never hit you again"), so that apologies appear meaningless; or (d) having been compelled to offer bogus apologies or grant false forgiveness ("Tell your sister you're sorry," or "You have to forgive me, because I won't be able to stop crying unless you do."), so that apologizing seems traumatically inauthentic.

Mutual and complex causation

A final, important impediment to offenders' apologizing is their belief that forgiveness means accepting *all* the blame and agreeing that their transgression is the *only* problem in the marriage. Apologizing for wrongdoing is made more difficult because, as research and clinical practice show, "victims often fail to acknowledge mitigating circumstances and their own contributions to the problem" (Baumeister et al., 1998, p. 85).

The betrayer's emotional needs

Betrayers will also be helped to apologize and repair to the extent that they feel the therapy is also about them. Therapists need to let betrayers know that eventually they will be able to tell their story, to be understood as not solely reprehensible, and to make their case that they can be trusted and let back into the fold. A complication here is that betrayers are frequently the ones whose needs were *not* being met in some important way in the marriage, but now they are being asked to wait still longer while their partner's needs, including for revenge and nurture, are front and center. Sensitive therapists will let them know that their time will come (as discussed in the next section) and, sometimes, will empathize with the specific hardships they may face in repairing the relationship (e.g., mourning the loss of the affair partner, repeatedly checking in with distrustful partners, being shamed by outsiders).

The stage of deeper understanding and personal growth

As the partners settle down, it becomes possible to explore antecedent events leading to the affair. Research confirms the benefits of this important step (Greenberg et al., 2010). Discussion and understanding are required if couples are to heal via genuine forgiveness, commit to avoid a recurrence, and (ideally) strengthen their marriage.

As with lesser offenses requiring repair, as partners approach each other and soften, each may be better able to acknowledge his or her contributions, in a process that becomes progressively more honest and revealing, and this may serve as a basis for making important changes in the marriage (Wile, 1993). Ultimately, some victims will acknowledge that they have been accomplices to the crime and then, continuing this metaphor, the partners work together toward crime prevention.

The initial goal of this stage is to jointly co-create a (usually) less traumatic narration than the "more negative, malicious, and often simplistic explanations often generated [earlier], such as 'You did this just to destroy me,' or 'I now realize you are a total liar and always have been'" (Baucom et al., 2009, p. 17). The couple must try to get past a totally contemptuous view of the offender's character. They must also avoid simplistic explanations from offenders, like "I just outgrew my (less evolved) partner and finally found my soulmate," that conceal important dynamics and appear in tandem with spouses who characterize offenders as irreparably immature or narcissistic. Getting past contempt and simplification will help couples reconnect. And re-narration will make life feel more predictable and controllable, since prediction can only come from understanding and control from altering causes.

In working out a diagnostic explanation of the affair, it helps to determine how much the affair was predominantly about sexual pleasure, opportunity, and reduced inhibition—as per Shirley Glass (1998, 2003), whose research found a frequent profile of sex between two late-working, inebriated co-workers; or to what extent it developed from deeper problems in the marital sexual relationship and/or in the partners' intimate support of each other; or whether it stemmed more from some unmet individual need in the offender. We want to know whether the affair is a "symptom" or a more superficial misstep. We should not assume that an affair is always a "systems" or marital issue, since 50% of men and 33% of women assert that their marriage was *not* the issue (Baucom, 2014)—although, in most of couples I have seen *who come for therapy*, that has turned out to be true.

Sorting this out can be complicated by the impact of the affair on the marriage. While not all affairs are due to marital problems, virtually all *create* marital crises, and these crises usually make partners appear more dysfunctional and less connected than they were prior to the affair.

It is easy to see how affairs can grow from the soil of chronic marital conflict. It is less obvious that affairs may emerge when the soon-to-be injured party has become deeply involved or preoccupied elsewhere, leaving their partner to find intimate connection outside the marriage. Such non-marital involvement can be as prosaic as excessive work, involvement with children, or assistance to other family members. Other forms of marital disengagement are less prosocial, including maladaptive "addictions," such as Internet gaming, TV sports watching, or casino gambling. Sometimes, spouses are involuntarily out of commission because of depression, a serious mental disorder, or physical illness. Usually, the soon-to-be-cheating partner's complaints about such absences have been minimized or have not been voiced loudly enough. Sometimes, both partners contribute to the absence of connection that grows insidiously without comment, perhaps because both believe it to be necessitated by role obligations (say, in dual-career marriages with young children).

Some affairs aim to supply other experiences that seem to be missing in the marriage (excitement, satisfying sex, or greater affirmation), while allowing the cheater to continue to reap some of the benefits of marriage (economic security, contact with children, social standing). Some nonparticipating partners collude in this, for instance, if they wish to avoid marital sex, dismissing evidence of the affair so as to maintain the benefits they also derive. Some such arrangements may "save a marriage" and allow it to continue, just as a wife's girlfriends or close family members sometimes stabilize couples by filling in for missing emotional support in the marriage. This was common in past centuries, when sexual satisfaction in marriage was assumed to be inadequate and men were viewed as understandably sexually frustrated. While some such arrangements may be stable compromises, the main problem is that they can suck intimacy out of the marriage, while risking distress and divorce should they come to light.[6]

Other affairs are better seen as flights from the rigors, inevitable challenges, or standard disappointments of marriage (see Finkel, 2014), such that the affair functions as a "vacation from marriage." Affair partners will be seen (usually erroneously) as superior for sex, fun, and understanding—qualities that are impossible to compare fairly when one is not sharing daily stresses presented by finances, home maintenance, and child-rearing. This will be more likely for those men who have trouble seeing their wives as sexual partners (per the Madonna–whore complex) or for those women who have trouble feeling sexual when in the role of wife or mother.[7] Others may flee what feels like excessive control/intrusion from their partners by attaching to affair partners whose demands are easier to keep at bay.[8] Those who conduct long-standing or serial affairs may be seeking affirmation through sex or be running from the vulnerability of dependency on a single partner.

The following condensed example from David Scharff (2014a) of an imagined affair illustrates the potential psychological complexity of affairs, as well as their adverse consequences for a marriage:

Throughout her marriage, Mrs. Thomas nursed a fantasy of love for a high school teacher she felt would always have been her ideal mate, never sharing this fantasy with her husband. Then, in community theatre, she met a man who fit the same mold. In her unspoken fantasy love affair, he unconsciously represented the exciting but dangerous man of her dreams who would never look at her in real life. These secret fantasies formed a wall against a close relationship with her unexciting, reliable husband whom she had chosen precisely because he did not represent the danger inherent in sexual excitement. She had been the apple of her father's eye, a man who had many affairs that denigrated her mother. In her fantasy affair, she triumphed over her defeated mother through being desirable. At the same time, by not living out an affair, she protected herself from the internally dangerous, sexual man. The secret distance from her husband had much the same effect as an actual affair.

(p. 257)

Scharff's example illustrates how a flight from marital intimacy to affairs can create an illusion of superior satisfaction elsewhere, reduce the potential pleasure of the marriage, and, as a result, perpetuate the inaccurate belief that the marriage is deficient.

As is well known, many affairs grow out of existential crises or a lack of zest for life—as in a "midlife crisis"—which may or may not derive from marital dissatisfaction and which may occur at any life stage, not just in midlife.[9] Such crises can be precipitated by awareness of aging, by illness, by the death of a friend or family member, by a career setback or success, or by some other life transition that makes clear that one's time on the planet is limited.[10] Perel (2017a) tells us, "The one theme that I hear above all else from those who have bitten into the forbidden apple is this: It makes them feel alive" (p. 173). And, as in many of the sexual fantasies discussed in an earlier chapter, some exhilaration can come from the transgressive nature of an affair, from the excitement of breaking the rules or coloring outside the lines, especially "for those who have lived responsible, dutiful, committed lives" (Perel, 2017a, p. 162).

Affairs in these circumstances can be seen as compromises—a way to hold onto the safety and stability of the marriage while experiencing the exuberance and novelty of an affair. In such cases, therapists can point out that the offending partner was not so much seeking a new *partner* as a new *self* and suggest working on how this might be achieved in some less damaging way.

After contributing influences have been assessed, therapy can proceed in many directions depending on the specifics but always toward examining values, deep existential worries, changed life circumstances, and issues of involvement and commitment. In cases where the marriage continues, the affair may ultimately be seen as a painful catalyst to re-evaluating the marriage and making plans for a better future.

Managing discussions of causes

In her discussion of Esther Perel's work, work that excels in exploring the dynamics of betrayal, Zoë Heller (2017) identifies the primary challenge we face when we set out to explore causes:

> In practice, it must be said, her method seems to demand heroic levels of forbearance on the part of faithful spouses. They are asked not only to forgo the presumption of their own moral superiority but to consider and empathize with what has been meaningful, liberating, or joyous about their partners' adulterous experiences. The affair that has caused them so much anguish may have been prompted by boredom or a longing for sexual variety, or it may have been a bid for existential "growth, exploration, and transformation." It's hard to imagine anyone being gladdened by the news that his or her spouse's adultery was an Odyssean quest for self-discovery.
>
> (p. 104)

Keeping this in mind, the main way to "sell" and frame discussions of the causes of cheating is by explaining that, as with many other life calamities, this is the only sure way to gain confidence that it won't happen again. As previously mentioned, a fundamental challenge is that such discussions may seem like blaming the victim. To avoid this, therapists should make clear that while certain things *contributed* to the affair, that is not to say that they *caused* it, since offenders could have found alternative, less hurtful ways to deal with their emotional needs. It may also help to explain that offenders may themselves not fully understand their motivations and that exploring contributions can thus pave the way to better solutions.

Having set the stage, therapists can proceed—as we do with other "home remedies" or "attempted solutions that cause problems," like drinking or gambling—to inquire how offenders experienced the affair, how it made them feel, and "how much the affair stemmed from something missing in your marriage—and how much from something missing inside you" (Leone, 2013b, p. 285). If Perel's questions in Table 12.1 have not yet been asked, therapists can ask some of them now (e.g., "Did you discover new parts of yourself or recover lost ones in that relationship?").

Additional complexities

Monogamy

Because sex outside committed relationships is so popular but creates so much havoc, especially in contemporary America, some authors have questioned whether the expectation of monogamous marriage isn't part of the problem (Perel, 2017a; Scheinkman, 2005). Noting greater acceptance of clandestine sex in other countries, they wonder whether mature people might not be more accepting, as in, "I hate that he steps out. I also hate that he leaves his socks on the floor." At bottom, this poses the question of whether couples can safely decouple sex from marital intimacy and trust. The answer would seem to be that some can, and some can't.

Men seem to be more capable of doing this. Studies cited in Green et al. (2016) confirm that (on average) men decouple sex from emotional attachment more than women and find that many gay male relationships can gravitate toward non-monogamy without negative consequences. Green et al.'s own interview study of straight, gay, and lesbian married Canadian couples found that most nonheterosexual couples view monogamy as something to be worked out on a case-by-case basis; only about half of the heterosexual couples saw it that way. Lest you think that lots of Canadians are OK with extramarital sex, however, these same heterosexual couples who had said that *in theory* it could be worked out almost universally said that monogamy was essential for them.

My experience, in cases of both straight and gay men (see the case example at the end of this chapter), is that infidelity in a partner can range from catastrophically upsetting (think O. J. Simpson) to almost a given. What makes the difference is whether the nonparticipating partner views sex with an outsider as threatening to the couple bond. Some think they won't mind but then do; others think they can't live with it but then come to accept it as the price of an otherwise satisfying marriage. While some famous couples have asserted that non-monogamy could work, only to find out otherwise (e.g., Alfred Kinsey; George and Nena O'Neill, the authors of *Open Marriage*), others seem to have done fine with "arrangements" (Lyndon Johnson, whose wife reportedly vetted his liaisons), if they were kept out of the public eye. Current interest in polyamory and consensual non-monogamy is beyond the scope of this chapter, but the consensus seems to be that some people can set up satisfactory, agreed-upon rules for extramarital sex (see LaSala, 2013). My experience in this area is limited, but I have treated gay couples who have been content with non-monogamy and straight couples who have tacitly accepted sex outside the marriage when partners differed greatly in age or when one was ill or otherwise disabled.

Ongoing affairs (secret or not)

Not all affairs are over or known about when therapy begins. Research (Korelitz, 1982; Baucom et al., 2009) and my own experience suggest that couple therapy is less effective, if not impossible, when an affair is ongoing, especially if it is unknown to the therapist (Marin et al., 2014).[11] This is mainly because ongoing affairs draw energy away from working on a shaky marriage and because no spouse can compete with an invisible affair partner.

I give each partner a chance to tell me about secret, ongoing affairs in the individual meeting I routinely have at the beginning of therapy. Without such meetings and their promise of confidentiality, clients may conceal important data. To manage such situations where confidentiality is a serious concern, I recommend the following:

Tell couples at the beginning of therapy that what is discussed in individual sessions is explicitly not the job of the therapist to share. The therapist may encourage sharing or exploring the pros and cons of sharing but won't be the one to do it.

Help secret-holders discuss their ambivalence about ending the affair. Regardless of how misguided the affair may seem to you—or to the secret-holder—try hard to discover its appeal. In one recent case, it was not so much that the affair partner was so beautiful or captivating, but that the affair led the husband to stop working so much and, instead, spend more time exploring new places in the city! The more traumatized or barren the childhood of offenders and the more they feel that their needs have never been met, the harder it can be for them to relinquish the benefits of the affair. All the motives discussed previously that power affairs can make them hard to give up.

If necessary, challenge the mistaken belief that the client can continue the affair while simultaneously working on the marriage or, worse, that he or she can continue the status quo by compartmentalizing the affair—Tony Soprano-like—without an adverse impact on the marriage.

Suggest that secret-holders put the affair on hold for a specified period during which they will put all their energy into improving the marriage. I usually suggest three months.

Help secret-holders understand the potential problems of nondisclosure and the potential benefits of sharing the secret. Be clear that nondisclosure may make things unworkable in the future when the truth comes out. Discuss these pros and cons for a relatively limited time since the clock is running for both of you.

Do not let countertransference disapproval of the person having the secret affair interfere with allowing that person to work on their feelings and plans in a nonjudgmental atmosphere. Remind yourself of times when you have had trouble being fully honest or decisive.

If clients decide to disclose the secret, help them plan how and when, and offer to help them do so in a therapy session.

Should the client prove unwilling to disclose the affair, refer both partners to individual therapists or, my preference, shift to "discernment counseling" (Doherty et al., 2016), as described in the next chapter on treating couples who are ambivalent about continuing their marriages. Delay and further reflection in individual sessions are often wiser than they might seem, including to therapists eager to move on to working on the marriage. I have seen individuals who took a year or more to decide on a course of action, sometimes returning with heightened commitment to their marriage, sometimes leaving with heightened certainty that this was what they truly desired (whether or not they stayed with the affair partner). Remember that our attempts to move things along quickly—by having the partner either disclose the secret or put the affair on hold—require the person conducting the undisclosed affair to quickly resolve ambivalence that may be intense. When this is not possible, we need to bow to reality and suggest a Plan B.

In making such a shift away from couple therapy (to Plan B), some experts recommend stating that the therapist has become aware of "some information" that makes it impossible to continue with couple therapy (e.g., Weeks et al., 2005) or that they have learned that the spouse is unwilling to continue for "reasons" that the partner is free to inquire about (Dimidjian et al., 2008). These options attempt to finesse the danger of the unaware client later holding the therapist responsible for not sharing the existence of an affair while honoring the pledge of confidentiality to the secret-holder. My method when recommending Plan B does not so obviously telegraph the presence of an affair. Rather than alluding to "some information" or "reasons," I simply note the secret-holder's extreme ambivalence about the marriage as my reason for recommending a different format better suited to that situation.

If I sense the presence of an undisclosed affair in an ongoing therapy, I will press a bit in a conjoint session for disclosure, but, failing that, will suggest individual sessions "to assess how things are going with each of you in private." This allows me to ask directly about an affair and to proceed one way or the other depending on what I hear.

Dealing with "the other woman" and ending affairs

Breaking up is (famously) hard to do. It will usually be painful for offenders, whether or not they are ambivalent about ending the affair. Perel (2017a), in a sensitive chapter on the psychology of affair partners, writes, "The other woman needs to be treated as a human being. . . . If the affair needs to be ended so the marriage can survive, it should be done with care and respect" (p. 251). To help these injured people, as well as guilty offenders, to accept the breakup, she frames it as an act of love, rather than a simple rejection, as "setting the affair partner free" to pursue other relationships.

Remarking that third parties in love triangles often present to us for individual treatment, David Scharff (2014a) adds insights about their psychology and points to positive developments for couples who end relationships with them sensitively:

> From the standpoint of the marriage, we see this person as the recipient of projections, a repository of split-off unconscious issues in the marriage. But as individual therapists, we see "other women" as patients. Many are drawn to unavailable partners for unconscious reasons that come from all developmental levels—issues of insecurity, needing to avoid feeling trapped or engulfed in a fully available relationship, and oedipal attraction to a parental object . . . . For many, the relationships result in a developmental dead end for which they seek our help . . . . *As we help [couples] toward an empathic yet dispassionate stance in relation to the third party, we also help them develop a capacity for concern and reparation towards each other.*
>
> (p. 260; italics added)

Divorcing couples

Most of this chapter has been about helping couples to forgive, apologize, and reconcile, but these may not always be possible or desirable. Some spouses will be so deeply wounded that they will be unwilling to continue the relationship. Some partners will reveal themselves to be unable to give up serial affairs or unwilling to break up with affair partners. In such cases, therapists need to shift gears and help the couple to disengage and accept the dissolution of their union. Sometimes, the partners will be able to maintain amicable contact, especially if they have children, but in other cases, hostility will remain. In these situations, even though full forgiveness and reconnection will not be achieved, it is still useful to work toward the lesser goal of acceptance.

Should the couple decide to separate, it helps if they do not use facts from the affair to retaliate or coerce the other person going forward, for instance, by telling children or coworkers about it. Keeping the painful secret private will be more difficult when they have decided to end the marriage and attempt to explain the divorce to family and friends, or if one behaves badly going forward, say, in the divorce proceedings. Nonetheless, therapists can again help the couple to discuss whom they will or won't tell. We will examine the topic of divorcing couples more fully in Chapter 14.

Unreasonable (neurotic) fears of an affair

Sometimes, one spouse is preoccupied about the existence of an ongoing affair, but the therapist is fairly confident that no secret sexual activity is happening. This is common in the wake of an actual infidelity or when jealousy has been present previously. In such situations, falsely accused spouses usually become defensive, angry, and withdrawn, all of which aggravate the complainant, as this creates even more emotional distance.

While I have been burned on occasion, falsely believing that nothing was afoot, I have found it useful to think of such complaints as akin to hypochondriasis: an inaccurate concretization of a real emotional problem. As with the hypochondriac who complains of a heart attack when the real problem is anxiety about aging, it helps to assess the facts independently (in that case, with an EKG) before assuming a concretized misrepresentation of a subjective truth. With a person complaining of an affair, assessment will include hearing the accused convincingly deny the affair to me *in private*—although some clients will lie even in that safer setting.

While some biologically based psychotic disorders can present this way, more often attachment insecurity is the basis for this complaint, with insecurity often aggravated by actual events (e.g., a husband now working late with an attractive assistant). The situation is improved by first helping the distancing spouse appreciate the subjective emotional truth behind their partner's false complaint. The couple can then be helped—in the ways that usually help pursuer–distancer couples—to heal the rift in their attachment bond (see Nielsen, 2016, pp. 63–69).

Therapy beyond the affair

Couples who move through the forgiveness and understanding phases of therapy and remain committed to each other may continue in conjoint therapy, now focusing on recurring negative interaction cycles or other specific areas of conflict. As Perel (2018) tells clients, this is an opportunity to "re-pair" and to experience the benefit of "feeling chosen by someone who has a choice."

When there has been recovery from an extramarital affair, therapists and spouses will need to pay special attention to the couple's sex life. And some partners may benefit from individual therapy aimed at addressing their propensities to act out.

Many couples who present with a serious betrayal turn out to have been emotionally distant from each other, leading parallel lives prior to the signal event. This distance is often what encouraged the acting out and what allowed it to remain secret. In helping these couples work toward greater happiness, trust, and stability, we must encourage them to increase their shared positive activities (see Nielsen, 2016, Chapter 14). They should be encouraged to get out together and to cultivate shared hobbies, friends, and community activities in the service of restoring a sense of companionship and togetherness. These experiences will help carry the couple beyond witnessing and apologizing to further healing and strengthening of their couple bond. Greater closeness and more fun together can also neutralize the distrust that can return when they are apart.

Never over and done

Therapists and clients must not hold overly idealized views of the forgiveness/recovery process, especially the belief that healing can take place once and for all. Serious betrayals are never forgotten. The best we can hope for is that they will be remembered in less painful, more complex ways. As Frommer (2005) points out:

> The state of forgiveness that we long for—free from residual anger, resentment, or ambivalence—is an ideal. In real life, forgiving often coexists with resurgences of doubt, bitterness, hurt, and the painful feeling that the relationship has been inextricably altered by what has happened. We forgive as best we can, which is to say, imperfectly.
>
> (p. 44)

As Greenberg's (2008, 2010) research has confirmed, even when there is considerable movement toward forgiveness, trust returns more slowly. In this regard, therapists should try to normalize this reality and attempt to immunize clients against undue disappointment when things do not progress as quickly as they wish. As pointed out by Macintosh et al. (2007), there is more to reconciliation after an affair than forgiveness. Rather, it is better to conceive of the goals as attachment security and mutual commitment, destinations that require both time and positive bonding experiences.

Therapists should also be on guard for couples who appear to have resolved their hurt but are mostly avoiding reopening a wound that continues to fester. We must use our judgment to decide when to revisit the subject and when to allow a respite from the intensity of reviewing the betrayal. I have erred in both directions. Sometimes, I have pressed too hard in this work when a break and discussion of other subjects might have been more productive, and sometimes, when I thought we were done and on the verge of ending a successful therapy, I have been surprised by a sudden resurgence of anger and defensiveness, showing that the old wounds were still raw and needed more attention.

A tale of two cases

Having already presented an extensive case of marital infidelity in the chapter on sexual problems and another chapter-length one elsewhere (Nielsen, 2019a), I've chosen to present and contrast two cases here: one where I succeeded (the couple moved beyond forgiveness and learned from the infidelity) and one where I failed (the couple remained stuck in an unforgiven stalemate). After presenting the cases, I will reflect on what made the difference.

Alan and Steven: A speedy recovery

Alan and Steven were a 30-something gay couple, married for two years, together for five, who came after Alan confessed—with considerable guilt—to several instances of sex with strangers in his gym's steam room, an offense made worse because he had contracted a sexual infection that he had transmitted to Steven. Although both had had helpful individual therapy previously, this was their first couple therapy experience.

Before their first session, Alan had expressed not only sincere shame and guilt, taking responsibility for his infidelities together with his strong admiration and love of Steven and his considerable fear that Steven might leave him because of this reprehensible behavior. Without much hesitation, Steven accepted Alan's apology. The incident had not so much shaken his moral compass (he could understand the temptation) as it had intensified his fear that Alan might prefer someone else. But because Alan's reassurance was so convincing, we were able to view some of this insecurity as unfounded, rooted in Steven's own self-criticism, with some stemming from his recent weight gain in the context of increased job stress. The conversation then turned to discussing problems in their relationship and sex life that might have contributed to Alan's lapse to infidelity.

This was the first serious, ongoing relationship for either man, and they both very much admired, appreciated, and loved each other. Both had been closeted until college, and both were delighted that they had found lifelong partners and were able to marry, something they had never dreamed possible. Alan's family was supportive of their union, and Steven felt at home with them. Steven had had a disruptive childhood: His parents fought frequently; his mother drank too much (eventually dying young from alcoholism); and his parents divorced when he was in high school, a trauma that he recovered from by working hard in school and, later, in his career. The couple had many interests in common: Both thought of themselves as "nerds who enjoyed videogames," loved their dog, and were planning, after COVID, to use a surrogate to start a family.

The sexual infidelity had an understandably jarring effect on their forward movement, but it also pushed them to discuss aspects of their relationship and sex life that they had been afraid to talk about, for fear of disrupting this oasis of happiness that they had found together. Having witnessed many fights between his parents, Steven, especially, was a serious conflict avoider.

Asking Alan what was exciting about the cheating proved a good beginning for our discussions of their more basic issues. Like many couples, Alan and Steven were somewhat shy about discussing sex. Some of this was due to their internalized homophobia and having come out quite late compared to their peers. But they had also shut down after a distressing incident during a Paris vacation when, at Steven's suggestion, they had visited a gay sex establishment and had been "grossed out" by events there, something they tacitly decided not to talk about again. But quite obviously, now was the time, with my help and encouragement, to revisit their sex life.

Alan confessed that what was exciting in the steam room was that he was the one pursued, the one who was the object of desire, the one who had only to sit still and allow himself to be jerked off by another man. This contrasted greatly with his usual roles at work, where he supervised a large team of engineers, and at home—in the marriage and in bed, where Alan almost always took the lead. In bed, the couple had gravitated, without discussion, into roles where Alan was always "dominant," including penetrating Steven for anal sex. More than either had previously registered or discussed, Alan wasn't always happy with this role: He often worried about maintaining his erection, used Viagra to help him "perform," and sometimes secretly wished he could take a more passive role.

Taking the lead in their relationship grew partly out of his being somewhat more secure and accomplished (he was taller, fitter, and made more money in a more prestigious job), which supported Steven's idealization of him. Steven's dependent relating was also maintained by his willingness to have Alan, who had grown up in more privileged surroundings, show him "how things were done" (e.g., in high-end restaurants and on their trip to Paris when Alan proposed, something both recalled with great fondness).

The upshot of Alan's steam room infidelity was that the couple, with my help, revisited their preferences in bed: What helped most was Steven telling Alan that he was happy to "take the lead" more often during sex; that overall, he was quite sexually satisfied; and that it didn't bother him if sex wasn't always perfect—thus reducing Alan's need to escape to steam room sex.

As the infidelity receded into the background, the men were able to discuss and support each other in other activities that bonded them—moving to a new condo in the middle of the pandemic (they proudly gave me a tour in one Zoom meeting), acquiring a puppy (a trial-run for a baby), and discussing Steven's stressful pandemic-related job. (Steven experienced Alan's non-directive support here as like "the mother I never had.") Equally important, the couple became explicitly aware of the dangers of avoiding conflict and of an unbalanced process in which Alan did too much of the work, the patterns that led to the steam room cheating. Instead, their collaborative process became more balanced, and their happiness grew.

Despite beginning with a major shock to the marriage, this therapy moved faster than most to a satisfactory conclusion after only ten sessions spread over four months.

David and Rebecca: A couple stuck in unforgiveness

By contrast, the following therapy ended recently, only slightly improved after 30 sessions spread over a year. It began in the wake of 72-year-old Rebecca's once more discovering a long-term, secret romantic (nonsexual) texting correspondence between her 79-year-old husband, David, and his former high school sweetheart (now widowed). The couple had been married 50 years and had two married children and one grandchild who lived far away. They presented in crisis with Rebecca obsessing about David's infidelity, thinking again of suicide, unable to sleep, and waking her guilty husband at night to beat him with her fists.

The couple had met when both were young and full of hope. She was a beauty (she showed me photos) who looked up to him as a dashing officer in their Israeli army unit. Both had traumatic past histories related to the Holocaust: David had been left with a Catholic family in Europe when his Jewish parents fled to Israel during the war. He was reunited with them in post-war Israel, growing up with a powerhouse, academically successful mother who never seemed satisfied with him (as he would later experience Rebecca), and who dominated his father. His father escaped to affairs (as David did later), which led to many scenes witnessed by David, including one in which his mother threw his father's belongings out a third-story window. Among other things, he became a lifelong conflict avoider, fleeing home to play with friends (a precursor of his later affairs).

When Rebecca was 4, her parents fled, with her, from Germany to Israel with barely the clothes on their backs. Impoverished and depressed, her parents neglected their daughter who, naturally shy and self-conscious, turned to books and art as solitary pursuits. As a result, from childhood on, Rebecca doubted others' reliability and loyalty. She had few friends and sometimes cut people out of her life when she felt slighted by them.

At age 18, she met and felt "rescued" by David, a calm, handsome officer, whom she idealized. After they married and moved to the United States, she gave up her artistic calling to raise their children, while he devoted himself to the successful career that made him famous. They met each other's needs, as she idolized and cared for him (unlike his mother) and as that devotion kept him happily invested in her and their family (unlike her parents). Their marriage seemed happy enough to her, even as she accepted that his obsessive personal style, which led to success in his work, meant that he would never talk to her in the romantic way she longed for. Receiving praise and given autonomy at work helped David accept Rebecca's sharp tongue and efforts to control him at home.

Late in life, they faced serious setbacks and disappointments reminiscent of their childhood years. They "lost" their children (their shared joy), who married and moved away. Both had major surgeries: She had cancer and knee replacements that interfered with mobility and caused her to gain weight, and he had prostate surgery that ended his sex life 12 years prior to their coming for therapy. Rebecca developed day/night reversal, which sleep therapy had not alleviated. The couple felt as though they lived in different time zones, as Rebecca soothed herself, as she had in childhood, by reading through the night. Equally important, after relocating to a new city with the promise of revitalizing an academic department, David was pushed out by a rival and forced into an unwanted semi-retirement. Unsurprisingly, it was during this time when she was often physically out of commission, that Rebecca discovered the first of David's two secret infidelities—romantic texting with a former classmate from his happy graduate school days.

Rebecca's jealousy of any friendly contact by David with other women had been a bone of contention throughout their marriage, but this secret connection threw Rebecca into a deep depression, which ultimately required electroconvulsive therapy. That David knew how devastated she had become before and yet went ahead a second time, in the same way, seemed unforgivable: How could he not realize this endangered her mental health?! David's repeated, sheepish response was that what Rebecca didn't know couldn't harm her, and, pretty obviously, he had been successfully concealing this second relationship for many years. Why couldn't she see it as he did, something harmless that was invigorating for him, like having a secret pen pal?

When she discovered his texts, Rebecca was especially disturbed to find out (a) that David had used terms of endearment with his "pen pal" that (they both agreed) he had rarely, if ever, used with her; and (b) that he had continued contact with this "whore" during trips Rebecca had planned for the family, and (c) that he had shared family photos and the autobiography he was writing with her. To Rebecca, these seemed unforgiveable acts, the meaning of which I tried to explore as I empathized with her disillusionment and pain.

Rebecca felt that her happy past was now all a fraud, no longer something she could draw on for succor in her final years. She described herself, in the journaling I suggested, as a puppet, playing the naïve wife, only a servant/manager for everyday life at home, while every day you bid your darling whore goodbye. My heart is sinking every time I think of the charade you played with me, in the next room of our house and in all the places we vacationed.

She felt some shame and self-doubt, mostly about having been trusting, but these feelings were minimized and fleeting. When David tried to explain his pleasure in texting with a woman who, unlike Rebecca, was *only* positive toward him, she replied, "It was not my fault! I had some crazy moments, but they related to everyday minutiae." She saw herself as a victim whose entire life was now fake, "prostituted to a simple, fucking whore who deserves a bullet." She lost all respect for David, "a spineless, weak person," deriding the "tremendous pride" she had felt for "his bright mind and achievements and, above all, for the almost symbiotic love between us." She was now

a different person with bitter emotions. I am so sorry to have become what I am today, to live like this, without a solution, at my age. There are days when despair for our future is so great that I want to cease being.

Reading this now, I can better forgive myself for not helping Rebecca get past this state of angry despair. Such "pain of a lifetime" might be too much for anyone to forgive. It may also explain why they remained together, David continuing in the role of ineffectual supplicant and neither of them able to cut what she called their symbiotic tie.

Rather than describing the therapy in detail, I will just enumerate what I tried. Above all, I tried, at first, to uncover the details of her pain and to empathize. When I grew tired of her incessant one-sided characterizations, I worked hard to keep in mind times when I had been betrayed, especially one time when I felt I had furthered a colleague's career, as Rebecca had. Later, I disclosed some of the details of my betrayal, which helped our alliance but didn't convince Rebecca that I knew how to help her move toward acceptance.

Most of all, I tried to help David apologize in a way that was detailed and convincing, conveying his understanding of Rebecca and his ongoing commitment. He said the words but the process in the room—with Rebecca loudly, incessantly attacking him—made his apologies seem lame and half-hearted. As I put it to them, "It's hard to convey sorrow and love when your partner is throwing bricks at your head." I worked to identify her "language of apology" (Chapman & Thomas, 2006) and assigned that so-titled self-help book. (Neither of them read it.) Outside the office, some of David's efforts to win her over (using words of endearment, bringing her flowers) helped, but mostly they proved insufficient to reduce Rebecca's anger, sometimes because they were done unromantically (e.g., when he gave her flowers and wanted credit for how many there were).

When David couldn't convince Rebecca of his attachment, I spoke for him (bringing tears to his eyes), telling her how he admired her, couldn't imagine losing her, and wanted her to see his texts as nothing more than an unreal fantasy escape. But Rebecca wouldn't accept my "flowers" either. And when I tried to recast his texting as a "home remedy" for the depression he felt due to his career collapse, or to explain the appeal of his texting relationships "to women who, unlike his mother, had not forgotten him," this did nothing for her, though at times she conceded that her defenses were "like the Mossad protecting me from additional pain."

I sought help from their individual therapist-psychiatrists and consultation from my own consultation group. Anti-anxiety medication helped her sleep, but antidepressants did little. When I referred Rebecca to a Jewish therapist, who I believed might be better able to break the logjam, Rebecca rejected this sensitive therapist almost on sight during their first meeting. I attempted to examine the steps in their vulnerability cycle, to show how, in a milder form, it had been the bane of the marriage previously; to link it to the past traumas and character defenses described previously; and to show how a similar pattern occurred with me (e.g., she criticized my English), but none of these interventions helped much, notwithstanding that they both seemed to respect me and what I had to say.

Rebecca's thoughts of suicide receded, and there were transient ceasefires and some good times together, especially when they visited their children or attended concerts. And she reported one hopeful dream: While on a hike in Israel, they were attacked by wolves. David protected her, and they recaptured some of their happy youth. Despite the wishful dream, the unforgiven state continued to haunt them.

Stymied, I asked Rebecca what her goals were for therapy and mentioned that forgiveness might be "a gift you give yourself," but this was too intellectual for her, as she claimed no control over her emotions. She just wanted me to make them less painful and "joked" about a woman who wouldn't get divorced because she preferred to make her husband suffer. Indeed, during the therapy, she had scared David with a suicidal gesture, pummeled him at night, destroyed his laptop, showed his texts to their children, and summoned the police, claiming falsely that he had locked her in her bedroom.

At times, David debated whether to move out to interrupt Rebecca's continuing punishment, but it seemed that his guilt and lifelong attachment wouldn't allow that. After a break during the pandemic, they tried two more sessions with me and, experiencing no change, called it quits.

Lessons from these cases

I've included these two contrasting cases to illustrate the extremes of this work and to convey some humility in the face of certain life tragedies. Table 12.3 compares the cases and suggests a multivariate explanation for why one case did so well and the other remained stuck.

Like some physical injuries, some marriages after infidelity can't be healed. Recall the study cited previously, which found that 43% of couples facing

Table 12.3 Comparing the Cases

	Alan & Steven	David & Rebecca
Outcome	Improved relationship	Stuck in unforgiveness
Description of the Event		
Actual sexual contact	Yes	No
Brief vs. extended "cheating"	Brief (two episodes)	Extended (six years)
Repeated	No	Yes, with a second partner
Prior experience of infidelity	None	Yes, devastating
Discussion of the Event		
Confessed vs. discovered	Confessed	Discovered
Apology	Strong, immediate	Weak, minimized
Acts of atonement	Considerable	Some, but qualified
Relationship Prior to Discovery		
Trajectory of relationship	Ascending	Stagnant, declining
Relationship tone	Positive, supportive	Adversarial, distant
Stress	Moderate for offended	Severe for both
Default relationship process	Offender took lead; both avoided conflict	Offended dominated; offender avoided conflict
Time spent together just prior to affair	Substantial, positive	"Different time zones"
Shared interests	Considerable overlap	Limited to their children
Prior criticism by offended	None/Idealization	Considerable
Individual Variables		
Prior trauma histories	Moderate in offended	Severe in both
Prior jealousy of offended	None	Considerable attachment insecurity
Self-esteem of offended	Some self-doubts	Denial of obvious insecurities
Self-esteem of offender	Fairly secure	Insecure, especially recently
Psychological mindedness	Offender high	Offender low
Empathic capacity	High in both	Offender obsessive; offended "paranoid"
Physical pain	None	Chronic back pain in offended
Sexual functioning	Adequate in both	Absent with physical limitations in both
Therapist/Therapy Variables		
Countertransference	Minimal challenge	Major challenge
Ability to create dialogue	Easy	Rarely achieved
Individual therapists	Not applicable	Consulted but not helpful
Journaling	Not applicable	Limited benefit
Self-help reading	Not applicable	Recommended, not read
Referral to separate individual therapist	Not applicable	Quit/declined after one session
Medication	Not applicable	Limited benefit

infidelity who attended therapy were divorced at five years. By presenting only successes, too many books and professional papers give the erroneous impression that all will turn out well if you just play your therapeutic cards right. While we must work to improve our results and try to learn from our failures, we should not blame ourselves for sometimes falling short.

A final point to avoid ending this chapter on such a sour note: While David and Rebecca ended up stuck in some circle of marital hell, their case history can serve as a catalogue of what to try, since when working with them, I used almost all the interventions that have worked with others. So, studying their case illustrates both what to try and the limits of those interventions to reverse the damage that infidelity can cause.

Notes

1. Regarding cultural variability, Feng and Yang (2016) reported that "mistress dispellers" have become a novel approach to infidelity in the People's Republic of China. In a country where marital therapy is unpopular, while keeping mistresses is common, betrayed wives can hire someone to "dispel" their husband's lover. As one such dispeller described her work: "Once we figure out what type of mistress she is—in it for money, love, or symptom—we draw up a plan" and then try to disrupt the affair from the mistress's side. She continued:

    > The counselor might move into the mistress's apartment building or start working out at her gym, getting to know her, becoming her confidante, and eventually turning her feelings against her partner. Sometimes, the counselor finds her a new lover, a job opening in another city or otherwise persuades her to leave the married man.

    Counselors also advise wives on "how to make themselves more attractive to their husbands." One company that "dispelled" 260 mistresses in a two-year period reported that this usually took three months and was 90% effective.

2. Forgiveness in everyday transactions, not just in the wake of betrayals, has been shown to correlate strongly with couple happiness (e.g., Bell & Fincham, 2019) or, in the words of Chapman and Thomas (2006, p. 22): "Good relationships are always marked by a willingness to apologize, forgive, and reconcile. The reason many relationships are cold and distant is because we have failed to apologize."

3. Making the subject even more complex, experts use different labels to differentiate these levels of coming to terms with the event and the perpetrator. Confirming the work of Worthington's group (2000), Greenberg et al. (2008) found that the state of "unforgiveness" can diminish *without* increasing "forgiveness," where *forgiveness* is defined as going beyond acceptance and letting go of the grievance to also include "an increase in positive emotions such as compassion, empathy, or understanding felt toward the injurer" (p. 187). By contrast, Luskin (2002) uses *forgiveness* to simply describe the shift out of the state of obsessive unforgiveness to that of acceptance, which he correctly notes does not require empathy with, or reparation from, the perpetrator, although empathy and repair can facilitate that shift. Spring (2004) refers to letting go of the grievance, as I do, as *acceptance*. When the victim adds empathic understanding, sometimes coupled with reconciliation with the offender, Spring calls this *genuine forgiveness*.

4. Chapman and Thomas (2006, p. 20) dispute the common Christian misconception that complete forgiveness does not depend on the offender's behavior:

Some, particularly in the Christian worldview, have taught forgiveness without an apology. They often quote the words of Jesus, "If you do not forgive men their trespasses, neither will your Father forgive your trespasses?" (Matthew 6:15) Thus, they say to the wife whose husband has been unfaithful and continues in his adulterous affair, "You must forgive him, or God will not forgive you." Such an interpretation of Jesus's teachings fails to reckon with the rest of the scriptural teaching on forgiveness. The Christian is instructed to forgive others in the same manner that God forgives us. How does God forgive us? The Scriptures say that if we confess our sins, God will forgive our sins. Nothing in the Old or New Testaments indicates that God forgives the sins of people who do not confess and repent of their sins.

5. Greenberg et al. (2010) found that offenders who acknowledged *shame* (that their action violated an internal norm) were more positively received that those who acknowledged *guilt* (that their action injured the other). In my clinical experience, victims vary with respect to what reassures them most. Some feel that if their partners are truly ashamed, they will be less likely to repeat the behavior. Others are more interested in hearing their partners talk about caring about them and are less reassured when offenders dwell on *their* internal struggles and values.

6. Illustrating the power of the unconscious mind to keep incompatible scenarios separated, some partners may surprise us when, having been obliviously content that sex had become infrequent in their marriages, they are shocked and gravely offended to learn that their partners have found it elsewhere.

7. For many women, affairs are an enticing escape from home and motherhood: "In the transition to marriage, too many women experience their sexuality as shifting from desire to duty. When it becomes something she should do, it no longer is something she wants to do" (Perel, 2017a, p. 184).

8. Sometimes, the man's motive is mainly to have unencumbered sex without intimacy or concern for the partner, especially when it is with sex workers, although this is now more socially frowned upon by wives who wonder what this says about the man they married. That said, such splitting off of sex from marriage may be the result of intrapsychic problems that diminish desire, as when a man's wife reminds him of his mother or when he feels obligated to "perform" in the marital bed. In such cases, women outside the marriage, paid or unpaid, may allow him to enjoy sex.

9. Affairs can serve as attempted "solutions" at any developmental crisis point: A 30-year-old client of mine cheated on his 29-year-old, longtime girlfriend when she pressed him to marry her, which he saw as forcing him to "grow up, get married, and become an adult."

10. Men or women distressed by aging or career stagnation frequently attempt to address this by "dating the solution," connecting with a young person, often one who admires their career accomplishments. For an excellent literary example, see Philip Roth's *The Dying Animal* (2001), in which Professor David Kepesh, distressed by aging, yet again pursues one of his graduate students and is especially captivated by her young body. The intriguing twist on the familiar story (spoiler alert) is that after growing emotionally attached to her, he lovingly supports her through her fatal illness.

11. Leone (2020) has presented an exception: a successful couple therapy in the presence of an ongoing long-distance affair. Among other things, the treatment was assisted by the offender coming to realize and take responsibility for what was missing in himself rather than in his marriage.

13 Couples Contemplating Divorce

About one-third of the couples who come for couple therapy are contemplating divorce (Doss et al., 2004; Owen et al., 2012). For some, the marriage is hanging by a thread and divorce seems imminent. Therapy is seen as a last-ditch effort, often long avoided, to save the day. Others have had prior unsuccessful couple therapies but are reluctantly willing to give it one more try. Often, one person is more intent on divorce, and the other is greatly distressed by the possibility; these are termed *mixed-agenda couples*. Sometimes, the latent goal is only to be able to say that therapy was tried—to make a ceremonial visit—to justify actions already decided upon. Such couples are more distressed at presentation, show less improvement in therapy, and (unsurprisingly) are more likely to be separated at six-month follow-up (Owen et al., 2012).

In many ways, initial assessment and therapy will be like that just described for extramarital affairs where the issue of divorce may also be on the table. Some partners will be in a state of crisis, feeling blindsided and shocked at the prospect of being abandoned, as described by K. Scharff (2014b):

> For the bereft spouse, life has taken on an unreal, nightmarish quality. For that man or woman, the central contract of their life has been broken, and the very person who they would normally turn to for solace is suddenly not only unavailable but the perpetrator of their torture.
>
> (p. 281)

Both partners will benefit from slowing things down before making any life-changing decisions. Therapists will want to know how far along the process has gone, whether the spouses are still living together, whether an affair is in progress, whether they have separated their finances, and whether lawyers are involved. As always, it will be crucial for the therapist to observe the couple's pattern of interaction.

Commitment

It is important to evaluate each client's level of commitment to their partner and to the therapy. The latter is assessed, in part, by asking about goals for the therapy: to improve the marriage or to decide whether to end it. I routinely ask about these topics, both in the first conjoint session and in my intake questionnaire. This allows all of us to learn each partner's level of commitment and whether both partners are clear on this. Even so, some partners will not be fully honest about their intentions. When commitment is low or divergent, this uncertainty will suffuse all discussions going forward.

Following the work of Stanley and Markman (1992), commitment can be analyzed by assessing how much staying in the marriage is determined by "dedication" (personal investment, willingness to sacrifice, a sense of couple identity or "we-ness") and how much by "constraint" (concerns related to children, finances, social consequences, religious convictions, or ethical values). Again, unsurprisingly, research has found that low levels of commitment (especially "dedication") predict poorer outcomes (Owen et al., 2014). While this might seem tautological, the components of commitment can become topics for discussion and therapeutic work. For instance, viewing commitment more as a process than as a static variable, we can sometimes help demoralized couples to recommit by helping them resurrect activities that once gave them shared satisfaction.

Initial alliance and encouraging therapy

In addition to the usual beginning moves, we should place a high priority on establishing an alliance with partners who are ambivalent about the value of therapy. To keep such clients involved, I enumerate ways therapy can help them even if they decide to divorce:

- Divorcing can be less painful and less contentious if jointly understood, even when one partner is opposed to it.
- Examining the pros and cons of divorce can make for a more informed choice and for less second-guessing later.
- If they have children or other reasons to continue to interact after the divorce, their interactions can be more amicable.
- Therapy can reduce the likelihood of repeating the same problems with future partners.

I point out that these assertions are backed by research (e.g., Bowman & Fine, 2000; Stanley et al., 1989) and explain that—while I have just come on the scene and do not know the history of their despair—research has shown that, at a certain point, couples throw what Gottman (2011) calls the *relationship history switch*, such that couples who had previously seen their marital narrative positively now view almost all past interactions, even positive ones, negatively. I explain that this may take time to reverse, but I have seen it happen. Following Wile's recommendation, I try to help the couple discuss this pervasive negativity by voicing what each might be thinking:

I find myself annoyed by practically everything you've been saying today, and it sounds like you feel the same way about me. That's the way it's been for a long time. What's happened to us? We started with so much love and respect and fun. It's enough to make me want to cry—which I might do if I weren't so irritated.

(Wile, 2012)

Countertransference and therapist goals

It is not only couples who may wonder whether it makes sense to continue their relationship. Therapists can also get caught up in the question and the strong feelings it evokes. We might think that we can stay out of this and let the couple make their own decision, but we will often feel pulled by one partner to help them bring the other back or by the other partner to give them permission to leave. Sometimes, we will feel more hope for the marriage than the clients and sometimes, we will have to help couples give up false hopes. How we decide these issues inside our heads will inevitably shape our body language, questions, and emphasis (Real, 2015).

Above all, we can remind ourselves that conjoint meetings can help even when couples divorce. The potential benefits are the ones I mentioned previously and were borne out by a large-scale study in which therapists viewed most of the outcomes positively, including in the one-third of couples who ended up separating (Stanley et al., 1989).

While it is not our call whether couples choose to divorce, in some situations that is probably best. Virtually, all therapists agree that divorce is beneficial in cases of extreme violence or other hurtful behavior when the offending partner refuses to accept responsibility or work toward change. Somewhat less obvious are cases where one person confesses that he or she "never loved" their partner but married them due to an unplanned pregnancy, the desire to escape a bad situation, or because of parental pressure. (Even in these situations, we should question whether such retrospective accounts are accurate or derived, instead, from current feelings.) Longitudinal research (see, especially, Hawkins & Booth, 2005) also confirms the long-term suffering that ensues when married couples remain, year after year, locked in combative or chilly relationships.[1] When assessing the results of my own practice, the outcomes I feel worst about are couples who have remained together unhappily. Some were out-and-out therapy failures; others limped sadly along in prolonged therapy; and a final group seemed to have benefited from treatment but then relapsed after termination. Such cases—some termed "gruesome twosomes" by family therapy founding father Chuck Kramer—have forced me to conclude that sometimes, therapists should point to the possible benefits of divorce and help couples move in that direction. This recommendation is strengthened because, like others, I have seen the long-term advantages of "good divorces" many times for those who have found more compatible partners or contentment as decoupled singles.

We should also not blame ourselves in cases where we tried our best to resuscitate a marriage that was close to death. Many couples who consult us are like some cancer patients who wait too long to consult their doctors and find that treatment that might have been effective earlier now fails. When couples have been unhappy for many years, it is a tall order to help them reverse the corrosive process we call *negative sentiment override*. Not infrequently, I see people whose areas of conflict seem workable and whose shared values, children, and history seem worth fighting for, but where one partner has just "had enough." Such clients are then unwilling to let their guard down and give therapy a reasonable chance. Instead, therapy is usually half-hearted, abbreviated, and disappointing. In other cases, I am the one who doubts that the years of acrimony and distrust can be overcome. For these reasons, Lebow (2014) suggests that we shouldn't beat ourselves up when we help mend only slightly more than 50% of marriages. And in some cases, helping couples divorce with minimal pain may have been their desired outcome.

Because treating couples on the verge of divorce often makes maintaining a neutral stance challenging, we must be even more alert than usual to our personal inclinations, especially concerning which of the two partners we like better or wish to protect more. As I will discuss shortly, the format of discernment counseling can help, but it does not eliminate some important challenges. One common dilemma is finding oneself thinking that one partner will indeed be happier if they leave a marriage but that the other will suffer as a result. Couple therapists like to think of the couple as the client, but, at times, the interests of the partners are clearly at odds. I sometimes manage this conundrum by reminding myself that, as in dating, the person who has been rejected, while injured in the short run, may do better long-term after separating from a dissatisfied partner. Experienced therapists recognize that some partners need our blessing to leave a personally injurious marriage and will not encourage a partner to stay in a marriage if they, themselves, would not (Real, 2015). While thinking along these lines can help us, sometimes we must simply work to help each person cope with the vastly different consequences of a painful divorce.

When working with couples contemplating divorce, it is particularly important to tease out how much their marital problems stem from individual psychopathology and how much they reflect systemic issues contributed to by both partners. The psychoanalyst Henry Friedman (2012) has presented two relevant cases of men who "despite considerable awareness of how much they had been damaged by their wives were unwilling or unable to protect themselves, either by setting appropriate limits or by separation or divorce" (p. 139). As their individual therapist, he believed that they were poorly served by couple treatments that stressed mutual causation and prioritized the marriages over the mental health of these mistreated husbands. Friedman compared the men to physically abused women and argued that their couple therapy failed to help them assign more responsibility to their wives and, possibly, to leave them. He thought that their concurrent couple therapy, with its commitment to seeing both partners as contributing, may have prolonged hope and denial in these men "who seemed unable to give up believing that they could turn the situation around and make their wives love and respect them" (p. 148). All experienced therapists have seen such cases. What Friedman is wondering is whether couple therapy for such clients is anti-therapeutic. Causal theories aside, Friedman's article also reminds us that we couple therapists, like the men he described, may be too captured by a wish to save all marriages.

Of course, Friedman is speaking from the perspective of an individual therapist, and individual therapists are prone to blame the unseen spouse for problems in the marriage (Gurman & Burton, 2014; Leone, 2013a). Perhaps, a combination of systemic therapy and attention to individual issues *in couple meetings* might have helped the marriages that Friedman described; perhaps not. Personally, I have successfully treated the marriages of abusive or excessively demanding spouses (both men and women), either by helping their partners respond better to their immediate needs (the squeaky wheel stops squeaking after getting the grease) or by helping the demanding, "abusive" partner take responsibility for their character pathology.[2]

The important point for this section on countertransference is that such divergent ways of assessing a disordered marriage—from the perspective of individual accountability and pathology, or from that of circular causation—will (and should) cause disturbance in the minds of therapists treating ambivalent spouses who are frequently struggling themselves with the same epistemological/ethical questions.

Therapists, especially those new to treating couples, should examine their own prejudices and experiences concerning divorce. Ideally, therapists will have had experiences with clients, friends, or lovers, where they have seen that breaking up was beneficial, and they will also have seen situations where people falsely pinned their hopes on finding a new, improved partner. Some therapists will have been through divorce themselves, and others will have benefited from couple therapy or learned that couples can constructively face their problems while staying together. Therapists whose parents have divorced can make use of that experience to help them empathize with clients and their children but should be careful not to overgeneralize from their own experiences. Therapists who entered the field with a semiconscious desire to heal their parents' marriage must be careful not to push too hard to save all marriages. Keeping such experiences in mind should help us remain open-minded while we help couples work out what seems best for them.

Format when couples are on the same page

When partners are almost equally uncertain about whether to divorce or when both have already pretty much decided to divorce (something I take up in the next chapter), I usually proceed conjointly as usual, but with the option of holding individual meetings when affairs are suspected or present, when emotion dysregulation is intense, or when discussions of ambivalence are hindered by the conjoint format. When one partner is markedly more intent on divorce than the other, I usually recommend discernment counseling.

Discernment counseling for *mixed-agenda couples*

William (Bill) Doherty (2011, 2016) has developed an important treatment option for mixed-agenda couples, those in which one, the *leaning-out partner*, inclines toward divorce and the other, the *leaning-in partner*, wants the marriage to continue. Doherty views this as a treatment stage, prior to a possible conjoint couple treatment. If, after several conjoint couple sessions, the mixed agenda becomes clear, the therapist should begin to work simultaneously with each client separately. Doherty also conducts brief conjoint meetings during which he and the partners report on where they stand. Couples are explicitly told not to expect much change in the marriage during this discernment phase, which has the following goals: (a) to *discern* whether to stay in the marriage and, if yes, whether to sign up for a course of conjoint couple therapy aimed at improving it; and (b) to develop narratives of each partner's personal contributions to the marital problems. If the partners decide not to go forward, attention turns to mourning the marriage and managing the divorce.

When compared to a format in which each client sees a different individual therapist to consider these decisions, discernment therapy has the advantage that the therapist has superior knowledge of both partners and their interactions. Unlike individual therapists, the discernment therapist is faced with the challenges of managing confidentiality and neutrality. Should individual therapists already be on the scene, it will be important to get permission to contact them to discuss the treatment.

Doherty notes that mixed-agenda cases are common but that the usual format of conjoint therapy has important structural flaws that interfere with successful treatment. Fearing that their honesty will only increase their partner's hurt or anger, leaning-out partners are commonly unwilling to discuss either their reasons for leaving or their continuing ambivalence. Many will just go through the motions and then use the failed therapy to further justify their leaving. Leaning-in partners, fearing that honesty about their despair and discontent will only make their partners more determined to leave, will also hold back. Individual meetings with the therapist, by contrast, are more likely to elicit frank discussion and meaningful self-examination.

The conjoint format also makes it harder for therapists to represent themselves as neutral concerning the decision to divorce—leaning-in partners will be exquisitely sensitive to evidence that we might favor divorce, while leaning-out partners may experience us as working to save the marriage at all costs.

Therapists, like many clients, may (incorrectly) believe that the best way to test whether a marriage should continue is a trial of couple therapy. The mistake here is that the constraints just mentioned do not always allow for a fair test. Doherty notes that therapists who, nonetheless, press ahead with conjoint sessions make three common errors: pursuing the leaning-out spouse too much, agreeing that the marriage cannot be revived, or trying to do couple therapy without a clear contract. This is not to say that one cannot work conjointly with such couples from the start; I have described one such case previously (Nielsen, 2019b) where I was able to quickly help one partner stop thinking that divorce would solve an internal problem she was inducing in her partner. Nonetheless, having made all the mistakes described by Doherty, I have shifted more often and more quickly to the format he advocates, which, I think, improves the likelihood of success.[3]

In the initial sessions that may determine the need for discernment counseling, Doherty recommends that therapists ask the following questions:

- The divorce narrative: "What has happened to your marriage that has gotten you to the point where divorce is a possibility?"
- The repair narrative: "What have you done to try to fix the problems?"
- The children question: "What role, if any, do your children play in your decision-making about the future of your marriage?"
- The best-of-times question: "What was the best of times in your relationship since you met?"

Individual work with leaning-out partners then aims to help them choose among three options: the status quo without therapy, separation or divorce, or committing to six months of couple therapy aimed at improving the marriage. When clients say that love or sexual desire has died, the therapist can ask, "Would you like to try to get it back?" knowing that such feelings are not as hopelessly gone forever as clients may think. Whichever choice leaning-out partners pick, they should become clearer and more confident about that choice and thus avoid second-guessing themselves later.

We also can help leaning-out spouses avoid thinking simplistically, "Sure I'm human and I make mistakes, but I was married to an impossible person," or "I married the wrong person," or "I just fell out of love." Instead, we can help them examine their ambivalence, their realistic future options, the maladaptive marital cycles they have fallen into, and their personal contributions (which are likely to continue regardless of which discernment option they choose). When affairs are ongoing, such individual work can help clarify what to do about them.

With leaning-in partners, the primary discernment counseling goal is usually the same as their stated goal: to see what can be done to save the marriage. Since they have given us license to work on this issue and are the more motivated of the two partners, Doherty points out that we can often confront them more forcefully about their contributions to the marital breakdown. This would be harder with the leaning-out partner present. We can share what we have learned from meeting with their partner about that person's complaints, doing so in a way that may make those criticisms easier to accept. Sometimes, this leads to a deeper appreciation of just how unhappy the leaning-out spouse has been and to discussion of possible steps that might reverse this, and thus to head off a divorce. Unfortunately and paradoxically, when faced with in-person criticisms from leaning-out partners, many leaning-in partners have failed to act, instead digging in and defending themselves. Therapists can now try to help them see what they might do, including by using suggestions proposed by "divorce buster" Michelle Weiner-Davis (2001) that encourage unilateral actions spouses can take to make their marriage more attractive to their partners.

Doherty reports that clients appreciated discernment counselors sharing data from their individual meetings with their partners. Clients also agreed that when feelings were running high, it would have been a mistake to have traditional conjoint couple therapy sessions. That said, Real (2015) describes a situation where conjoint meetings have proven helpful with *mixed-agenda couples*. These are times when he has taken sides—agreeing with the leaning-out partner that change is overdue—and confronted the leaning-in partner on how they must change and then worked with that partner to do so.

Seeing their own contributions more clearly often makes leaning-in and leaning-out spouses more hopeful, since they now see possibilities for change that they had not considered previously. If the couple decides to start couple therapy, Doherty asks them to begin by writing a "reconciliation plan" stating what they have agreed to do to make the marriage a success (e.g., attend AA or Al-Anon meetings; do couple therapy for six months; stop seeing their lover).

If the leaning-out spouse decides to divorce, the therapist can help the couple cope, including by challenging the assumption that one can be happy with a partner who is staying in a marriage reluctantly, possibly only out of a sense of guilt. Overall, Doherty reports that divorces following discernment counseling are more amicable, with less ongoing projection of blame and claims of victimhood.

Peter Fraenkel's contributions for working with *last chance couples*

Possibly because, like Doherty, he is a recognized expert and often the last resort for couples who have failed in prior therapy, Peter Fraenkel (2019) has also given much thought to how to work with *last chance couples*, those with one partner on the verge of leaving the marriage. Fraenkel notes that these couples come in four varieties. His useful typology applies to many of the couples we see, but *last chance couples* are more demoralized and even closer to calling it quits:

- High-conflict couples.
- Couples in which one partner has violated the values and expectations of the other or has threatened the other's personal safety.
- Couples with mismatched ideas about what they want to have happening in their lives now and in the future.
- Low-intensity, low-desire couples.

While therapy must be tailored to each type—including by working on forgiveness and apologies in cases of betrayal—Fraenkel emphasizes getting off to a good start, since some couples may come only once. Like doing battlefield surgery, the goal is to stop the bleeding on the spot to prevent the imminent death of the marriage. Time is of the essence and therapists must move fast, often without the luxury of obtaining a detailed history. Instead, Fraenkel believes that the focus of the first session must be on the question, "What would be one change that you'd need to see today, in this session (or in the next week), that would lead you to think that you might want to return for a second session?" (p. 581). Therapists should ask this question first of the more ambivalent spouse. Some of Fraenkel's additional recommendations for initial sessions include:

Ask about prior therapies and what went wrong. You don't want to make the same mistakes, and you want to know what to avoid in the short run.

Allow the couple to tell you the full extent of their suffering and avoid asking them too early to recall good times. The second part of this recommendation differs from that of Doherty, who recommends asking about the "best of times" to revive hope and gain understanding, so judgment is required here. Fraenkel does want to know what first attracted the partners to each other, since that will often be part of their problem, though asking about this can also recall good times.

*Focus on **actions** that may change the pattern of interaction soon*, what he calls "revealing and transforming meaning through motion," "creative relational movement," or "experiments in possibility." Fraenkel wants partners to gain hope by doing things differently, by listening to music, drumming, or, more prosaically, talking to each other using the speaker–listener technique. Early in therapy, he encourages couples to engage in simple, shared pleasurable activities: hugging, telling a joke, reading a poem, sharing daily statements of appreciation, or taking a silent walk in a new place. See, also, my discussion of the timing and pragmatics of encouraging such positive activities (Nielsen, 2016, Chapter 14).

For most couples, move quickly to psychoeducation, including teaching the speaker–listener technique and emotion regulation skills, acknowledging that these will feel awkward at first.

Challenge partners' hopelessness based on the idea that the other is not "motivated to change" by noting that motivation may increase once each partner sees the other participating in new patterns. Have clients recall how their low motivation to, say, go to the gym, to begin a work project, or to practice a musical instrument increased once they got started.

Support clients in the middle of change who worry that, while behaviors are new and beneficial, they can feel artificial or incomplete. Reframe this as the experience of "doing something new" such that if they *didn't* feel awkward, it might not truly be new!

Make clear that, while positive change in therapy might encourage a partner to remain in the marriage, it does not necessitate it, and that there may be other benefits. It is important to say this because some partners may be unwilling to engage in any effort to improve things if they believe that positive results will weaken their resolve to leave.

Fraenkel's sage advice can boost hope, not only in *last chance couples* but in others who come to us in despair.

Mixed-agenda and last chance couples: meet separately or conjointly?

My clinical experience supports all the practical recommendations offered by Fraenkel, mixed and matched with those of Doherty. Where I differ with them is on the technical question of how often and for how long to meet with clients separately versus conjointly. As noted earlier, the main advantages of discernment counseling are that we slow the process and get greater depth of understanding by meeting with the partners separately. This has helped me in many cases, with the qualification that sometimes I have met for far longer than the five sessions Doherty recommends as standard. I also do not usually meet with the partners individually on the same day and follow/combine those meetings with a conjoint review session, as he recommends. Instead, my conjoint review sessions are full-length and less frequent than the individual sessions. When I meet for more individual sessions than Doherty recommends, it is because the work on ambivalence sometimes takes longer and because I have not felt a need to rush the process or to make such a sharp distinction between what is a prelude to couple therapy and what counts as the real deal.

Fraenkel does not usually meet individually for long with his *last chance couples*, and sometimes I have found that works just fine for me, as well, even when divorce is on the table (e.g., as noted in Chapter 12, on extramarital affairs, where this is my preference). In an email conversation with me concerning these issues (April 3, 2021), Fraenkel wrote:

> Just another thought for you for the chapter, at least in describing the rationale for my approach versus Bill D[oherty]'s. As you know, I think the key thing for last chance couples and especially the "leaning out" partner is to see actual change in the other partner before they decide to engage in a longer course of therapy. My concern with Bill's extensive individual sessions is that those sessions are likely focused on what's happened thus far, and that means there are few challenges to the negative scripts and attributions partners have developed about each other. My strong belief is that the only thing that can change long-standing negative beliefs about the other partner and the possibility of a better relationship going forward is for the leaning-out partner to see with her or his own eyes actual change; these changes then begin to disrupt the power of negative beliefs. Otherwise, I would imagine that in those individual meetings, you're just getting a history of how bad things have been for a long time, and essentially "rehearsing" and strengthening the negative narrative.

Here, Fraenkel is flagging the power of in-the-room, here-and-now conjoint sessions to provide corrective experiences. It's worth noting that this is always a potential advantage of the conjoint format over individual sessions. It may also be true that less experienced therapists with more volatile or difficult clients might do better with individual meetings, while Peter Fraenkel, with his years of experience, can move quickly to restore hope in the aforementioned ways.

Doherty and Fraenkel aside, there are always pros and cons to meeting individually or not with clients who come for help with their marriages. After the diagnostic phase, I favor working almost exclusively conjointly *unless the conjoint sessions are either unmanageably destructive or unhelpfully guarded*, both of which are common when couples are strongly contemplating divorce.

Working with ambivalence

Contemplating and vacillating about divorce is common: One study found that 25% of married people had recently thought about divorce, and another 28% had thought about it in the past but were still married (Hawkins et al., 2015). As noted by Allen and Hawkins (2017), deciding whether to divorce resembles other difficult decisions that are challenging because they are made rarely and their outcomes are not immediate. As just discussed, individual meetings with clients on the brink of divorce are especially useful forums for discussing their ambivalence. When doing this, most therapists can draw on similar experiences working in individual therapy with clients who were contemplating divorce or ending a romantic relationship. For most people on the verge of divorce, the state of ambivalence is painful, as they remain stuck, uncertain whether to commit to the status quo or pursue a different future. These people need our assistance to make what are often gut-wrenching decisions about fundamental and irreversible life changes.

Before clients can commit to a course of action, it will help to explore both options in depth. Deciding whether to divorce means considering both practical concerns (the impact on children, living arrangements, finances, career, and social relationships) and potential psychological dangers (shame, guilt, loss, and loneliness). We can help clients speculate about alternative futures, assisting them in uncovering unexamined assumptions (e.g., "Marriage equals success; divorce means failure." "Leaving a partner means you are a bad person." "My partner will never change."). Some clients' images of what their lives will be like post-divorce are overly rosy; others are excessively pessimistic. Divorce can be a new beginning, or it can start a replay of the same problems with a new partner. For many, it will mean serious new challenges due to lost identity, friends, and financial security. For some, it will be worth it. Most clients will deeply appreciate our helping them navigate these turbulent waters.

Planned separations

Planned separations can help some partners resolve their ambivalence. Unlike the spontaneous variety (where someone leaves unilaterally), trial separations are structured by the couple and have the explicit goal of assessing whether divorce or reunion is best. Partners can work on self-improvement that might allow the marriage to continue and can evaluate the amount of stress and loss that a finalized divorce might bring. For many people, a planned separation fosters cooling off and self-reflection. For leaning-out partners, it gives space to reconsider their decision. Planned separations also allow spouses who have been left—sometimes for understandable reasons, like problem drinking—to focus less on the narcissistic injury and more on their role in the marital problems.

Planned separations interrupt vicious cycles that may be the main source of marital trouble. They also make it harder to blame one's partner for one's unhappiness. Projective identification is not as easy without a partner close by to represent the problem. Overadequate–underadequate or pursuer–distancer clients will need to manage without their familiar dance partners. Partners may become aware of what they would lose if they divorced, or conversely, of how they can make it on their own.

In my practice, the details of such arrangements have varied greatly, though discussion of particulars with the couple has been valuable. One experienced clinician (Phillips, 1981) recommends that the partners (a) live apart with minimal contact for a minimum of three months, (b) work on family-of-origin issues, and (c) spend time alone thinking and journaling about how to improve their lives. He recommends that partners avoid all romantic relationships, though other clinicians disagree with this recommendation and think that dating during the separation can be helpful. Ideally, both partners should pursue individual therapy aimed at personal growth and insight into their contributions to marital problems. As the trial separation goes forward, couples can renegotiate terms, including about going on dates and reinstituting sex if they are moving closer, or by working out more defined boundaries if they are moving apart. Some partners will continue to join in some family meals and events; for others, this is not a good idea. Phillips believes that most couples mistakenly get back together too soon, which reduces potential gains. In all cases of trial separation, I counsel people against being swayed excessively by early loneliness or by the agendas of friends or relatives.

My clinical experience with trial separations is limited. I have seen some couples for whom such a formal trial period proved helpful, in keeping with the enthusiastic advocacy of Raffel (1999), whose self-help book includes many practical suggestions. Raffel recommends four- to six-month separations, during which partners agree not to divorce. Noting that many couples just "muddle through," she distinguishes *trial separations* from *controlled separations*, in which couples agree to follow written ground rules, like agreeing to tell others, "We have separated and are working things out. That's all we can say for now." She finds that working out detailed ground rules reduces *separation shenanigans* like making harassing phone calls at 2 a.m., "forgetting" to pick up the kids, emptying a shared savings account, flaunting a new lover, and other forms of acting out common to divorcing couples. Controlled separations also reduce repeated episodes of brief separations followed by a return to the same old unsatisfactory marriages.

The case against trial separations is that couples living separately have fewer opportunities to work on issues and enjoy time together and that new problems may arise due to finances, logistics, access to children, and insecurity about contact with alternative partners. These problems should be balanced against the advantages mentioned previously, especially the opportunity to cool things down. To my knowledge, there are no randomized trials to assess trial separations, so we don't know whether they might improve on national statistics, which find that 80–90% of couples who separate eventually divorce (Tumin et al., 2015).

Transitions out of couple therapy

When one or both partners have decided to divorce, I suggest that we have some meetings to work out practicalities, especially what to tell children. Children should be reassured that it's not their fault; that the parents are not divorcing them; and that, ideally, their lives will continue as close as possible to what they were previously. In this phase, I also try to help partners deal with continuing feelings of anger, shame, guilt, loss, or disillusionment. Most often, couples come only a few times, but sometimes we continue with "divorce therapy," as described in the next chapter.

There are several other transitions that are common. While I favor discernment therapy in the short run and often longer than the five sessions recommended by Doherty, I find it problematic to continue what amounts to two simultaneous individual therapies beyond a few months. Maintaining neutrality becomes almost impossible when the partners hold onto divergent agendas, just as it can be for a divorce lawyer to simultaneously represent opposing sides. Therapists can become even more conflicted about what they believe is best for each of the partners, sometimes feeling that divorce would be better for one but disastrous for the other. Consequently, when partners remain ambivalent and deadlocked, I recommend that each client work with an individual therapist who can be unconflicted and aligned only with the needs of that client. The couple then continues to see me only for conjoint work.

As described in Chapter 12, on extramarital affairs, I also recommend separate therapists much earlier, often after only a few individual sessions, when one person wishes to continue an affair. If the affair is still secret, I do not share that fact, but say only that I believe that the partners are currently too far apart and that it would be best if they work things out separately.

In an ideal world, the couple therapist would always remain the "therapist for the couple," but there are exceptions. When leaning-in partners are abandoned against their will, everyone may agree that they need continuing help and that the best person for the job is the couple therapist. Sometimes, this was the covert agenda of the leaning-out partner from the beginning; other times, it evolves organically. It may also happen with couples moving toward divorce that one partner already has an individual therapist and thinks it would be fine for the couple therapist to continue individual sessions with the other one. The upside here is continuity with one partner; the downside is the loss of a neutral therapist in the future, for instance, if the partners get back together or wish to work out some area of post-divorce conflict. In either of these transition variations, therapists should be careful to explain this trade-off and obtain consent from the partner who will not continue with you. (I discuss such a case in the next chapter.) When continuing like this in individual therapy, it's important to review your client's assessment of your performance as a couple therapist. Almost always, they see you positively—otherwise they would not have continued—but they may harbor some lingering disappointments that should be aired.

Notes

1. Using data from four waves of the Marital Instability Over the Life Cycle Study, with the initial wave of data collected in 1980 and the last in 1992, Hawkins and Booth (2005) found that married people who scored below average on marital happiness at each of four points in time were lower on life satisfaction and self-esteem than those who divorced. They concluded that divorce only rarely improved the mental health of unhappily married couples.

2. The wives Friedman presented were extremely clingy and dependent and then angry and vengeful when their husbands failed to do as they wished. As their couple therapist, I would have tried to hold them more responsible for their attachment and other emotional needs and for managing their dysregulated emotions. As per DBT's eponymous "dialectic," I would have tried to help them voice their desire for unconditional love while also taking responsibility for becoming less in need of reassurance.

3. Doherty has published results (2016) for 100 consecutive "highly distressed" couples with one partner leaning toward divorce and reluctant to enter couple therapy. He found that 47% chose to proceed with couple treatment, and 55% of these remained married an average of 28 months later. Of the 41% who chose separation or divorce, only 10% got back together. For the small group who chose to stay together without therapy, 35% later divorced. These data suggest benefits, but since there was no control group, it's hard to know just how this format compares to standard conjoint treatment, though my clinical experience agrees with Doherty's that this is a better way to begin with most mixed-agenda couples. A more recent intensive study of discernment therapy with 11 couples who chose to divorce (Emerson et al., 2020) found overall, though not universal, benefits at follow-up. Couples especially credited discernment therapy with achieving greater clarity and honesty, acceptance and reduced ambivalence, awareness of personal contributions, less animosity during the divorce, and greater cooperation after the divorce, especially related to more amicable coparenting.

14 Divorcing Couples

Most therapy is simpler . . . . These were families in great pain, as much as any I had seen. . . . Most often, one person's bad behavior begat another person's worse behavior and so on, and those efforts that did appear on someone's part to act better were ignored. And, so often, family members described being caught up in a Kafkaesque legal system in which they were relentlessly misconstrued and under attack . . . . Most of all, there were the children . . . most of whom were deeply wounded and troubled.

— Jay Lebow (2019, p. viii)

This chapter takes up where the last one left off, with couples who have manifestly decided to divorce. Some will remarry and form stepfamilies, the topic of the next chapter. Everything we have discussed so far is relevant when working with divorcing couples and stepfamilies, but these two chapters will focus on unique features that make these cases so challenging. Above all, we will try to help clients let go of the past, do what's best for their children, and interact constructively with many subsystems (lawyers, angry ex-partners, partisan therapists, friends, and family) so that they can finalize their divorces and create satisfying, if more complex, new lives.

Therapists may enter the scene at various points: when couple therapy ends with the decision to divorce, during a *difficult divorce*, or when a stepfamily is having trouble. In all these situations, it is essential to keep in mind the systemic contributions and biases of unseen actors; we will often want to hear their version of events and will sometimes want to include them in therapy.[1]

Divorce: frequency, reasons, and outcomes

Divorce is common. Approximately 20% of first marriages in the United States will end within the first five years, and 40–50% of first marriages ultimately end in divorce (Copen et al., 2012). Despite these challenging odds, 70–75% of people remarry (Cruz, 2012). For reasons we will discuss shortly, such remarriages fare somewhat worse, with 50–60% divorcing (Ganong et al., 2006). Creating added stress for older adults, *gray divorces*, defined as those by people over age 50, now account for 25% of U.S. divorces (Brown & Lin, 2012).

DOI: 10.4324/b22905-19

The most common reasons people give for divorcing are infidelity, substance abuse, spending money irresponsibly, physical aggression, painful arguments, "incompatibility," "growing apart," or being unable to talk to each other (Lebow, 2019). These are encompassed by Fraenkel's categories of "couples on the brink" mentioned in the previous chapter: high-conflict couples; couples in which one partner has violated the values and expectations of the other or has threatened the other's personal safety; couples with mismatched ideas about what they want to happen now or in the future; and low-intensity, low-desire couples.

Divorce is almost always traumatic in the short run for both adults and children, who show overall increases in distress, depression, and other mental and physical disorders. Nonetheless, most people (80%) are resilient, and some in chronically low-quality marriages show gains in overall well-being (Sharra et al., 2019).

Importantly, there is no evidence that adults who divorce or their children do any worse than those living in non-divorcing families where the parents are unhappy with each other (Booth & Amato, 2001; Cummings & Davies, 1994; Greene et al., 2003; Greene et al., 2012; Hetherington, 2003). Obviously, outcomes vary as a function of the pre-divorce maturity of the partners ("selection"), their financial resources, how often they must change residence, and whether an adult becomes significantly depressed—among other things.[2] One consistent research finding is that children's adjustment is strongly related to how well their parents manage the breakup, including by not involving them in it (e.g., Hetherington, 2003; Isaacs et al., 2000).

"Divorcing" is best viewed as a process rather than a single event at a courthouse, and, as with extramarital affairs, often involves a crisis stage. There will be both external changes—in living arrangements, finances, and relations with children and extended family—and internal changes related to the meaning of the divorce. Incomes fall for many, more often for women, and fathers routinely spend less time with their children (Rice, 2005). In the longer term, divorce is a benign force for change and growth for some, whereas others experience it as a lingering disaster from which they never recover.

Divorce after couple therapy

In my informal review of a series of 67 cases that I treated in couple therapy (Nielsen, 2016), divorce was a surprisingly rare outcome (about 15% at the time, but somewhat higher after adding couples who divorced years after therapy had concluded). Divorce was more common for couples who came only a few times or who had long-standing problems and when motivation was low or secretly absent in one partner.[3] On the other hand, divorce was uncommon when couples persisted in therapy past three months. Most such couples stayed married, and most benefited from the therapy.

When divorce can help

After the institution of unilateral or "no fault" divorce in the 1970s and the subsequent increase in divorce, the rate leveled off at 40–50% by the 1980s. During this time, the rates of wives' suicides, domestic violence, and spousal homicide declined substantially (Rutter, 2015). So, when thinking about divorce outcomes, Rutter correctly asks, "Compared to what?" and suggests the relevant comparison should be between unhappily married couples (of various sorts) who stay together and unhappily married couples who split up. Her research found that people who left distressed marriages were less depressed going forward than people who stayed in distressed marriages (but not when compared to happily married couples).

In reviewing my cases, I discovered a substantial minority of clients, about half the divorcing group, who saw divorce positively as they extricated themselves from a chronically maladaptive, conflictual, violent, or otherwise dysfunctional form of marital bondage. As a woman in a TV sitcom put it when asked about her "broken" marriage: "It was broke until I fixed it by ending it!" In theory, one might expect such improvement from many types of unhappy, mismatched pairs. In fact, I observed two common patterns in which divorce both required and evidenced personal growth by one or both partners. In *conflictual couples*, the couple came to therapy maintaining an imperfect stability by fighting with each other. These couples exhibit the psychology of individual borderline clients, achieving "warmth via friction," and maintain a sense of bounded identity and goodness via episodes of paranoid projective fighting with a simultaneously loved and hated significant other. A second type, *identified patient couples*, were stuck in varieties of an overadequate–underadequate dance, including where symptomatic behavior of one spouse was matched by enabling from the other.

Ending such conflictual or unbalanced relationships frequently led to improvement, often in *both* partners. The likely reason is that breaking such a pathological bond requires the ego strength, self-esteem, and courage to face an unfamiliar, stressful, and possibly lonely future. When clients are helped in that direction, they often become happier, stronger, and grateful.

Similarly, Esther Perel (2017a) remarks, "We need a concept of terminated marriage that doesn't damn it—one that helps to create emotional coherence and narrative continuity" (p. 286). To facilitate this, she invites couples to write goodbye letters to each other that "capture what they'll miss, what they cherish, what they take responsibility for, and what they wish for each other" (p. 287).

Couples stuck in marital hell

My real failures as a therapist were with couples who remained married and were unable to curb their maladaptive processes. These couples most often made me lament my limited power to improve marriages. Perhaps,

I should have confronted them more than I did and discussed the possibility and attendant challenges of divorce. In what follows, I take up how to help people who have chosen to exit their unsatisfactory marriages.

Divorce therapy: overview

Some of the couples who chose to divorce while in therapy with me stayed *after* the decision to divorce had been manifestly settled, to continue to work out the details. Rarely have couples come to me *initially* to work on their divorcing process—though such work is a specialization for others and for divorce mediators and has many of the same goals (see, especially, Lebow, 2019). In both situations, this work has generally proved beneficial, as it has helped couples contain their pathological processes, mourn the relationship, and deal with ongoing parenting and financial issues. When possible, I try to do as much work as possible before the partners consult attorneys, since attorneys tend to move the process in an adversarial direction. I have found Constance Ahrons's (1994) work useful in conceptualizing this phase of therapy and recommend her book, *The Good Divorce*, to clients who have decided to divorce. In addition to Lebow's book cited above, the following are valuable *for therapists* working with divorcing couples: Baris et al. (2001); Isaacs, Montalvo, and Abelsohn (2000); and Pam and Pearson (1998).

Individual or conjoint therapy?

It is unclear whether individual or conjoint couple therapy is preferable for working on the emotional fall-out of divorce (guilt over leaving, narcissistic injury over being left, shame for failing, loss of an identity and a life partner, guilt and concern about the impact on children, and generalized anxiety about the future) and the many practical problems posed by divorce. Each has advantages and limitations. Preliminary research reported by Sprenkle and Storm (1981) found that conjoint therapy was optimal for uncertain couples who stayed together, while individual therapy was better for those who divorced. The same article found conjoint sessions superior to individual therapy for handling child custody issues.

If I have been seeing a couple previously, I generally prefer to continue conjointly for as long as seems productive. Many of these couples tend to drop out after a short time and continue with individual therapists, which allows them to be more honest about their feelings, although this makes it harder to work out practical matters and arrive at compromises with their partners.

In situations where one person has an individual therapist already, I prefer *not* to continue working individually with the other partner, even when I have the other spouse's approval to do so, since unbalancing the alliance will make it harder for the couple to return to discuss couple issues in the future. Sometimes, however, as noted in the previous chapter, a spouse's acute emotional needs, financial limitations, or belief that I alone can help them, have led me to continue to see one of the spouses alone. When I have done this, it has usually meant the end to any therapy with the other partner.

The challenges of conjoint divorce therapy

Working conjointly with clients is difficult. Working conjointly with clients who are divorcing is even harder. The commitment bond has been severed and countless new stressors are on the scene. Frequently, unending conflict over the particulars of the divorce serve simultaneously to continue the connection and enact revenge. Some guilty partners fail to act with reasonable self-interest, making decisions that later fuel their resentment. Unresolved problems with intimacy and conflict resolution that plagued the marriage will also plague the divorce. Children can become triangulated and injured. Lawyers, sometimes unaware of these problems or financially motivated to ignore them, can aggravate conflict—although helpful attorneys can calm the waters.

The central goals of divorce therapy

In all these situations, therapy—conjoint or individual—can often expose, clarify, and help manage these issues so that clients can mourn and move on. Arriving at a three-dimensional narrative of the marriage, one that is not exclusively about suffering and victimization, will help. Therapists, aware of the future costs of behaving badly, will want to encourage their clients to behave ethically. In the words of Baucom et al. (2009):

> Overall, we try to help couples end their relationship in a manner in which both people are able to maintain a sense of personal dignity, and each partner not only respects the way that the other person has handled the situation but also concludes, "I liked the way that I handled the situation. I acted within my own value system. And although it was tempting at times to get dirty, I didn't do that."
>
> (p. 315)

Selling divorce therapy

When couple therapy fails to improve a marriage and divorce is looming, many couples wish to flee therapy ASAP. If the therapeutic alliance is still solid and not unbalanced, I encourage them to stay for a while. I do so by appealing to their (nearly universal) desire to do well by their children (if they have them) and to their (less universal) desire to end the war and move ahead with their lives, that is, to have a "good divorce." It is also easy to point to the many practical problems that now present themselves (e.g., who will live where and how to apportion childcare) and to suggest that they might use me to propose and discuss some "best practices" and help with negotiations.[4]

Some practical suggestions for divorce therapy

As with conjoint couple therapy generally, therapists will need to focus on making the process safe and productive, often by taking still more of a leadership role by steering discussions and (if they haven't done this before) teaching rules for speaking, listening, emotion regulation, timeouts, and problem solving (see Nielsen, 2016, Part IV).

Therapists should explicitly ask each partner what issues he or she hopes to address. Topics may include parenting, visitation, finances, mental health of a partner, boundaries, breakdowns in communication, or simply calming things down. It helps to have clients describe their greatest post-divorce fears and concerns: Are these about kids, money, loneliness, guilt, getting along with friends or relatives, or something else? Unlike mediation (discussed later), couple therapy can have a broader range of goals, including reviewing the relationship and working out issues between parents and children. Like mediation, goals should focus on the future, rather than on rehashing the past.

Working out detailed parenting agreements can do more than just settle arrangements; it can allow the divorcing couple to work together on a shared, constructive task. When successful, the co-parenting plan can serve as a transitional object—like the stuffed animals that make separations from parents bearable for children—as the couple give up their attachments as lovers and replace them with that of functioning co-parents (Iscoff, 2021). Parenting arrangements worked out by attorneys or the court will not provide that benefit and may aggravate the demonized splitting seen in high-conflict divorces if the goal is to determine who is the "best" parent.

In addition to helping the couple work together to set goals and co-parent, the following have proven helpful in divorce therapy:

- When tensions are particularly high, therapists can begin and end sessions with a calming mindfulness meditation. With extremely volatile couples, separate individual sessions may help.
- Therapists can encourage clients to avoid discussing loaded topics outside sessions, including in contentious emails, and to minimize contact in situations that stir up arguments (exchanges of children, shared school and social events).
- Therapists can help clients work out rule-driven methods of communication, since these become more challenging when parents no longer live together. In difficult divorces, written messages (emails, texts) may be preferable to voice messages since they can be better thought out and less emotional. The downside of these written formats is that they can be misconstrued or used against partners in litigation, which undermines their utility.
- Separate from such work on pragmatics, some work can be done, along the way, to develop a more complete, less demonic narrative of the divorce. As therapy progresses, therapists can help clients avoid viewing

their partners with undue suspicion when they behave *positively*, and to not mislabel their children as irreparably damaged when they report some foreseeable trouble or frustration with the other parent.

- Because some of this work can't be done conjointly, some clients should be referred to individual therapy to help them process the loss, review their contributions to the failed marriage, and plan their future.
- When individual therapists are involved, it can help to coordinate with them, as one should also do with mediators or lawyers. In such cases, couple therapists can act as information hubs or quarterbacks for the entire system (Lebow, 2019).
- As will be discussed in more detail shortly, therapists can help clients understand and work with the legal system, while also noting its limitations for resolving disputes.[5]
- If the partners are already involved in legal action, therapists should obtain a signed agreement early on concerning goals, functions, confidentiality, and reporting to lawyers and the court.
- Therapists should be clear that, in most cases, what is said will not be available as evidence in court battles, for instance, to modify existing custody agreements or as evidence concerning the "fitness" of either parent. These may be latent agendas, but unless you are specifically aware of them and experienced in this area, there are real dangers, including malpractice suits against you, unless you state your boundaries up front.
- Therapists can help couples avoid two common mistakes: It may be best to discourage *some* partners (usually husbands) from seeking 50:50 custody, which may be more childcare than they can realistically handle. Other partners can be encouraged to pay for their ex's education, a short-term expense that could lead to long-term reductions in financial support to, and increased self-esteem for, the beneficiary.
- Because parenting is a common and important topic for divorcing couples, it will sometimes help to involve the children directly in the therapy; other times, therapists can work with the parents alone to improve parenting skills and help their children cope. When possible and accurate, therapists can compliment parents on their parenting to soften the narcissistic blows that divorce entails.

Additional suggestions when a couple presents in the middle of a difficult divorce

- First meetings with partners should be individual to allow each to tell their story without being sidetracked by arguments over differing versions of facts.
- Payment: While it is customary for each person to pay half, it is best to work this out prior to the first session—via their attorneys, if they have them.

Modifications for when you are seeing only one of the divorcing partners

Whether you are treating partners together or individually in an ongoing divorce, you must keep in mind the systemic nature of what is going on (Lebow, 2019). As in other situations when therapists meet with only one party in a marriage, there is a strong likelihood that individual therapists will be co-opted by their client's demonization of their partner.[6] Systemic thinking doesn't come naturally for humans, and people easily default to blaming individual actors too much and taking at face value what they hear from a client, even from children. It is not uncommon for disagreements between individual therapists to parallel disagreements between their respective clients (Graller et al., 2001). As noted by Lebow (2019), some well-meaning therapists who express "empathy" for their clients may inadvertently fuel the fires of polarization.

Unsuspecting therapists may report events in court that clients told them that were not factual. The risks are considerable in difficult divorces and greatest when children are brought to therapy by only one parent, whose agenda and facts are often biased. Consequently, especially when working with individual clients, it is critical to communicate with others involved in the case, while respecting details clients may designate as off limits. These other people may include new partners, who can be a force for good by stabilizing the divorced partners. In other cases, a new partner, either at the time of separation or later, may destabilize and complicate things. Similarly, while legal professionals can impede progress, courts can also help, including by mandating therapy when it would not occur otherwise.

Countertransference and personal requirements for therapists

Divorce may evoke clinicians' own experiences of separation and loss and "serves as a stark reminder that even the best-laid plans for a shared life of closeness and joy can fall apart" (Ehrlich, 2014, p. x). As noted in the previous chapter, when conducting this work, it helps if one is philosophically neutral about divorce as an outcome. Even more than in couple therapy aimed at improving a relationship, therapists working with divorcing couples need to work hard not to jump to moralizing conclusions, deciding too quickly who is the villain and who is the victim. Thinking systemically and sometimes "siding with the least likeable partner" (Nielsen, 2016) may help, as will realizing that offensive, insensitive misbehavior is often secondary to a failure of the other partner to meet selfobject needs and provide "psychological oxygen" (Leone, 2008).

Patience will help, and so will the acceptance of some painful truths. After working for many years in a clinic specializing in difficult divorces (The Family Divorce Project of the Philadelphia Child Guidance Clinic, hereafter FDP), Isaacs and associates (2000) observed, "The therapist must have a clear realization that life is unfair, that symmetrical, balanced endings are rare, and that situations where both members land safely are unusual. Ordinarily, somebody gets more, somebody gets less" (p. 125). And Lebow (2019) adds the painful truths that "Not all co-parents can co-parent, not all divorced partners should be allowed to have contact with each other, and not all parents should be allowed to be in contact with their children" (p. 228).

Unsurprisingly, then, Lebow (2019), speaking after many years of experience with difficult divorces, suggests that some therapists are not suited for this work, specifically, "those who have a strong preference for less structured treatment, cherish having positive emotional connections to all their clients, frame all therapy as about growth, or primarily focus on raising clients' level of emotional experiencing" (p. 226). He strongly recommends that anyone working in this area should attend relevant workshops and obtain supervision from an experienced mentor. After reading Lebow's book, with its many complex examples, I would recommend you read it as a start, and second his advice that inexperienced therapists should seek expert assistance.

Mourning: the heart of the matter

> Divorcing grown-ups often have no idea how to bear grief; some do not even know they *are* grieving. Children in distress rarely have the words for their sorrow and anger and most divorcing parents lack means for helping them deal with their troubling feelings. We can think of the people, then, who approach therapists for help around divorce—an adult consumed with bitterness, a child acting out angrily at school, a parent and child unable to connect emotionally— as stuck or partially stuck around the tasks of mourning.
>
> —Joshua Ehrlich (2014, p. 74)

> Whereas an adult whose gradual acceptance of loss leads to the conclusion, "what happened, happened," a Mr. Neal [a client unable to mourn] insists that what happened should not have happened: It was unfair, immoral, or just plain wrong. Such people, then, do not see their task post-divorce as mastering internal struggles over loss. They believe, instead, that they must fight to rectify injustice.
>
> —Joshua Ehrlich (2014, p. 30)

The preceding quotes come from the best book I've found on the topic of how to help clients accept (i.e., mourn) the loss of their marriages. With many telling examples, Ehrlich illustrates how couples, especially in stalled difficult divorces, defend against the painful feelings engendered by divorce, most notably via perpetual conflicts that enact vengeance while maintaining a tie and sometimes represent an unconscious hope for reconciliation. Children also need to mourn, and this is more difficult when their parents are unable to manage their own grief.

As with other tragedies that we help our clients accept, progress will depend on assisting them to (a) reduce their defenses; (b) face and manage feelings of shame, guilt, and loss; and (c) find new satisfactions and resources elsewhere. Unfortunately, the popular defense of exaggerating the negative qualities of one's partner can mute painful feelings attending a divorce—guilt and second-guessing in the person who left and narcissistic injury in the person who was abandoned. Letting go of such negative views of the "troublesome other" (Stokkebekk et al., 2020), of defensive projections (Nielsen, 2019b), and of "grievance stories" (Luskin, 2002) will sometimes be made more difficult by litigation that rewards these defenses and by further painful experiences of perceived selfishness by partners who were previously primary love objects.

Finding the meaning

Ehrlich makes the key point that to help people mourn a loss, one must discover what it means to them; the significance can vary greatly from person to person and explains why divorce is far more distressing for some people than for others. For many people, a divorce shatters the hopeful belief that two people can remain in love and care for each other as they face life's challenges, "in sickness and in health," on into old age, ending only when "death do us part." Mourning signals a lost future, so well described by Judy Wallerstein (quoted in Ehrlich, 2014):

> Even the most miserable marriage embodied some expectation of a better life, companionship, love, and esteem, and although no tears may be shed for the lost partner, the symbolic meaning of the marriage should be put to rest with gentleness.
>
> (p. 17)

People also enter marriage with *fears* of what might happen: that it will end in divorce like that of their parents, or that one's chosen mate, like a parent or prior lover, will become depressed, take to drinking, or have affairs. Coupled with these feared "ghosts from the past" (see my Christmases Past case in Nielsen, 2016), partners enter with hopes for healing. They wish for partners who will not replay past traumas but who will, instead, provide emotional support and bolster self-esteem as they leave their families of origin. So, when marriages come apart, these past fears and future hopes (now dashed) can come online again. Some of these are illustrated in the following case example from Ehrlich (2014):

> Mr. Berger was stunned by his wife's decision to end their marriage. A driven and accomplished businessman, Mr. Berger harbored the fantasy that he could control the world, a fantasy bolstered by business successes. Delighted by his wife's idealization of his accomplishments, he felt crushed as she became disillusioned with his lack of commitment to the family. Her decision to leave him shattered his fantasy of control and his enlivening experience of being admired, leaving him feeling small,

inadequate, and ashamed. Alongside that terrible injury to his pride, Mr. Berger struggled to manage intense sorrow over losing a woman he had deeply loved. He engaged in a series of brief affairs that left him feeling even lonelier . . . .

Because his wife served soothing selfobject functions for him, bolstering his self-esteem, losing her meant losing important psychological *functions* she provided. Mr. Berger also was *attached* to his wife, appreciating her as a strong woman whose passion for the arts and child-rearing capacities he valued and appreciated. They had taken great pleasure in raising their children, and Mr. Berger especially cherished memories of family trips to his childhood home on the California coast. Thus, he was losing a person he valued, relied on, and shared with. In addition, his wife's decision to end the marriage re-evoked painful childhood experiences of powerlessness and inadequacy when Mr. Berger had been rendered helpless by forces outside his control.

(pp. 7–8)

By comparing divorce to an "ambiguous loss" (Boss, 1999)—a situation unlike death, with its clear-cut finality—we can see how some people can harbor the hope that the loss of a living former partner is not permanent and might be reversed. We see this especially in children's wishes that parents reunite. Accepting the finality of divorce is made harder because, for parents with children, there is never a complete "death" of the relationship, as it continues through shared parenting. Shared children can also delay mourning because their very existence is a reminder of the marriage, especially if they resemble one of their parents. Unsurprisingly, research shows that the presence of children, with the need for continued co-parenting, makes recovery from divorce harder and that parents' problems accepting divorce correlate with children's internalizing and externalizing problems (DeAnda et al., 2020).

The future

Moving on also involves "relinquishment of the familiar" (Steiner, 2005), as people change residences, take on new parenting roles, and alter routines that have long been taken for granted. For many, finding a new partner feels daunting. The stress of reordering their lives makes many people cling to the past, to the "devil they know." Therapists see this problem frequently when trying to help people leave unrewarding jobs or unsuitable dating relationships. For many people, "It feels better to have shoes that don't quite fit than no shoes at all." Facilitating this aspect of mourning involves helping people imagine and then create a satisfying new future.[7]

Mourning therapeutics

By now, you should have a general idea about how to help clients mourn. Here's a more condensed outline with some particulars not yet mentioned:

- *Begin by validating the client's distress, normalizing what you can, and offering hope* that they can bear the pain and create a better future. Keep in mind that you are providing the support and "holding" that will make this work tolerable and productive.
- *Work to uncover and diminish guilt and shame.*
- *Inquire about personal meanings,* including those derived from earlier traumatic losses and events. Help clients see connections between prior events and the current divorce that sensitize them and make letting go more difficult.
- *Gently challenge defenses* that serve to protect clients from deeper distress. Help them see that they can get by without recourse to maladaptive "survival strategies." Accept that "immature defenses" (Vaillant, 1993) will slow the work and require special care.
- *Allow verbal expressions of anger* that, if suppressed, may lead to depression or aggressive actions.
- *Look for hurt and sadness as primary emotions that are concealed behind secondary expressions of anger and wishes for revenge.*
- *Try to forestall destructive acting out* that—while providing a temporary sense of agency—may delay reality acceptance and mourning. Uncover the hurt that powers this. Look for envy when a client perceives an ex-spouse as happy, successful, or having "moved on," since uncontained envy can motivate vengeful acts intended to spoil the ex's perceived happiness.
- *Help clients accept that compromising with ex-partners is not the same as "selling out."* Challenge all-or-nothing, zero-sum thinking when it occurs.
- *Praise clients when they show the courage to bear the pain and move on* without resorting to vindictiveness or endless wrangling.
- *Encourage clients not to collude with those who offer praise to children for being falsely "mature"* by not showing distress or intense feelings, or who criticize them for "not getting over it."
- *Help parents cope with the guilt and distress that can interfere with helping their children discuss and process the divorce.*
- *Encourage clients to gain support from family, friends, and religious leaders but warn them about the dangers that can come from biased outsiders.*

A note on projective identification

Projection and projective identification (see Nielsen, 2019b) are often the core problems blocking mourning in contentious, never-ending difficult divorces. This may start when one party projects all the malevolence, badness, and failings onto the other and thereby induces the recipient of the projection either to counterattack or to collapse into induced incapacity. Other scenarios may be more mutual, as partners engage in what Bion (1961) termed a defensive "fight group," as anxiety is managed by a never-ending battle that conceals and delays facing the actual problems at hand.

Some projectors may not be people with severe personality disorders but only "normal" people in the throes of a divorce, who:

in the same way that couples idealise each other in order to manage the anxieties attendant with marriage, [now when] . . . choosing to divorce must de-idealise the other in order to manage the pain of the attendant losses. The result is that the reluctant spouse feels unimaginably betrayed.

(K. Scharff, 2014b, p. 281)

And, of course, both partners may default to de-idealizing the other, not just the one who was rejected, and both may then feel unfairly injured.

The therapeutic challenge here—as in all cases of severe personality disorders where splitting and projective identification are in play, and in healthier couples caught in such death spirals of projective identification—is to try to help clients "contain" the feelings/attributions that they are locating in their partners. Often, this is not possible, especially when projectors do not see the need for therapy, as in the following tragic example from Ehrlich (2014):

Mr. Neal, severely under-parented as a child, struggled throughout adolescence and early adulthood with social isolation and pervasive feelings of inadequacy. He was astonished in his early thirties when a woman found him attractive and wanted to marry him. However, when his wife became fed up with his controlling, jealous mode of interacting and left after eight years, Mr. Neal became seriously depressed and then consumed with bitterness. He initiated a ferocious court battle for custody of his daughter, Chloe, which he eventually won . . . Controlled and articulate, Mr. Neal managed to convince the judge that his ex-wife posed a grave threat to Chloe. In contrast, as he presented it, he was essentially flawless. The passage of time had done nothing to ameliorate Mr. Neal's outrage. He could not talk about his ex-wife without spitting venom . . . By attributing all disturbance to his wife and exaggerating his own virtues, Mr. Neal disowned a role in the demise of his marriage, protecting his fragile self-esteem. By viewing his wife as disturbed, he also could invalidate his reasons for having loved her (i.e., how could he possibly love someone so awful?), thus assuring himself there was no reason to feel sad about losing her. Fully defended against awareness of the hurt and sadness he did feel, Mr. Neal focused on his righteous mission to protect his daughter from her "crazy" mother. . . . Mr. Neal is not mourning. We see no awareness of sorrow or guilt, no rewriting of a "divorce script" that reflects increasing awareness of his role in the marital problems or empathy for his ex-wife's travails. The psychological imperative to keep sorrow and hurt out of conscious awareness takes precedence over—and renders impossible—a goodbye. Projective defenses—which place intolerable feelings outside oneself—invariably impede mourning because mourning, by definition, means working with them internally.

(pp. 29–30)

Stem sentences to counter demonization

Not all divorces end so tragically, although countering demonization can be therapeutically difficult. Nelson (2015), working conjointly with couples, offers the following exercise designed specifically to diminish natural (if not long-standing) inclinations to demonize partners. She prints out the following stems and asks partners to complete them (separately) between sessions. They then share them during divorce therapy:

- "One thing I appreciated about our marriage was . . ."
- "One dream I'm letting go of is . . ."
- "One thing I'm deeply sorry for is . . ."
- "One way I'll always care for you is . . ."
- "I'm helping you move forward by . . ."

To keep this exercise from deteriorating into a fight that will erase its benefits, she limits what the other can say mainly to registering and repeating what was said.

Some additional practical matters

What to tell family and friends

As with affairs, therapists can (sometimes) help couples agree not to overly demonize their partners to mutual friends and family members (especially their children).

Residence issues

Although my experience is limited, there are two residential setups that have not worked well: *nesting*, where the children stay in one home and the parents move in and out; and *cohabitation*, where both parents stay in the home and alternate parenting duties. Cohabitation may result from limited funds or fear of losing leverage in custody disputes if a partner moves out, but over time, it creates too many opportunities for painful interacting. What is preferable is moving as quickly as possible to two equivalent domiciles that can accommodate the children, rather than a home base and a satellite.

What to tell the kids

Ideally, parents should co-author and then share a jointly acceptable, non-pathologizing narrative of the divorce, keeping in mind that the children may remember this conversation forever. They should say that they are both very sad about the divorce, that they tried hard to avoid it, and that they had enjoyed good times in the marriage and as the family grew and will miss those.

Parents should be clear that, even though they may have been seen fighting about parenting, the children are loved and are not to blame for the divorce.

Parents should say that they expect that the children will be sad and angry, and that they hope they can help them with those feelings. They should explain what will happen next concerning living space, visitation, holidays, and other logistics, with an eye to the children's needs and interests. In doing this, they should not sugarcoat or mislead children about the challenges ahead and the adjustments they will have to make. Along the way and at the end, parents should ask their children what they know about divorce and how they are thinking about it now, after listening to what the parents have said.

Parents should not consider this a one-and-done event but should be prepared to continue to field distress, questions, and complaints going forward.

Therapists can warn parents to avoid denigrating each other, since research shows this harms children and, paradoxically, can boomerang and adversely impact the relationship between the child and the denigrating parent (Rowen & Robert, 2014). That said, parents should validate realistic complaints their children make about their ex-spouses, like excessive drinking or failing to keep promises about visiting. When doing so, however, parents should be mindful of possible hidden agendas from the child (e.g., playing the parents against each other, bonding with the listener) and of preferring to have a child validate an experience they share. In the following example, a mother has trouble seeing her daughter's disappointment with her father, and reacts poorly:

> Upon returning from a weekend with her father, Staci, ten, complained to her mother that her father spent most of Saturday afternoon watching college football. Her mother responded, "Yeah, big surprise, that was one of the reasons I had to get out of the marriage." Optimally a mother might say, "That sounds hard. Did you try to let your dad know how you felt about it?" . . . Over time, Staci came to feel that there was no real point in speaking to her mother about frustrating features of life at her father's home and stopped doing so . . . . More ominously, Staci might come to feel that complaining about her father would be the most reliable avenue for connecting emotionally with her mother and the quality of her relationship with her father may erode. Alternatively, she may come to feel estranged from her mother because her mother refuses to support her relationship with her beloved (if frustrating) father.
>
> (Ehrlich, 2014, p. 55)

When faced with parents who hold divergent views of each other and events, children are taxed to find an explanation. Some can be helped by what we couple therapists know and communicate to couples daily: that there is usually truth on both sides, even if the failure to accept the other side's truth leads to a standoff. Without help, too many children in high-conflict divorces end up choosing sides.

Helping children with mourning

Whether consumed by their own problems or basking in the excitement of living with a new partner, many divorcing parents reduce vigilance and overall involvement in parenting, leaving children to fend for themselves. Many parents will misread their children as "doing just fine" or as "simply misbehaving." Others will heedlessly involve them in loyalty conflicts or custody battles.

Ideally, parents should encourage their children to share how they are doing and, without being too dramatic, share their own grief as a model that normalizes this for their kids. There are many reasons parents and children commonly avoid these conversations. Parents who cannot face their own feelings will not be able to help their children do so; they may not notice signs of distress in their kids and won't welcome discussions initiated by the children.

Additionally, parent–child conversations about feelings are difficult. Many parents either push too hard or give in too easily when children don't want to talk and when children falsely say they are "Just fine!" Feeling guilty about the divorce, parents may be too ready to accept at face value their child's assertion that things are OK, and children may not want to stress their parents with the truth. Therapists can help by encouraging, coaching, and sometimes directly facilitating dialogue. While referrals for child therapy can help, parents should not simply farm out the task of helping their children through this stressful time.

Like grown-ups, children institute defenses against mourning and facing the new reality. Common defenses include denial and affect suppression (especially, anger at parents), self-blame, withdrawal, somatic distress, being excessively "good," defiant acting out in many forms, and, for older kids, promiscuity, drug use, and delinquency. Many children displace their anger, directing their hostility at peers and teachers. Such acting out should be reframed as a cry for help. Many children will become depressed or lose traction in school.

Parents telling children not to blame themselves for a divorce does not solve the problem of children feeling helpless in a world where they have no say in whether a divorce will happen. Just as natural disasters outside people's control may elicit fantasies that misbehavior caused them (cf., the story of the flood in Genesis), so too, having no control may feel worse than imagining that one's misbehavior caused the problem.

Like kids who blame themselves to cope, "parentified children" help out too much in a reversal of the usual parent–child caretaking hierarchy. Parents contribute to this pattern if they misuse or overuse children as confidants, companions, bed partners, or childcare workers. Such children may later have trouble separating from parents and establishing independent lives of their own.

Fathers may not only have difficulty discussing distressing feelings with their kids but may have trouble simply being with them and enjoying time together, since doing so can trigger heart-rending memories of happy times as a family prior to the divorce. Events that previously were pleasurable (attending a school play or sharing a holiday) can now cause pain. Some fathers cope by further distancing from their children, who then miss them even more.

Visitation and custody arrangements

Parents who are angry at their ex's or who are denying their own wishes to stay married can make this situation worse by minimizing their children's needs to see their ex and by making it hard for them to be together. This will have the most negative impact on children who were close to the other parent, who will now have to choose between working to maintain contact or giving them up to escape the custodial parent's anger.

Often, when parents argue intensely about parenting or custody agreements, they are arguing about what is best for *them*, while discounting their children's needs and preferences. Therapists can point to the mental health needs of children to continue contact with the other parent, and—in situations where one parent is vindictively discouraging access—they can use additional arguments based on self-interest and likely consequences. The following interventions were suggested by hardened veterans of the FDP: "The children will never learn how difficult he really is; then they're yours completely, and he gets off the hook; then you will get no help from him, while he enjoys himself and takes no responsibility for their care," or "If they have no contact with their father, they'll blame it on you and hate you. It will destroy your relationship with your children" (Isaacs et al., p. 190). These interventions sneakily engage the mothers' vindictiveness and self-interest in the service of a better future for all. Gentler versions that still encourage shared custody and allow contemplation of the dangers ahead ask the parent, "What kind of childhood do you want your child to remember years from now?" and "What kind of relationship do you want to have with your child years from now?"

Therapists treating only the custodial parent may sometimes help by reaching out to the noncustodial parent, fostering trust and their participation in therapy. Sometimes, lawyers or court orders mandate participation of both partners. Should a partner continue to be unavailable, the therapy can shift to helping everyone accept that painful reality.

Therapists assisting discussion of custody and visitation arrangements should avoid a rush to judgment that decides too quickly who is "the best parent" or that the child(ren) should live with the parent they think best since, as noted by the FDP experts:

> Every clinician and every divorce lawyer is familiar with the situation in which the parent who looks best "psychologically" and with whom the child obviously wants to stay is in fact overtly or covertly blocking the child's relationship with the other parent. Also commonplace is the situation in which it becomes clear over time that a child's insistence on living with a particular parent is based on the belief that he or she must save that parent from falling apart.
>
> (Isaacs et al., p. 222)

Another problem that can be flagged so as to avoid trouble later is a custody decision that generates so much resentment that the "losing" parent either fails to comply or endlessly returns to relitigate the agreement. *Moral: When possible, work toward equitable and realistic agreements, ones that are more likely to stick.*

Mom's house, Dad's house, and a businesslike relationship

Ideally, divorcing partners can set up two households that come to be seen as resources rather than threats in a zero-sum game. The goal should be to give the children "two homes with no fighting" (Ricci, 1997, 2012). This requires that parents give up being lovers and continue as co-parents. Separate from the work of mourning, Ricci thinks parents can be helped to make this shift by offering them the metaphor of a business relationship. She tells divorced partners, "You don't have to love your former mate to have a businesslike relationship any more than you have to love your mechanic to get your car fixed" (1997, p. 36). Such relationships are characterized by: (a) a focus on the business at hand; (b) formal, courteous, cordial, and public interactions; (c) high personal privacy and low personal self-disclosure; and (d) attention to building and maintaining trustworthiness.

When a client responds to this with, "I hate my ex so much there is no way I could ever do business with him [or her]!" Ricci (1997) counters with,

> Pretend you need to obtain insulin for your diabetic child, and you are living on a frontier outpost. The only source of insulin, by a twist of fate, is controlled by someone you distrust. If you don't find a way to do business with this person, you are courting a serious medical emergency with your child.
>
> (p. 85)

She wants to jettison the destructive myth that if the couple couldn't work together when married, they won't be able to do so after divorce. While couples who were not good at managing conflict before will often have the same problems post-divorce, it is also true that many people do better with friends than with roommates, and that people can work together in business and not want to be friends. Former spouses can join around the shared, agreed-on task of parenting, while not wanting to spend time with each other in other ways. Children can benefit as they watch two people they love work together despite feelings of anger, hurt, and resentment. This makes them feel safe and teaches them by example.

For some couples, a business relationship is all we can expect. Others may gradually resume friendship, and some may eventually treat each other as extended family, but a business relationship baseline often gets things off to a good start.

Ricci also offers clients a positive way to characterize their post-divorce situation: Rather than "I have a failed marriage and am raising my kids part-time," they can say, "I have a family with three kids who live with me during most weeks and alternate weekends, and with their father (mother) the rest of the time. The children have two homes." Ricci offers the following specific recommendations for parents living separately:

- Make both homes feel like *homes* for the kids (not hotels), regardless of how much time the kids are there.
- Maintain your own "territory" and respect the autonomy of your co-parent, including their privacy and right to decide what goes on in their home on their watch
- Respect the other parent's time with the children. Even if things come up (say, tickets to a basketball game), you must get an OK from the other parent before mentioning it as a possibility to the kids. If the other parent is adamant and you really want to smooth the waters, give those tickets to him/her.
- Try hard to be flexible, reliable, and helpful.
- Interfere only when a child needs your protection. In such cases, get outside help. It's unreasonable to expect perfect parenting or total agreement on how it should be done.
- Do not make assumptions about what the other parent will do; write things down and send written plans/understandings back and forth. If emotions are running high and you trigger each other easily, try to do most communicating in writing, by email or text.
- Kids should be allowed to talk about what went on at the other home, as they would about other events, like what went on at school.

Some additional co-parenting suggestions for divorcing parents

Ideally, parents should choose their battles, respond promptly and amicably to requests for schedule changes, and try to build a collaborative relationship that respects differences and prioritizes the needs of the children. For many fathers, it may be the first time they have been solely responsible for children; for many mothers, it may be the first time they are not overseeing the father's caretaking. Therapists can encourage and help partners to be patient as they adjust and learn new roles. The following can help reduce mayhem:

- No spontaneous discussions when making handoffs of kids.
- No significant discussions in the presence of kids.
- Find a regular time to talk each week by phone. If this is likely to be heated, set a co-parenting agenda ahead of time by email and stick to it.
- Allow children to communicate freely back and forth between households.
- Follow Karen Bonnell's advice: "If I borrow a cup of sugar, I'm going to bring you a piece of pie," by which she means when requesting a favor, parents should ideally return it with a little more sweetness. When a co-parent obliges a schedule change request, show appreciation. When

they don't, accept it gracefully (cited in Bonnell & Papernow, 2019, p. 214).

- Try to reduce the stress of kids living "between two worlds" by discussing and agreeing on expectations and consequences that apply in both households. Parents can let this go if it becomes too snarled in conflict, and, instead, draw clearer boundaries concerning differences. Couples often think this will confuse children, so it helps to point out that rules at school or at their friends' homes may be different, and that isn't fatal. When a child says, "But Mommy lets me drink Coke!" Dad can respond, "I know. At Mommy's you can drink Coke. At Daddy's we drink milk. When you grow up you can decide which is better." Not: "Mommy never did care about nutrition" (Papernow, 2018a, p. 41).
- Don't assume that what your child says happened at the other house is absolutely the case but remain curious about it.
- When a child complains about the other parent or relays a criticism from that parent, consider coaching the child on how to cope directly with the other parent.

While sharing these "best practice" recommendations, therapists can encourage fathers to stay involved with their children, meet with parents together to work out details, and, when feelings are running hot, engage in "shuttle diplomacy" between them.

Children with problems

In addition to the recommendations mentioned already, including in Chapter 8, therapists asked to work with children during a divorce should avoid the countertransference tendency to try to become a better parent for the child, something that can push parents to the side and minimize their importance to their children. Therapists should also resist pressure from one parent to exclude the other parent when treating a child. Not only are there legal dangers in doing this, but even if one believes a client's story that the absent parent is the problem, it still makes more sense to involve that person in the therapy, at minimum in the assessment phase.

When you do this, first ask the parents if they can be in the same room together for a meeting; if not, meet with them separately. If you do meet together, limit the agenda to talking about the child's needs and problems and intervene when things drift toward unfinished marital issues, while remaining sensitive to how hard this may be to do.

Special considerations regarding adolescents

Adolescents can be even harder to reach because of their flight from dependency on parents, their normative de-idealization of parents, and their claims of needing time with their peers. Compared to younger children, they are also more skilled in playing one parent off against the other. Parents, tempted to give in too easily to the idea that teens don't need closeness with parents, should be warned about this mistake. As noted by the FDP clinicians,

> The distancing adolescent may find an anchorage in socially acceptable areas—schoolwork in preparation for college, sports, or religious activities, or a stable relationship with a boyfriend or girlfriend. But there is also the strong possibility that he or she will latch onto delinquent groups and activities or drift perilously alone.
>
> (Isaacs et al., 2000, p. 184)

Therefore, ideally, parents should be helped to work together to set limits, counsel about dangers (sex, drugs, and driving), and, above all, provide emotional support.

Resources for parents

Two excellent self-help books for parents are:

- R. E. Emery (2016). *Two Homes, One Childhood: A Parenting Plan to Last a Lifetime.* New York, NY: Avery.
- I. Ricci (2012). *The CoParenting Toolkit: The Essential Supplement for Mom's House, Dad's House.* San Ramon, CA: Custody and CoParenting Solutions.

Dealing with the legal system

Couples in difficult divorces involve lawyers and courts as they battle over finances and parenting agreements. At minimum, this adds stress due to time and money spent. While such involvement is not inevitably bad and is always necessary to finalize the divorce and give legal standing to eventual agreements, it presents complications that even experienced therapists find challenging. Ideally, I discourage clients from rushing to lawyers or making lasting decisions while their emotions are running hot; I try to help them first mourn and work out some initial details concerning living arrangements and parenting. Once the legal system becomes seriously involved, its win–lose environment and focus on fault-finding can interfere with mourning and, ironically, with reaching acceptable compromises, per the following quote from Lebow:

> [T]he adversarial context of much of the judicial system provides endless opportunities for confrontations in pleadings, subpoenas, depositions, and court appearances, which frequently engender conflict at a personal level as well as within the legal system. Statements made by attorneys, text in pleadings, and behavior around such issues as the

sharing of financial information or a parent's conduct readily become the focus of arguments and bad feelings.

(2019, p. 166)

There is, however, some good news: In situations where therapists feel it will interfere with therapy to testify (most cases!), they can usually avoid this by "letting the attorney who wants the therapist's participation know that it will not be helpful to their client's case" (Lebow, 2019, p. 183). And, contrary to what you might think, sometimes courts can be quite helpful to therapists, especially by providing leverage that forces clients to attend treatment and not end it prematurely. Sometimes, the simple requirement to report on attendance can help.

To navigate these waters, therapists should (a) learn how to communicate and with whom, (b) establish a relationship with a trusted attorney to consult with as needed, and (c) find a reliable way to learn about court developments. Attorneys for the children are often the best conduits of information between the court and therapists, although sharing information with attorneys must be done with caution.

If clients will allow it, therapists should contact their attorney(s). As when talking to other therapists, this can head off demonization of unseen partners and flag sensitive issues that lawyers may not be aware of. Sharing information with a client's attorney should only be about what you have witnessed and should be balanced with sharing with the other client's attorney.

Therapists can help clients prepare for meetings with their lawyers, mediators, and spouses. Therapists can help clients prioritize their goals, discuss their options, and identify triggers that may throw them off their game. Role-playing of difficult conversations can help clients feel more confident and prepare ways to present their desires so that they will be heard. Some clients can be encouraged to take a friend with them when they meet with their lawyer, as they might when going to a potentially unsettling doctor's appointment, since clients may have difficulty hearing what is said and remembering it later.

As you play your part in assisting with these negotiations, keep in mind the advantages and limitations of legal documents: While detailed agreements that have been worked out in therapy, in mediation, or between lawyers can help avoid future disagreements (say, over who pays for camp or college), they can never be complete enough to avert the need to manage all future disputes especially if underlying feelings have not been settled. Sometimes, mandated mediation can be written into agreements, which may help when post-divorce disputes ensue.

Mediation

Divorce mediation has become a popular format for divorcing couples to work out legal matters. In most situations, a trial of mediation is superior to partners going straight to separate lawyers. Since legal agreements that will stand up in court must be worked out, mediators who are knowledgeable in the law and skilled in facilitating negotiations can help as they meet simultaneously with the partners. Mediation is private, gives parties more time to talk to each other than shuttling documents between lawyers, and is usually less expensive. While many people believe that they will do better in a litigation process with a lawyer who will "fight" for them against a self-centered opponent, mediation usually allows more control and protection, especially since it is far less likely to create an escalating, paranoid, adversarial process.

Research supports the efficacy of mediation (Sharra et al., 2019), including one long-term follow-up study (Emery et al., 2001), which found that three-quarters of couples in litigation were able to resolve conflicts over child custody in mediation versus only one-third who proceeded without it.

When lawyers are preferred

The principal difficulty when working with any divorcing couple is helping people who could not manage conflict while married to do so while separating, when they are usually even more traumatized and angry with each other. Consequently, and unsurprisingly, clinical experience and limited research (Bickerdike & Littlefield, 2000) find that mediation is less effective for couples who have failed to accept that the marriage is over and misuse mediation sessions to rehash their marital issues. For some people, mediation serves as a litmus test, identifying couples for whom it doesn't work, those who will require lawyers to represent them in what are likely to be difficult divorces. There are also rare cases (intimate partner violence, sociopathy, and extreme dishonesty) where a full-scale, litigated divorce is preferable from the outset.

For cases unsuitable for mediation or ones that fail at it, lawyers may serve as "sane communicators," who shuttle back and forth between the parties. As skilled negotiators, lawyers may also draw up "one plan solutions" (Fisher et al., 1981) that shorten what might otherwise be endless negotiations. Some of these cases will also involve lawyers for the children or parenting coordinators appointed by the court. Model lawyers will know how to calm the waters and help their clients manage the trauma they are experiencing. Top-notch therapists will continue to think systemically as they try to work with this complex system.

The Just-Tell-Us-What-to-Do Couple: lessons from a divorce therapy

What can you do when a marriage is about to go over a cliff? What issues come up? How can you help to minimize the damage? How do you manage your countertransferences? I will try to illustrate these and other issues covered in this chapter with the following case that began with the wife 95% sure that she "had had it" after 15 years in a loveless marriage.

A short trial of discernment counseling ended abruptly after Sheri confessed to a recent, brief affair and Todd ceased (manifestly) trying to have her stop divorcing him. Unlike many couples, they continued with me for the next six months in the format we had begun with: I met with each of them weekly and with both together almost as often. When it became clear that my neutrality was stretched to the limit, I polled them on options, learned that Todd had already sought the services of two other therapists/coaches (!), and then, with their blessing, continued individual therapy with Sheri, though with some intermittent email and phone contacts with Todd. Sheri's therapy continued for three years as we dealt with the extended divorcing process, problems with their children, and her post-divorce love life. What follows is a condensed description of three years of therapy, something that could easily be a 300-page noir novel. After setting the stage, I'll discuss some topics we worked on, focusing on lessons learned.

Presentation and background

Sheri, a stylish business consultant for an international firm, had married Todd, a consultant engineer, when both were in graduate school. Neither had dated much prior to that. They had grown up in similar suburbs, with many interests in common. They began slowly, as friends. She was attracted to him as financially promising and smart, a man with a plan, and a man unlikely to leave her—all the opposite of her father. He was attracted to her as smart, outgoing, sexy, and strongly attached to him—very much the opposite of his socially awkward, obsessional family and his own personal style. They had three children, ages 12, 10, and 6, the oldest and youngest with emotional problems.

Both came from unpromising backgrounds. Sheri's parents divorced when she was 5. Her engineer father remarried twice. Sheri was shuttled between homes and suffered from the lack of financial and emotional stability. Her first "wicked stepmother" preferred her own children over Sheri. Her second "wicked stepmother" convinced her father to pull the plug on Sheri's college tuition at a prestigious university, forcing her to switch to a much less desirable state school. Outgoing and sociable, Sheri had always had friends, but had been insecure, especially with boys.

Todd's background was worse than he, at first, related, apparently with an autism gene running in the family: His mother and sister were always socially inept and embarrassing. Todd had been a nerd, insecurely attached, with few close friends and the manager of his high school golf team. Not good at day-to-day relationships in business, he, nonetheless, had developed a convincing, methodical style that helped him sell software systems.

Though drawn to each other by powerful wishes for a sort of marital cure (see Nielsen, 2019b), neither had been "in love" with the other (or anyone else). Their honeymoon was remembered for a problem that plagued their marriage: Todd's insecurity had been so powerful that he had forbidden Sheri from spending any time alone with friends who had coincidentally been vacationing at the same resort. Despite this inauspicious start, Sheri had been drawn to him as successful and, unlike her, sure of his life course. Both had focused on their careers and on the children who came soon after they married. As time went by, however, Sheri complained that Todd worked too much and was never home. Re-evaluating his (concretized) belief that their bond depended most on his making lots of money, and worried about losing her, Todd changed course and pulled back, and the couple relocated to Chicago. As it turned out, this destabilized their "marriage contract" (Sager, 1994), as they reversed roles: Todd now became more the intrusive pursuer, upset, as on their honeymoon, by any evidence that Sheri didn't love him or that he was a lower priority than her friends, their kids, or her work. Now more convinced that their relationship depended more on money earned than on time spent together, Todd felt used and angrily told her so. Thinking concretely and behaviorally about their love life, Todd gave Sheri an ultimatum that they must have "intimacy" at least 30 minutes per day or he would leave.

Although Sheri had married Todd, in part, because she was sure he "wouldn't leave her," now his barnacle-like, insecure attachment style was driving her nuts. Feeling beset and oppressed by his insults, his sexual ultimatum, and what had long seemed his lack of empathy, Sheri would blow up, defensively, confirming Todd's fears by telling him how relieved she was when he wasn't around and how, possibly, he should go have an affair to let her off the sexual hook.

First session

In keeping with their putting off therapy till their marital cancer was about to kill it—Todd out of psychological deafness, Sheri out of "hysterical" blindness—Sheri came 15 minutes late for this session that she had finally convinced Todd to attend. She blamed Todd for this lateness, mentioning things he had failed to handle at home that had held her up. Todd, who had arrived on time, had been eager to get started without her and had already completed my questionnaire on his iPad. (This would be a pattern going forward: Todd trying hard to follow directions while oblivious to the needs of others.)

Sheri was thin, fit, severe, dressed in attractive business attire. She was highly emotional, alternating between angrily defending herself and crying intensely as she conveyed her hopelessness. Todd was slightly overweight, schlumpy, and more casually dressed. He sulked angrily during most of the session in which I obtained their history. Todd softened when I suggested that he would appreciate some empathy from Sheri ("You panic, doubting that you matter to Sheri."). However, while relating to me like a good student, and listening when I described their circular dynamics (his chasing/harassing her that caused her to flee or angrily refuse to give him what he wanted), Todd remained unmoved, viewing himself as the victim of an ungrateful wife and equally skeptical that their marriage could be saved.

Discernment phase

We agreed to a few more diagnostic meetings, after which we began discernment counseling. During that time, I tried to help Todd acknowledge his role in driving Sheri away, without success. While he listened, he kept returning to his suspicion that she was cheating on him, something that might explain the inconsistency in her behavior; he showed me "documentary evidence" of her love in cards she had written him in the last year that contrasted with her recent statements of disgust. Since Sheri had denied an affair to me in our individual meetings, I initially suggested to Todd that Sheri's inconsistent behavior reflected her ambivalence, coupled with her fear of revealing how unhappy she was.

As it turned out, Sheri was very unhappy, but she was also lying to both of us about a brief affair. She had taken up four months previously with their dog trainer (not quite the "pool boy," but close), a 30-year-old married man. He was the opposite of Todd's near Asperger-like behavior, a "dog whisperer" who skillfully tuned in to Sheri's feelings and knew how to make her feel sexy and admired. She knew this relationship was crazy and impossible, but she was smitten and told me about it only after she had ended it and told Todd.

Sadly, this was pretty much the end of productive work with Todd, who now found it easier to locate all their problems in Sheri's cheating and, before that, her years of lying to him about her unhappiness (which was, indeed, partly correct, just as she had also lied to me). When Todd asked me if he should still send a thank you card to that dog trainer, who had taken care of their dog during a recent vacation (!!), I got a taste of how Todd could ask weird questions that, on reflection, concealed and projected his rage (concealed, since sending poison would have better matched his feelings; projected, since sending a complimentary card might prevent retaliation from a jealous rival).

Therapy with Todd

In the six months that followed, when I met with Todd weekly and the couple almost weekly, it was easy to see that Sheri was not coming back to the marriage. Todd had trouble handling this. He fell apart and was unable to sleep or work. I helped steady him through this as I have done with others shocked in the wake of a partner's affair and the prospect of divorce.

But my assistance was never enough, so that Todd now enacted a similar dance with me as he did with Sheri: sending me long, detailed, obsessive emails, many as emergencies on weekends, asking for direction on how to manage. (Feeling his pain, I took time to respond, but I also charged him, to cool my countertransference annoyance.) Some of Todd's questions seemed practical and understandable, although he used them to counter the powerlessness he felt as his world was falling apart. But most of the time, his proposals for the couple's "planned separation" failed because he focused so much on behavior ("When should we date other people?" "Should we take our rings off now?") while ignoring the feelings that made them impossible to follow (e.g., he couldn't bring himself to vacate their home). After acting out with Sheri by coming into the bathroom when she was dressing, he wrote me detailed questions about what was wrong with this, as he would later inquire about obviously inappropriate conduct with his daughters. His Asperger brain cried out for "Rules to Live By," so that Todd reminded me of Sheldon on the sitcom, *Big Bang Theory*, whose mother, faced with similar social cluelessness, had taught Sheldon to "Always offer upset people a warm drink." Todd had great trouble leaving our sessions; most went over time and ended only when I had to almost kick him out physically, again showing his attachment insecurity and his inability to absorb what I had to offer.

As with others who obsess following an attachment injury, I talked with him about ways to calm himself and encouraged reaching out to friends. It was sad to learn that he had no close friends, having relied on Sheri for that function, something that made her loss even more poignant and painful. He resisted my suggestion that he join a group for divorcing fathers, instead refocusing on his work, even as trouble concentrating made that hard for him.

What was it, I often wondered, that Todd needed that might have helped him feel incrementally satisfied and able to leave our sessions feeling better? I offered lots of empathy and, in keeping with my understanding of what makes for prolonged difficult divorces, I tried to help him face and then manage his shame and humiliation at being left. It was easy to see how a person would feel terrible, especially as he continued to try so hard "to stay on the team" but now, as in high school, was relegated to the limited role of team manager (i.e., co-parent). I also tried to console him for not having seen this coming, though he mostly blamed Sheri for not telling him about her dissatisfaction.

But Todd, like other obsessional, nonpsychological types, kept his focus on his "grievance story" and concrete logistics, details of the divorce agreement, and lengthy communication emails back and forth. He also defended himself by triangulating his kids into the fray, as either attempted allies or stand-ins for Sheri, whom he could control, berate, and talk to endlessly. At times, I was able to help him mentalize and understand the inner life of Sheri, himself, their children, and others, but this would rarely last long, giving me the feeling that I was writing on sand and again giving me a taste of how frustrating marriage to Todd might have been. While I also had countertransference experiences with Sheri that caused distress, those with Todd began to feel uncontainable. When I tried to sell him on the idea of therapy as a "laboratory" where he could explore his relationship with me in order to understand his relationship with others, he didn't get it. Worse, it seemed likely that he had been picking up on my increasing negative vibes, so that when I raised the problem of my mixed allegiance as the divorce proceeded and asked him what we should do (one option was just to meet conjointly with the two of them), he revealed that he had already been seeing two other therapists/coaches. He indicated it was fine with him to stop our sessions and for me to continue with Sheri. He planned to use mediation for the remaining conjoint couple work.

Even though Todd remained stuck and still angry at Sheri three years later, it seems likely that our longer-than-average "divorce therapy" reduced the intensity of his vengeful wishes and acting out, keeping them at bay long enough for lawyers to lay the foundation for the divorce settlement that, after he and I stopped meeting, dragged on for several years.

Therapy with Sheri prior to individual therapy

In our conjoint and individual sessions, I tried to help Todd and Sheri process her fling and add to our understanding of why their marriage was failing. After it became clear that both wanted to divorce, I suggested that this understanding could help them in future relationships and in working together as co-parents.

Mostly, they remained stuck, with Todd blaming Sheri, as she defended herself and gradually lost interest, even as she apologized to him for not telling him sooner about the intensity of her unhappiness. It seemed that these conjoint sessions gradually taught Sheri, at least, how to interact with Todd in the businesslike manner that I advocated. In our individual sessions, I role-played with her and showed her how to use counter-projective communications that might reduce Todd's vengeful acting out by presenting herself as accommodating and not completely exiting from his life.

Her individual therapy went better, though the problem was not so much about mourning the deceased marriage, as about what to do now that it was dead. Partly, Sheri had kept herself defensively oblivious to her dissatisfaction so as to remain in a relatively stable family situation (unlike her childhood) with a man whose insecurity and social undesirability guaranteed that *he* would not leave *her* and to protect her children from experiencing the pain she had felt when her parents had divorced and fought for years over custody. But, as Todd had suspected, her romantic fling with the dog trainer awakened her to what she'd been missing. Now she wanted more of what she had tasted.

Sheri now concluded that she had stayed way too long with a man who was insensitive, annoying, and socially embarrassing. Given her character structure, it's possible that she was seeking validation of this from me—to add to that of her girlfriends and family members, some of whom had warned her against marrying Todd in the first place—but mostly, I experienced her as ready to leave her marriage.

Nonetheless, she did need to work on her excesses of dependency on others (Todd, girlfriends, family, coworkers), which tended to blind her to distressing realities (not only in her marriage but also at work and with friends) and prevented her from asking for what she needed. (Toward the end of our therapy, we laughed as she reported that she no longer found herself asking her kids what flavor of ice cream she should choose.) In contrast to Todd's transference to me as some sort of computer that could provide antiseptic, easy-to-follow answers, Sheri's dependent idealization of me allowed her to listen when I interpreted the many ways she tried to blind herself to what was going on, especially with her children and, later, with her several boyfriends. Still stung by her having consciously withheld the fact of her affair from me, I used this to keep in mind how hard it was for her to "face facts." Doubting that others would give her what she asked for, she didn't ask for what she needed, didn't get it, remained stuck depending on what others provided spontaneously, and then had to pretend that she was OK. This difficulty with asking others for what she wanted (rather than only what she should do) and not denying her desires came up many times, including with us, as I noted how she routinely waited till the end of our sessions before she asked for help on "the big stuff."

These two clients—The Just-Tell-Us-What-to-Do Couple—both wanted and needed help and direction. Both were excessively dependent in their outside lives, not just in their failing marriage. The intensity of this dependent need partly explained their willingness to come to therapy longer than most couples after they had decided to divorce. However, their ability to listen and absorb my assistance differed greatly. Sheri's idealization of me and willingness to listen made the therapy quite valuable to her. Todd's distrust, concrete thinking, and trouble mentalizing limited the ability of a once-a-week therapy to help him. That I personally experienced Todd's difficulty in listening and collaborating helped me in my work with Sheri.

Mediation

This is a short section because, as with other mediations that fail, this one looked much like the failed conjoint couple therapy. Todd used the time to rail at Sheri, and the sessions—like those he had with me—exhausted everyone, going hours past their scheduled endings. The mediators, Sheri told me, "threw up their hands" and referred them to the lawyers, who then took control of negotiations.

Co-parenting during the divorce

I spent considerable time coaching Sheri on parenting during the divorce. Like other hysterics who run away from their thoughts about what is happening (Shapiro, 1965), she wasn't consistently picking up what her children were experiencing. Her oldest daughter, Laura, was suffering in school. Laura's pre-divorce tendency to boss her friends around (as her father did to her) led to her being ostracized by her friend group and to intense clinging to her mother. For a long time, Laura wasn't willing to see a therapist, viewing this as too stigmatizing. Laura's reluctance helped me to encourage Sheri, who traveled frequently for work, not to farm out her daughter's need for help to a therapist. Just as Sheri had needed (and missed) her mother in childhood, Laura needed her mom. As we talked about what she could do to help Laura, we discovered things that got in the way: Laura's social miscues reminded

Sheri of Todd and his "autistic" family members and of some of her own childhood experiences of painful rejection by peers (which she didn't want to recall). Checking with Laura's teachers, we discovered that Sheri's fear that Laura was on the spectrum was unwarranted. Accessing her own childhood memories helped Sheri talk to Laura, rather than simply setting limits on "misbehavior" as she and Todd had been doing.

More generally, as we reviewed Sheri's near-total amnesia of her childhood, she became more aware of what was going on and less apt to cope via impulsive actions, including shopaholism. Soon after we began to focus intently on her childhood, with all its relocations and parental divorces, Sheri—who had had an eating disorder in high school—found herself eating a kind of cookie she had not allowed herself since she was 13! Intriguingly, it turned out that, like Proust's famous narrator with the madeleine, recalling the past helped Sheri recover some of its pleasures, as well as its pain.

Over the years, we frequently discussed the challenges of co-parenting with Todd. As mentioned, he kept involving the children in the marital drama. The girls would often complain that their father kept them up long after their bedtimes, talking to them about his suffering, criticizing their mother, and giving them bad advice (e.g., telling Laura to deal with her ostracizing peers by angrily telling them that they were "screwing her," topping it off by criticizing and controlling them). The following selections from a more extensive email that Todd sent Laura illustrate the managerial, controlling, insensitive parenting that upset Laura, while revealing Todd's obliviousness to his own needs, represented and seen as excessive in his daughter:

> I will not be approving any food delivery this weekend. I also will not be approving any additional food purchases from the grocery store this weekend. I will not be providing you any transportation to other plans this weekend. Also, I have put in place a number of programs to help support you and your independence including your fitness subsidy and meal subsidy that I am suspending until further notice.
>
> I requested that every day you think about 2 to 3 things you are grateful for and I have not seen your list . . . . Also, there is a little exercise that I would like you to complete on gratitude [the web address was listed here]. In addition to the gratitude, I hope that you will review this list of signs for entitled children and reflect upon them. [I've listed only 4 of 9.]
>
> - Expects bribes or rewards for good behavior.
> - Is more concerned about himself than others.
> - Passes blame when things go wrong.
> - Can't handle disappointment.
>
> I love you, Laura, and I am confident we can work through these issues.

After Sheri vetoed a meeting I proposed we have with Todd to discuss parenting, Todd vetoed my meeting with Sheri and Laura. What helped, nonetheless, was coaching Sheri in how to talk to Todd about Laura and the other two children (their youngest was also symptomatic; the middle child was coping as an overcompliant "well sibling") in ways that he could hear and that aimed to extricate them from being "middled" by Todd.

One particularly challenging event that we processed took place when Todd and Laura were visiting his sister and the sister's "autistic daughter." The children got into a yelling match, in what I came to view as a proxy war between Todd and Sheri, one that took considerable time to defuse and relocate back in the parents.

As I do with other divorcing families, we worked on setting up reliable methods of communication between the parents, allowing family rules to differ between the two households, and coping with the anger stirred by Todd's dragging the divorce out, and threatening not to pay agreed-upon support and alimony by falsely claiming impoverishment. Many of the co-parenting issues were aggravated whenever Todd received news that Sheri was involved with a new boyfriend.

Sheri's dating

Much of my individual therapy time with Sheri was spent reviewing her dating. She was understandably afraid of repeating her mistaken choice of Todd. With each boyfriend, she sought my reactions and those of her girlfriends. Given the challenges of finding a suitable mate for a mid-40s career woman who often traveled for work and had three challenging children, this period of her life sometimes resembled those montages in romcoms where the newly single mom runs through one flawed suitor after another. There were many near misses.

After a time, Sheri settled on one man, David, whom she was still dating when we terminated our therapy. She was strongly attracted to David, who resembled her in many ways—sometimes I thought of them as a literal example of Kohut's twinship selfobject relationship (1971, 1977). David was a handsome businessman, divorced after a long marriage to an emotionally unstable woman, with three children almost identical in ages and gender to Sheri's kids, with the oldest—like Laura—suffering the most with emotional problems and intense dependency on him. It helped a lot that David and Sheri shared so much, not only their ethnic/religious backgrounds but also their similar anxieties and hopes for a better future.

Like other couples who contemplate merging their lives (see the next chapter), they struggled most with how to find time for each other, given their many responsibilities with work and children. I met with them several times to see if I could identify problems and offer help. In person, their strong attraction to each other and his neurotic anxieties were more apparent than I would have known from just listening to her talk about him. Their fights assumed a recurring pattern and tended to confirm their transference fears:

hers that he would not prioritize her, like her family of origin (unlike Todd, "the barnacle"); and his that, feeling slighted, she would blow up and attack him as his "crazy" wife had for many years. It helped her to learn to accept that some of the times when he seemed disloyal to her were truly situational, related to his realistic devotion to his children (a typical "stepfamily" loyalty challenge), while others related to her trouble being clear with him about what she needed. At one point, following advice from some of her friends who weren't that keen on him, they split up for six months. When they got back together, they did better, in part because the separation had led him to seek twice-weekly psychotherapy, which had reduced his anxious reactivity to Sheri when she was upset (and evoked thoughts of his ex-wife).

Sheri at work

As in other individual therapies, we spent some time talking about her professional life, which, at times, resembled her marriage. As an example of how therapy helped her, she was able to ask her (competitive, female) boss—whom she had previously avoided in a stepmother transference—about her chances for promotion. When her boss made clear that this was not in the cards, Sheri hired a headhunter, talked to higher-ups at her firm, and arranged a transfer and promotion to a different division. Therapy and her divorce had helped her learn that she needn't sit still and accept what life sent her way.

Termination

As time went by, Sheri felt less need to consult with me, and our sessions moved to about once monthly, when she was in town and had a specific problem to discuss. Money and time were tight, so when she requested that I refer her to a colleague who charged less and had an office close to her home, I made that referral to a trusted female friend. That was several years ago and, as far as I know, Sheri is maintaining the gains from her therapy. I am less sanguine about Todd, but given the stoicism he was capable of, his close local family ties, and how his hassling of his wife and children gradually diminished in the last year of this work, he may also have reached a reasonable level of acceptance and emotional stability.

Commentary on the case

This case illustrates a protracted, difficult divorce that was beneficial for one party, unresolved for the other, and troubling to everyone, including the children. The therapy started when the marriage was too far gone to save and in the presence of a hidden affair. Discernment counseling confirmed the leaning-out partner's decision to divorce and the affair sealed the deal for the other partner. A trial of mediation failed, as it replayed issues in the therapy. The protracted, simultaneous treatment of the couple—for the first six months—may have decreased some of the injury and vindictiveness of the leaning-in partner and facilitated the legal process, which, somewhat surprisingly, though protracted (it felt most like stalling), was not excessively impeded by entitled or unrealistic requests.

The divorce therapy that preceded the individual therapy certainly assisted the later therapy of the partner who continued, since the therapist knew from personal experience what she was up against. The therapist was blocked from doing family therapy but helped the mother to work with her children and to interrupt displaced enactments involving them and her ex-husband. While the children regressed during the divorce, we should note that two of them had been struggling prior to the parents' decision to divorce, in keeping with research showing that unhappy marriages, not just divorcing ones, contribute to childhood distress. The wife's individual therapy also assisted her in her post-divorce dating and professional life, specifically as these were informed by problematic behaviors present in her marriage and learned in childhood.

This therapy also illustrates the virtual impossibility of one therapist treating both partners all the way to the final chapter of a contentious divorce. We gave it a go, but met an impasse, after which it seemed best, as in some legal proceedings, for each partner to have their own advocate. While it's pretty obvious why I ended up with Sheri (she was a far more malleable and appreciative client), my experience with Todd stirred some of the sad disillusionment described earlier in this chapter for therapists working in this area who must accept that divorces are not always fair or therapies equally beneficial, especially when a divorce seems clearly to benefit one partner more than the other.

Notes

1. While most divorces are difficult, *difficult divorce* has become a term of art (Lebow, 2019), one signifying a divorce that is stuck, protracted, and full of pain and acrimony. Many qualify as *high-conflict divorces,* another term of art. In what follows, I have chosen not to italicize *difficult* every time I refer to such divorces, but I want readers to know that I have that connotation in mind.

2. Generalizing about the impact of divorce is difficult because of selection effects, such that people who are more psychologically unstable *prior* to marriage divorce more often and might then be expected to have more difficulty post-divorce, independent of the stressful consequences of the divorce. This includes people who have had a major depressive episode prior to divorce who, unsurprisingly, have been shown to have a far greater chance of having another one after a divorce (Sharra et al., 2019).

3. Jacobson and Christensen (1996, pp. 6–8), reviewing outcomes in traditional behavioral couple therapy, found that couples coming later for therapy or hovering on the brink did worse. The prognosis was better when couples were "committed to making it work"; possessed "convergent goals"; were more "equal" in their relationship; and were more "emotionally engaged," including doing things together (importantly, sex). Couples who were still arguing did better than ones showing mutual withdrawal. Sue Johnson (2008) has also reported less success with couples who

waited till the last minute to come for EFT; she attributed this to the accumulation of attachment injuries that made it hard to restore attachment bonds.

4. In their Structural Family Therapy approach to difficult divorces, Isaacs and associates (2000) go a bit further than I usually do to encourage clients to stay on task. Noting that, "The complainants seldom express a sense of total defeat" and are slow to move on, they paint a dire picture of the future to motivate them, saying, for instance, "You may have to be prepared for this to go on for another five or six years, and the kids will have to put up with the consequences," or "I'm sure that late at night, you will think of all the trips to Puerto Rico you could have taken with the money you spent on lawyers!" (pp. 104–105).

5. The following example of a couple arguing about visitation time illustrates how adversarial negotiating in the legal system can inadvertently go awry: "A husband may ask for far more than he wants because he is certain that his wife will never give him as much as he really wants. She in turn interprets his asking for so much as his wanting everything. She sees him as greedy, out to take advantage of her, just as she felt he did in the marriage. She therefore resolves to give him very little, which confirms her husband's belief that she will be unreasonable and that he had better grab whatever he can get. The impasse persists" (Isaacs et al., 2000, p. 7).

    This is a good example of interlocking negative transferences previously present in the marriage, now "confirmed" during the divorce; it also illustrates a naive misapplication of certain negotiation tactics to the divorce setting.

6. While demonization is the order of the day in divorces, the opposite can occur. On several occasions, I have been shocked when meeting partners of individual clients to find them *more* distasteful than I had been led to believe. So, while many clients exaggerate the faults of their partners, others blind themselves to obvious problems.

7. For a hilarious country and western song that simplistically illustrates how a new future helps cope with loss, listen to Steve Holy sing "Brand New Girlfriend," on YouTube.

15 Stepfamily Couples

Using a first-time family map to navigate stepfamily relationships is a bit like trying to drive around Los Angeles with a map of Boise, Idaho.

—Patricia Papernow (2018a, p. 27)

Remarried couples with stepchildren are a minefield, even for experienced therapists, because the partners almost always come with parenting issues, not just couples' problems, and because many therapists miss the nuances of stepfamily dynamics.

—William Doherty (2002)

As these quotes from two experts in this field warn us, stepfamily life adds considerable complexity to the couple therapy of remarried clients. In this chapter, I review the territory and make suggestions for treating these clients, who are at high risk for divorce.

Some statistics

- At present, about 40% of marriages are remarriages for one or both partners and, since close to two-thirds of these adults have children, stepfamilies are quite common (Ganong & Coleman, 2018; Guzzo, 2016).
- Most remarried couples are less happy with each other than first-married couples (Bray, 2019).
- Divorce occurs sooner and more often in remarried couples (DeLongis & Zwicker, 2017).
- Stepfamily couples cite conflicts over children as the leading cause of their marital problems (Bray, 2019; Browning & Artelt, 2012; Stanley et al., 2002), though finances, legal problems, and trouble with former partners also cause stress (Sweeney, 2010).
- *Complex stepfamilies*, in which both parents have children from prior families living with them, have the highest divorce rates, while stepfamilies with a mutual child do much better if they had stabilized before that child was born (Vishner et al., 2003).

DOI: 10.4324/b22905-20

- Lack of parenting experience is a risk factor for divorce (Vishner et al., 2003).
- Stepparents who try to assert parental authority too early—even optimal "authoritative parenting"—are more likely to get into trouble than stepparents who act more as friends or camp counselors (Bray, 2019; Vishner et al., 2003).
- Overall, children benefit from having resident stepparents (Sweeney, 2010).
- There is no firm consensus on long-term outcomes. The bad news seems to be that "stepchildren are at 50% greater risk for developing significant emotional and behavioral problems compared with children in first-marriage families." The good news is that "most children in step-families do not experience long-standing adjustment problems; they are able to adapt to their new family structure and become competent individuals" (Bray, 2019, p. 711).

Terminology and varieties

The following terms can help us categorize stepfamilies: *First-marriage couples* or *first marriages* are contrasted with *stepfamilies* (much preferred to *blended families*), in which *co-parents* most often do their parenting in *binuclear families*. Parents and stepparents can be characterized as *residential* versus *nonresidential* or as *custodial* versus *noncustodial*—though, since most situations are not binary, I will often use *residential* simply to refer to the adult who *at the time being discussed* shares a roof with a child. *Simple stepfamilies* are ones in which only one of the adults has children, as contrasted with *complex stepfamilies*, where either both parents bring children to the marriage or where they add one or more children after marrying. None of these situations is actually "simple," and still more variations exist, including couples who are cohabiting, those that involve other relatives, and those where partners are in different developmental life stages (e.g., a divorced father with two teenage daughters who marries a younger, never-married woman, after which they have a baby).

Structural differences among stepfamilies add to the complexity of treating them (Coleman & Ganong, 2015). *Stepfather families* (in which the mother has custody) are the most frequent variety, making up 69% of stepfamilies (Bray, 2019). *Stepmother families* are generally more tense for everyone, and daughters in such families have the most difficulty, even more than when they live in stepfamilies with their mothers (Vishner et al., 2003). Stepfamilies also differ in how recently and how amicably the parents' marriages have ended, and in whether prior marriages ended by death, divorce, or divorce following an affair.

Children as a core issue

Above all, stepfamilies differ from first-time families because the children and their parents have established relationships, and the children and their stepparents are just getting started. For most parents, forming a new marriage is a joyful event full of hope for a better future, but for many children, it feels like a loss: a reduction in attention from their parents and the end of dreams of seeing their parents reunited. Parents and children usually hold quite different attitudes toward the other biological (divorced) parent, not just toward the new stepparent. Adding to the parenting complexity, some stepparents are completely new to parenting, some are tired of it, and some want to have more children in the new marriage.

For children who spend time living with each biological parent, the challenge is like maintaining dual citizenship in two disparate countries (Vishner et al., 2003). Ideally, children can benefit if the two families offer diverse experiences and support, as described by one of Connie Ahrons's daughters in Ahrons's landmark book, *The Good Divorce* (1994), where one family was athletic and the other more intellectual. But if the "countries" remain hostile to each other, children will suffer if forced to pick sides. Consequently, stepfamilies do best when children and adults form mutually satisfying relationships between families. Often, a painful surprise to couples and their therapists is that many stepcouples divorce despite having formed solid parent–stepparent bonds because they have been unable to form solid stepparent–stepchildren bonds.

Transitioning to a stepfamily

The first two years after a remarriage—especially if teenagers are involved and later, when the children become teens—are almost universally more stressful than parents expect (Hetherington, 1999). Couples who were doing fine when dating may wonder if they overlooked some serious character flaw in their partners. Far more often, they have minimized what this change of formal roles means to the participants: Stepparents now see that their well-being is tied to that of their stepchildren, stepchildren now see stepparents more as some sort of "parent," and biological parents become more aware of being caught between people they love.

Above all else, experts advise what research confirms: Parents should avoid rushing this transition. Therapists need to reassure couples that it will take time and that much of what will happen is normative—if challenging—including that parents will usually be feeling better and children worse. Parents will have to accept that relationships can't be forced.[1]

As when parents divorce, when parents remarry, children should be told what to expect ahead of time, and parents should listen to what their children tell them about how it's going for them. Most of the time, adults will want to go faster than kids can handle. Common mistakes are pressuring children, including adult children, to accept the new reality and neglecting the inner distress that can surface when a parent remarries. To maintain their emotional tie to their biological parent, many children will direct all the anger they feel about the remarriage toward the stepparent ("the wicked stepmother"). If a parent had died, children may view the new marriage as an act of disloyalty.

Therapists can facilitate conversations between the soon-to-be spouses about children and parenting but also about finances, in-laws, religion, etc.—as one might with a dating couple who have decided to marry. Adults who had become used to living alone and making unilateral decisions must now, once again, share power. An extended period of "living apart together" (LAT) may allow time for everyone to adjust and decide whether the new relationship will work. In some cases, extra time will help children still reeling from the divorce; in others, the challenge will be about getting used to adding another adult and possibly stepsiblings or yet another housing change. As noted by Papernow, forming a new family takes time and is less like the quick and simple "blending" of ingredients in a blender and more like the challenge of a Japanese and an Italian family coming together for meals.

While most books on stepfamilies focus on problems with children, therapists should be on the lookout for other problems. First among these for stepcouples are often fears that problems they had with their ex-spouses will repeat, so that ghosts of ex-partners often haunt new marriages. The wife whose husband cheated may be overly suspicious of her new husband. The man who divorced his spendthrift wife may fear the same out-of-control spending by his new wife.

Remarriage can also destabilize or aggravate an already-shaky post-divorce situation. The new couple should be alert to competitiveness from noncustodial parents. Stepparents should avoid showing undue overt affection to their stepchildren when the other parent is around. Parents can offer reassurance to their co-parent about the stepparent's character, including that the stepparent acknowledges that the co-parent will always be their children's parent. As when working with one client who is divorcing, therapists should continue to think systemically and try to maintain empathy for people they have not met.

Goals and formats for stepfamily therapy

Since divorce is so common in stepfamilies, preventing one should be a prime goal. Confession: I have sometimes been slow to see divorce coming, having underestimated what might happen to the initially amicable stepparents who presented to me. Be on guard! Everything we know about helping couples handle conflict, improve shared happiness, and parent their children can help, but it's easy to miss the power of established biological bonds to disrupt newer marital ones. At the same time, therapists should be careful not to blame children or nonresidential adults for hidden marital problems. Another overarching idea: While psychoeducation about "best practices" is frequently beneficial and appreciated, therapists should watch for what makes good advice hard to follow, including hurt feelings from prior experiences, transferences, and unfinished mourning.

The importance of subsystems

One of the most important recommendations from Scott Browning (2012) regarding treating stepfamilies is *not* to follow the rigid prescription from the early years of family therapy that all family members must be included in every session. Instead, Browning came to see the advantages of meeting with subgroups and sometimes with individuals, while keeping an eye on the overall system.[2] Like the Vishners, who pioneered stepfamily therapy, he advocated beginning with the stepcouple and, later, adding meetings with family subgroups.

Assessment and sequencing of meetings

Most therapy begins with a phone call from one parent. During that call, I try to get the lay of the land and, most often—like Browning, Papernow, and the Vishners—I suggest meeting first with the stepcouple. Since these two people are usually struggling with each other, not just with the children whom they complain about, this initial format avoids an overheated, less workable session with kids present. It also supports a hierarchy of parental leadership and helps parents be frank about their concerns about the children.

I then do my standard couple assessment, giving special attention to likely stepfamily problems. Because this is a stepfamily, I want to be sure to ask about what caused trouble in their previous marriage(s), and what parenting was like in those marriages and in their families of origin. Throughout, I express empathy, highlight issues, and provide some psychoeducation to normalize the situation.

Depending on what I learn, I follow Browning's recommendations for sequencing additional diagnostic/therapeutic meetings with relevant subsystems:

- The stepcouple.
- The custodial parent and the child (or children) with problems—to assess the child, but not to bash the stepparent. Should that start to happen, I switch to an individual meeting with the child.
- The sibling subsystem(s).
- The stepparent–stepchild subsystem.
- Selected members of the binuclear family.
- Others (e.g., grandparents) may be included, and the frequency of various subgroup meetings can be weighted according to the family structure and problems.

Some individuals may need to be seen alone to obtain their stories and build trust. Meetings between co-parents will go better with a preapproved agenda and a set number of meetings. It might be assumed that some subsystems are strong and don't need extra attention, but this is often a mistake, especially since biological parents and their children, while sometimes appearing fine, often need help to heal a developing rift.

Just as most individual therapists are wary about doing couple therapy, the prospect of wading into the unknown, less controlled territory of multiple subgroup meetings still frightens me, partly because I don't see many children in my practice. But experience has shown that, although the slow march of weekly individual (or couple) therapy sessions feels safer, family subgroup meetings get the job done faster and better.

I will now discuss in more detail the most common problems stepfamilies face and some suggestions for handling them; most of which come from Ahrons (1994), Browning and Artelt (2012), Papernow (2013, 2015, 2018a, 2018b), and Vishner and Vishner (1991; Vishner et al., 2003).

Maladaptive wishes and myths

As in first marriages, there are some predictable disillusionments and rude awakenings that family members may not be prepared for. Therapists can help by naming and normalizing likely challenges and unique complexities. Papernow calls these "invisible burdens" and credits the Vishners with identifying wishes for an "instant family," including one where stepmothers will quickly become caretaking, nurturing "mothers," and stepfathers will quickly become rule-enforcing "fathers." (This common fantasy is made worse if the stepfather feels that, as "the man," he should assert authority over the children and/or if the mother is hoping that her new husband will rescue her from unruly teenagers.) The Vishners—two mental health professionals who married in 1959—apparently learned about such fantasies the hard way, as they struggled to find ways to manage a family to which each brought four children.

Another unhelpful expectation is that stepparents should love their stepchildren, that stepchildren should love their stepparents, and that grandparents should love all their grandchildren and stepgrandchildren equally. Such wishes deny the realities of actual experience. As Browning (2012) notes,

> Some stepmothers enter a stepfamily prepared to love a child, only to find that the child neither wishes for nor will accept love from her. Some stepmothers continue to love against all odds; for others, the child's rejection is simply too painful to ignore.
>
> (p. 90)

Exposing such expectations as unrealistic will help decrease the intensity of many family arguments. Over time and with hard work, some family members will grow to love and respect one another; others can wish each other success and happiness even if a strong affectionate bond never develops.

A related erroneous belief, expressing a wish, is that things will go better if "everyone would just do more things together," but as Papernow points out, dyads are not anti-family and are frequently the best way to develop, strengthen, and maintain relationships. Further, across many situations, therapists can work against overly rosy expectations that interfere with accepting what would simply be annoying in first-marriage families, like teens preferring peer activities to family events. Another example: If children return home less controlled after a visit with Dad, Mom need not view that as a catastrophe requiring that the children stop seeing Dad; the same thing could have happened after a camping trip with Dad if they were still married.

Insider–outsider and conflicting loyalty problems

Loyalty issues loom large in stepfamilies. While the prototypical conflict is the biological parent torn between their new partner and their biological child (Cartwright, 2010), many other loyalty conflicts are possible, including (as discussed previously) children caught between their biological parents and (even) parents torn between a former partner and a new spouse. Children may feel like second-class citizens when not living in their primary residence, when new children are born into a stepfamily, or when more money is spent on children with different parentage. Stepfathers may wonder if they are only valued for their money, and their wives may fear criticizing them, lest they lose financial support for their children. In truth, any pairing in these complex systems can generate distress in other family members, who may feel neglected, excluded, or unimportant. Therapists can help uncover, identify, and normalize the feelings of family members in such situations and help them express this in ways that other family members can understand.

A father can help reduce loyalty binds by telling his children, "Your mom's place in your heart, and hers in yours, is permanent. Like the mountains. Like the sun. I hope sometime you come to care about [stepmom's name]. But even if you do, it will be in a separate place in your heart from your mom's place" (from Papernow, 2018a, p. 34). Alert to how non-resident, biological parents can undercut relationships between their children and stepparents, parents can attempt to reassure them, as well.

A useful nomenclature that helps clarify foreseeable stepfamily problems is that of *insiders* and *outsiders*. Vis-à-vis children, biological parents are insiders, and stepparents are outsiders. Insiders typically feel caught between their children and their outsider partners, not just about practical decisions concerning their children, but—more basically and significantly—about how to divide time between them. The challenge is to balance the needs of biological children with those of the outsider partner and to empathize with whomever feels they are not getting enough (usually everyone!). A common trap arises when friends or therapists try to be supportive but, having heard only one side of the story, are overly sympathetic to unbalanced behavior ("You're so right: Of course, your children should come first!").

The outsider–insider difference helps explain why stepparents often label their stepchildren as rejecting and disrespectful, whereas parents see them as understandably stressed or as normal teenagers. Both may have a point, and this common disagreement leads to our next topic: stepfamily parenting and discipline.

Parenting and discipline

Stepparenting is more difficult than parenting. Unlike biological parents, stepparents come on the scene not knowing any of the (often traumatic) history of the children whom they hope to relate to. Some have no parenting experience, and many harbor unrealistic developmental expectations. And children often reject stepparent authority, asserting, "You're not my mother [father]!" In this demanding situation, all experts agree that stepparents should prioritize "connection rather than correction" and should take a back seat to biological parents in discipline.

Optimally, stepparents should try to connect with their stepchildren, recognizing that this is a long-term process and accepting that it is unrealistic to begin in the role of authority figure, a status that is earned, not acquired. This will be more difficult for residential stepmothers, who often spend more time with their stepchildren in the absence of the children's fathers. Stepparents should work toward establishing a role that is less disciplinarian and more that of a friendly companion, benevolent coach, or admired camp counselor. They should look for opportunities to compliment their stepchildren and to spend time together in low-key activities—accepting that some snarky comments come with the territory. Younger children will usually be easier to bond with, whereas adolescents are generally more ambivalent toward stepparents, not wanting another adult around to tell them what to do and objecting more often to let's-feel-like-a-family activities.

Even with these recommendations in mind, working out parenting plans in stepfamilies is challenging because: "Stepparents everywhere seem to want more limits and structure with their stepchildren. Parents everywhere seem to want more love and understanding for their children" (Bonnell & Papernow, 2019, p. 189). Kids may contribute to tension by acting out and challenging authority more than usual due to the many adaptations they have had to make, not just to the stepparent, often relocating, changing schools, and losing friends.[3] The result is that the common parenting polarization over discipline and rules versus unconditional love is almost inevitable. As Browning (2012) sees it:

> The parent believes that the stepparent is focusing on the more negative aspects of the child and somehow missing the child's talents and goodness. The stepparent often feels that he or she is viewing the

child . . . from the perspective that will be taken later by teachers, admissions officers, and future bosses.

(p. 60)

Browning points out that parents are wrong to think that this disagreement will go away completely if the stepparent would just have a deeper, more accurate view of the child. While this is sometimes true, other times, as in most marital conflicts, both sides have a point.

Making this polarization still worse, stepparents who are doing a lot for the kids (making meals, doing laundry, paying bills) may feel that their stepchildren take them for granted and believe there should be consequences. And parents, feeling depressed or guilty, may let rule enforcement slip. In these situations, stepparents who notice and feel unappreciated may step into what they see as a parenting vacuum and try to provide discipline. This almost always makes things worse, as the kids rebel and misbehave still more, pushing the couple apart. Not only will the adults continue to squabble, but the stepparent may avoid dealing with the stepchildren and, thus, diminish *positive* interactions. Ideally, and instead, stepparents can serve as advisors behind the scenes, a more limited parental role. Optimally, in their discussions together, stepparents can help parents be firmer and parents can help stepparents be kinder and more understanding.

What should a stepparent do when the parent isn't home? Parents should make clear that when they are absent, the stepparent is in charge—taking a role like a sitter who has "borrowed authority"—and anticipate what issues might come up, as in the following example from Papernow (2015):

> When Theresa is going to be out of the house, she can say to Tanya, "Joe is in charge. The rule is no social media before homework. I expect a good report from Joe!" If Joe catches Tanya texting, he can say calmly, "You know the rule! No texting before homework!" Joe then reports to Theresa, and Theresa imposes any consequences.

(p. 475)

Stepparents, thus authorized to enforce House Rules, can acknowledge, "I'm not your dad," and follow that with, "but I am the adult in charge. Your mom wants your room picked up, and I'm here to make sure her wishes are followed."

Forming a new family culture

Obviously, there is more to creating satisfying stepfamily life than bonding between stepparents and stepchildren and working out discipline. I can only touch on some additional issues here, but work in this direction begins, as mentioned earlier, by realizing that "blending" is often more like the experience of people moving to a foreign country where unfamiliar customs are taken for granted. There will be more struggle around holidays when people want to do things as they've "always" been done, but clients can be warned to expect more mundane surprises as well (e.g., disagreements over what counts as being "late" or "loud"). Many things that had previously been taken for granted will have to be discussed, negotiated, and sometimes revised. Everyone should expect surprises and to "learn by goofing" (Papernow, 2015) when they encounter a taken-for-granted difference about how things ought to be done. Parents should pick their battles, go slow with new changes, and retain important established routines, objects, and rituals.

Stepfamily members will also often have to deal with competition, crowding, sexual stimulation, financial stress, religious differences, less time to go around, and the overarching problem of balancing the needs of more people living together. Money and how to spend it can become a particularly loaded topic, including when related to major expenses for children with different parents.

Perhaps less obviously, parents should keep adult physical affection private since it can trigger distress in children still unhappy about their parents' divorce. Stepsiblings should not be expected to become best buddies right away (or ever): They didn't choose each other; their parents did. Parents should accept that kids are in a different place than they are and not move too quickly by making empty reassurances ("It's a nice house, and you get your own bedroom.") or going to fix-it mode ("If you'd just be nicer, the other kids will like you.").

To help create a sense of warmth and belonging, Browning and Papernow offer several practical suggestions, including setting up a "curiosity jar" into which family members place fun questions that help everyone get to know each other better, telling family stories (with the same goal), creating shared family rituals (e.g., a tree-planting ceremony), and simply (gradually) doing fun things together.

Two households and ex-spouses

I discussed the separate households of divorced parents in the previous chapter. Here, I will mention some additional problems that commonly emerge when divorced parents remarry and form stepfamilies. The most common are that exes can become more upset when their former partners remarry and that children can become even more stressed about loyalty. Nonresidential father–child relationships often become more vulnerable and distant if fathers drop from sight as they focus on their new family. And parents who think their children are now getting a better parent may fail to understand children who show heightened desire to remain connected to nonresidential parents, even to those whom others deem unworthy or unloving.

Therapists may then be called in to work on acting out or conflict about these issues, some of which may have seemed settled. Again, assisting with mourning and acceptance will often be critical to success. Mixed feelings should be acknowledged and accepted ("I bet part of you is relieved that you don't have to be scared by Daddy's drinking anymore. But I bet another part of you misses him a lot!"—from Papernow, 2015). As always, therapists should be cautious when hearing about misbehavior by exes whom they haven't met.

Additional complexity and varieties

As if things weren't complicated enough in stepfamily life, there are a few more nuances worth noting. As previously mentioned, complex stepfamilies are ones where children are merged from more than one family or where parents add them to an existing stepfamily. (Some couples will present in conflict over whether to add children.) In such cases, resources (money, time, and space) can be stretched to the limit, and there will be even more subsystems to keep in mind. Browning and Artelt (2012) provide wonderful case examples of such complex cases, which show how genograms can help keep the players straight and highlight coalitions, cutoffs, and problems across and between generations. Among other things, they recommend, if possible, coordinating visitation so that all children are away at the same time, thus giving parents some couple alone time.

Some stepfamilies form after a parent has died. Children and remarried adults generally want to keep the deceased parent in mind, and loyalty issues can surface. Possibly more than in other situations, items in the house (not just photos) connected with the parent who died will take on special significance.

LGBTQ stepfamilies generally face the same problems as other stepfamilies. Added problems can surface with outsiders (in-laws, friends, coworkers) concerning whether partners are "out," and stepparents with a history of rejection due to stigma may feel even more acutely the pain of rejection by stepchildren (Papernow, 2015).

African American stepfamilies often do better due to traditions of "child keeping" or "cross-household parenting," such that parenting tasks are shared within larger family configurations and nonresidential fathers expect to maintain relationships with their children (Papernow, 2015).

While grandparents often argue with their children in first marriages about how they parent their grandchildren and about how much time they spend together, these issues are often exacerbated in stepfamilies, partly because some parents are ambivalent about encouraging ties with the families of former spouses. Ideally, parents should keep in mind that stepgrandparents can be emotional, financial, and child-care resources (Browning & van Eeden-Moorefield, 2019).

Finally, stepfamily *divorces* can add still more complexity and people to the mix. Things can be particularly sad if a stepparent has developed a bond with a stepchild but, not having adopted that child, finds that they have no legal standing concerning continuing contact. As in all the aforementioned situations, therapists may be called upon to mediate between partners and should not shy away from group meetings when treating a distressed member of a divorced couple.

Resources for families and therapists

To help couples familiarize themselves with the territory and learn about stepfamilies more systematically than is possible in therapy sessions, I recommend the following self-help books and websites. These resources not only provide practical suggestions but also normalize many problems, thus removing some of their sting:

- K. Bonnell & P. L. Papernow (2019). *The Stepfamily Handbook: From Dating to Getting Serious to Forming a "Blended Family."* United States: KDP.
- E. B. Vishner & J. S. Vishner (1991). *How to Win as a Step-Family.* New York: Brunner/Routledge.
- www.stepfam.org (National Stepfamilies Resource Center).
- www.stepfamilyrelationships.com/ (Patricia Papernow's website).
- www.stepfamilies.info/smart-steps.php (a research-validated, 12-hour curriculum).

Lessons from my stepfamily couples

After searching through my files for a case to illustrate my work with stepfamilies, I came away somewhat surprised and disheartened. I found that I didn't have many successes. Partly, this seemed to be due to selection bias in that, as stated earlier, second-marriage couples have already failed once, usually for good reasons. More than most first-marriage couples I see, these clients came with serious character pathology that had caused them lifelong trouble in maintaining all their relationships, not just intimate partnerships. Also, having become somewhat the go-to therapist in my community, I was seeing many people who had already failed at couple therapy two or three times. Almost all those clients were skeptical and ambivalent about therapy. The majority were *last chance couples* with one foot out the door, and many didn't stay long enough for a fair test of treatment. Almost all my cases also faced substantial external problems that would have stressed any marriage: limited finances, contentious ex-spouses, and children with serious emotional problems.

Studying those cases and finding my less-than-stellar results made me wish that I had known then what I know now. That review strengthened my conviction that therapists treating stepfamily couples must be on their toes and keep the following in mind:

- Pay attention to problems with stepchildren! Do this even if you are not skilled in child therapy.
- Do not minimize external challenges. Help couples face them sooner than you might otherwise think necessary. Left unresolved, they may make partners decide that they would be better off going it alone.
- Keep in mind the "ghosts of earlier marriages" that haunt the minds of the remarried couple.

I will now illustrate these recommendations in the successful therapy of a complex stepfamily that formed and survived in the wake of a difficult divorce. I call them the Can-Do Couple because of their many strengths, which helped us navigate very challenging waters.

Case example: The Can-Do Couple

Course of therapy

After reviewing my notes on this lengthy, complex therapy, I decided that the best way to describe it was by giving snapshots of sessions along the way. This will show clearly how problems kept resurfacing—very few were "over and done"—and will give a taste of how external events/stressors intersected with internal hopes and fears.

Referral and family members

This was the first couple therapy for Ben (a biochemist) and Jill (a senior manager at a not-for-profit), both in their mid-40s, both divorced (she four years before; he two months before, after a long separation), with nine (!) children between them, living separately and not yet married as the therapy opened. The couple were referred by Ben's individual therapist, who had helped him greatly in the previous four years, during his lengthy difficult divorce from his wife. Jill had had a brief, unhelpful therapy with her husband prior to their divorce.

Ben and his ex-wife, Nancy, had three children: David (17, a high school junior doing OK, though with some problems with his mother), Todd (14, an 8th grader struggling, with anxiety and low self-esteem), and Sophie (13, a 7th grader). These children alternated living at Ben's and Nancy's houses.

Jill's children included her sister's daughter, Lauren (33, raised by Jill from age 5, now self-sufficient and about to move out of Jill's house to live on her own); her oldest son, Aaron (20, doing fine as a college junior); her middle son, Noah (18, a "poster boy for ADHD," doing great as a college freshman); and two children living almost exclusively with her: Zach (14, also with ADHD) and Kelly (12, bipolar, struggling in many ways).

Over the course of their year-long, once-weekly therapy, we worked together to merge their families, cope with their children's problems and Ben's ex, move into a new shared house, reconnect with friends, and marry.

Session 1

The couple came on time. Both were spunky, attractive, dressed perhaps overly casually, in keeping with their manner. Both talked extremely fast, reasonably clearly, in earnest, mostly in sync with each other, allowing themselves to be influenced by what the other said. Unlike many couples I see, their interpersonal process was mainly positive and affectionate. Ben kept telling me how great Jill was, how great their sex life was, and how committed he was to her. One process problem, which she complained about and I observed in this session, was that when she complained, he would try to argue her out of it with "glass half-full," can-do comments. This tended to invalidate her complaints, and sometimes resulted in them talking at cross purposes and not hearing each other, for example, when she complained about a recent family event, and he too quickly pointed out that he had done things with her in mind, which she didn't seem to hear or acknowledge. I thought this could use some work.

They seemed to value taking time to talk about their situation, with their main concern that external events might wear them down, leading each to run away to alternative partners they each imagined might quickly replace them.

Here's what they told me about their history: As one might imagine, given all their children with problems, the couple had met (four years previously) at a talk on the topic of ADHD. They soon started dating on the tail end of their failing marriages. They were strongly attracted to each other physically and, more important, to each other as "responsible" adults, devoted to their children (unlike how they viewed their former spouses). They had many interests in common: working out, travel, eating out, and conducting occasional dinners for drug companies (she planned them; he was a speaker).

The precipitating event for their coming to therapy now was their fear that incidents like those surrounding Sophie's recent bat mitzvah—it had required interaction with Nancy, whom they compared to a Taliban terrorist intent on blowing up their union—would "chip away" at their developing, committed relationship. This fear was heightened by experiences in childhood and in their prior marriages: Both doubted that any romantic relationship could last or provide support. Ben had had to interact more with Nancy in planning the bat mitzvah, which Nancy had banned Jill from attending, and that had added to Jill's insecurity. Even as the couple would later succeed in managing their boundary with Nancy as co-parent to Ben's kids, Jill would worry, as she did in this first session, that Ben might cheat on her, as he had confessed he'd done with Nancy for years. This had been a focus of his individual therapy and, as they both knew, had included Jill for a short time as "the other woman."

Jill's insecurity was also sometimes fueled when she felt like the outsider to Ben's insider in a loyalty conflict with his children, as in the following example: Jill had accidentally cut herself and had called Ben for help but—partly because she didn't really convey how much she needed him (to help with the kids more than herself)—he had stayed at Todd's baseball game (Nancy was also there), which angered Jill. On other occasions, too, Jill played the "overadequate" person, which created problems: Recently she had agreed to do a last-minute Passover seder for everyone but then became over tired and resentful. She recognized this tendency and said she had been working to be clear that she wasn't Superwoman, while remaining the strong, can-do person Ben admired.

Like Jill, Ben showed some insight into his own problematic behavior. He saw himself (correctly, I thought) as a high-energy person with ADHD. He thought that having lost two siblings—a brother during childhood and a sister more recently—combined with a mother who was rarely available, had led to his "reach for all the gusto you can today" attitude, one that had included promiscuous sex. That last, understandably, worried both of them, though they assured me (externalizing/locating their doubts in me) that this would not be a problem in their marriage, noting that Ben had been faithful during the four years they had been together.

Nancy had been an extremely poor sport during the extended divorcing process and continued to angrily spread lies about Ben—that he wasn't a good parent and didn't provide financial support—and to tell all their friends that he had cheated on her with Jill and others. While downplaying the impact of their cheating, Ben and Jill described Nancy as self-centered, entitled, unwilling to seek employment, inflexible on parenting arrangements, and intent on poisoning Ben's kids against him and Jill. They mentioned some litigation to limit Nancy's intrusion into their lives, but Jill wanted still more help with this boundary.

The couple were also stressed (and joined) around anger at Jill's ex-husband, Steve, who reneged on support payments and, despite claiming to be a great dad, was pretty much absent as a father. (Finances would continue to be a source of strain, and sometimes conflict, throughout the therapy.) Steve was described as a sociopathic salesman, intermittently employed, often in debt, such that his house had been foreclosed on twice—the last time being the final straw that led Jill to leave him. The couple also described Steve as "pathetic," characterizing himself as "poor me," a victim who, nonetheless, always managed to wriggle out of responsibilities. Most recently, he was not making court-ordered, minimal child support payments.

Listening to this, I wondered if Steve might be depressed and saw Nancy as stuck in an unforgiving state, reeling from her husband's years of cheating. Ben and Jill seemed to like each other in many ways, most importantly as two overadequate spouses who had, in part, enabled their underadequate partners, and who had eventually given up and escaped to find partners they could respect and hoped to rely on.

In addition to problems with money and their exes, the couple was stressed daily by their children—five now living at home, three of whom had substantial emotional problems that the couple considered mostly biochemical. They clearly cared about their kids, but I thought it might be hard for them to acknowledge the children's reactions to the divorce, given these parents' need to minimize their guilt and lay all the responsibility on their exes.

As concerned countertransference, I felt mostly positive toward this couple, who seemed well matched and ready to work. I found it a bit wearing to fight for airtime with them in the session (this gave me a taste of their overadequate, take-charge style, which may have caused problems with their exes) and to listen to their repetitive declarations of love and idealization.

I cautioned myself not to mess with that since I saw it mainly as a defense that helped them bond as teammates facing real challenges. My biggest anxiety as we began concerned whether we could manage all their external problems (with exes, kids, finances, and more), typical of nascent stepfamilies. With that in mind, I cautioned them against the unrealistic (stepfamily) wish that they could easily "blend" their families into a Brady Bunch that resembled a far less complex first marriage.

As our first session drew to a close, I told them, as I usually do, that I was glad they had come for help and sympathized with their situation. They listened, nodding agreement, as I summarized their problems, especially the challenge of stabilizing their developing relationship as it was buffeted by problems with their exes, finances, and children, who were also hurting. Therapy would be a safe place where we could discuss options and come up with plans. I noted their fears of the past repeating, especially Ben's cheating, but more fundamentally, the worry both had that the other person would let them down, even though they had little evidence for that, seeing each other, realistically, as capable, responsible people. When I asked if that was how they saw things and whether they thought they could work with me, they agreed, and it seemed we were off to a good start. I gave them my intake questionnaires to complete before our next session.

Some additional background

In the next few sessions, I learned some relevant information about their backgrounds. Ben was the third of four siblings who grew up in a traditional family where his father was often absent for work and his homemaker mother was a worrywart who bragged about her son's academic accomplishments but never really listened to what he said—all of which seem to have contributed to his inordinate need for admiration, including via affairs. When his oldest brother died of leukemia when Ben was 13, his mother became even more worried about him and his health. At first, he liked this and used it to get special care, but he soon found it oppressive, especially when he was ill. He became more aloof from her and more self-sufficient, believing that he "always had to be on top of his game." Most likely, his choice of a career as a spokesperson in medical biochemistry derived from wishes for attention combined with a desire to master the trauma of his brother's death and his mother's anxiety.

Jill resembled her strong, long-suffering homemaker mother, who struggled with Jill's much older siblings, while her lovable truckdriver father was often absent on the road. Her brother, now chronically mentally ill (violent, probably bipolar), terrorized her. Her older sister was also troubled and functioned poorly, which explained how Jill later came to raise this sister's daughter, Lauren. The legacy of this was that Jill, like Ben, was insecurely attached, though motivated to work hard to show that she, unlike her siblings, could be responsible. I came to see her, also, as trying to master her past with her bullying brother, as she had first worked as assistant to a wealthy, sociopathic, sexist entrepreneur; married a dysfunctional sociopath; and now worked for a boss with a bad temper, though in a charitable foundation. Her strong family history of serious mental illness might have been the genetic root of some of her children's problems, as well as her ambivalence about caring for them—sometimes excelling, sometimes "going on strike."

Ben's questionnaire

Among other things, Ben complained about not having enough time with Jill and accurately noted that Jill complained about his "spinning things too positively."

Jill's questionnaire

Like Ben, Jill worried that they wouldn't have enough time together (including for sex), which made her feel loved, as this was crowded out by their numerous responsibilities. She sometimes doubted Ben's commitment and worried that he might cheat on her. Above all, she was disturbed by Nancy's aggressiveness and by Kelly's illness. She thought she and Ben needed a long-term plan. She worried that her contributions as a homemaker–partner and her lower salary wouldn't be enough for Ben, who made far more money. But she also thought that Ben appreciated and "deserved" her maternal/caretaking services and that these would be "easy" for her to do.

Session 2

In addition to gathering additional background data, we discussed Ben's younger sister's death, two years before, from breast cancer. This was especially painful because his sister had endorsed them as a couple and challenged Ben to give up philandering. She had also supported them when Nancy was giving them a hard time and very few of Ben's friends were comfortable with them.

Session 3

The focus was a topic that would be ongoing: Jill's children. Kelly, age 12, had been in therapy since age 6, first for depression and ADHD and now with a diagnosis of rapid cycling bipolar disorder. She had a "terrible temper" and got very upset when her mother diverted her attention elsewhere. Her father was no help with her. This had a negative impact on Jill's 14-year-old son, Zach, who would retreat to his bedroom. Zach also had ADHD.

In this session, Jill was explicit that Ben could help her by being more involved with Zach, as his father was a constant disappointment, and she was preoccupied with Kelly. Ben agreed to help, and he and Zach grew closer. I suggested that the couple might want to get more outside help for the kids. (I would repeat this suggestion many times to this couple, who could afford it but dragged their feet. Eventually, they got afternoon help from a local high school girl, which was a big plus.)

They reported doing pretty well protecting their time together, but it was hard living apart, as Ben had only finalized his divorce two months before. The main impediment to merging households, they said, was Kelly. Jill made herself vulnerable by telling Ben her fear that he would leave her because Kelly was more than he had bargained for. She wondered whether she (Jill) should not impose such stress on anyone and should remain single. Ben reassured her that he was with her in trying to help with Kelly, and we discussed what they might do when Kelly had tantrums or couldn't manage separations from Jill. I encouraged them to talk to Kelly—and not just when she was upset—about her feelings about Ben, the two of them, and her difficulties at school.

Conversation with Ben's individual therapist

As I routinely do, I got permission to talk to other therapists involved with the family. Ben's therapist, a senior colleague whom I trusted, saw things as I did, viewing Ben as an "essentially good," hyperkinetic, overadequate man, who took over tasks in his family of origin after his older brother died and kept this sort of caretaking up in his first marriage, while escaping to affairs. He told me that Ben felt genuinely guilty about his affairs and was relieved and delighted to have found Jill. The external problems of their kids (especially Kelly), money, and his ex were real and needed to be discussed. Ben had told him that they looked forward to therapy sessions with me.

Session 4

We now opened another topic that would continue: money, including how it impeded their full commitment and their joining households. Ben described his long-term plan, including how things would be different when he stopped paying child support/maintenance, in five years and when all the kids were away at school, in six years. With my encouragement, they agreed to work on the details of a budget that weekend. They felt good that Jill's persistence in attaching her ex-husband's salary had paid off to the tune of $1,700/month. I learned how Ben had lent Jill money to help her with a down payment for her current home, something that helped her believe in his commitment and capacity to contribute financially.

They then talked of plans to consolidate households, should the situation with Kelly improve (Jill now agreed with my suggestion to get more childcare help). On the psychological front, we all agreed that Jill sometimes overdid helping others.

Session 5

Noting that their kids' problems sometimes came between them, they returned to talking about Kelly. Jill was getting burned out. At this point, they still hadn't located an extra helper but had more incentive to do so now that Lauren, who had provided some babysitting, had moved out. Kelly had become more upset in the past year, which suggested to me some psychological shift (though Jill blamed the hormones of puberty). They reported that Kelly dreaded visiting her father and that he had always been "abusive and psychologically insulting" to her. Again, I found myself validating how difficult Kelly could be, followed by advocating more psychological attention to Kelly, who they tended to see too concretely as upset simply "because of her father" or "because of her rapid cycling."

Session 6

Jill wanted to talk about their long-term "plan." Possibly feeling safer in therapy, she angrily blamed Ben for never "finding time to discuss details," comparing him to Steve as "delinquent." Ben apologized and they agreed, without apparent difficulty, to create a budget that week. We all agreed that Jill had an expectation/transference that Ben would let her down on such tasks, as Steve had. Ben could trigger and confirm this transference, I suggested, in a way that was hard for him to appreciate: When "juggling too many balls" in his hyperkinetic, overadequate state, he sometimes "dropped some of them," and then seemed not to be there for her, as occurred that week, when he forgot to give Jill the summer schedules for his kids, although he had put them together as she had requested.

Session 7

Jill repeated that it would help her if they worked out a set of household rules for their families and interactions—something neither of them had had in their first marriages. Ben and I agreed, and we all set to work on this project in the session. Along the way, I confronted Ben's "everything's fine" remarks/attitude as sometimes helpful, but sometimes experienced by Jill (and me) as a false attempt to forestall discussion. It might also be, I wondered, that his ADHD sometimes made it hard for him to focus.

Session 8

This session confirmed the value of therapy to help even well-intentioned people take time to focus on core issues: At this session, we returned to finances, after Ben and Jill confessed that they still hadn't worked out a budget or discussed long-range plans. Finances were intertwined with issues of commitment. Part of what was causing the delay was that Ben feared that getting married would raise Jill's income and endanger college scholarships for her kids. They agreed that while Jill would feel more solid once they were married, the practical side of both won out as they chose to delay their wedding. This was made easier by Ben's convincing assurance of his love for Jill and their excitement about a planned vacation together to New Orleans. Jill was also reassured by the reception she received from his friends, who had invited *the two of them* to a ribfest at their home.

The ever-present fear of Ben's infidelity was further reduced when Ben showed his vulnerability by directly expressing his need for, and pleasure in, receiving compliments and dependent care from Jill (she told him that she loved his body and cooking for him)—needs that had not been met in his marriage, which he linked to his escape to affairs.

Sessions 9–10

As if the couple didn't have enough to deal with, Jill—more distracted than usual after catching her two teenage boys drinking—had a bicycle accident that resulted in a concussion, followed by dizziness, insomnia, "brain fog," and irritability that persisted for several weeks. Ben was a big help during this time, and, for this, Jill gave him the recognition he so appreciated. Sex also helped both of them but was sometimes limited by privacy concerns with their children.

We discussed some additional stresses—for Jill, at work; and for Ben, with his parents—and things were generally harder now that the kids were back from camp. Kelly continued to be very demanding and often angry, though she had improved on new medications (they had been working more closely with Kelly's psychiatrist). Jill cried thinking about Ben's daughter, who is one year older, but "far easier to love."

Both now felt that the status quo was rather good and were wary of upsetting it by moving to one household. Both expressed fears of repeating the failures of their prior marriages, which may explain why Jill so wanted Ben to buy an engagement ring—to test him as financially responsible, unlike Steve.

Session 12

They arrived 15 minutes late due to their self-denying, magnanimous desire to check in on Lauren, who had been depressed recently. Ben had paid attention during the last session and took steps toward purchasing an engagement ring during their upcoming New Orleans vacation.

Kelly was terribly upset about their going away, so angry that she hit Ben and was now worried that they hated her. I encouraged them (yet again) to talk to Kelly to undercut thoughts that they are going away *because they can't stand her and need a rest*, thoughts that, for someone with Kelly's psychology, might make separations even worse. Nonetheless, Kelly was growing more accepting of Ben and was less upset with the idea that he shared space with her mom.

Session 13

They had a great time vacationing in New Orleans and did pretty well after returning, managing various crises: Steve's late support payment, Kelly having a tantrum with Steve's mother, Steve's mother sending them an upsetting email, and general stress getting the kids ready for school/college.

They returned to Jill's fear about their future and her dislike of Ben's too-optimistic "glass half full" defense, which accompanied his not telling her (or himself) what was bothering him. We agreed that while Ben's optimistic enthusiasm worked to enliven things, sometimes he could scare people when, as I put it, "he says he could get out of the middle of the Sahara Desert with only a Swiss army knife." Ben agreed, including by acknowledging that it had been "a pretty tough" (!) return from vacation.

Sessions 14 and 15

They discussed options for a jointly shared house, including scaling back from the idea of building one (!) to buying one they had found that seemed perfect, with its separate third floor for his kids and a "Bat Cave" for Ben. This, again, raised concerns about finances, including their mild polarization concerning spending money. Jill was far more cautious; Ben wanted to spend it and "enjoy the fruits of their labors" (recall his "reach for all the gusto" mantra). To help with financial planning, I recommended that they consult a professional planner.

Sessions 16 and 17

They were excited to show me Jill's engagement ring, to tell me how they finally became engaged, had sent out formal announcements, and were about to go public, letting everyone know at a local party the next weekend. They were also in contract negotiations for the house they had mentioned before. I supported their shared wish to have a formal wedding ceremony with their kids, friends, and relatives all present to witness, validate, and give a great send-off to their union.

Ben was reluctant to tell the news to Nancy on the phone, fearing that she might take her rage out on their kids and, once more, label Jill "that whore he's marrying." We agreed that he should try to meet with Nancy in person to try to calm the waters. Mostly, both presented his relationship with Nancy as unworkable and not something they wanted to discuss. In retrospect, I might have pressed more for Nancy and Ben to meet with me to see if the war could be called off, at least to spare the children further distress.

They mentioned that it had been helpful to sit down and make plans together between sessions (as they had learned to do in therapy), to divvy up tasks and review how things were getting done. This seemed to be news to them, possibly because they didn't do it with their prior spouses.

Kelly and the other children seemed relatively OK, although Jill mentioned anger/upset that Zach, her high school freshman, was recently caught smoking both cigarettes and pot. Otherwise, he seemed to be doing OK. Despite the "he's OK" comment, and possibly because of it, I encouraged Jill to find time to hear more about how Zach was doing from the inside rather than to see him only as either OK or delinquent. Again, because I thought they might be missing how stressful their engagement and upcoming move to a shared house might be, we role-played how and what to tell their kids.

Sessions 18–20

They were delighted to tell me (a skeptic about their planning) that their housing situation was working out extremely well, with both their houses likely to sell at or near the time they closed on their new house. We then discussed some concerns about merging their two families, especially Jill's fear of being drained by childcare with Ben's boys (a stepmother role assumption), including by the need to chase after them to clean up, given that their mom was a slob. Ben reassured her that he would manage his boys and do whatever she needed him to do—including helping her carve out some alone time—to make their unified home a success.

As we so often did, we reviewed his past sexual unfaithfulness and her fear of it repeating. He was clear that what he most needed was the kind of appreciation he was getting from Jill and joked that when he thought of other women, he imagined them dying to have him and envious of Jill (his near-perfect partner), who did!

We spent more time talking about Kelly, including Jill's fear that Ben didn't like her. She agreed that some of this was a projection of her own disavowed feelings. I did some psychoeducation about stepfathers, how they must go slow to establish relationships, and how "liking" isn't essential, especially at first. Kelly's meds were helping her mood swings and Jill, with encouragement, but without direct intervention from Ben, had become better at setting limits and "catching her when she's doing well." I labeled Jill as Kelly's "human pacifier," first calming her, then helping her "regulate" her frustration by putting it into words, and then working out plans to help her cope (per Plan B discussed in Chapter 8). As time went by, I heard that Kelly was confiding in her mother about what sounded like typical early teen problems in school and with her friends.

Sessions 21–24

Ben sold the house he had been living in with his kids and moved into a short-term rental apartment. As expected, this evoked acts of aggression from Nancy, who collected some items of his remaining at her house and, *War of the Roses* style, cut them up and deposited them on Jill's lawn. Ben, perhaps overreacting, took out a restraining order on Nancy and worried that she might try to spoil their wedding. Possibly contributing to Nancy's acting out was that Ben, having worked out his guilt, was so obviously and publicly delighted to be with Jill and to have Nancy out of his life.

Ben and Jill continued to do well despite multiple stresses: his court case to allow him to share a home with Jill before they married; Nancy's continuing rage, expressed in angry emails and exchanges with the kids; and the delay in moving to the new house, during which Ben and his three kids were cramped together in their rental space. Therapy gave the couple a place to complain, work out plans (including for their wedding), and discuss how their children were reacting to the disruptions.

Amid all this, the main potential psychological roadblock continued to be Jill's transference to Ben as not pulling his weight—something that seemed palpably false, but which, once she got some evidence for it, could lead them to escalating fights, with the threat that they might call everything off. Jill's fear came from a combination of experiences that undercut trust and encouraged her can-do, "I'll do it myself!" behavior, which could then exhaust her and cause resentment. In childhood, her older brother had bullied her, her older sister was "useless", and her father was "well-meaning, but absent," off driving his truck, all these encouraging her to identify with her long-suffering mother. Later, her bosses and Steve continued a pattern of people taking advantage of her and letting her down. She also knew that Ben's heart had not been in his first marriage, but outside, with his career and other women. To cope, she took over and took action. Unlike the Energizer Bunny, Jill's overdoing it often led her to "run out of gas" and be resentful after she reached her limit. During the therapy, this became easier to flag, and even mildly humorous for the three of us, after Jill reported that she had literally run out of gas three times in the previous year when driving, necessitating rescue from Ben each time. Helping them see this coming—so that they could take steps to prevent both Jill's exhaustion and a seeming confirmation that Ben was "just like Steve"—was a central focus in these sessions and throughout the treatment.

Session 25

Our focus was again on Kelly, who had been difficult and evoked shame as well as frustration in Jill. Kelly seemed to think that happiness came only from acquiring things: clothes, food, Mom. She was relentless in pursuit of these, oblivious to how this affected others and inconsolable when she didn't get what she thought she needed. She was better at school, however, and when out of the house. This suggested to me—more than Jill and Ben were willing to acknowledge at first—that some of her upset was situational, including the impending move to a new house as the stepfamily became a single-residence reality. While at times I worried, along with Jill, that Kelly might need residential treatment, on this day, I pushed for more activities that could develop self-esteem and internalize ideas of things she could *do*, rather than *get*. Two that came up as we brainstormed were dance classes and family walks with their dog. I also suggested that Jill find time to read with Kelly, something more engaging than passively watching TV together.

Session 26

Once more, Jill was upset, thinking that Ben wasn't working hard enough, wasn't with her enough, and had his heart somewhere outside the family. As discussed earlier, this felt mostly like transference insecurity, but it failed to go away when Ben pointed out how her "mindreading" was unfair and misjudged his intentions. Jill's doubts had become worse as their wedding approached. I suggested that the coming wedding both stirred her fear that the past might repeat *and* tended to confirm that fear, since with so many pre-wedding tasks to complete, Ben was certain to let her down occasionally and to have less quality time available to spend with her. My interpretation seemed to help Jill but, as with other couples, I think what did the job more than my offer of intellectual insight was a combination of her relating some painful moments from her past (she cried intensely as she recalled how her father had missed her high school graduation) and having Ben listen sympathetically and then hug her as he voiced his commitment to love and care for her.

Session 27

This was a wide-ranging session, again touching on the danger of the past repeating as their wedding approached. Ben had paid attention in the last session and soon had opportunities to take proactive action to counter Jill's transference: He had explained to Jill that the reason he hadn't put some things away was because he knew she would want to do it herself and assured her that his watching football earlier wasn't to avoid her since he was looking forward to shared time later that day. On her own, Jill had figured out that some of the imperfections she objected to in Ben were projected self-criticism, flavored with crabbiness from feeling overworked. She could see that this created a vicious cycle and tried to be more forgiving of both Ben and herself.

Jill was also being more thoughtful in her interactions with Kelly, and Kelly was loving it. Positivity was reverberating throughout this soon-to-be married stepfamily.

Session 28

Another unexpected bomb threatened, but the couple showed resilience in working together to defuse it. With only two weeks until the wedding, Ben's brother (who had become a Chasidic rabbi) informed Ben that he could not perform their wedding as planned because Jill was not "converted enough." This upset them in different ways, which we worked through. For Ben, the main thing was a further "loss," now as his older brother's withdrawn support reminded him of the death of his supportive sister two years before. Ben had always looked up to his brother, idealizing him, and had tagged along behind him in childhood. But as they grew older, he came to see his brother, like his ex (and like Jill's view of her older siblings), as "high maintenance." When his brother had become strictly Orthodox, this had created more distance between him and the rest of Ben's family, whose Judaism was less strict. Ben also felt guilty about "letting Jill down," contributing to her view of him as "a fuck-up husband," since he had been assuring her (overconfidently, as we had seen him do before) that this would be "no problem."

For Jill, beyond the need to find an alternative officiant, Ben's brother's decision felt like a rejection and stirred up the lifelong self-doubt she had tried to quell by always trying to "get the award for trying the hardest." In Catholic school, she had received top grades and graduated at age 16. Later, she studied Judaism, long and hard, prior to converting from Catholicism to Judaism in order to marry Steve. Now she was being told that that wasn't enough! In addition, I suggested she might have an underlying hope for their wedding: that Ben would confirm his deep admiration for her and that they would finally escape the stigma of their affair and divorces and be recognized as "good enough" by their friends and family. Her brother-in-law, I said, should not be given the power to spoil that legitimate plan.

Sessions 29–34

The couple rebounded, found a rabbi to marry them, and very much enjoyed their wedding and honeymoon. Aware of Jill's insecurity, Ben was especially attentive to her at the wedding. Seeking a testimonial, he introduced her to his individual therapist, whom he had invited, and got him to "validate the work I've done," including on his cheating.

Before and after the wedding, Nancy created some unpleasantness, including (symbolically) when she made their daughter, Sophie, throw out some waffles she had brought from Ben and Jill's house. Ben followed my previous advice to try to help his daughter understand what was going on without unduly pathologizing Nancy, while noting that it wasn't fair for her to make Sophie a pawn in the continuing unpleasantness between her parents.

Returning from their honeymoon, Ben was touched by the care with which Jill carried back a vase they had purchased, unlike how his ex, under similar circumstances, had brought back a gift for Sophie: in pieces. In our meetings after their honeymoon, I continued to try to help them to articulate what forces—resembling Jill's care of that vase—could help Ben remain devoted to her rather than straying to other women. During this discussion, Jill told us for the first time that Steve had cheated on her, which was also in the back of her mind when she wondered if she could depend on Ben.

It now became OK for both to reveal that they liked the attention of the opposite sex. When I warned that they would lose their "young bodies" over time, Ben responded that he wasn't interested in younger women, loved the way Jill looked, and imagined that "she won't let herself go," which seemed likely to me, as well.

As their therapist, I was gratified to watch them work out, by themselves, what had caused a fight the previous Saturday night. As her 50th birthday approached, Jill had thrown out the accusation that Ben might not "still love me when I'm 64." She could see that she had been triggered by his change in mood, after what she thought had been a good time out to dinner. Ben responded that he had been hurt, first by her taking three cell phone calls from Kelly during dinner, and then by her rejecting his suggestion that they train for and run in a marathon in Italy. He had then silently worried that she might also reject his proposing sex after they got home. Ben said he could accept that Jill needed to attend to Kelly, whom they both worried about, but he wanted Jill to know how important her attention was to him, how a lack of attention had made him stray from Nancy, and that failing to get responsiveness from Jill could put him in a funk, something she had noticed, but then misinterpreted as a sign of future loss of interest (when she was 64).

Some of these sessions also returned to the topic of Jill's exhausting herself and then growing resentful. If only she could recognize this earlier, others might not have to face her self-righteous nagging or what she termed her "hanging up" on them when she ended conversations and fled to be by herself. This would also help Ben not to stray since he would be more likely to look forward to time with her in a good mood at the end of the day.

Sessions 35 and 36

These sessions dealt with Kelly's bat mitzvah, two weeks hence, an event like Sophie's which had brought them to therapy. They were both mad at Nancy, who was trying to forbid her kids from attending (which was especially painful for Kelly, who didn't have many friends), while telling them that "Dad ruined our lives." Simultaneously, Steve was not paying his share of the cost and lied to his kids, explaining, falsely, that their mom hadn't invited his best friend. It was helpful for them to vent their anger, after which they were able to settle down and plan steps to get all the children to the event. Once more, we briefly role-played what they might say to the kids, with an eye to honesty, requiring some violation of the excessively limiting rule to "never say anything negative about the other parent."

Ben was stressed by expenses (the new house, their wedding, Kelly's bat mitzvah) and wanted Jill, appropriately I thought, to free up some of her deferred income from work. Still a bit distrusting, she had wanted to reserve that money for her kids' education but acceded to his request. She had some trouble being charitable after seeing him, now that they all lived under one roof, criticizing and disciplining her kids (seemingly more than his). We discussed how this might be illusory since his kids weren't around as much and noted the contribution of Jill being the protective "insider" parent. We also reviewed the "stepparent discipline" challenge ("connection before correction") that I had flagged before.

Sessions 37 and 38

A bit sooner than I might have preferred, the couple decided to set a date to stop their therapy. During this year-long therapy, they had managed many external stressors, got married and received approval from friends and family (if not their exes, who remained stuck in the past), and were now living agreeably together in their dream house with their kids getting along and mostly enjoying one another. Kelly was bonding with Sophie and benefiting from that friendship. Todd and Zach, also close in age—who had taken up more of our therapy time than I have recounted here—were also doing fine and playing video games together. Moving in together may have helped both Jill and Ben with their continuing neurotic doubts about the other—she, that he would stray and be irresponsible; he, that she would fail to pay attention, admire him, and enjoy him sexually. Their many expenses were another reason to stop, even though their stepfamily culture was still forming.

Session 39, the last session

The couple asked for my summary of the therapy, and we reviewed it together. I congratulated them on the many challenges they had met together and pointed to the insecurities just mentioned. Jill reported that therapy had helped her become closer to Kelly and reduced her fear that people would think that she, Jill, got a good deal, but Ben got a lemon (because of Kelly).

As sometimes happens in final sessions, more information came out about prior losses—at this session, about the death of Ben's brother and how that had changed his life (reported earlier in this summary).

We also got a taste of their core interpersonal insecurity. Ben, who had been overworked and stressed by a visit from his mother, had developed a cold. As a result, he was more distant, subdued, and "cranky" than usual. When Jill was gone overnight on a trip with Kelly, Ben had felt her "disconnecting," reminding him of times when she would literally hang up the phone on him when they were fighting. For her part, seeing Ben less like himself, reminded Jill of her ex and older siblings and sent a temporary shiver through her.

Building on this incident and their insight into it, I tried to "immunize" them about similar situations in the future. The main danger, I said, would come when one of them was not so upbeat, so high functioning, so connected, so good looking, so sexy—at these times, they might panic, rather than thinking that this was just an inevitable part of life. This fit, I said, with Jill's fear, expressed in our first session, that if she married, the marriage would inevitably deteriorate to "a husband in bed in his boxers, eating Oreos." They agreed that they had to scale back their images of a blissful future with unflappable partners. Jill, as Ben had done recently, reassured us that when she recently saw an old boyfriend, she felt less interest in flirting and attributed this to closeness and confidence in her marriage. Ben said that he had been helped by the therapy and was looking forward to his future with Jill.

I wished them well and told them that, should they need to consult me, my door would always be open. That was 15 years ago and, as far as I know, they have by now passed age 64 and are still loving each other.

Comments on the case

No single case can illustrate the complexities of treating any problem seen in couple therapy, possibly least of all the treatment of stepfamilies, but I think this extended account does illustrate much that I wanted to highlight, not only about the problems of stepfamilies but also about how to manage other practical problems covered in earlier chapters.

As concerns stepfamily couples, one must not underestimate the challenges of forming a second family and preventing another divorce. There were times when this couple almost threw in the towel. Instead, couple therapy helped defuse many of the potential stepfamily landmines: children with reactive and prior problems; stepparenting issues (loyalty, discipline, favoritism); parental fantasies of escape to a stress-free, Brandy Bunch life coupled with children who see it differently and act out; managing finances and division of labor; consolidating households and melding siblings; coping with still-angry ex-spouses; and, all the while, convincing the couple that their past would not necessarily repeat.

This case history, reconstructed using my session notes taken at the time, also illustrates how problems are rarely settled once and for all. Instead, problems surfaced and resurfaced many times, and some sensitivities that were present in the first session were still present at the very end, though Ben and Jill were far more alert to their issues and able to manage them better.[4]

One regret I have about using this case to illustrate work with stepfamilies is that, while we spent much time discussing how to work with exes and children, I never convened subgroups to assess and treat ongoing problems with those people. The main reason is that I treated this family long ago, before I had read Browning's work and come to see, from my own work as well, the value of such meetings, especially to consolidate subgroups and counter demonization. In this case, it may have been true that the exes were unworkable, as the couple described them with convincing evidence. Unlike our discussions of how to deal with the exes, who remained unchanged, the therapy conducted at a distance with the children seemed helpful and possibly sufficient. If I were to treat this couple today, I would meet with Kelly and would invite each of the other children to at least one meeting.

The couple described here brought considerable strengths and resources to this situation, one reason I labeled them The Can-Do Couple. Their interpersonal process was admirable; they were energetic problem-solvers who listened to my suggestions and rarely blamed each other when the going got tough; and, despite little help from their exes, they could afford to finance what they needed. In this way, they were more emotionally capable (though still scarred) than many whose first marriages have failed because of serious character pathology that they bring to subsequent relationships. Possibly, only such capable people could have successfully coped with the large number of challenges this couple faced.

Because their interpersonal process was mostly positive, the therapy didn't need to focus so much on maladaptive vulnerability cycles, and instead, more often took the form of what I have called the basic "talk to each other model" or Couple Therapy 1.0, described in Chapter 1. In this straightforward model of conjoint therapy, partners benefit, as these two did, from setting aside time, away from distractions, to discuss pressing problems in a safe space. The therapist symbolizes the task, offers some suggestions, and serves as an incentive to show up weekly—like appointments with a personal trainer. Here, I want to register the value of this sort of thing for stepcouples, like this one, who face myriad challenges.

Jill and Ben did bring baggage from their childhoods and from their first marriages, mostly their sense that they could not rely on others who they expected would let them down or fail to love them. Without therapy, their survival strategies—overadequacy and minimizing of psychological causes of distress (both of them), martyrdom alternating with "hanging up" and exhaustion (Jill), and excessive confidence coupled with avoidance of planning and potential infidelity (Ben)—might have endangered their hope for something different. Instead, those strategies were a constant focus in this treatment, which softened their defenses, helped them be more vulnerable, and tended to correct their negative expectations (transferences). As an example of this work, recall that Ben's optimism and can-do manner had initially drawn Jill to him. But whenever he failed to plan, took on too much, and dropped the ball, she would worry that he was like Steve and couldn't be counted on. My slowing Ben down and exposing the anxieties concealed beneath his "glass half full" optimism helped him plan and then act in ways that moved the ball toward marriage and gradually convinced Jill that he was the real deal. Exposing Ben's desire to be mirrored and appreciated also helped. Growing more confident that he could be counted on, and now knowing what he wanted, Jill was happy to give Ben the praise that enlivened him, prevented his relapsing to affairs, and kept their positive cycle going.

Finally, this extensive case report, the last one in this book, illustrates the value of therapeutic integration—Integrative Couple Therapy in Action—as I made use of systemic understanding, psychodynamic interventions, and concrete behavioral/educational instruction, each as needed, during a year-long, successful therapy.

Notes

1. For a moving, award-winning film that portrays a divorce and remarriage from the child's perspective, see Richard Linklater's film *Boyhood* (2014), in which a remarried mother tells her son, "But now we have a family," and he responds (sadly), "We already had a family."

2. As we continue this discussion of stepfamily therapy, you will see that Browning deserves credit for several other deviations from prior family therapy dicta. Like others, he found that the situation for stepfamilies could be aggravated if therapists clung to the Structural Family Therapy belief that happy, functioning families require two parents with equal power, joined in a unified parental hierarchy with no differentiated closeness (coalitions) between a parent and their children. Similarly, he noted no need for consistent "family rules" between households or even, sometimes, within them. And, in stepfamilies, with their ever-present fear of divorce, he found little need for "enactments" to increase emotional intensity in therapy sessions.

3. Again, the film *Boyhood* (2014) provides a painful, compelling example: The eponymous boy of the film copes, year after year, by passive-aggressively resisting direction from his mother, stepfathers, and teachers in the wake of the many stressors imposed on him. The film also shows a stepfather, and, later, mother's new boyfriend, overreacting to this behavior, which then negatively impacts their relationships with the boy's mother.

4. Follow-up studies of "successful" psychoanalyses reveal similar outcomes: Clients retain their sensitivities but, now aware of them, are better at bouncing back when knocked down (e.g., Schlessinger & Robbins, 1983).

Concluding Remarks

My earlier book on couple therapy (Nielsen, 2016) offered a road map for working with couples. It mined the best thinking and interventions from the three main approaches to couple therapy—systemic, psychodynamic, and behavioral/psychoeducational—and showed how they could be integrated and sequenced. The goal was to create a model that was flexible, comprehensive, and user-friendly and *not* a new brand name (Nielsen, 2020). Instead, I thought of each approach as adding *upgrades* to the basic conjoint model that I called Couple Therapy 1.0.

Domain-specific upgrades

As I came to the end of that book, it was clear that I had more to say. What was missing was domain-specific knowledge, that is, more upgrades about the most common problems and situations that couples bring us. So, I began researching and writing what, for years, I simply called *Book 2*, the volume you have now finished. While my first book provided an aerial view of work with couples, somewhat independent of their particular complaints, this one aimed for a closer look, offering detailed suggestions concerning how to think beyond therapeutic techniques and methods when applying them to specific cases. Again, I tried to mine the best of what was available, reading the recognized experts in each field and often talking with them in person, and comparing their ideas and research with my own experiences. The chapters in this book might count as academic reviews of each topic, but my principal goal has, again, been to provide a practical guide to help therapists navigate each challenging situation. As before, when I was writing *The Roadmap*, I found that the process of trying to specify best practices in each of the areas reviewed here sharpened my thinking and improved my own results. I hope that, after studying these pages, you will have the same experience.

What was left out and could help still more

Topics on the cutting room floor

Sadly, some important topics did not make the cut, mostly due to limited space in a book that was already busting its britches: clients coming with

DOI: 10.4324/b22905-21

depression, intimate partner violence, serious medical conditions, and severe personality disorders. I had written chapters on minority couples, intercultural couples, and same-sex couples, but space did not allow their inclusion here. All these situations present unique challenges and deserve careful study. Fortunately, all have been studied and written about by others.

Earlier and better access

Despite declining stigma and the fact that people find it easier to come for "marriage counseling" than for individual psychotherapy, most studies show only a small percentage of couples getting treatment prior to divorcing (Jacobson & Addis, 1993; Johnson et al., 2002). Additionally, given how gradual the downward slide is, many couples do not recognize how compromised their marriage is until it's too late (Doss et al., 2003; Gottman et al., 2020). As noted by Morrill et al. (2011):

> Couples who have not yet begun to self-evaluate as distressed often have low motivation to seek treatment. On the other hand, severely distressed couples often believe it is too late for their relationships to improve. Thus, couples are often caught in the paradox of perceiving that their relationship is either too distressed or not distressed enough to benefit from existing treatments.
>
> (p. 472)

To address this problem, these authors created an opportunity for couples to come for a less stigmatized, easier access, sooner-than-later "Marriage Checkup" and found that they drew in many couples in the distressed range who were otherwise unlikely to have sought therapy.

Online programs

Because some couples may hesitate to seek help due to the cost or time involved, online programs might provide access. One such program based on Interpersonal Behavioral Couple Therapy, available at www.OurRelationship.com (Doss et al., 2013), fills this need. Compared to self-help books, online resources can provide videotaped examples, as well as contact in online meetings with therapists/educators in mix-and-match formats.

Relationship/marriage education

Another way to improve matters is to provide destigmatized relationship education at predictable stages of life. Ideally, programs would become as routine for couples as Lamaze is for childbirth preparation. Current examples are *The First Dance* (Doherty & Doherty, www.thefirstdance.com) and *Bringing Baby Home* (Gottman & Gottman, 2007; *www.gottman.com/product/*

bbh-new-parents-workship-couples-materials-set/), programs designed for couples who are, respectively, about to get married or about to have or have just had a baby. Many religious groups offer forms of premarital education immediately prior to marriage. Other programs—like PREP, PAIRS, Prepare-Enrich, and Relationship Enhancement—offer marriage education to those who seek it, either before or after they marry. These programs have been shown to improve communication and conflict management skills, increase commitment and positive feelings about marriage, and reduce intimate partner violence and the odds of divorce (Carroll & Doherty, 2003; Stanley, 2001; Stanley et al., 2020). A recent meta-analytic review of *online* relationship education programs found that these were generally quite helpful in improving both individual and relationship functioning (Spencer & Anderson, 2021).

While marriage education has been shown to be beneficial during marriage, reaching people sooner, as with sex education, is also desirable, especially to head off the unions of mismatched couples. Currently, many high schools and some elementary schools offer programs in relationship education. The for-credit program I developed for college students at Northwestern University (Nielsen et al., 2004), now in its 21st year, has served as a model for similar courses at other universities, and contributes to the growing, but still underutilized, field of marriage education for young adults.

Other factors that limit treatment success

Success in treating couples is also limited by comorbid Axis I disorders (especially depression and alcohol and drug addictions), by severe personality disorders, and by a society that places undue pressures on families while offering them insufficient support (as discussed in Chapter 11). While social stressors could be worse, and are in many parts of the world, improvement in these areas would help.

Therapist maturity and well-being

Success in couple therapy depends on more than the therapist's knowledge. Research on the outcomes of couple therapy consistently finds that therapist factors are crucial—often more important than the interventions applied (Sprenkle et al., 2009). A bedrock principle in psychoanalytic training is that personal mental health is indispensable to therapist performance, and that personal therapy is an important—possibly essential—path to that end. As the therapeutic process unfolds, our personal maturity and overall well-being can be decisive, especially when we are challenged to be a container for difficult emotions or when we are under fire from critical, demoralized clients. Sensitivity to divergent cultural values and differences is also essential. My final recommendation to my readers, then, is to work on yourself: Read great literature, pay attention to your own areas of stress, try to understand your family of origin, work on your relationships and other sources of fulfillment, pay attention to what helps *you*, and gain humility as you see how hard it is to change yourself and those you love. This also applies to those of us who have been at this work for years: We also need to keep emotionally fit and avoid burnout.

Closing thoughts

Treating couples is an adventure. People share their deepest hurts and fears with us so that we can help them cope. In doing this, they offer us a gift that can enrich our lives, as well. Even when terribly sad or frustrating, they give us a front-row seat for many of life's otherwise hidden dramas. As we engage with couples, we gain invaluable wisdom and perspective on life. When we make a difference in our clients' lives, we feel the profound satisfaction that comes from serving others and the gratifying sense that we are on this planet for a reason.

Couple therapy will always be a clinical art form that relies on the ability to synthesize our storehouse of knowledge with our experience, intuition, and wisdom. I hope that this book has added to your personal storehouse and helps as you engage in this challenging and worthwhile enterprise. I salute all of you who, like me, have taken up this challenge.

References

Ablow, J. C., Measelle, J. R., Cowan, P. A., & Cowan, C. P. (2009). Linking marital conflict and children's adjustment: The role of young children's perceptions. *Journal of Family Psychology, 23*, 485–499.

Abrahamson, I., Hussain, R., Khan, A., & Schofield, M. J. (2012). What helps couples rebuild their relationship after infidelity? *Journal of Family Issues, 33*, 1494–1519.

Ahrons, C. R. (1994). *The good divorce: Keeping your family together when your marriage comes apart.* New York: HarperCollins.

Akhtar, S. (2002). Forgiveness: Origins, dynamics, psychopathology and technical relevance. *Psychoanalytic Quarterly, 71*, 178–212.

Allen, S., & Hawkins, A. J. (2017). Theorizing the decision-making process for divorce or reconciliation. *Journal of Family Theory & Review, 9*, 50–68.

Amato, P. R., Johnson, D. R., Booth, A., & Rogers, S. J. (2007). *Alone together: How marriage in America is changing.* Cambridge, MA: Harvard University Press.

American Psychological Association (2019 and 2020). *Stress in America.* Retrieved on 5/12/2020.

Ananat, E. O., & Gassman-Pines, A. (2021). Work schedule unpredictability: Daily occurrence and effects on working parents' well-being. *Journal of Marriage and Family, 83*, 10–26.

Archuleta, K. L. (2013). Couples, money, and expectations: Negotiating financial management roles to increase relationship satisfaction. *Marriage & Family Review, 49*, 391–411.

Atkins, D. C., Marin, R. A., Lo, T. T., Klann, N., & Hahlweg, K. (2010). Outcomes of couples with infidelity in a community-based sample of couple therapy. *Journal of Family Psychology, 24*, 212–216.

Atkins, D. C., Yi, J., Baucom, D. H., & Christensen, A. (2005). Infidelity in couples seeking marital therapy. *Journal of Family Psychology, 19*, 470–473.

Atkinson, B. J. (2005). *Emotional intelligence in couples therapy: Advances from neurobiology and the science of intimate relationships.* New York: W.W. Norton.

Atwood, J. D. (2012). Couples and money: The last taboo. *The American Journal of Family Therapy, 40*, 1–19.

Badawy, P. J., & Schieman, S. (2021). With greater power comes greater stress? Authority, supervisor support, and work—family strains. *Journal of Marriage and Family, 83*, 40–56.

Bader, M. J. (2002). *Arousal: The secret logic of sexual fantasies.* New York: Thomas Dunne Books.

Baris, M. A., Garrity, C., Coates, C. A., Duvall, B. B., & Johnson, E. T. (2001). *Working with high-conflict families of divorce: A guide for professionals.* Northvale, NJ: Jason Aronson.

Barish, K. (2012). *Pride and joy: A guide to understanding your child's emotions and solving family problems.* Oxford: Oxford University Press.

Barton, A. W., Futris, T. G., & Nielsen, R. B. (2015). Linking financial distress to marital quality: The intermediary roles of demand/withdraw and spousal gratitude expressions. *Personal Relationships, 22*, 536–549.

Basson, R. (2007). Sexual desire/arousal disorders in women. In S. R. Leiblum (Ed.), *Principles and practice of sex therapy* (4th ed., pp. 25–53). New York: Guilford Press.

Basson, R. (2010). Women's difficulties with low sexual desire, sexual avoidance and sexual aversion. In S. B. Levine, C. B. Risen, & S. E. Althof (Eds.), *Handbook of clinical sexuality for mental health professionals* (2nd ed., pp. 159–179). New York: Routledge.

Baucom, D. H. (2014). *Treating affair couples: An integrative approach.* Workshop at The Family Institute at Northwestern University, 9/13/2014.

Baucom, D. H., Epstein, N. B., Taillade, J. J., & Kirby, J. S. (2008). Cognitive-behavioral couple therapy. In A. S. Gurman (Ed.), *Clinical handbook of couple therapy* (4th ed., pp. 31–72). New York: Guilford Press.

Baucom, D. H., Hahlweg, K., & Kuschel, A. (2003). Are waiting-list control groups needed in future marital therapy outcome research? *Behavior Therapy, 34*, 179–188.

Baucom, D. H., Snyder, D. K., & Gordon, K. C. (2009). *Helping couples get past the affair: A clinician's guide.* New York: Guilford Press.

Baumeister, R. F., Exline, J. J., & Sommer, K. L. (1998). The victim role, grudge theory, and two dimensions of forgiveness. In E. L. Worthington, Jr. (Ed.), *Dimensions of forgiveness: Psychological and theological perspectives* (pp. 79–104). Philadelphia: Templeton Press.

Beck, L. A., & Clark, M. S. (2010). What constitutes a healthy communal marriage and why relationship stage matters. *Journal of Family Theory & Review, 2*, 299–315.

Bell, C. A., & Fincham, F. D. (2019). Humility, forgiveness, and emerging adult female romantic relationships. *Journal of Marital and Family Therapy, 45*, 149–160.

Bianchi, S. M., & Milkie, M. A. (2010). Work and family research in the first decade of the 21st century. *Journal of Marriage and Family, 72*, 705–725.

Bickerdike, A. J., & Littlefield, L. (2000). Divorce adjustment and mediation: Theoretically grounded process research. *Conflict Resolution Quarterly, 18*, 181–201.

Bion, W. (1961). *Experiences in groups.* New York: Basic Books.

Bond, J. C., Thompson, E. G., & Prottas, D. (2003). *Highlights of the 2002 national study of the changing workforce.* New York: Families and Work Institute.

Bonnell, K., & Papernow, P. L. (2019). *The stepfamily handbook: From dating to getting serious to forming a "blended family."* United States: KDP.

Booth, A., & Amato, R. (2001). Parental predivorce relations and offspring post-divorce well-being. *Journal of Marriage and Family, 63*, 197–212.

Boss, P. (1999). *Ambiguous loss: Learning to live with unresolved grief.* Cambridge, MA: Harvard University Press.

Bowman, L., & Fine, M. (2000). Client perceptions of couples therapy: Helpful and unhelpful aspects. *American Journal of Family Therapy, 28*, 295–310.

Bradbury, T. N., Fincham, F. D., & Beach, S. R. H. (2000). Research on the nature and determinants of marital satisfaction: A decade in review. *Journal of Marriage and Family, 62*, 964–980.

Bradbury, T. N., & Karney, B. R. (2010). *Intimate relationships.* New York: W.W. Norton.

Bradford, A. B., Drean, L., Sandberg, J. G., & Johnson, L. N. (2019). They may disapprove, but I still love you: Attachment behaviors moderate the effect of social disapproval on marital relationship quality. *Family Process, 59*, 1530–1551.

Bray, J. H. (2019). Remarriage and stepfamilies. In B. H. Fiese (Ed.), *APA handbook of contemporary family psychology* (Vol. 1, pp. 707–724). Washington, DC: American Psychological Association.

Breunlin, D. C., Pinsof, W., Russell, W. P., & Lebow, J. (2011). Integrative problem-centered metaframeworks therapy I: Core concepts and hypothesizing. *Family Process, 50*, 293–313.

Breunlin, D. C., Schwartz, R. C., & MacKune-Karrer, B. (2001). *Metaframeworks: Transcending the models of family therapy.* San Francisco: Jossey-Bass.

Brown, E. (2001). *Patterns of infidelity and their treatment.* New York: Routledge.

Brown, S. L., & Lin, I. F. (2012). The gray divorce revolution: Rising divorce among middle-aged and older adults, 1990–2010. *The Journals of Gerontology Series B: Psychological Sciences and Social Sciences, 67*, 731–741.

Browning, S., & Artelt, E. (2012). *Stepfamily therapy: A 10-step clinical approach.* Washington, DC: American Psychological Association.

Browning, S., & van Eeden-Moorefield, B. (2019). Stepfamily therapy with stepgrandparents and their adult children. In P. Pitta & C. Datchi (Eds.), *Integrative couple and family therapies: Treatment models for complex clinical issues* (pp. 219–236). Washington, DC: American Psychological Association.

Butler, M. H., Harper, J. M., & Mitchell, C. B. (2011). A comparison of attachment outcomes in enactment-based versus therapist-centered therapy process modalities in couple therapy. *Family Process, 50*, 203–220.

Campione-Barr, N., & Smetana, J. D. (2019). Families with adolescents. In R. E. Larzelere, A. S. Morris, & A. W. Harris (Eds.), *Authoritative parenting: Synthesizing nurturance and discipline for optimal child development* (pp. 593–601). Washington, DC: American Psychological Association.

Carr, D., Freedman, V. A., Cornman, J. C., & Schwarz, N. (2014). Happy marriage, happy life? Marital quality and subjective well-being in later life. *Journal of Marriage and Family, 72*, 743–761.

Carroll, J., & Doherty, W. (2003). Evaluating the effectiveness of premarital prevention programs: A meta-analytic review of outcome research. *Family Relations, 52*, 105–118.

Cartwright, C. (2010). Resident parent–child relationships in stepfamilies. In J. Pryor (Ed.), *The international handbook of stepfamilies: Policy and practice in legal, research, and clinical environments* (pp. 208–230). Hoboken, NJ: Wiley.

Castleman, M. (2016). Dueling statistics: How much of the Internet is porn? *Psychology Today*, Blog posted November 3, 2016, downloaded 1/1/2018.

Catherall, D. (1992). Working with projective identification in couples. *Family Process, 31*, 355–367.

Chambers, A. (2014). Ask a TFI couples expert: Money and marriage. https://thefamilyinstitute.wordpress.com/2014/06/03/ask-a-tfi-couples-expert-money-marriage-with-anthony-chambers-phd-abpp/ (accessed 5/30/16).

Chapman, G., & Thomas, J. (2006). *The five languages of apology: How to experience healing in all your relationships.* Chicago, IL: Northfield.

Cherlin, A. J. (2004). The deinstitutionalization of American marriage. *Journal of Marriage and Family, 66*, 848–861.

Christensen, A., & Jacobson, N. (2000). *Reconcilable differences.* New York: Guilford Press.

Çineli, B. (2020). Money management and gender equality: An analysis of dual-earner couples in Western Europe. *Family Relations, 69*, 803–819.

Coleman, M., & Ganong, L. (2015). Stepfamilies as they really are: Neither Cinderella nor the Brady Bunch. In B. J. Risman & V. E. Rutter (Eds.), *Families as they really are* (2nd ed., pp. 343–357). New York: W. W. Norton.

Collett, J. (2010). Integrating theory, enhancing understanding: The potential contributions of recent experimental research in social exchange for studying intimate relationships. *Journal of Family Theory & Review, 2,* 280–298.

Coontz, S. (2005). *Marriage, a history: How love conquered marriage.* New York: Penguin Books.

Cooper, A. M. (1987). Changes in psychoanalytic ideas: Transference interpretation. *Journal of the American Psychoanalytic Association, 35,* 77–98.

Cooper, A. N., May, R. W., & Fincham, F. D. (2019). Stress spillover and crossover in couple relationships: Integrating religious beliefs and prayer. *Journal of Family Theory & Review, 11,* 289–314.

Copen, C. E., Daniels, K., Vespa, J., & Mosher, W. D. (2012). First marriages in the United States: Data from the 2006–2010 National Survey of Family Growth. *National Health Statistics Reports, No. 49,* March 22, 2012.

Cowan, P. A., & Cowan, C. P. (2012). Normative family transitions, couple relationship quality and healthy child development. In F. Walsh (Ed.), *Normal family processes: Growing diversity and complexity* (4th ed., pp. 428–451). New York: Guilford Press.

Cowan, P. A., & Cowan, C. P. (2015). Beyond family structure: Family process studies help to reframe debates about what's good for children. In B. J. Risman & V. E. Rutter (Eds.), *Families as they really are* (2nd ed., pp. 358–379). New York: W. W. Norton.

Cruz, J. (2012). *Remarriage rate in the U.S., 2010* (Family Profile No. Family Process 12–14). Bowling Green, OH: National Center for Family & Marriage Research.

Cummings, E., & Davies, P. (1994). *Children and marital conflict: The impact of family dispute and resolution.* New York: Guilford Press.

Cusk, R. (2015). The mother of all problems: On raising teenagers. *New York Times Sunday Magazine,* 3/22/2015, pp. 38–43, 64.

DeAnda, J. S., Langlais, M. R., Anderson, E. R., & Greene, S. M. (2020). After the marriage is over: Mothers' separation distress and children's postdivorce adjustment. *Family Relations, 69,* 1113–1127.

de Botton, A. (2016). *The course of love: A novel.* New York: Simon & Schuster.

DeLongis, A., & Zwicker, A. (2017). Marital satisfaction and divorce in couples in stepfamilies. *Current Opinion in Psychology, 13,* 158–161.

Dennerstein, L. (2010). The sexual impact of menopause. In S. B. Levine, C. B. Risen, & S. E. Althof (Eds.), *Handbook of clinical sexuality for mental health professionals* (2nd ed., pp. 215–227). New York: Routledge.

Dew, J. (2015). The many interfaces between money and marriage. *National Council on Family Relations Report, 60*(1), F12–13.

Dew, J., Dean, L., Duncan, S. F., & Britt-Luttier, S. (2020). A review of effectiveness evidence in the financial-helping fields. *Family Relations, 69,* 614–627.

Dimen, M. (2003). *Sexuality, intimacy, power.* New York: The Analytic Press.

Dimidjian, S., Martell, C. R., & Christensen, A. (2008). Integrative behavioral couple therapy. In A. S. Gurman (Ed.), *Clinical handbook of couple therapy* (4th ed., pp. 73–103). New York: Guilford Press.

Doherty, W. J. (2002). Bad couples therapy: Getting past the myth of therapist neutrality. *Psychotherapy Networker,* November/December 2002 issue, downloaded from www.psychotherapynetworker.org, 9/1/2014.

Doherty, W. J. (2003). *Take back your marriage: Sticking together in a world that pulls us apart.* New York: Guilford Press.

Doherty, W. J. (2011). In or out: Treating the mixed-agenda couple. *Psychotherapy Networker, 35,* 45–50, 58–60.

Doherty, W. J., Galston, W. A., Glenn, N. D., Gottman, J., Markey, B., Markman, H. J., Nock, S., Popenoe, D., Rodriguez, G. G., Sawhill, I. V., Stanley, S. M., Waite, L. J., & Wallerstein, J. (2002). *Why marriage matters: Twenty-one conclusions from the social sciences. A report from family scholars.* New York: Institute for American Values.

Doherty, W. J., Harris, S. M., & Wilde, J. L. (2016). Discernment counseling for "mixed-agenda" couples. *Journal of Marital and Family Therapy, 42,* 246–255.

Doss, B. D., Atkins, D. C., & Christensen, A. (2003). Who's dragging their feet? Husbands and wives seeking marital therapy. *Journal of Marital and Family Therapy, 29,* 165–177.

Doss, D. D., Benson, L. A., Georgia, E. J., & Christensen, A. (2013). Translation of integrative behavioral couple therapy to a web-based intervention. *Family Process, 52,* 139–153.

Doss, B. D., Rhoades, G. K., Stanley, S. M., & Markman, H. J. (2009). The effect of the transition to parenthood on relationship quality: An 8-year prospective study. *Journal of Personality and Social Psychology, 96,* 601–619.

Doss, B. D., Simpson, L. E., & Christensen. A. (2004). Why do couples seek marital therapy? *Professional Psychology: Research and Practice, 35,* 608–614.

Edwards, M. (2013). *Knowing self, knowing others, being known.* Address at the annual meeting of the American Family Therapy Academy, Chicago, IL, 6/7/2013.

Ehrlich, J. (2014). *Divorce and loss: Helping adults and children mourn when a marriage comes apart.* London: Roman & Littlefield.

Eickmeyer, K. J., Manning, W. D., & Brown, S. L. (2019). What's mine is ours? Income pooling in American families. *Journal of Marriage and Family, 81,* 968–978.

Ellison, C. R. (2002). A research inquiry into some American women's sexual concerns and problems. *Women and Therapy, 24,* 147–159.

Emerson, A. J., Harris, S. M., & Ahmed, F. A. (2020). The impact of discernment counseling on individuals who decide to divorce: Experiences of post-divorce communication and coparenting. *Journal of Marital and Family Therapy, 47,* 36–51.

Emery, R. E., Laumann-Billings, L., Waldron, M. C., Sharra, D. A., & Dillon, P. (2001). Child custody mediation and litigation: Custody, contact, and coparenting 12 years after initial dispute resolution. *Journal of Consulting and Clinical Psychology, 69,* 323–332.

Enright, R. D., & Fitzgibbons, R. P. (2000). *Helping clients to forgive: An empirical guide for resolving anger and restoring hope.* Washington, DC: American Psychological Association.

Falconier, M. K. (2015). TOGETHER—A couples' program to improve communication, coping, and financial management skills: Development and initial pilot-testing. *Journal of Marital and Family Therapy, 41,* 236–250.

Falconier, M. K., Jackson, J. B., Hilpert, P., & Bodenmann, G. (2015). Dyadic coping and relationship satisfaction. *Clinical Psychology Review, 42,* 28–46.

Felmlee, D. H. (1998). "Be careful what you wish for . . .": A quantitative and qualitative investigation of "fatal attractions." *Personal Relationships, 5,* 235–253.

Feng, E., & Yang, C. (2016). Cheating husbands fuel a new industry in China: Scorned wives hire "mistress dispellers." *New York Times,* 7/30/2016, p. A8.

Ferreira, L. C., Fraenkel, P., Narciso, I., & Novo, R. (2015). Is committed desire intentional? A qualitative exploration of sexual desire and differentiation of self in couples. *Family Process, 54,* 308–326.

Fife, S. T., Weeks, G. R., & Stellberg-Filbert, J. (2013). Facilitating forgiveness in the treatment of infidelity: An interpersonal model. *Journal of Family Therapy, 35,* 343–367.

Fincham, F. D., & Beach, S. R. H. (1999). Conflict in marriage: Implications for working with couples. *Annual Review of Psychology, 50,* 47–77.

Finkel, E. J. (2014). The all-or-nothing marriage. *New York Times Sunday Review*, 2/16/14, p. 1.

Fishbane, M. D. (2005). Differentiation and dialogue in intergenerational relationships. In J. Lebow (Ed.). *Handbook of clinical family therapy* (pp. 543–568). Hoboken, NJ: Wiley.

Fishbane, M. D. (2009). "Honor your father and mother": Intergenerational values and Jewish tradition. In F. Walsh (Ed.), *Spiritual resources in family therapy* (2nd ed., pp. 174–193). New York: Guilford Press.

Fishbane, M. D. (2010). Relational empowerment in couple therapy: An integrative approach. In A. S. Gurman (Ed.), *Clinical casebook for couple therapy* (pp. 208–231). New York: Guilford Press.

Fisher, R., Ury, W., & Patton, B. (1981/2011). *Getting to yes: Negotiating agreement without giving in* (3rd ed.). New York: Penguin Books.

Foran, H. M., Whisman, M. A., & Beach, S. H. (2015). Intimate partner relationship distress in the DSM-V. *Family Process, 55*, 423–442.

Forgatch, M. S. (1994). *Parenting through change: A training manual*. Eugene, OR: Oregon Social Learning Center.

Forgatch, M. S., & Kjøbli, J. (2016). Parent management training—Oregon Model: Adapting intervention with rigorous research. *Family Process, 55*, 500–553.

Fosco, G. M., & Grych, J. H. (2010). Adolescence triangulation into parental conflicts: Longitudinal implications for appraisals and adolescent parent relations. *Journal of Marriage and Family, 72*, 254–266.

Fosco, G. M., Lippold, M., & Feinberg, M. E. (2014). Interparental boundary problems, parent–adolescent hostility, and adolescent–parent hostility: A family process model of adolescent aggression problems. *Couple and Family Psychology: Research and Practice, 3*, 141–155.

Fraenkel, P. (2009). The therapeutic palette: A guide to choice points in integrative couple therapy. *Clinical Social Work Journal, 37*, 234–247.

Fraenkel, P. (2011). *Synch your relationships, save your marriage*. New York: Palgrave MacMillan.

Fraenkel, P. (2019). Love in action: An integrative approach to last chance couple therapy. *Family Process, 58*, 569–594.

Fraenkel, P., & Capstick, C. (2012). Contemporary two-parent families: Navigating work and family challenges. In F. Walsh (Ed.), *Normal family processes: Growing diversity and complexity* (4th ed., pp. 78–101). New York: Guilford Press.

Fraiberg, S., Adelson, E., & Shapiro, V. (1975). Ghosts in the nursery: A psychoanalytic approach to the problem of impaired infant–mother relationships. *Journal of the American Academy of Child Psychiatry, 14*, 387–421.

Framo, J. L. (1976). Family of origin as a therapeutic resource for adults in marital and family therapy: You can and should go home again. *Family Process, 15*, 193–210.

Freud, S. (1905). Three essays on the theory of sexuality. In J. Strachey (Ed. and Trans.), *The standard edition of the complete psychological works of Sigmund Freud* (Vol. 7, 130–244). London: Hogarth Press.

Friedlander, M. L., Escudero, V., & Heatherington, L. (2006). *Therapeutic alliances with couples and families: An empirically informed guide to practice*. Washington, DC: American Psychological Association.

Friedman, H. J. (2012). Destructive women and the men who can't leave them: Pathological dependence or pathological omnipotence. *Journal of the American Psychoanalytic Association, 72*, 139–151.

Frommer, M. S. (2005). Thinking relationally about forgiveness: Commentary on paper by Stephen Wangh. *Psychoanalytic Dialogues*, *15*, 33–45.

Gambrell, L. E., & Piercy, F. P. (2015). Mindfulness-based relationship education for couples expecting their first child—Part 1: A randomized mixed-methods program evaluation. *Journal of Marital and Family Therapy*, *41*, 5–24.

Ganong, L., & Coleman, M. (2018). Studying stepfamilies: Four eras of family scholarship. *Family Process*, *57*, 7–24.

Ganong, L., Coleman, M., & Haas, J. (2006). Divorce as a prelude to stepfamily living and the consequences of redivorce. In M. A. Fine & J. H. Harvey (Eds.), *Handbook of divorce and relationship dissolution* (pp. 406–434). Mahwah, NJ: Erlbaum.

Gassman-Pines, A., & Schenck-Fontaine, A. (2019). Economic strain and job loss. In B. H. Fiese (Ed.), *APA handbook of contemporary family psychology* (Vol. 2, pp. 457–470). Washington, DC: American Psychological Association.

Gladwell, M. (2000). *The tipping point: How little things can make a big difference*. New York: Little, Brown.

Glass, J., Simon, R., & Anderson, M. (2016). Parenthood and happiness: Effects of work–family reconciliation policies in 22 OECD Countries. *American Journal of Sociology*, *122*, 886–929.

Glass, S. H. (1998, July–August). Shattered vows: Getting beyond betrayal. *Psychology Today*.

Glass, S. H. (2003). *Not "just friends": Protect your relationship from infidelity and heal the trauma of betrayal*. New York: Free Press.

Gobodo-Madikizela, P. (2008). Trauma, forgiveness, and the witnessing dance: Making public spaces intimate. *Journal of Analytical Psychology*, *53*, 169–188.

Goldberg, A. (1999). *Being of two minds: The vertical split in psychoanalysis and psychotherapy*. Hillsdale, NJ: The Analytic Press.

Goldstein, A., & Brandon, M. (2004). *Reclaiming desire: 4 keys to finding your lost libido*. New York: Rodale.

Gordon, K. C., & Baucom, D. H. (1998). Understanding betrayals in marriage: A synthesized model of forgiveness. *Family Process*, *37*, 425–449.

Gordon, K. C., Baucom, D. H., & Snyder, D. K. (2005). Forgiveness in couples: Divorce, infidelity, and couples therapy. In E. L. Worthington (Ed.), *Handbook of forgiveness* (pp. 407–421). New York: Routledge.

Gottman, J. M. (2011). *The science of trust: Emotional attunement for couples*. New York: W. W. Norton.

Gottman, J. M., Coan, J., Carrera, S., & Swanson, C. (1998). Predicting marital happiness and stability from newlywed interactions. *Journal of Marriage and Family*, *60*, 5–22.

Gottman, J. M., & Gottman, J. S. (2007). *And baby makes three*. New York: Crown.

Gottman, J. M., & Gottman, J. S. (2010). Gottman method couple therapy. In A. S. Gurman (Ed.), *Clinical handbook of couple therapy* (4th ed., pp. 138–164). New York: Routledge.

Gottman, J. M., & Gottman, J. S. (2017). The natural principles of love. *Journal of Family Theory & Review*, *9*, 7–26.

Gottman, J. M., Gottman, J. S., Cole, C., & Preciado, M. (2020). Gay, lesbian, and heterosexual couples about to begin couples therapy: An online relationship assessment of 40,681 couples. *Journal of Marital and Family Therapy*, *46*, 218–239.

Gottman, J. M., Katz, L., & Hooven, C. (1996). *Meta-emotion*. Hillsdale, NJ: Erlbaum.

Gottman, J. M., & Levenson, R. W. (1999). What predicts change in marital interaction over time? A study of alternative models. *Family Process*, *38*, 143–158.

Graller, J., Nielsen, A. C., Garber, B., Davison, L. G., Gable, L., & Seidenberg, H. (2001). Concurrent therapies: A model for collaboration between psychoanalysts and other therapists. *Journal of the American Psychoanalytic Association, 49*, 587–606.

Gray, J. (1992). *Men are from Mars, women are from Venus.* New York: HarperCollins.

Green, A. I., Valleriani, J., & Adam, B. (2016). Marital monogamy as ideal and practice: The detraditionalization thesis in contemporary marriages. *Journal of Marriage and Family, 78*, 416–430.

Greenberg, L. S., & Goldman, R. N. (2008). *Emotion-focused couples therapy: The dynamics of emotion, love, and power.* Washington, DC: American Psychological Association.

Greenberg, L. S., & Johnson, S. M. (1988). *Emotionally focused therapy for couples.* New York: Guilford Press.

Greenberg, L. S., Warwar, S. H., & Malcolm, W. M. (2008). Differential effects of Emotion-Focused Therapy and psychoeducation in facilitating forgiveness and letting go of emotional injuries. *Journal of Counseling Psychology, 55*, 185–196.

Greenberg, L. S., Warwar, S. H., & Malcolm, W. M. (2010). Emotion-Focused Couples Therapy and the facilitation of forgiveness. *Journal of Marital and Family Therapy, 36*, 28–42.

Greene, R. W., & Ablon, J. S. (2006). *Treating explosive kids: The collaborative problem-solving approach.* New York: Guilford Press.

Greene, S. M., Anderson, E. R., Forgatch, M. S., DeGarmo, D. S., & Hetherington, E. M. (2012). Risk and resilience after divorce. In F. Walsh (Ed.), *Normal family processes: Growing diversity and complexity* (4th ed., pp. 102–127). New York: Guilford Press.

Greene, S. M., Anderson, E. R., Hetherington, E., Forgatch, M. S., & DeGarmo, D. S. (2003). Risk and resilience after divorce. In F. Walsh (Ed.), *Normal family processes: Growing diversity and complexity* (3rd ed., pp. 96–120). New York: Guilford Press.

Grubbs, J. B., & Gola, M. (2019). Is pornography use related to erectile functioning? Results from cross-sectional and latent growth curve analyses. *Journal of Sexual Medicine, 16*, 111–125.

Gurman, A. S. (Ed.). (2008a). *Clinical handbook of couple therapy* (4th ed.). New York: Guilford Press.

Gurman, A. S. (2008b). Integrative couple therapy: A depth psychological approach. In A. S. Gurman (Ed.), *Clinical handbook of couple therapy* (4th ed., pp. 383–423). New York: Guilford Press.

Gurman, A. S. (Ed.). (2010). *Clinical casebook of couple therapy.* New York: Guilford Press.

Gurman, A. S. (2011). Couple therapy research and the practice of couple therapy: Can we talk? *Family Process, 50*, 280–292.

Gurman, A. S., & Burton, M. (2014). Individual therapy for couple problems: Perspectives and pitfalls. *Journal of Marital and Family Therapy, 40*, 470–483.

Gurman, A. S., & Fraenkel, P. (2002). The history of couple therapy: A millennial review. *Family Process, 41*, 199–260.

Guzzo, K. B. (2016). *Stepfamilies in the U. S.* (Report No. FP-16–09). Retrieved from www.bgsu.edu/ncfmr/resources/data/family-profiles/guzzo-stepfailies-women-fp-16-09.html.

Hahlweg, K., Baucom, D. H., Grawe-Berber, M., & Snyder, D. K. (2010). Strengthening couples and families: Dissemination of interventions for the treatment and prevention of couple distress. In K. Hahlweg, M. Grawe-Gerber, & D. Baucom (Eds.), *Enhancing couples: The shape of couple therapy to come* (pp. 3–29). Cambridge, MA: Hogrefe.

Hardy, J. H., & Lucas, A. (2010). Economic factors and relationship quality among young couples: Comparing cohabitation and marriage. *Journal of Marriage and Family, 72*, 1141–1154.

Hare-Mustin, R. (1978). A feminist approach to family therapy. *Family Process, 17,* 181–194.

Harris, S. M., & Hays, K. W. (2008). Family therapist comfort with and willingness to discuss client sexuality. *Journal of Marital and Family Therapy, 34,* 239–250.

Hawkins, A. J., & Erickson, E. E. (2015). Is couple and relationship education effective for lower income participants? A meta-analytic study. *Journal of Consulting and Clinical Psychology, 76,* 723–734.

Hawkins, D. N., & Booth, A. (2005). Unhappily ever after: Effects of long-term, low-quality marriages on well-being. *Social Forces, 84,* 451–471.

Heintzelman, A., Murdock, N. L., Krycak, R. C., & Seay, L. (2014). Recovery from infidelity: Differentiation of self, trauma, forgiveness, and posttraumatic growth among couples in continuing relationships. *Couple and Family Psychology: Research and Practice, 3,* 13–29.

Heller, D., Watson, D., & Ilies, R. (2004). The role of person versus situation in life satisfaction: A critical examination. *Psychological Bulletin, 130,* 574–600.

Heller, Z. (2017, December 16 & 25). Infidels: A couples therapist gives adultery a chance. *New Yorker,* pp. 101–105.

Helmeke, K. B., & Sprenkle, D. H. (2000). Clients' perceptions of pivotal moments in couples therapy: A qualitative study of change in therapy. *Journal of Marital and Family Therapy, 26,* 469–484.

Hetherington, E. M. (1999). *Coping with divorce, single parenting, and remarriage: A risk and resiliency perspective.* Mahwah, NJ: Erlbaum.

Hetherington, E. M. (2003). Intimate pathways: Changing patterns in close personal relationships across time. *Family Relations, 52,* 318–331.

Hibbs, B. J. (2010). *Try to see it my way: Being fair in love and marriage.* New York: Avery.

Hinchliff, S., & Gott, M. (2004). Intimacy, commitment, and adaptation: Sexual relationships within long-term marriages. *Journal of Social and Personal Relationships, 21,* 595–609.

Iasenza, S. (2010). What is queer about sex? Expanding sexual frames in theory and practice. *Family Process, 49,* 291–308.

Isaacs, M. B., Montalvo, B., & Abelsohn, D. (2000). *Therapy of the difficult divorce: Managing crises, reorienting warring couples, working with the children, and expediting court processes.* Northvale, NJ: Jason Aronson.

Iscoff, D. (2021). Co-parent therapy and the parenting plan as transitional phenomena: Working psychoanalytically with high-conflict separating and divorcing couples. *Couple and Family Psychoanalysis, 11,* 14–26.

Jackson, G. L., Krull, J. L., Bradbury, T. N., & Karney, B. R. (2017). Household income and trajectories of marital satisfaction in early marriage. *Journal of Marriage and Family, 79,* 690–704.

Jacobson, N. S., & Addis, M. E. (1993). Research on couples and couples therapy: What do we know? Where are we going? *Journal of Consulting and Clinical Psychology, 61,* 85–93.

Jacobson, N. S., & Christensen, A. (1996). *Acceptance and change in couple therapy: A therapist's guide to transforming relationships.* New York: W. W. Norton.

Jenkins, N. H., Stanley, S. M., Bailey, W. C., & Markman, H. J. (2002). *You paid how much for that?! How to win at money without losing at love.* New York: Jossey-Bass.

Johnson, A. M. (1949). Sanctions for superego lacunae of adolescents. In K. R. Eissler (Ed.), *Searchlights on delinquency: New psychoanalytic studies.* Oxford, England: International Universities Press.

Johnson, C. A., Stanley, S. M., Glenn, N. D., Amato, P. A., Nock, S. L., Markman, H. J., & Dion, M. R. (2002). *Marriage in Oklahoma: 2001 baseline statewide survey of marriage and divorce.* Oklahoma City: Oklahoma State University.

Johnson, S. M. (2008). Emotionally focused couple therapy. In A. S. Gurman (Ed.), *Clinical handbook of couple therapy* (4th ed., pp. 107–137). New York: Guilford Press.

Johnson, S. M., & Greenberg, L. S. (1985). The differential effects of experiential and problem solving interventions in resolving marital conflict. *Journal of Consulting and Clinical Psychology, 53,* 175–184.

Jones, A. C., Robinson, W. D., & Seedall, R. B. (2017). The role of sexual communication in couples' sexual outcomes: A dyadic path analysis. *Journal of Marital and Family Therapy, 44,* 606–623.

Kahr, B. (2007). *Who's been sleeping in your head: The secret world of sexual fantasies.* New York: Basic Books.

Kahr, B. (2009). Psychoanalysis and sexpertise. In C. Clulow (Ed.), *Sex, attachment, and couple psychotherapy: Psychoanalytic perspectives* (pp. 1–23). London: Karnac Books.

Kaplan, H. S. (1974). *The new sex therapy.* New York: Brunner/Mazel.

Kaplan, H. S. (1995). *The sexual desire disorders: Dysfunctional regulation of sexual motivation.* New York: Brunner/Mazel.

Kazdin, A. (2008). *The Kazdin Method for parenting the defiant child.* Boston: Houghton Mifflin.

Keizer, R., & Schenk, N. (2012). Becoming a parent and relationship satisfaction: A longitudinal dyadic perspective. *Journal of Marriage and Family, 74,* 759–773.

Kernberg, O. F. (1991). Aggression and love in the relationship of the couple. *Journal of the American Psychoanalytic Association, 39,* 45–70.

Kernberg, O. F. (2011). Limitations to the capacity to love. *International Journal of Psychoanalysis, 92,* 1501–1515.

Kessel, D. E., Moon, J. H., & Atkins, D. C. (2007). Research on couple therapy for infidelity: What do we know about helping couples when there has been an affair? In P. R. Peluso (Ed.), *Infidelity: A practitioner's guide to working with couples in crisis* (pp. 55–69). New York: Routledge.

Killewald, A. (2016). Money, work, and marital stability: Assessing change in the gendered determinants of divorce. *American Sociological Review, 81,* 696–719.

Kimmes, J. G., & Durtschi, J. A. (2016). Forgiveness in romantic relationships: The roles of attachment, empathy, and attributions. *Journal of Marital and Family Therapy, 42,* 645–658.

Kinsey Institute (2013). FAQ: Infidelity www.kinseyinstitute.org/resources/FAQ. html#Infidelity, downloaded 9/9/2013.

Kleinplatz, P. J. (2010). Lessons from great lovers. In S. B. Levine, C. B. Risen, & S. E. Althof (Eds.), *Handbook of clinical sexuality for mental health professionals* (2nd ed., pp. 57–72). New York: Routledge.

Knopp, K., Rhoades, G. K., Allen, E., Parsons, A., Ritchie, L. L., Markman, H. J., & Stanley, S. M. (2017). Within- and between-family associations of marital functioning and child well-being. *Journal of Marriage and Family, 79,* 451–461.

Knudson-Martin, C. (2013). Why power matters: Creating a foundation of mutual support in couple relationships. *Family Process, 52,* 5–18.

Kohut, H. (1971). *The analysis of the self.* New York: International Universities Press.

Kohut, H. (1977). *The restoration of the self.* New York: International Universities Press.

Korelitz, A. Z. (1982). Dealing with secrets in conjoint therapy. In A. S. Gurman (Ed.), *Questions & answers in the practice of family therapy* (Vol. 2, pp. 105–107). New York: Brunner/Mazel.

Krueger, D. W. (1986). Money, success, and success phobia. In D. W. Krueger (Ed.), *The last taboo: Money as symbol & reality in psychotherapy and psychoanalysis* (pp. 3–16). New York: Brunner/Mazel.

Kurdek, L. A. (1993). Predicting marital dissolution: A 5-year prospective longitudinal study of newlywed couples. *Journal of Personality and Social Psychology, 64*, 221–242.

Lafrance, A., & Miller, A. (2020). *What to say to kids when nothing seems to work: A practical guide for parents and caregivers.* New York: Routledge.

Landers, A., Dimitropoulos, G., Mendenhall, T. J., Kennedy, A., & Zemanek, L. (2020). Backing the blue: Trauma in law enforcement spouses and couples. *Family Relations, 69*, 308–319.

Landripet, I., & Stulhofer, A. (2015). Is pornography use associated with sexual difficulties and dysfunctions among younger heterosexual men? *Journal of Sexual Medicine, 12*, 1136–1139.

Lansky, M. R. (2007). Unbearable shame, splitting, and forgiveness in the resolution of vengefulness. *Journal of the American Psychoanalytic Association, 55*, 571–593.

LaSala, M. (2013). *Monogamy not required: Lessons from gay male couples.* American Family Therapy Academy annual meeting, Chicago, IL, 6/8/2013.

Laumann, E., Paik, A., & Rosen, R. (1999). Sexual dysfunction in the United States: Prevalence and predictors. *Journal of the American Medical Association, 281*, 537–544.

Lebow, J. L. (1997). The integrative revolution in couple and family therapy. *Family Process, 36*, 1–17.

Lebow, J. L. (2013). Editorial: Couple therapy and family therapy. *Family Process, 52*, 1–4.

Lebow, J. L. (2014). *Couple and family therapy: An integrative map of the territory.* Washington, DC: American Psychological Association.

Lebow, J. L. (2019). *Treating the difficult divorce: A practical guide for psychotherapists.* Washington, DC: American Psychological Association.

Lebow, J. L., Chambers, A. L., Christensen, A., & Johnson, S. M. (2012). Research on the treatment of couple distress. *Journal of Marital and Family Therapy, 38*, 145–168.

Lederer, W., & Jackson, D. D. (1968). *The mirages of marriage.* New York: W. W. Norton.

Lee, G. R., Seccombe, K., & Sheehan, C. L. (1991). Marital status and personal happiness: An analysis of trend data. *Journal of Marriage and Family, 53*, 839–844.

Leone, C. (2008). Couple therapy from the perspective of self psychology and intersubjectivity theory. *Psychoanalytic Psychology, 25*, 79–98.

Leone, C. (2013a). The unseen spouse: Pitfalls and possibilities for the individual therapist. *Psychoanalytic Dialogues: The International Journal of Relational Perspectives, 23*, 324–339.

Leone, C. (2013b). Helping couples heal from infidelity: A self psychological, intersubjective approach. *International Journal of Psychoanalytic Self Psychology, 8*, 282–308.

Leone, C. (2019). Self psychology-informed family therapy: Increasing selfobject experience between family members—An important component of psychoanalytic treatment of children and adolescents. *Psychoanalysis, Self and Context, 14*, 292–305.

Leone, C. (2020). When couple therapy has started but an affair is continuing: Key clinical moments, curative factors and lucky breaks in a self psychological couple therapy and its context. *Psychoanalysis, Self and Context, 15*, 152–169.

Lepore, J. (2021, January 18). We work: Labor without end. *New Yorker*, pp. 65–69.

Levine, S. B. (1999). *Sexuality in mid-life.* New York: Plenum Press.

Lewis, J. T., Parra, G. R., & Cohen, R. (2015). Apologies in close relationships: A review of theory and research. *Journal of Family Theory & Review, 7*, 47–61.

Lindemann, D. J. (2017). Individualism and interdependence in the commuter marriage. *Journal of Marriage and Family, 79*, 1419–1434.

Linehan, M. M. (1993). *Skills training manual for treating borderline personality disorders*. New York: Guilford Press.

Lochman, J. E., Boxmeyer, C. L., Andrade, B., & Kassing, F. (2019). Coping power. In B. H. Fiese (Ed.), *APA handbook of contemporary family psychology* (Vol. 3, pp. 361–376). Washington, DC: American Psychological Association.

Lodge, A. C., & Umberson, D. (2012). All shook up: Sexuality of mid- to later life married couples. *Journal of Marriage and Family, 74*, 428–443.

Lower, L. M. (2005). Couples with young children. In M. Harway (Ed.), *Handbook of couples therapy* (pp. 44–60). New York: Wiley.

Luskin, F. (2002). *Forgive for good*. New York: HarperCollins.

Lyubomirsky, S. (2013). *The myths of happiness: What should make you happy, but doesn't; what shouldn't make you happy, but does*. London: Penguin Books.

Macintosh, H. B., Hall, J., & Johnson, S. M. (2007). Forgive and forget: A comparison of Emotionally Focused and Cognitive-Behavioral models of forgiveness and intervention in the context of couple infidelity. In P. R. Peluso (Ed.), *Infidelity: A practitioner's guide to working with couples in crisis* (pp. 127–147). New York: Routledge.

Maltz, W., & Maltz, L. (2008). *The porn trap: The essential guide to overcoming problems caused by pornography*. New York: Harper.

Marcus, I. D. (2010). Men who are not in control of their sexual behavior. In S. B. Levine, C. B. Risen, & S. E. Althof (Eds.), *Handbook of clinical sexuality for mental health professionals* (2nd ed., pp. 383–399). New York: Routledge.

Margolies, E. (2001). *Men with sexual problems and what women can do to help them*. Northvale, NJ: Jason Aronson.

Marin, R. A., Christensen, A., & Atkins, D. C. (2014). Infidelity and behavioral couple therapy: Relationship outcomes over 5 years following therapy. *Couple and Family Psychology: Research and Practice, 3*, 1–12.

Mark, K. P., & Lasslo, J. A. (2018). Maintaining sexual desire in long-term relationships: A systematic review and conceptual model. *Journal of Sex Research, 55*, 563–581.

Markman, H. J., Stanley, S. M., & Blumberg, S. L. (2001). *Fighting for your marriage* (2nd ed.). San Francisco: Jossey-Bass.

Masarik, A. S., Martin, M. J., Ferrer, E., Lorenz, F. O., Conger, K. J., & Conger, R. D. (2016). Couple resilience to economic pressure over time and across generations. *Journal of Marriage and Family, 78*, 326–345.

Masters, W. H., & Johnson, V. E. (1970). *Human sexual inadequacy*. Boston: Little, Brown.

McCarthy, B. W., Ginsberg, R. L., & Fucito, L. M. (2006). Resilient sexual desire in heterosexual couples. *The Family Journal, 14*, 59–64.

McCarthy, B., & McCarthy, E. (2014). *Rekindling desire: A step-by-step program to help lowsex and no-sex marriages*. New York: Brunner-Routledge.

McCarthy, B. W., & Thestrup, M. (2008). Couple therapy and the treatment of sexual dysfunction. In A. S. Gurman (Ed.), *Clinical handbook of couple therapy* (4th ed., pp. 591–617). New York: Guilford Press.

McCullough, M. E., Pargament, K. I., & Thorsen, C. E. (Eds.). (2000). *Forgiveness: Theory, research, and practice*. New York: Guilford Press.

McCullough, M. M., Worthington, E. L., & Rachal, K. C. (1997). Interpersonal forgiving in close relationships. *Journal of Personality and Social Psychology, 73*, 321–336.

Meana, M. (2010). When love and sex go wrong: Helping couples in distress. In S. B. Levine, C. B. Risen, & S. E. Althof (Eds.), *Handbook of clinical sexuality for mental health professionals* (2nd ed., pp. 103–120). New York: Routledge.

Meneses, C. W., & Greenberg, L. S. (2011). The construction of a model of the process of couples' forgiveness in emotion-focused therapy for couples. *Journal of Marital and Family Therapy, 37*, 491–502.

Metz, M. D., & McCarthy, B. W. (2003). *Coping with premature ejaculation: How to overcome PE, please your partner and have great sex.* Oakland, CA: New Harbinger.

Mikulincer, M., & Shaver, P. (2007). A behavioral systems perspective on the psychodynamics of attachment and sexuality. In D. Diamond, S. Blatt, & J. Lichtenberg (Eds.), *Attachment and sexuality* (pp. 51–78). New York: The Analytic Press.

Miller, A. S., & Byers, S. E. (2004). Actual and desired duration of foreplay and intercourse: Discordance and misperceptions within heterosexual couples. *Journal of Sex Research, 41*, 301–309.

Minuchin, S. (1974). *Families and family therapy.* Cambridge, MA: Harvard University Press.

Minuchin, S., & Fishman, H. C. (1981). *Family therapy techniques.* Cambridge, MA: Harvard University Press.

Mitchell, S. A. (2002). *Can love last? The fate of romance over time.* New York: W.W. Norton.

Morin, J. (1995). *The erotic mind: Unlocking the inner sources of sexual passion and fulfillment.* New York: HarperCollins.

Morin, J. (2012). *Long-term erotic couples: Discoveries from those who've made it work.* Presented at The Society for Sex Therapy and Research (SSTAR) annual meeting, Chicago, IL, 3/30/2012.

Morrill, M., Eubanks-Fleming, C., Harp, A., Sollenberger, J., Darling, V., & Cordova, J. V. (2011). The marriage checkup: Increasing access to marital health care. *Family Process, 50*, 471–485.

Morrill, M., Hines, D., Mahmood, S., & Cordova, J. V. (2010). Pathways between marriage and parenting for wives and husbands: The role of coparenting. *Family Process, 49*, 59–73.

Morris, A. S., Jespersen, J. E., Cosgrove, K. T., Ratliff, E. L., & Kerr, K. L. (2020). Parent education: What we know and moving forward for greatest impact. *Family Relations, 69*, 520–542.

Murray, S. H. (2019). *Not always in the mood: The new science of men, sex, and relationships.* Lanham, MD: Rowman & Littlefield.

Murray, S. H., Milhausen, R. R., Graham, C. A., & Kuczynski, L. (2017). A qualitative exploration of factors that affect sexual desire among men aged 30 to 65 in long-term relationships. *Journal of Sex Research, 54*, 319–330.

Mustillo, S., Li, M., & Wang, W. (2021). Parent work-to-family conflict and child psychological well-being: Moderating role of grandparent coresidence. *Journal of Marriage and Family, 83*, 27–39.

Neilson, J., & Stanfors, M. (2018). Time alone or together? Trends and trade-offs among dual-earner couples, Sweden 1990–2010. *Journal of Marriage and Family, 80*, 80–98.

Nelson, N., Peleg-Koriat, I., & Ben-Ari, R. (2018). Perceived procedural justice and conflict management in intimate relationships: The moderating effects of anxious attachment and personal power. *Couple and Family Psychology: Research and Practice, 7*, 34–46.

Nelson, T. (2015). The intentional divorce: Helping couples let go with dignity. *Psychotherapy Networker, 36*, 33–37, 48.

Nemeth, J. M., Bonomi, A. E., Lee, M. A., & Ludwin, J. M. (2012). Sexual infidelity as trigger for intimate partner violence. *Journal of Women's Health, 21*, 942–949.

Nielsen, A. C. (2016). *A roadmap for couple therapy: Integrating systemic, psychodynamic, and behavioral approaches.* New York: Routledge.

Nielsen, A. C. (2017a). From Couple Therapy 1.0 to a comprehensive model: A roadmap for sequencing and integrating systemic, psychodynamic, and behavioral approaches. *Family Process, 56,* 540–557.

Nielsen, A. C. (2017b). Psychodynamic couple therapy: A practical synthesis. *Journal of Marital and Family Therapy, 43,* 685–699.

Nielsen, A. C. (2019a). Couples in the digital age: An integrative systemic-psychodynamic-behavioral model of couple therapy. In P. Pitta & C. Datchi (Eds.), *Integrative couple and family therapies: Treatment models for complex clinical issues* (pp. 111–133). Washington, DC: American Psychological Association.

Nielsen, A. C. (2019b). Projective identification in couples. *Journal of the American Psychoanalytic Association, 67,* 593–624.

Nielsen, A. C. (2020). Couple therapy integrated: A commentary on couple impasses—three therapeutic approaches. *Clinical Social Work Journal, 48,* 313–318.

Nielsen, A. C., Pinsof, W., Rampage, C., Solomon, A., & Goldstein, S. (2004). Marriage 101: An integrated academic and experiential undergraduate marriage education course. *Family Relations, 53,* 485–494.

Olson, D. H., & Olson, A. K. (2000). *Empowering couples: Building on your strengths* (2nd ed.). Minneapolis, MN: Life Innovations.

Olson, M. M., Russell, C. S., Higgins-Kessler, M., & Miller, R. B. (2002). Emotional processes following disclosure of an extramarital affair. *Journal of Marital and Family Therapy, 28,* 423–434.

Orlinsky, D. E., & Ronnestad, M. H. (2005). *How psychotherapists develop: A study of therapeutic work and professional growth.* Washington, DC: American Psychological Association.

Ornstein, A. (2015). Why Kohut's ideas will endure: The contributions of self psychology to the treatment of children and to the practice of psychotherapy. *International Journal of Psychoanalytic Self Psychology, 10,* 128–141.

Owen, J., Duncan, B., Anker, M., & Sparks, J. (2012). Initial relationship goal and couple therapy outcomes at post and six-month follow-up. *Journal of Family Psychology, 26,* 179–186.

Owen, J., Rhoades, G., Shuck, B., Fincham, F. D., Stanley, S., & Markman, H. (2014). Commitment uncertainty: A theoretical overview. *Couple and Family Psychology: Research and Practice, 3,* 207–219.

Owen, J., Rhoades, G. K., Stanley, S. M., Markman, H. J., & Allen, E. S. (2019). Treatment-as-usual for couples: Trajectories before and after beginning couple therapy. *Family Process, 58,* 273–286.

Pacey, S. (2019). Should 'sensate focus' have a place in couple psychoanalytic psychotherapy? *Couple and Family Psychoanalysis, 92,* 181–197.

Paine, E. A., Umberson, D., & Reczek, C. (2019). Sex in midlife: Women's sexual experiences in lesbian and straight marriages. *Journal of Marriage and Family, 81,* 7–23.

Pam, A., & Pearson, J. (1998). *Splitting up: Enmeshment and estrangement in the process of divorce.* New York: Guilford Press.

Panksepp, J. (1998). *Affective neuroscience.* New York: Oxford University Press.

Papernow, P. L. (2013). *Surviving and thriving in stepfamily relationships: What works and what doesn't.* New York: Routledge.

Papernow, P. L. (2015). Therapy with couples in stepfamilies. In A. S. Gurman, J. L. Lebow, & D. K. Snyder (Eds.), *Clinical handbook of couple therapy* (5th ed., pp. 467–488). New York: Guilford Press.

Papernow, P. L. (2018a). Clinical guidelines for working with stepfamilies: What family, couple, individual, and child therapists need to know. *Family Process*, *57*, 25–51.

Papernow, P. L. (2018b). Recoupling in mid-life and beyond: From love at last to not so fast. *Family Process*, *57*, 52–67.

Papp, L. M., Cummings, E. M., & Goeke-Morey, M. C. (2009). For richer, for poorer: Money as a topic of marital conflict in the home. *Family Relations*, *58*, 91–103.

Park, B. Y., Wilson, G., Berger, J., Christman, M., Reina, B., Bishop, F., . . ., & Doan, A. P. (2016). Is Internet pornography causing sexual dysfunctions? A review with clinical reports. *Behavioral Science* (Basel), *6*, 17.

Parker-Pope, T. (2010). *For better: How the surprising science of happy couples can help your marriage succeed*. London: Plume Books.

Patterson, G. R. (1982). *Coercive family process*. Eugene, OR: Castalia.

Patterson, G. R. (2005). The next generation of PMTO models. *The Behavior Therapist*, *28*, 24–32.

Patterson, T., & Datchi, C. C. (2019). Money, power, and gender in intimate relationships: Cognitive Behavioral Couple Therapy. In P. Pitta & C. Datchi (Eds.), *Integrative couple and family therapies: Treatment models for complex clinical issues* (pp. 91–109). Washington, DC: American Psychological Association.

Peloquin, K., Byers, E. S., Callaci, M., & Tremblay, N. (2019). Sexual portrait of couples seeking relationship therapy. *Journal of Marital and Family Therapy*, *45*, 120–133.

Perel, E. (2006). *Mating in captivity: Reconciling the erotic with the domestic*. New York: HarperCollins.

Perel, E. (2017a). *The state of affairs: Rethinking infidelity*. New York: HarperCollins.

Perel, E. (2017b): Infidelity resource guide. https://thestateofaffairs.estherperel.com/infidelity-resource-guide/

Perel, E. (2018). *Podcast: "Where Should We Begin?" Season #1, Episode #1 "I've Had Better."* http://esther.audible.libsynpro.com/ep-1-ive-had-better-0

Perry-Jenkins, M., & Schoppe-Sullivan, S. (2019). The transition to parenting. In B. H. Fiese (Ed.), *APA handbook of contemporary family psychology* (Vol. 1, pp. 463–482). Washington, DC: American Psychological Association.

Pew Research Center (2007). *Modern marriage. I like hugs. I like kisses. But what I really love is help with the dishes*. Washington, DC: Pew Research Center.

Pew Research Center (2015). Social and demographic trends. Retrieved 9/30/2018 from www.pewsocialtrends.org/2015/12/17/1-the-american-family-today/

Phillips, C. E. (1981). Guidelines for separation counseling. In A. S. Gurman (Ed.), *Questions & answers in the practice of family therapy* (pp. 290–296). New York: Brunner/Mazel.

Pines, A. (1996). *Couple burnout: Causes and cures*. New York: Routledge.

Pinsof, W. (1995). *Integrative problem-centered therapy: A synthesis of family, individual, and biological therapies*. New York: Basic Books.

Pinsof, W., Breunlin, D. C., Russell, W. P., & Lebow, J. (2011). Integrative problem-centered metaframeworks therapy II: Planning, conversing, and reading feedback. *Family Process*, *50*, 314–336.

Platt, R. A. L., Nalbone, D. P., Casanova, G. M., & Wetchler, J. L. (2008). Parental conflict and infidelity as predictors of adult children's attachment style and infidelity. *The American Journal of Family Therapy*, *36*, 149–161.

Pollmann-Schult, M. (2014). Parenthood and life satisfaction: Why don't children make people happy? *Journal of Marriage and Family*, *76*, 319–336.

Preisner, K., Neuberger, F., Posselt, L., & Kratz, F. (2018). Motherhood, employment, and life satisfaction: Trends in Germany between 1984 and 2015. *Journal of Marriage and Family*, *80*, 1107–1124.

Proulx, C. M., Helms, H. M., & Buehler, C. (2007). Marital quality and personal well-being: A meta-analysis. *Journal of Marriage and Family*, *69*, 576–593.

Raffel, L. (1999). *Should I stay or go? How controlled separation (CS) can save your marriage*. Lincolnwood, IL: Contemporary Books.

Rancourt, K. (2016). *Are we out of touch? Responses of women with and without sexual problems to partner touch*. Presentation to Society for Sexual Therapy & Research annual meeting, Chicago, IL, 4/16/2016.

Rasmussen, K. R. (2016). A historical and empirical review of pornography and romantic relationships: Implications for family researchers. *Journal of Family Theory & Review*, *8*, 173–191.

Rathgeber, M., Bürkner, P.-C., Schiller, E.-M., & Holling, H. (2019). The efficacy of emotionally focused couples therapy and behavioral couples therapy: A meta-analysis. *Journal of Marital and Family Therapy*, *45*, 447–463.

Real, T. (2015). Rowing to nowhere: When is enough enough? *Psychotherapy Networker*, *36*, 27–31, 46–47.

Ricci, I. (1997). *Mom's house, Dad's house: Making two homes for your child* (Rev. ed.). New York: Simon & Schuster.

Ricci, I. (2012). *The coparenting toolkit: The essential supplement for Mom's House, Dad's House*. San Ramon, CA: Custody and CoParenting Solutions.

Rice, J. K. (2005). Divorcing couples. In M. Harway (Ed.), *Handbook of couples therapy* (pp. 405–430). New York: Wiley.

Ringstrom, P. A. (2014). *A relational psychoanalytic approach to couples psychotherapy*. New York: Routledge.

Risen, C. B. (2010). Listening to sexual stories. In S. B. Levine, C. B Risen, & S. E. Althof (Eds.), *Handbook of clinical sexuality for mental health professionals* (2nd ed., pp. 3–20). New York: Routledge.

Roberts, N. A., Leonard, R. C., Butler, E. A., Levenson, R. W., & Kanter, J. W. (2013). Job stress and dyadic synchrony in police marriages: A preliminary investigation. *Family Process*, *52*, 271–283.

Roddy, M. K., Nowlan, K. M., Doss, B. D., & Christensen, A. (2016). Integrative behavioral couple therapy: Theoretical background, empirical research, and dissemination. *Family Process*, *55*, 408–422.

Rosen, I. C. (2007). Revenge—the hate that dare not speak its name: A psychoanalytic perspective. *Journal of the American Psychoanalytic Association*, *55*, 595–620.

Roth, P. (2001). *The dying animal*. New York: Vintage Books.

Rowen, J., & Robert, E. (2014). Examining parental denigration behaviors of co-parents as reported by young adults and their association with parent–child closeness. *Couple and Family Psychology: Research and Practice*, *3*, 165–177.

Russell, S. T., Mallory, A. B., Bishop, M. D., & Dorri, A. (2020). Innovation and integration of sexuality in family life education. *Family Relations*, *69*, 595–613.

Rutter, V. E. (2015). The case for divorce. In B. J. Risman & V. E. Rutter (Eds.), *Families as they really are* (2nd ed., pp. 329–340). New York: W. W. Norton.

Sager, C. J. (1994). *Marriage contracts and couple therapy: Hidden forces in intimate relationships*. Northvale, NJ: Jason Aronson.

Sanders, M. R., & Turner, K. M. T. (2019). The Triple P system: Parenting support for every family. In B. H. Fiese (Ed.), *APA handbook of contemporary family psychology* (Vol. 3, pp. 409–424). Washington, DC: American Psychological Association.

Scharff, D. E. (2014a). Working with affairs. In D. E. Scharff & J. S. Scharff (Eds.), *Psychoanalytic couple therapy: Foundations of theory and practice* (pp. 254–265). London: Karnac Books.

Scharff, K. (2014b). Divorce and parenting wars. In D. E. Scharff & J. S. Scharff (Eds.), *Psychoanalytic couple therapy* (pp. 279–294). London: Karnac Books.

Scheinkman, M. (2005). Beyond the trauma of betrayal: Reconsidering affairs in couples therapy. *Family Process, 44,* 227–244.

Scheinkman, M. (2008). The multi-level approach: A road map for couples therapy. *Family Process, 47,* 197–213.

Scheinkman, M. (2019). Intimacies: An integrative multicultural framework for couple therapy. *Family Process, 58,* 550–568.

Scheinkman, M., & Fishbane, M. D. (2004). The vulnerability cycle: Working with impasses in couple therapy. *Family Process, 43,* 279–299.

Schlessinger, N., & Robbins, F. P. (1983). *A developmental view of the analytic process.* New York: The Analytic Press.

Schnarch, D. (1991). *Constructing the sexual crucible: An integration of sexual and marital therapy.* New York: W.W. Norton.

Schnarch, D. (1997). *Passionate marriage: Keeping love and intimacy alive in committed relationships.* New York: Henry Holt.

Segraves, R. T. (1982). *Marital therapy: A combined psychodynamic–behavioral approach.* New York, NY: Plenum Medical Book Co.

Sears, J. S., Repetti, R. L., Reynolds, B. M., Robles, T. F., & Krull, J. L. (2016). Spillover in the home: The effects of family conflict on parents' behavior. *Journal of Marriage and Family, 78,* 127–141.

Shaddock, D. (2000). *Contexts and connections: An intersubjective systems approach to couples therapy.* New York: Basic Books.

Shapiro, D. (1965). *Neurotic styles.* New York: Basic Books.

Shapiro, M. (2007). Money: A therapeutic tool for couples therapy. *Family Process, 46,* 279–291.

Sharra, D. A., Bourassa, K. J., & Manvelian, A. (2019). Marital separation and divorce: Correlates and consequences. In B. H. Fiese (Ed.), *APA handbook of contemporary family psychology* (Vol. 1, pp. 687–705). Washington, DC: American Psychological Association.

Siegel, D. J., & Bryson, T. P. (2015). *No-drama discipline: The whole-brain way to calm the chaos and nurture your child's developing mind.* London: Scribe.

Siegel, D. J., & Hartzell, M. (2003). *Parenting from the inside out: How a deeper self-understanding can help you raise children who thrive.* New York: Penguin Books.

Silveri, A., & Samayoa, M. F. (2018). Beyond the honeymoon: Physical attraction and its role throughout marriage. In C. C. Weisfeld, G. E. Weisfeld, & L. M. Dillon (Eds.), *The psychology of marriage: An evolutionary and cross-cultural view* (pp. 211–222). Lanham, MD: Rowman & Littlefield.

Snyder, D. K., & Mitchell, A. E. (2008). Affective-reconstructive couple therapy: A pluralistic, developmental approach. In A. S. Gurman (Ed.), *Clinical handbook of couple therapy* (4th ed., pp. 353–382). New York: Guilford Press.

Sobolewski, J. M., & Amato, P. R. (2005). Economic hardship in the family of origin and children's psychological well-being in adulthood. *Journal of Marriage and Family, 67,* 141–156.

Solomon, A. (2012). *Far from the tree: Parents, children, and the search for identity.* New York: Scribner.

Solomon, A. (2020). How to talk with your partner about porn, and why you should: Proven strategies for having this important conversation. *Psychology Today,* online. Posted 5/13/2020, downloaded 5/18/2020.

Solomon, M., & Tatkin, S. (2011). *Love and war in intimate relationships: Connection, disconnection, and mutual regulation in couple therapy.* New York: W.W. Norton.

Sorkhabi, N., & Mandara, J. (2013). Are the effects of Baumrind's parenting styles cultur-ally specific or culturally equivalent? In R. E. Larzelere, A. S. Morris, & A. W. Harris (Eds.), *Authoritative parenting: Synthesizing nurturance and discipline for optimal child devel-opment* (pp. 113–135). Washington, DC: American Psychological Association.

Spencer, C. M., & Anderson, J. (2021). Online relationship education programs improve individual and relationship functioning: A meta-analytic review. *Journal of Marital and Family Therapy, 47,* 485–500.

Spock, B. (1954). *Dr. Spock talks with mothers.* Cambridge, MA: Riverside Press.

Sprenkle, D. H., Davis, S. D., & Lebow, J. L. (2009). *Common factors in couple & family therapy: The overlooked foundation for effective practice.* New York: Guilford Press.

Sprenkle, D. H., & Storm, C. (1981). The unit of treatment in divorce therapy. In A. S. Gurman (Ed.), *Questions & answers in the practice of family therapy* (pp. 284–289). New York: Brunner/Mazel.

Spring, J. A. (2004). *How can I forgive you?* New York: HarperCollins.

Sroufe, L. A. (2000). Early relationships and the development of children. *Infant Mental Health Journal, 21,* 67–74.

Stanley, S. M. (2001). Making a case for premarital education. *Family Relations, 50,* 272–280.

Stanley, S. M., Carlson, R. G., Rhoades, G. K., Markman, H. J., Ritchie, L. L., & Hawkins, A. J. (2020). Best practices in relationship education focused on intimate relationships. *Family Relations, 69,* 497–519.

Stanley, S. M., & Einhorn, L. A. (2007). Hitting pay dirt: Comment on "Money: A ther-apeutic tool for couples therapy." *Family Process, 46,* 293–299.

Stanley, S. M., Lobitz, C., & Markman, H. J. (1989, May). Marital therapy in Colorado. *Colorado Psychological Association Bulletin,* 12–18.

Stanley, S. M., & Markman, H. J. (1992). Assessing commitment in personal relation-ships. *Journal of Marriage and Family, 54,* 595–608.

Stanley, S. M., Markman, H. J., & Whitton, S. (2002). Communication, conflict, and commitment: Insights on the foundations of relationship success from a national sur-vey. *Family Process, 41,* 659–675.

Stanley, S. M., Rhodes, G. K., & Whitton, S. W. (2010). Commitment: Functions, for-mation, and the securing of romantic attachment. *Journal of Family Theory & Review, 2,* 243–257.

Steiner, J. (2005). The conflict between mourning and melancholia. *Psychoanalytic Quar-terly, 74,* 83–104.

Stephens-Davidowitz, S. (2015). Searching for sex: What big data reveals and conceals about our desires, our bodies and our many insecurities. *New York Times Sunday Review,* 1/25/2015, pp. 1, 6.

Stokkebekk, J., Iversen, A., Hollekim, R., & Ness, O. (2020). "The troublesome other and I": Parallel stories of separated parents in prolonged conflicts. *Journal of Marital and Family Therapy, 47,* 52–68.

Stoller, R. J. (1991). *Pain & passion: A psychoanalyst explores the world of S & M.* New York: Plenum Press.

Stone, P. (2010). *Opting out: Why women really quit careers and head home.* Berkeley, CA: University of California Press.

Sullivan, L. J., & Baucom, D. H. (2005). Observational coding of relationship-schematic processing. *Journal of Marital and Family Therapy, 31,* 31–43.

Summers, F. L. (1999). *Transcending the self: An object relations model of psychoanalytic therapy.* Hillsdale, NJ: The Analytic Press.

Sweeney, J. M. (2010). Remarriage and stepfamilies: Strategic sites for family scholarship in the 21st century. *Journal of Marriage and Family*, *72*, 667–684.

Swindel, R., Heller, K., Pescosolido, B., & Kikuzawa, S. (2000). Responses to nervous breakdowns in America over a 40-year period: Mental health policy implications. *American Psychologist*, *55*, 740–749.

Taffel, R. (2012, January–February, 22–29). The decline and fall of parental authority. *Psychotherapy Networker*, pp. 52–54.

Tansey, M. J., & Burke, W. F. (1989). *Understanding countertransference: From projective identification to empathy*. Hillsdale, NJ: The Analytic Press.

Taormino, T. (2008). *Opening up: A guide to creating and sustaining an open relationship*. San Francisco, CA: Cleis Press.

Teti, D. M. (2019). Parenting at risk and contemporary family systems. In B. H. Fiese (Ed.), *APA handbook of contemporary family psychology* (Vol. 1, pp. 503–519). Washington, DC: American Psychological Association.

Titelman, P. (2010). A clinical format for Bowen family systems therapy with highly reactive couples. In A. S. Gurman (Ed.), *Clinical casebook for couple therapy* (pp. 112–133). New York: Guilford Press.

Trail, T. E., & Karney, B. R. (2012). What's (not) wrong with low-income marriages. *Journal of Marriage and Family*, *74*, 413–427.

Trillingsgaard, T., Baucom, K. J. W., & Heyman, R. E. (2014). Predictors of change in relationship satisfaction during the transition to parenthood. *Family Relations*, *63*, 667–679.

Tumin, D., Han, S., & Guian, Z. (2015). Estimates and meanings of marital separation. *Journal of Marriage and Family*, *7*, 312–322.

Vaillant, G. E. (1993). *The wisdom of the ego*. Cambridge, MA: Harvard University Press.

Verghese, A. (2010). *Cutting for stone*. New York: Vintage.

Vishner, E. B., & Vishner, J. S. (1991). *How to win as a step-family* (2nd ed.). New York: Brunner/Routledge.

Vishner, E. B., Vishner, J. S., & Pasley, K. (2003). Remarriage families and stepparenting. In F. Walsh (Ed.), *Normal family processes: Growing diversity and complexity* (3rd ed., pp. 153–175). New York: Guilford Press.

Vowels, L. M., & Mark, K. P. (2020). Partners' daily love and desire as predictors of engagement in and enjoyment of sexual activity. *Journal of Sex & Marital Therapy*, published online by Taylor & Francis, January 9, 2020, https://doi.org/10.1080/009 2623X.2019.1711274

Wachtel, E. F. (2017). *The heart of couple therapy: Knowing what to do and how to do it*. New York: Guilford Press.

Wachtel, E. F., & Wachtel, P. L. (1986). *Family dynamics in individual psychotherapy: A guide to clinical strategies*. New York: Guilford Press.

Wachtel, P. L. (2014). *Cyclical psychodynamics and the contextual self: The inner world, the intimate world, and the world of culture and society*. New York: Routledge.

Waite, L., & Gallagher, M. (2000). *The case for marriage: Why married people are happier, healthier, and better off financially*. New York: Doubleday.

Wallerstein, J., & Blakeslee, S. (1995). *The good marriage*. New York: Warner Books.

Wallerstein, J., Lewis, J., & Blakeslee, S. (2000). *The unexpected legacy of divorce: A 25-year landmark study*. New York: Hyperion.

Walsh, F. (Ed.). (2012a). *Normal family processes: Growing diversity and complexity* (4th ed.). New York: Guilford Press.

Walsh, F. (2012b). The new normal: Diversity and complexity in 21st-century families. In F. Walsh (Ed.), *Normal family processes: Growing diversity and complexity* (4th ed., pp. 3–27). New York: Guilford Press.

Walsh, F. (2016). Reconnection and reconciliation: Healing relational wounds. In F. Walsh (Ed.), *Strengthening family resilience* (3rd ed., pp. 327–355). New York: Guilford Press.

Weeks, G. R., & Gambescia, N. (2015). Couple therapy and sexual problems. In A. S. Gurman, J. L. Lebow, & D. K. Snyder (Eds.), *Clinical handbook of couple therapy* (5th ed., pp. 635–656). New York: Guilford Press.

Weeks, G. R., Odell, M., & Methven, S. (2005). *If only I had known . . . Avoiding common mistakes in couples therapy.* New York: W. W. Norton.

Weiner, L., & Avery-Clark, C. (2017). *Sensate focus in sex therapy: The illustrated manual.* New York: Routledge.

Weiner-Davis, M. (2001). *The divorce remedy: The proven 7-step program for saving your marriage.* New York: Fireside.

Weiner-Davis, M. (2003). *The sex-starved marriage: Boosting your marriage libido: A couple's guide.* New York: Simon & Schuster.

Weiner-Davis, M. (2017). *Healing from infidelity.* Woodstock, IL: Michele Weiner-Davis Training Corporation.

Wenning, K. (1996). *Winning cooperation from your child! A comprehensive method to stop defiant and aggressive behavior in children.* Northvale, NJ: Jason Aronson.

Whisman, M. A., & Uebelacker, L. A. (2003). Comorbidity of relationship distress and mental and physical health problems. In D. K. Snyder & M. A. Whisman (Eds.), *Treating difficult couples: Helping clients with coexisting mental and relationship disorders* (pp. 3–26). New York: Guilford Press.

White, M. (2007). *Maps of narrative practice.* New York: W. W. Norton.

Whitehead, B., & Popenoe, D. (2002). *The state of our unions: The social health of marriage in America.* Piscataway, NJ: The National Marriage Project, Rutgers University.

Wiebe, S. A., & Johnson, S. M. (2016). A review of the research in emotionally focused therapy for couples. *Family Process, 55,* 390–407.

Wile, D. B. (1993). *After the fight: Using your disagreements to build a stronger relationship.* New York: Guilford Press.

Wile, D. B. (2002). Collaborative couple therapy. In A. S. Gurman & N. S. Jacobson (Eds.), *Clinical handbook of couple therapy* (3rd ed., pp. 281–307). New York: Guilford Press.

Wile, D. B. (2012). Creating an intimate exchange. Retrieved from *Collaborative Couple Therapy Newsletter,* http://danwile.com/2012/07/creating-an-intimate-exchange/ Retrieved 11/20/2012.

Wile, D. B. (2013). Opening the circle of pursuit and distance. *Family Process, 52,* 19–32.

Williams, J. C., & Boushey, H. (2010, January). *The three faces of work–family conflict: The poor, the professionals, and the missing middle.* Washington, DC: Center for American Progress.

Williamson, H. C. (2020). Early effects of the COVID-19 pandemic on relationship satisfaction and attributions. *Psychological Sciences, 31,* 1479–1487.

Wolf, A. E. (2000). *The secret of parenting: How to be in charge of today's kids—from toddlers to preteens—without threats or punishment.* New York: Farrar, Straus & Giroux.

Wolf, A. E. (2002). *Get out of my life, but first could you drive me & Cheryl to the mall: A parent's guide to the new teenager* (Rev. ed.). New York: Farrar, Straus & Giroux.

Worthington, E. L., Jr., Sandage, S. J., & Berry, J. W. (2000). Group interventions to promote forgiveness: What researchers and clinicians ought to know. In M. E.

McCullough, K. I. Pargament, & C. E. Thoresen (Eds.), *Forgiveness: Theory, research, and practice* (pp. 228–253). New York: Guilford Press.

Worthington, E. L., Jr., & Wade, N. G. (1999). The psychology of unforgiveness and forgiveness and implications for clinical practice. *Journal of Social and Clinical Psychology, 18*, 385–418.

Yorgason, J. B., Seidel, A., Rauer, A., & Polenick, C. R. (2021). Are you awake? Why sleep matters in marriage and what couples can do about it. *National Council on Family Relations Report, 65*, F21—F23.

Young, M., & Schieman, S. (2018). Scaling back and finding flexibility: Gender differences in parents' strategies to manage work–family conflict. *Journal of Marriage and Family, 80*, 99 118.

Zeytinoglu, S., Davey, M. P., Cleland, C., Fisher, K., & Akyil, Y. (2017). Experiences of couples caring for a child born with cleft lip and/or palate: Impact of the timing of diagnosis. *Journal of Marital and Family Therapy, 43*, 82–99.

Zuccarini, D., Johnson, S. M., Dalgleish, T. L., & Makinen, J. A. (2013). Forgiveness and reconciliation in emotionally focused therapy for couples: The client change process and therapist interventions. *Journal of Marital and Family Therapy, 39*, 148–162.

Index

Note: Page numbers in italics indicate a figure and page numbers in bold indicate a table on the corresponding page. Page numbers followed by "n" indicate a note.